Martin Whittingham

A History of Muslim Views of the Bible

Studies of the Bible and Its Reception

Edited by
Constance M. Furey, Steven McKenzie,
Thomas Römer, Jens Schröter,
Barry Dov Walfish, and Eric Ziolkowski

Volume 7

Martin Whittingham

A History of Muslim Views of the Bible

The First Four Centuries

DE GRUYTER

ISBN 978-3-11-099144-4
e-ISBN (PDF) 978-3-11-033588-0
e-ISBN (EPUB) 978-3-11-038927-2
ISSN 2195-450X

Library of Congress Control Number: 2020943470

Bibliographic information published by the Deutsche Nationalbibliothek
The Deutsche Nationalbibliothek lists this publication in the Deutsche Nationalbibliografie; detailed bibliographic data are available on the Internet at http://dnb.dnb.de.

This volume is text- and page-identical with the hardback published in 2021.
Logo: Martin Zech
Printing and binding: CPI books GmbH, Leck

www.degruyter.com

To Helen, Anna and Saskia, with love

Acknowledgements

It is a pleasure to record the many debts of gratitude involved in bringing a book to completion, even though 'completion' is perhaps a relative term as I look ahead to work on a second volume.

Stimulating and gracious colleagues at the Centre for Muslim-Christian Studies, Oxford, have listened to presentations of parts of this work. In particular I wish to thank Ida Glaser, David Coffey, Richard McCallum, Georgina Jardim and Shabbir Akhtar for their encouragement along the path. I am also grateful to the trustees of the Solomon Academic Trust, which runs CMCS, for their support and encouragement. Some of this material has been presented at research seminars at CMCS, as well as at various other venues, and I am grateful for helpful comments from people too numerous to mention. I am also thankful for my involvement in the community of Regent's Park College, Oxford, where I am a research fellow and where I have always received such a warm welcome. Fellows there have listened to earlier versions of some of these chapters, and I thank in particular Professor Paul Fiddes for his encouragement and interest. Belal Abo al-Abbas and Janan Izadi have both given valuable input, which I truly appreciate. Others have helped me towards the finish line in a variety of supportive ways. These include Richard McArthur, Sr Dorothee Grupp, Angela and Nigel Bamping, Neil and Megan Heath, Margaret Hanson, Gordon Tubbs, Loraine and Alasdhair Hedges, Dave and Helen Jackson, Sylvia Kempshall, Matthew Kempshall and Kirstin Gwyer. My daughter Anna provided wonderful help with bibliography at just the right time. Responsibility for views expressed and any errors is of course my own.

I am grateful to A.J. Droge and to Equinox Press for permission to quote from *The Qur'ān: a New Annotated Translation.*

It has been a pleasure to work with my editors at De Gruyter, Albrecht Doehnert and Aaron Sanborn-Overby, who both combine warmth and professionalism in equal measure.

Lastly, it is a delight to thank my family for their love and presence in my life. My father died two months before I submitted the manuscript for review, but my final year with him was a special one. My mother, my wife Helen, and our daughters Anna and Saskia have a place in my life greater than words can express – even for someone who works with words every day.

https://doi.org/10.1515/9783110335880-001

Contents

A Note on Conventions — XIII

Abbreviations — XV

1 Introduction — 1
1.1 Aims and Scope — **6**
1.1.1 Aims — **6**
1.1.2 Scope — **6**
1.2 Setting the Scene — **9**
1.2.1 The Availability of the Bible to Muslims — **9**
1.2.1.1 Arabic — **9**
1.2.1.2 Persian — **12**
1.2.2 Other Debates About the Falsification of Scripture — **14**
1.2.2.1 Jewish-Christian Debates — **14**
1.2.2.2 Sunni-Shia Debates — **15**
1.2.3 Some Qur'anic Terms — **17**
1.2.4 Previous Discussions — **17**
1.2.5 Design of the book — **19**

2 Views of the Bible in the Qur'an and Earliest Commentaries — 21
2.1 Introduction — **21**
2.2 Qur'anic Terms — **22**
2.2.1 *Tawrāt* — **22**
2.2.2 *Zabūr* — **22**
2.2.3 *Injīl* — **23**
2.2.4 Other Terms for Previous Scriptures — **24**
2.3 Positive verses — **25**
2.4 Negative verses — **26**
2.5 Early Qur'an Commentary — **27**
2.5.1 Commentary on Positive Verses — **28**
2.5.1.1 Muqātil b. Sulaymān — **28**
2.5.1.2 Al-Ṭabarī — **30**
2.5.1.3 Al-Qummī — **32**
2.5.2 Commentary on Negative Verses — **34**
2.5.2.1 Muqātil b. Sulaymān — **35**
2.5.2.2 Al-Ṭabarī — **36**
2.5.2.3 Al-Qummī — **37**

2.5.3 Conclusion — 38
2.6 Excursus: The Question of Abrogation: Does the Qur'an Abrogate the Bible? — 39
2.6.1 Introduction — 39
2.6.2 Abrogation in the Qur'an — 40
2.6.3 Abrogation in Classical Scholarship — 41
2.6.4 Supersession — 42
2.6.5 Abrogation of law — 43
2.6.6 The Bible and Internal Qur'anic Abrogation — 43
2.6.7 Conclusion — 44

3 Hadith and Biographical Literature — 46
3.1 Hadith and Biographical Literature — 46
3.1.1 Understanding Hadith and Biographical Literature — 46
3.1.2 Attitudes to Jews and Christians in Hadith Literature — 49
3.1.3 Some Important Individuals — 50
3.2 Attitudes to Biblical Material — 51
3.2.1 Acceptance — 51
3.2.2 Neutrality — 52
3.2.3 Negative Views — 53
3.2.4 Twelver Shia Views — 54
3.2.5 *Taḥrīf* — 56
3.2.5.1 Textual Corruption — 57
3.2.5.2 Corruption of interpretation — 60
3.3 Using the Bible — 61
3.3.1 Attestation of Muhammad — 62
3.3.2 Establishing the role of the Muslims in God's purposes — 66
3.3.3 The Role of 'Umar — 71
3.3.4 Legitimisation of conquest — 73
3.3.5 Apocalyptic Literature — 76
3.4 Biblical elements in Hadith Literature — 78
3.4.1 Old Testament — 78
3.4.2 New Testament — 80
3.4.2.1 Biography — 81
3.4.2.2 Teaching — 81
3.5 Conclusion — 84

4 Engaging on Many Fronts: Other Writings from the Early Centuries — 86
4.1 Introduction — 86

4.2 Proofs of Prophethood — **87**
4.3 Historical Writing — **96**
4.4 Ismāʿīlī Use of the Bible — **104**
4.4.1 Iranians — **105**
4.4.2 The Fāṭimids — **107**
4.4.3 The Brethren of Purity — **108**
4.5 Qur'anic Exegesis — **109**
4.6 Tales of the Prophets (*Qiṣaṣ al-Anbiyāʾ*) — **112**
4.7 Renunciant Literature — **114**
4.8 Disputation (*Kalām*) — **116**
4.9 Law — **120**
4.10 Philosophers — **126**
4.11 Views from Non-Muslim Sources — **128**
4.11.1 Jewish Responses — **129**
4.11.2 Christian Responses — **129**
4.12 Conclusion — **134**

5 A Tale of Three Critics – and one Apostle — 136
5.1 Qāḍī ʿAbd al-Jabbār — **136**
5.1.1 Biography and context — **136**
5.1.2 Works — **137**
5.1.3 The Gospels — **138**
5.1.4 Paul and his Letters — **138**
5.1.5 Use of the Bible — **139**
5.1.6 Influence and Evaluation — **140**
5.2 Excursus: Paul in Classical Islamic and Other Traditions — **141**
5.2.1 Paul in the Qur'an — **141**
5.2.2 Paul in Early Islamic Literature — **142**
5.2.3 Paul in Jewish Literature — **144**
5.2.3.1 Toledot Yeshu — **145**
5.2.3.2 Other works — **148**
5.2.4 Implications — **149**
5.3 Ibn Ḥazm — **150**
5.3.1 Biography and context — **150**
5.3.2 Works — **151**
5.3.2.1 The Book of the Distinction (*Kitāb al-Faṣl fi'l-milal wa'l-ahwāʾ wa'l-niḥal*) — **152**
5.3.2.2.1 Ibn Ḥazm and the Old Testament — **153**
5.3.2.1.2 Ibn Ḥazm and the New Testament — **155**
5.3.5.1.3 Methods — **157**

5.3.2.1.4 Motivation — 158
5.2.3.1.5 Influence — 160
5.4 Al-Juwaynī — 161
5.4.1 Biography and context — 161
5.4.2 Al-Juwaynī and the Old Testament — 162
5.4.3 Al-Juwaynī and the New Testament — 162
5.4.4 Reflection — 163
5.5 Conclusion — 165

6 Conclusions and Prospects: Looking Back and Looking Ahead — 167

Appendix: Qur'anic Verses on the Previous Scriptures — 172
1 Positive Attitude — 172
2 Some Form of Corruption Assumed — 179

Bibliography — 181
Primary Sources — 181
Secondary Sources — 187

Index of Subjects and Names — 209

Index of Biblical References — 211

Index of Qur'anic References — 213

A Note on Conventions

The terms "Hebrew Bible" and "Old Testament" are used interchangeably. While Jews would not regard the Hebrew scriptures as the "Old Testament," Christians have traditionally done so, and both designations will be used.

Arabic transliteration is normally given in full, according to the system of the *International Journal of Middle East Studies*. However, some Arabic words which have become common in English usage are not transliterated, or not fully transliterated, for example, Qur'an, hadith, Sunni and Shia. Muhammad is likewise not fully transliterated, unless it occurs as part of an otherwise fully transliterated name of an author.

In the main text titles of works are given first in English, to enhance readability, then in their original language. In references, the original language title is employed, with the translation also given for texts not already mentioned in the main text. In this, and in providing references to translations and reference articles as needed, I have sought to make this book accessible to those from a Biblical studies background who may be unfamiliar with the terrain of Islamic studies.

Dates involving Muslim people or events are given in AH/CE format. Other dates are given in CE format.

Translations of the Bible are taken from the *New Revised Standard Version*. Translations of the Qur'an are taken from A.J. Droge, *The Qur'ān: a New Annotated Translation* (Sheffield: Equinox, 2013, reprinted with corrections 2017).

https://doi.org/10.1515/9783110335880-002

Abbreviations

AAIW	Arts and Archaeology of the Islamic World
AAJR	*American Academy for Jewish Research*
AJSR	*Association for Jewish Studies Review*
ANT	Arbeiten zur neutestamentlichen Textforschung
AOS	American Oriental Series
BA	Biblia Arabica
BEO	*Bulletin d'études orientales*
BSOAS	*Bulletin of the School of Oriental and African Studies*
CBC	*Catholic Biblical Quarterly*
CIS	*Comparative Islamic Studies*
CMR	*Christian-Muslim Relations: a Bibliographical History*
CSCO	Corpus Scriptorum Christianorum Orientalium
CSCOSA	Corpus Scriptorum Christianorum Orientalium, Scriptores Aethiopici
CSCOSAr	Corpus Scriptorum Christianorum Orientalium, Scriptores Arabici
DLB	*Dictionary of Literary Biography*
DRLAR	Divinations: Rereading Late Ancient Religion
EI	*Encyclopaedia Iranica*
EI2	*Encyclopaedia of Islam, second edition*
EI3	*Encyclopaedia of Islam, THREE*
EJM	*Études sur le judaïsme medieval*
ELN	*English Language Notes*
EQ	*Encyclopaedia of the Qur'an*
ESAE	Edinburgh Studies in Apocalypticism and Eschatology
GBIC	Great Books of Islamic Civilization
HCMR	The History of Christian-Muslim Relations
HOS	Handbook of Oriental Studies
HUCA	*Hebrew Union College Annual*
ICMR	*Islam and Christian-Muslim Relations*
IHC	Islamic History and Civilization
IHIW	*Intellectual History of the Islamicate World*
IJMES	*International Journal of Middle East Studies*
ILS	*Islamic Law and Society*
IOS	*Israel Oriental Studies*
IPTS	Islamic Philosophy, Theology and Science: Texts and Studies
IS	*Islamic Studies*
JA	*Journal asiatique*
JAOS	*Journal of the American Oriental Society*
JCMAMW	Jews, Christians and Muslims from the Ancient to the Modern World
JECS	*Journal of Eastern Christian Studies*
JGH	*Journal of Global History*
JHMR	Judaica: Hermeneutics, Mysticism and Religion
JIS	*Journal of Islamic Studies*
JJS	*Journal of Jewish Studies*

https://doi.org/10.1515/9783110335880-003

JLARC	*Journal for Late Antique Religion and Culture*
JNES	*Journal of Near Eastern Studies*
JQR	*Jewish Quarterly Review*
JQS	*Journal of Quranic Studies*
JRAS	*Journal of the Royal Asiatic Society*
JSAI	*Jerusalem Studies in Arabic and Islam*
JSJ	*Journal for the Study of Judaism*
JSQ	*Jewish Studies Quarterly*
JSS	*Journal of Semitic Studies*
JTS	*Journal of Theological Studies*
LCE	Library of the Christian East
LCL	Loeb Classical Library
LAL	Library of Arabic Literature
ME	*Medieval Encounters*
MEMIW	The Medieval and Early Modern Iberian World
MES	*Middle East Studies*
METI	Middle Eastern Texts Initiative
MIDEO	*Mélanges de l'Institut dominicain d'études orientales*
MMW	Makers of the Muslim World
MUS	*Le Muséon*
MW	*The Muslim World*
NEIS	New Edinburgh Islamic Surveys
NTS	*New Testament Studies*
OC	*Oriens Christianus*
OSAR	Oxford Studies in the Abrahamic Religions
RHR	*Revue de l'histoire des religions*
RQR	*Review of Qur'anic Research*
RSO	*Rivista degli Studi Orientali*
RSQ	Routledge Studies in the Qur'an
SAL	Studies in Arabic Literature
SHCT	Studies in the History of Christian Traditions
SIU	*Studia Iranica Upsaliensia*
SLAEI	Studies in Late Antiquity and Early Islam
SMJR	Studies in Muslim-Jewish Relations
SPNPT	Studies in Platonism, Neoplatonism, and the Platonic Tradition
SSLL	Studies in Semitic Languages and Linguistics
TGUOS	*Transactions of the Glasgow University Oriental Society*
TQS	Themes in Qur'anic Studies
TSAJ	Texts and Studies in Ancient Judaism
TSMEMJ	Texts and Studies in Medieval and Early Modern Judaism
TSQ	Texts and Studies on the Qur'an
TTH	Translated Texts for Historians
VG	Vigiliae Christianae
ZDMG	*Zeitschrift der deutschen morgenländischen Gesellschaft*
ZGKIO	Studien zur Geschichte und Kultur des Islamischen Orients
ZKG	*Zeitschrift für Kirchengeschichte*

1 Introduction

> Knowledge is the object of a quest for the believer, and it will benefit him, from wherever he takes it, and it will not detract from the truth to hear it from unbelievers (...). Whoever declines to take a beautiful thing from its place lets an opportunity slip, and opportunities pass by like the clouds.[1]

These are the words of Ibn Qutayba (d.276/889), a Baghdad judge who regularly used the Bible in his writings. He is not typical in his openness to sources outside of the Qur'an and other traditional reservoirs of knowledge used by Muslim scholars. But nor is he entirely atypical. In the first four centuries of Islam, the period in view in the present work, there are plenty of examples of Muslims making use of the Bible in various ways, Muslims who might therefore give at least qualified support to this remark of Ibn Qutayba. Both criticism of the Bible and use of it in these early centuries of Islam form part of the process of Muslim identity formation, as will become clear.

Reception history is not a phrase that would have been familiar to early Muslim (or other) writers. Nonetheless they provided ample material with which to construct a history of Muslim reception of Biblical materials, one dimension of a rapidly growing interest in Biblical reception history. The purpose of this work and a future second volume is to attempt to tell the story of Muslim responses to those previous scriptures. Volume 1 aims to trace the key developments from the emergence of Islam to the death of the Iberian Muslim Ibn Ḥazm in 994/1064. His death date provides an appropriate breakpoint since it ushers in a period of more extensive and often hostile criticism of the Bible, although a critical approach was present in less dominant form in the preceding centuries. The second volume will follow Muslim ideas as they spread to the lands of the Ottomans, Iran, India, Africa and South-East Asia, and on into the complex terrain of the nineteenth and twentieth centuries, concluding with twenty-first century works. Although the story takes us right back to the emergence of Islam it is also of pressing relevance in contemporary interreligious relations. The important origins, developments, variations and indeed surprises shed fascinating light on the nature of Muslim reception of Biblical material.

1 Ibn Qutayba, *'Uyūn al-Akhbār* (*Choice Reports*), vol. 1 (Beirut: Dār al-Kutub al-'Ilmiyya, 1986), 28. I translate *ḍālla* here as "object of a quest". The sense is of something persistently sought; cf. the translation in Camilla Adang, *Muslim Writers on Judaism and the Hebrew Bible*. IPTS. (Leiden: Brill, 1996), 33. For more on Ibn Qutayba see Chapter 4.

https://doi.org/10.1515/9783110335880-004

I write from outside the fold of Islam, as a Christian who seeks to present the range of Muslim views as fairly as possible. This range can be strikingly wide, as two twenty-first century comments illustrate. Abdullah Saeed writes:

Since the 'authorized' scriptures of Jews and Christians remain very much today as they existed at the time of the Prophet, it is difficult to argue that the Qur'anic references to Tawrat and Injil were only to the 'pure' Tawrat and Injil as existed at the time of Moses and Jesus, respectively. If the texts have remained more or less as they were in the seventh century CE, the reverence the Qur'an has shown them at the time should be retained even today.[2]

By contrast, Muhammad al-A'ẓamī describes the disparity between the preservation of the Qur'an and the corrupted state of the Biblical text as "midday sunshine versus the darkest shades of night".[3] Most views fall somewhere between these two, but the question presents itself – what can have led to such a range of reactions? This book and its companion second volume attempt to answer that question.

The Qur'an includes verses which could potentially seem positive about the previous scriptures. "Guidance and light" is one of the Qur'anic descriptions of what the Torah (*Tawrāt*) and the Gospel (*Injīl*) offer (Q5:44, 46). The complex issue of what "Torah" and "Gospel" are understood to mean in these verses is explored below. Some might be surprised at such an apparently positive description being given to the scriptures of Jews and Christians. Yet there are many such verses (all listed in the Appendix) alongside a smaller number of a more negative hue. To complicate matters further, note the following Qur'anic statements. "No one can change the words of God. That is the great triumph" (Q10:64). Furthermore, "Surely We have sent down the Reminder, and surely We are indeed its Watchers" (Q15:9). These words are clearly applied primarily to the Qur'an. To what extent this "triumph" and guardianship also extend to Jewish and Christian scriptures existing before the advent of Islam is a question underlying the story presented here.

My approach will be to look at particular writers and their contexts, in order to illuminate two broader trends of response. One is Muslim charges that Jews and Christians have corrupted either their interpretation or the very text of their scriptures. These acts of alteration are referred to as *taḥrīf al-maʿnā* (corruption of the meaning) or *taḥrīf al-lafẓ* (corruption of the text). The second trend is

2 Abdullah Saeed, "The Charge of Distortion of Jewish and Christian Scriptures," *MW* 92 (2002), 434. Cf Saeed, chapter 8 of *The Qur'an: An Introduction* (Abingdon: Routledge, 2008), 144–56.
3 Muhammad al-A'ẓamī, *The History of the Qur'anic Text* (Leicester: UK Islamic Academy, 2003), 299.

Muslim use of the Bible – for a variety of purposes, usually involving seeking background or support for Islamic beliefs. So while one approach is wary or explicitly critical, the other is apparently more positive. These two trends can sometimes co-exist in the same work. A Muslim writer's use of the Bible does not necessarily indicate trust in the reliability of the Biblical text in general. This should not be assumed, as the same writer can both use and question the text.

I have already used the term "writer" several times. This work is necessarily dependent on writers who left a record of views.[4] These views were revealed, directly or indirectly, in Quranic commentaries, works of apologetics or polemics, histories of the world, arguments in support of Muhammad's prophethood, hadith reports and legal works, to name but some of the genres discussed in this volume. Two points need making about such writings. First, much Muslim writing exhibits no engagement with the Bible. Large tracts of Qur'anic commentary, legal works and Sufi mystical manuals are not focussed on the previous scriptures, so it is important to avoid an exaggerated picture of Muslim writers' interest in Biblical texts. Having said that, the evidence for that interest is plentiful. The works presented here employ various kinds of use and critique of the Bible which show that it was seen both as a resource and a challenge.

Secondly, the views of an elite educated group in a period of widespread illiteracy are not of course representative of the whole of their society. In regard to early Christian-Muslim interaction, this point has been richly illustrated by Jack Tannous.[5] We cannot reconstruct levels of awareness of the previous scriptures, or interest in them, among the wider Muslim population, and the present work focusses on the development of beliefs and ideas as we have them recorded for us, rather than illuminating social history amongst the majority who had no opportunity to preserve their views for posterity. However, it would be simplistic to assume that early Muslims would have had no knowledge of Jewish and Christian scripture. Many of those Muslims would have been converts from a Jewish or Christian background, or the children of the same, and could thus have carried into their new faith knowledge of the rites, beliefs and symbols of their previous faith. This may not have been extensive in some cases, but there would have been an inevitably wide range of familiarity with or experience of Judaism and Christianity. In fact, glimpses of more widely-held attitudes and of concrete situations can be gained from written clues, as will become clear. While we can-

4 Information on the lives and works of many relevant figures is now available in the many volumes of David Thomas et al (eds.), *Christian-Muslim Relations: A Bibliographical History* (Brill: 2009–).

5 Jack Tannous, *The Making of the Medieval Middle East: Religion, Society and Simple Believers* (Princeton: PUP, 2018).

not claim to know the attitudes of the many from the writings of a few, the writings of a small number help to shape the ideas of many others. This is seen clearly in modern websites and writings on a topic such as Biblical proofs of Muhammad. These often employ proof texts taken from works written during the early centuries of Islam.[6]

What is meant by the term "Bible"? This question needs approaching both in terms of the boundaries of a concept of written canon, and secondly regarding how Muslims would likely have received Biblical information. This second point is particularly pertinent in the earliest period of Islam, when canonical texts would have circulated in approximate form as part of oral traditions, or in other ways which made it difficult for them to be distinguished from texts usually regarded as non-canonical.

The compilation of the Biblical canons of the Hebrew Bible/ Old Testament and the New Testament is one of many areas encountered in this book where debates continue. By the time of the rise of Islam in the seventh century CE a solid core of canonical texts had long been established, but there continued to be minor variation over certain books, such as in the Syrian and Ethiopian Churches.[7] In order to provide some boundaries for the present study, this enquiry will focus on responses to written material widely deemed canonical as the seventh century and the new faith of Islam dawned. This means, for example, that 1 and 2 Peter, Jude and Revelation are included, while the Deutero-canonical works of Tobit, Judith, 1 and 2 Maccabees, The Wisdom of Solomon and Ben Sira (also termed Ecclesiasticus) are not. However, works not seen as canonical will surface from time to time in exploring sources for Muslim writers' discussions of a particular Biblical figure, such as Isaiah. There seems no Muslim engagement with challenging the canonicity of the books which some Christian churches questioned.

Instead it is more pertinent to this study to consider how the intertwining of canonical and other traditions impacted Muslim writers. It may not always have

6 See for example 'Proofs of Muhammad's Prophethood in the New and Old Testament,' available at http://www.waytotruth.org/prophetmuhammad/proofs.html, accessed 12 May 2020, which mentions the same traditions about Moses and David and the future Muslim community as found in the *Proofs of Prophethood* of the traditionist al-Bayhaqī (d. 458/ 1066), on whom see Chapter 3.

7 For a careful survey setting out a variety of viewpoints on both testaments, see Edmon Gallagher and John Meade, *The Biblical Canon Lists from Early Christianity: Texts and Analysis* (Oxford: OUP, 2018), the first chapter of which summarises at length the conclusions of the rest of the book. See also Lee McDonald and James Sanders, eds., *The Canon Debate* (Peabody, MA: Hendrickson, 2002), for a variety of perspectives.

been clear to early Muslims in particular where the boundaries between canonical and non-canonical Biblical material lay – not least because this may not have been either clear or important to some of the Jews and Christians with whom they had contact. The same is true for those Muslims who were themselves converts from Judaism or Christianity.[8] The value placed in Judaism on the Oral Torah (The Midrash and Talmud) as well as the Written Torah would have further complicated the issue of discerning the boundaries of the written scripture in any discussion or oral transmission of "Biblical" content. In relation to both faiths, it is difficult to know how the mass of ordinary Jews and Christians would have regarded the authority of different texts and traditions in circulation, especially as theological and general literacy (not necessarily the same thing, of course) cannot be expected to have been widespread.

Related to these practical considerations is the question of how far scripture functioned in practice as written as opposed to oral material, both for its devotees and for those interacting with them. As William Graham puts it, "The spoken word of scripture has been overwhelmingly the most important medium through which religious persons and groups throughout history have known and interacted with scriptural text."[9] Graham also notes the "interpenetration of the written and spoken word."[10] If Jews and Christians responded to scripture by hearing it, reciting it or, in Christian contexts, seeing some of its focal points depicted in images (such as a crucifix), how did this affect Muslim encounters with the scriptures of the other faiths? It is impossible to know the answer to this for the distant past, but the issue at least reminds us that Muslims were learning about texts in ways which may have involved not only conversation with Jews and Christians, but also by perhaps hearing their scripture recited or proclaimed, if they encountered such an occasion, or from accounts of the same. Awareness of such possible experience helps to inform our understanding when Muslim authors appear to be drawing on oral and at times imprecisely remembered sources.

The geographical spread of writers engaging Biblical texts in the early centuries is not as wide as the geographical spread of Islamic rule, which extended rapidly via conquest westward to Spain (by 92/711) and eastward to the borders of India. Around half of the people featuring in the ensuing pages are based in present-day Iraq, or at least spent time there, the centre of power of the 'Abbāsid dynasty (132–656/750–1258), even though many originated elsewhere, including

---

8 See Tannous, *Medieval Middle East.*

9 William Graham, *Beyond the Written Word: oral aspects of scripture in the history of religion* (Cambridge: CUP, 1987),155.

10 Graham, *Beyond the Written Word*, 156.

Medina, Khurasan (north eastern Iran), and Rayy (on the edge of modern Tehran). Only in the fourth/eleventh century is there a major figure from Spain, who despite being on the geographical edge of the Muslim majority world, proves central to the story. In the course of that story we shall see how Muslim writers express various aspects of their religious identity by their relationship to previous scriptures.

1.1 Aims and Scope

1.1.1 Aims

Three issues underpin Muslim views of the Bible, namely, abrogation, corruption and usage of the Bible. First, is the Bible abrogated, that is, superseded or cancelled by the advent of the Qur'an? This is discussed in a section of Chapter One devoted to the issue. The other two themes will run throughout the story of responses told here. The second theme concerns to what extent, if any, Muslim writers think that the text and/or interpretation of the Bible is corrupted. This issue of corruption is commonly referred to as *taḥrīf*. The vast majority of Muslims today assumes that the Biblical text itself is corrupted to a lesser or greater extent, but Muslim views of corruption have historically been more varied and complicated than this, and the foundations of the notion of *taḥrīf* are explored below. Thirdly, in what ways is the Bible used by Muslims, and why has it proved useful to writers of polemics, history, Qur'anic exegesis and a range of other works?

The availability of Biblical texts to any given Muslim writer in a language they could understand is an issue discussed below. In addition, we must ask what factors in Muslims' experience or society caused them to bring the Bible into view. What kind of contacts would Muslims have had with Jews or Christians? And to what extent are there different Sunni and Shia responses to questions about the Bible?

1.1.2 Scope

Some interesting areas of enquiry fall outside the framework of this study. First, Biblically-related material in the Qur'an itself, such as Qur'anic accounts of figures who also occur in the Bible, constitutes a separate field of study, and is only examined where Muslim writers link it to Biblical material.[11] At such points the understandings of those Muslim writers will be the main focus.

A second excluded area concerns the question of alternative texts. If the text of the Bible preserved today is not the original text sent down by God, do Muslims think that they have located the genuine article? Sometimes parts of the original Bible are said to have been found.[12] There are also manuscripts of Muslim versions of the Psalms of David which are not attempting to be rewritten Bible, and in fact are more akin to rewritten Qur'an. These engage primarily Muslim intrareligious concerns.[13] There are also Twelver Shia explanations of how component parts of the previous scriptures disappeared, along with other important items, at the time of the disappearance of the Twelfth Imam in Samarra in 260/874.[14] A further example of a text sometimes claimed as a genuine gospel, or else the closest we have to such a gospel, is the *Gospel of Barnabas*. This work exists in an Italian manuscript probably dating from the turn of the seventeenth century, with a large portion of the text also extant in a Spanish manuscript. It purports to be by Barnabas, the Cypriot Christian whom the Biblical Book of Acts describes as working alongside Paul (see Acts 9:27–15:41). The Gospel of Barnabas presents Muhammad as the messiah, but carries clear evidence of being a product of the medieval period, though there is as yet no consensus over its exact origins within that period.[15] It appeared in Arabic translation very soon

---

11 Amongst many studies in this field, see Gabriel Said Reynolds, *The Qur'an and its Biblical Subtext* (Abingdon: Routledge, 2010).

12 Joseph Sadan, "Some Literary Problems Concerning Judaism and Jewry in Medieval Arabic Sources," in *Studies in Islamic History and Civilization in Honour of David Ayalon* (Jerusalem: Cana, 1986), 353–98; Arthur Jeffery, "A Moslem Torah from India," *MW* 15 (1925), 232–39.

13 David Vishanoff, "An Imagined Book Gets a New Text: Psalms of the Muslim David," *ICMR* 22 (2011): 85–99; and Vishanoff, "Why do the Nations Rage? Boundaries of Canon and Community in a Muslim's Rewriting of Psalm 2," *CIS* 6 (2010): 151–79. However, these "Psalms of the Muslim David" can contain material bearing on discussion in the present study; see Vishanoff, "Images of David in Several Muslim Rewritings of the Psalms," forthcoming. I am grateful to the author for making available to me a pre-publication copy of this article. Cf. the discussion of David's sin in Chapter 4, below.

14 Khalid Sindawi, "'Fāṭima's Book': a Shīʿite Qur'ān?" *RSO* 78 (2004), 58.

15 Gerard Wiegers, "Gospel of Barnabas," in: EI3, consulted online on 03 July 2019 http://dx.doi.org/10.1163/1573-3912_ei3_COM_27509 See also Jan Joosten, "The *Gospel of Barnabas* and the Diatessaron," *HTR* 95 (2002): 73–96; Jan Slomp, "The 'Gospel of Barnabas' in Recent Research," *Islamochristiana* 23 (1997): 81–109. For the text in English, see Lonsdale and Laura Ragg, *The Gospel of Barnabas* (Oxford: Clarendon, 1907). This is regularly reprinted without the Raggs' critical introduction; see for example *The Gospel of Barnabas* (New Delhi: Islamic Book Service, 1998). For the Arabic translation see *Injīl Barnābā*, trans. Khalīl Saʿādah (Miṣr: Maṭbaʿat al-Manār, 1908). For the role of the *Gospel of Barnabas* in Muslim-Christian exchanges,

after its appearance in English translation in 1907, and while some Muslims, including the Egyptian writer Maḥmūd 'Abbas al-'Aqqād (d.1964) and contemporary American Muslim Yusuf Estes have stated their rejection of its authenticity, these are minority voices amongst those either endorsing it or remaining silent on the issue.[16]

A third excluded area is the traditions allegedly from Jewish or Christian sources, (and sometimes Zoroastrian) which came to be known to Muslims as *Isrā'īliyyāt*. Such traditions, widely circulated in hadith and Quranic commentaries (*tafsīr*), were derived from a blend of canonical material mixed with Jewish and Christian oral or non-canonical sources, often reworked into a distinctively Muslim form. Sometimes they did not in fact derive from the supposed source traditions.[17] These will not in general be in focus in the present study, as the majority of their material is non-canonical. However, they are relevant to Chapter 3, on tradition literature, as they help to shed light on the range of attitudes to notions of previous scriptures in this literature. It is worth noting that the label *Isrā'īliyyāt*, not used in the first three centuries of Islam for this material (which circulated widely in those centuries), is typically used today to criticise traditions that an author regards as unreliable. Such traditions have fallen out of favour amongst modern Muslim commentators, one reason being concern that they encourage discussions by non-Muslims of possible Qur'anic borrowings from previous scriptures or from Jewish and Christian tradition. A second reason is the heightened hostility, since the emergence of the state of Israel, towards material of possible Jewish origins.[18]

---

see Oddbjørn Leirvik, "History as a Literary Weapon: The Gospel of Barnabas in Muslim-Christian Polemics," *Studia Theologica – Nordic Journal of Theology* 56 (2002): 4–26.

16 Slomp, "The Gospel in Dispute," 68 n. 1, mentions al-'Aqqād. Yusuf Estes writes here about the Gospel of Barnabas: http://www.islamnewsroom.com/news-we-need/730-gospelofbarnabas-factorfake [accessed 21/3/2019].

17 On the history of the use of the term, see Roberto Tottoli, "Origin and Use of the Term *Isrā'īliyyāt* in Muslim Literature," *Arabica* 46 (1999): 193–210, and Shari Lowin, "Isrā'īliyyāt", in: *EI3*, consulted online on 08 May 2020 http://dx.doi.org/10.1163/1573-3912_ei3_COM_32621. Ibn Taymiyya (d.728/1328) and Ibn Kathīr (d. 774/1373) later helped to popularize generalized suspicion towards such material.

18 Roberto Tottoli, *Biblical Prophets in the Qur'an and Muslim Literature* (Richmond: Curzon, 2002), 180–88.

1.2 Setting the Scene

1.2.1 The Availability of the Bible to Muslims

In an age when information seems endlessly available, it is important to remember the very practical issue of the availability or otherwise of information, texts and other types of report. Access to the ideas in a scripture does not depend entirely on written texts and translations, as information would have circulated orally through discussion, transmission of reports, and perhaps even by hearing parts of the religious observances of those of other faiths. A hadith in the collection of al-Bukhārī states, "Jews and Christians would read the *Tawrāt* in Hebrew and translate and explain it in Arabic to the Muslims'."[19] Nevertheless, written versions are an important factor in ensuring continuing availability, and an overview of the emergence of Biblical translations in significant languages of the Muslim majority world helps provide some context for Muslim responses. Here the focus is on the beginnings of Arabic and Persian biblical translations, while Volume 2 will also outline the emergence of the Bible in other languages, including Ottoman Turkish and Malay, as well as its continued spread in Arabic and Persian.

1.2.1.1 Arabic

The question of how soon Biblical texts were translated into Arabic is of particular interest. This is because it relates to the possibility of Muhammad being familiar with Biblical information in written form, as opposed to oral transmission. It is commonly thought that no such texts were available in Arabic at the time of Muhammad.[20] Griffith argues that the gospels appeared in Arabic around the early eighth century in the milieu of Palestine and Syria, having a liturgical function as well as a theological role, positing an earlier date in his monograph than

---

19 Al-Bukhārī, *Ṣaḥīḥ*, vol. 9 (Riyadh: Darussalam, 1997), *Kitāb al-I'tiṣām bi'l-Kitāb wa'l-Sunna* (*The Book of Holding Fast to the Qur'an and the Sunna*), no. 7362. As seen in this hadith, Biblical scripture was not a remote concept only found in faraway places. For perceptions of rather more faraway places, see Daniel König, *Arabic-Islamic Views of the Latin West: Tracing the Emergence of Medieval Europe* (Oxford: OUP, 2015).

20 Sidney Griffith, *The Bible in Arabic*, JCMAMW (Princeton: PUP, 2013). See also Griffith, "When did the Bible Become an Arabic Scripture?," *IHIW* 1 (2013): 7–23. These works build on his "The Gospel in Arabic: an Inquiry into its Appearance in the First 'Abbāsid Century," *OC* 69 (1985): 126–67, reprinted in idem, *Arabic Christianity in the Monasteries of Ninth Century Palestine* (Aldershot: Variorum, 1992).

in his previous articles.[21] An argument for the existence of Arabic gospel translations emerging before, or at the time of the rise of Islam, and in that region, has recently been made by Kashouh.[22] However, this seems to go beyond current evidence.[23] What is agreed is that the earliest extant Arabic Bible translation is a version of Matthew, along with parts of Mark and Luke, in a manuscript known as Vatican Arabic 13.[24] Extensive discussion of the emergence of gospel translations has been provided by Vollandt, along with his discussion of Arabic translations of the Hebrew Bible.[25]

The Hebrew Bible seems to have appeared in Arabic a little later than the gospels, in 9th century translations written initially in Judeo-Arabic (Arabic written using Hebrew letters). The factors underlying this development are obscure, but early sources refer to oral contexts before written texts are produced.[26] The most famous early Arabic translation of the Hebrew Bible is by Saʿadya Gaon (d.942), an Egyptian Jew who became "head of the school" ("*Gaon*") of one of the two important rabbinic schools in Baghdad. Translations by unknown authors preceded this, and co-existed with Saʿadya's until they were eclipsed in

21 Griffith, *Bible in Arabic*, 122, 126. See also David Cook, "New Testament Citations in the Ḥadīth Literature and the Question of Early Gospel Translations into Arabic," in *The Encounter of Eastern Christianity with Early Islam*, eds E. Grypeou, M. Swanson, D. Thomas, HCMR 5 (Leiden: E.J. Brill, 2006): 185–223. For a translation of a relevant text from Ibn ʿAsākir, see 218–23.

22 Hikmat Kashouh, *The Arabic Versions of the Gospels: the manuscripts and their families* (Berlin: Walter deGruyter, 2011).

23 See Griffith, *Bible in Arabic*, 114–18, for challenges involving the date of the emergence of extended writing in Arabic, and the strong likelihood of translation occurring in the monasteries of Syria/ Palestine.

24 Kashouh, *Arabic Versions*, 138. In a forthcoming article, Andrew Persson will argue that the gospel translations preserved in Vatican Arabic 13 do not originate from a South Palestinian milieu on the basis of translational style, language and the use of some Persian terms. I am grateful to Andrew for this information. On Paul's letters in Arabic, see Vevian Zaki, "The Textual History of the Arabic Pauline Epistles: One Version, Three Recensions, Six Manuscripts," in *Senses of Scripture, Treasures of Tradition: the Bible in Arabic among Jews, Christians and Muslims*, ed. Miriam Hjälm (Leiden: Brill, 2017): 392–424, and Sara Schulthess, "Liste des manuscrits arabes des lettres de Paul: Résultats Préliminaires," *JECS* 66 (2014): 153–67.

25 Ronny Vollandt, *Arabic Versions of the Pentateuch* (Leiden: Brill, 2015), 40–89. For wider reflection on the state of research into Arabic Bible translations see also Vollandt, "The *Status Quaestionis* of Research on the Arabic Bible," in *Studies in Semitic Linguistics and Manuscripts: a Liber Discipulorum in Honour of Professor Geoffrey Khan*, eds. Nadia Vidro, Ronny Vollandt, Esther-Miriam Wagner, Judith Olszowy-Schlanger (Uppsala: University of Uppsala, 2018): 442–67. See also Tamar Zewi, *The Samaritan Version of Saadya Gaon's Translation of the Pentateuch*, BA 3 (Leiden: Brill, 2015), 7–17.

26 Vollandt, *Versions*, 73. See also Polliack, Meira. *The Karaite Tradition of Arabic Bible Translation*, EJM 17 (Leiden: E.J. Brill, 1997).

the twelfth century.[27] Sa'adya's translation, which was extensive but not of the entire Hebrew Bible, became known as the *Tafsīr* (Arabic for "commentary", or "explanation") since it existed originally in a long form which also included a great deal of commentary. But a short form, with commentary removed, came to replace the circulation of the longer version.[28] It is possible that one of the reasons prompting Sa'adya's translation was criticisms by the famous Baghdad writer al-Jāḥiẓ (d. 255/ 869) of previous attempts to render the Hebrew scripture in Arabic. There is also evidence that some of Sa'adya's deviations from the Hebrew original reflect the influence of Islamic terms and sources.[29]

Translation of parts of the Hebrew Bible was not confined to Jews. A translation of the Psalms by Ḥafṣ al-Qūṭī, the Christian judge of his community in Cordoba, Spain, dates from 889. This translation was based on Jerome's Vulgate Latin text, and likewise carried evidence of Qur'anic linguistic influence.[30] The study of the Bible in Arabic, in formative stages and beyond, is receiving increased momentum from a major project, *Biblia Arabica*. This provides a bibliog-

27 Vollandt, *Versions*, 76.

28 Vollandt, *Versions*, 81.

29 David Friedenreich, "The Use of Islamic Sources in Saadiah Gaon's *Tafsir* of the Torah," *JQR* 93 (2003), 353–95; Miriam Goldstein, "Sa'adya's *Tafsīr* in Light of Muslim Polemic Against Ninth–Century Arabic Bible Translations," *JSAI* 36 (2009): 173–99. More generally on Sa'adya's translation see Richard Steiner, *A Biblical Translation in the Making: the Evolution and Impact of Saadia Gaon's* Tafsīr (Cambridge, MA: Harvard University Press, 2011), along with the review by Ronny Vollandt in *JJS* 64 (2013), 209–13. See also Nathan Gibson, "A Mid-Ninth Century Arabic Translation of Isaiah? Glimpses from al-Jāḥiẓ," in Hjälm, ed., *Senses*, BA 5, 327–69. On manuscripts of Sa'adya's translation see Berend Jan Dikken, "Some Remarks About Middle Arabic and Saadia Gaon's Arabic Translation of the Pentateuch in Manuscripts of Jewish, Samaritan, Coptic Christian, and Muslim Provenance," in *Middle Arabic and Mixed Arabic: Diachrony and Synchrony*, eds. Liesbeth Zack and Arie Schippers, SSLL 64 (Leiden: Brill, 2012): 51–81. For Sa'adya's critique of Christianity and Islam see Daniel Lasker, "Saadya Gaon on Christianity and Islam," in *The Jews of Medieval Islam: Community, Society and Identity*, ed. Daniel Frank, EJM 16 (Leiden: Brill, 1995): 165–177.

30 For the Arabic text with French translation, see Ḥafs al-Qūṭī, *Le Psautier Mozarabe de Hafs le Goth*, ed. and trans. Marie-Thérèse Urvoy (Toulouse: Presses Universitaires du Mirail, 1994). See also discussion in Jeffery Einboden, *The Qur'ān and Kerygma: Biblical Reception of the Muslim Scripture across a Millennium*, TQS (Sheffield: Equinox, 2019), 9–34, a chapter entitled "From Al-Fātiḥa to Hallelujah: The Qur'ānic Psalter of Ḥafs al-Qūṭī"; Arie Schippers, "Ḥafṣ al-Qūṭī's Psalms in Arabic Rağaz Metre," in *Law, Christianity and Modernism in Islamic Society*, eds. U. Vermeulen and J.M.F. van Reeth (Leuven: Peeters, 1998): 133–46; and Vollandt, *Versions*, 70.

raphy of hundreds of resources for the study of the Bible in Arabic, alongside generating new scholarship.[31]

1.2.1.2 Persian

Discussion of Persian Bible translations will extend here beyond what is otherwise the chronological scope of this volume. Reaching beyond 1064 CE, into the fourteenth century, is useful in sketching the emergence of Persian translations since they appear more slowly than translations into Arabic.[32] Old Persian, written in Aramaic script, prevailed up to the era of the Sassanians, who ruled from 224 CE onwards. Middle Persian, a form of Pahlavi, and written in an Aramaic-derived script, emerged in the Sassanian era, and the earliest extant Persian Bible translations occur in this language. Short sections of the Book of Psalms in Middle Persian were found in a Chinese monastery in 1905, and the manuscripts can be dated to the mid-6th to 7th century CE. The actual translation is likely to be from the late 5th century, quite possibly by Ma'na of Shiraz, who became Nestorian Metropolitan of Persia.[33] There is a reference by John Chrysostom, writing in 391 as Patriarch of Constantinople, to Christian doctrines being translated into various languages including Persian, and a similar brief comment by Theodoret, 5th century bishop of Cyrrhus (in present-day Turkey), but the basis for these remarks remains unclear. It is possible that John Chrysostom could in fact be referring to Syriac.[34]

No Persian translation of any part of the Bible has been found in Iran earlier than the 14th century, but 9th-10th century commentaries on various books of the Hebrew Bible include Biblical text. These commentaries, found in Egypt, are written in Judeo-Persian (Persian written in Hebrew letters), and were used by Persian-speaking Jews.[35] During the 11th-13th centuries, a period of great political turmoil, no manuscript evidence of translations exists, but there is a new rise of translation in the 13th-14th centuries. A Persian diatessaron, or harmony of the

---

31 The Biblia Arabica project can be found at https://biblia-arabica.com/ (accessed 1.4.2019). For the bibliography section, see https://biblia-arabica.com/bibl/index.html (accessed 1.4.2019).

32 A major new survey of Persian translations of the Bible traces their emergence and development. See Kenneth Thomas, *A Restless Search: A History of Persian Translations of the Bible* (Atlanta: SBL Press/ Nida Institute for Biblical Scholarship, 2015).

33 Thomas, *Search*, 13ff, 38–39. The translation found in the Chinese monastery is based on the Syriac translation known as the *Peshitta* (Thomas, *Search*, 41).

34 Thomas, *Search*, 16. See also "Bible" (multiple authors), in: *EI* 4, ed. Ehsan Yarshater, London: Routledge, 1990.; Walter Fischel, "The Bible in Persian Translation,"*HTR* 45 (1952): 3–45.

35 Thomas, *Search*, 50–52.

four gospels written as one document, was produced at the end of the 13th century. The translator himself explains that this was as a result of the forcible displacement of Christians from western Iran to the east by the Mongols.[36] As a result of this displacement the children and grandchildren of the displaced Christians lost the ability to use Syriac and urged the translator to produce a work in Persian, their newly acquired language.[37] Also from the late 13th century comes a translation of the Gospel of Matthew, from a manuscript dated to 1312, while translations of all four gospels were copied in 1318 and 1341.[38] The earliest known translations of the Hebrew Bible by Jews are a translation of the Psalms from 1316 and of the Pentateuch from 1319. Translations of all other books of the Hebrew Bible also date from the 14th and 15th centuries. However, these translations remained unknown outside Jewish communities until the 1600's as they were all written in Judeo-Persian.[39] The story of Persian translations beyond what has been discussed here will be continued in volume 2, and includes interesting developments under the Safavids (907–1148/1501–1736).

This discussion of Arabic and Persian translations shows that widespread access amongst Muslims to Biblical ideas via written texts would have been very limited for an extended period. Access via oral transmission, through personal interaction, would have been much more influential for the vast majority of Muslims.[40] In addition, as already noted, many early Muslims would have been former Jews or Christians, and would have carried some knowledge of their former faith and scriptures into their lives as Muslims.[41] In the context of Christians, Syriac would have been particularly important as a medium of transmission of Biblical knowledge.

---

36 The Diatessaron (from the Greek, '*tò dià tessárōn euangélion*" or "the gospel through four,") was produced by Tatian, in the third quarter of the second century CE, but as it was widely suppressed in late antiquity, even the original language of its composition is not known. See William Petersen, *Tatian's Diatessaron: its Creation, Dissemination, Signicance and History in Scholarship*, VG 25 (Leiden: Brill, 1994).

37 Thomas, *Search*, 74–80. On a newly discovered manuscript of the Persian Diatessaron see Mahmoud Hassanabadi, Roubik Jahani and Carina Jahani (eds.), with English preface by Robert Crellin, *A Unified Gospel in Persian: An Old Variant of the Gospels along with Exegetical Comments*, SIU 33 (Uppsala: University of Uppsala, 2018). The Diatessaron was also translated into Arabic; see Peter Joosse, "An Introduction to the Arabic Diatessaron," *OC* 83 (1999): 72–129.

38 Thomas, *Search*, 84.

39 Thomas, *Search*, 97.

40 Griffith, *Bible in Arabic*, 43.

41 As noted frequently by Tannous, *Medieval Middle East*.

1.2.2 Other Debates About the Falsification of Scripture

Although not all Muslim discussion of the Bible is about its alleged falsification, it is an important aspect of the overall picture. In this context, charges of falsification existing in two other contexts merit comment, one being debates between Jews and Christians, the other intra-Muslim debates over the text of the Qur'an.

1.2.2.1 Jewish-Christian Debates

Before the rise of Islam, Christians sometimes criticised Jews for falsifying parts of the Old Testament. This occurred in the context of two differing Christian views of the reliability of the Hebrew Scriptures. The majority view up to the twelfth century was exemplified by Augustine, Bishop of Hippo in present-day Algeria (d. 430). This view maintained that Jews should be tolerated within areas ruled by Christians since they had providentially preserved the authentic texts of their Scriptures.[42] However, a more negative view claimed that Jews had deliberately altered passages which would otherwise affirm Christian understandings, where there was discrepancy between the Hebrew text and Greek translations of it.[43] It is possible that such views provided sources for later Muslim discourse against the Bible. For example, it has been suggested that Syriac Christian criticisms of Jews' failure to read scripture properly influenced the Qur'an's own criticism of Jews.[44]

In some Muslim writings the charge is made that Ezra had produced a new, false scripture after the return of the Jews from exile in Babylon beginning in 538 BCE. It is possible that the idea of Ezra as author of the Torah became known to Muslims through Jewish-Christian disputes, such as Justin Martyr's *Dialogue with Trypho*, although the same charge that Ezra is the real author of the Torah is found in the pagan Porphyry's *Against the Christians*.[45] The role of *4 Ezra*, an apocalyptic Jewish text with Christian elements, is also influential in this re-

42 See Irven Resnick, "The Falsification of Scripture and Medieval Christian and Jewish Polemics," *ME* 2 (1996), 344–47. For Augustine see *City of God* (*De civitate Dei*), XI–XXII, 18.46 (Turnhout: Brepols, 1955); English translation in Philip Schaff, ed., *A Select Library of the Nicene and Post-Nicene Fathers of the Christian Church*, Series 1, vol. 2 (Edinburgh: T&T Clark, 1819–93), 892.
43 Resnick, "Falsification," 353–60.
44 Gabriel Said Reynolds, "On the Qur'anic Accusation of Scriptural Falsification (*taḥrīf*) and Christian anti-Jewish Polemic," *JAOS* 130 (2010): 189–202.
45 Robert Berchman, *Porphyry Against the Christians*, SPNPT 1 (Leiden: Brill, 2005), 198.

gard.[46] The alleged role of Ezra as composer of the Torah provides an example of a Muslim criticism of the Bible which might have grown from Jewish, Christian or pagan roots, such are the porous boundaries of different traditions when criticising others.

1.2.2.2 Sunni-Shia Debates

Sunni-Shia debates demonstrate that the accusation of falsifying scripture was alive in internal Muslim disagreements of the early centuries. Shia Muslims differ from Sunnis over the issue of leadership of the Muslim community. They believe that of the first four caliphs, whom Sunnis term "rightly guided", only the fourth, 'Alī, was entitled to rule the community, since only he was a relative of Muhammad. This dispute over the status of 'Alī is reflected in attitudes to the Qur'anic text in the early centuries of Islam, because of the absence of the name of 'Alī from the text. (Searching for 'Alī in the Qur'an has parallels to seeking Muhammad in the Bible). Sunni Muslims traditionally hold that 'Uthmān established a standardised version of the Qur'an around 30 – 31/650, ordering all variant versions to be destroyed.[47] In the early centuries of Islam, however, the standard Shia view of the 'Uthmānic codex was that it omitted passages which confirmed the leadership of the fourth caliph 'Alī and the Imams, hereditary leaders following 'Alī and revered by Twelver Shia, the majority branch of Shi'ism.[48] This is evident in a Shia tradition attributed to the sixth Imam Ja'far al-Ṣādiq (d.148/765), which links Shia suffering at the hands of Sunnis, and Sunni alteration of the Qur'an, with the experience of Jews and Christians. "Just as the Jews and Chris-

46 See Martin Whittingham, "Ezra as the Corrupter of the Torah? Re–assessing Ibn Ḥazm's role in the Long History of an Idea," *IHIW* 1 (2013): 253 – 71. For broader reflection on the Bible in Jewish–Christian interactions see Anna Sapir Abulafia, "The Bible in Jewish-Christian Dialogue," in *The New Cambridge History of the Bible, vol. 2, From 600 – 1450*, eds. Richard Marsden and Ann Matter (Cambridge: CUP, 2012), 616 – 37.

47 Literature on the formation of the Qur'an is of course vast. See as an introduction Nicolai Sinai, "When did the Consonantal Skeleton of the Qur'an Reach Closure?" in *BSOAS* 77 (2014): 273 – 92 and 509 – 21, and more generally his *The Qur'an: a Historical-Critical Introduction*, NEIS (Edinburgh: EUP, 2017).

48 See Rainer Brunner, "The Dispute About the Falsification of the Qur'ān Between Sunnīs and Shī'īs in the 20th Century," in *Studies in Arabic and Islam*, eds. Stefan Leder et al (Leuven: Peeters, 2002): 437– 46; idem, *Die Schia und die Koranfälschung* (Würzburg: Ergon Verlag, 2001), 1 – 11. On the theme of Shia rejection of the Uthmanic codex, see also Etan Kohlberg and Mohammad Ali Amir–Moezzi (eds.) *Revelation and Falsification: the* Kitāb al-Qirā'āt *of Aḥmad b. Muḥammad al-Sayyārī*, TSQ 4 (Leiden: Brill, 2009), and Amir–Moezzi, "The Silent Qur'an and the Speaking Qur'an: History and Scriptures through the Study of Some Ancient Texts," *SI* 108 (2013): 143 – 74.

tians altered and falsified the book of their prophet after him, this community [i.e. the Muslims] shall alter and falsify the Qur'an after our prophet – may God bless him and his family – for everything that happened to the Children of Israel is bound to happen to this community."[49]

At the end of the tenth century CE the Shia began to moderate their view. The first important figure in this change was Ibn Bābawayh (d. 381/991), who emphatically denied that the Shia believed the Uthmanic codex to have been falsified, though he did affirm that there was much more revelation not included in the Qur'an.[50] From this period onwards the Shia developed a position of support for the 'Uthmānic codex. The solution was widely embraced that any omissions affected only the true explanation written in 'Alī's copy of the Qur'an, not parts of the scriptural text itself.[51]

As previously noted, searching for 'Alī in the Qur'an has parallels to searching for Muhammad in the Bible. There are three Shia approaches to the problem that 'Alī and the Shia in general are not mentioned by name in the Qur'an, and the first two of these correspond to Muslim explanations for the lack of explicit reference to Muhammad in the Bible. One approach is to claim that the Qur'an has been falsified by cutting out relevant references. A second teaches that Qur'anic texts contain hidden meanings, which once discerned through correct interpretation or direct spiritual revelation reveal support for Shia beliefs. So either the text has been falsified, or such references are implicit, and depend on the reader correctly interpreting the passage in question.[52] Discussions about finding Muhammad in the Bible, drawing on the same approaches, are discussed later in this work.

---

49 Quoted in al-Nūrī al-Ṭabarsī (d. 1320/1902), *Faṣl al-khiṭāb fi ithbāt taḥrīf kitāb rabb al-arbāb* (*Judgement regarding Proof of the Corruption of the Book of the Lord of Lords*), lithographed, 1298/1880, 35; translated in Meir Bar–Asher, "Shī'ism and the Qur'ān," in: *EQ* 4.

50 Ibn Bābawayh al-Qummī, *Risālat al-i'tiqādāt* (*Epistle on Beliefs*) published in Shaykh al-Mufīd, *Muṣannafāt al-Shaykh al-Mufīd* (*The Works of Shaykh al-Mufīd*), vol. 5, (Qom: al-Mu'tamar al-'Ālamī bi-Munāsabat Dhikrā Alfīyat al-Shaykh al-Mufīd, 1413/ 1993), 84; English translation in *A Shi'ite Creed*, tr. A. Fyzee (Tehran: World Organization for Islamic Services, 1402/1982 revd. edn), 77.

51 Brunner, "Dispute," 437.

52 Bar-Asher, "Shi'ism and the Qur'an," in: *EQ* 4. The third approach is that the Qur'an teaches principles, which tradition expands into greater detail.

1.2.3 Some Qur'anic Terms

The Qur'an refers to the previous scriptures of Jews and Christians by a number of terms, discussed more fully in Chapter 2. The most important are *Tawrāt* (Torah), *Zabūr* (Psalms) and *Injīl* (Gospel). Since these original scriptures are understood in the Qur'an to be sent down by God to a prophet in a manner parallel to the sending down of the Qur'an upon Muhammad, their original form must, in Muslim understanding, be in accord with the Qur'an. The question of the meanings imparted by writers to the terminology of *Tawrāt, Zabūr* and *Injīl* is further complicated by the fact that the extant Biblical texts at the time of Muhammad were the same texts as were prevalent before, and up to today (with the obvious exception of textual variants discerned through analysis of manuscripts). As a result of this situation, Muslim writers use the Qur'anic terms *Tawrāt*, *Zabūr* and *Injīl* (Gospel) in a variety of ways. The terminology can refer to works regarded as completely lost and replaced by inauthentic versions. Secondly, these terms can describe the authentic elements thought to be present in the extant canonical texts, such that, for example, the authentic *Injīl* can be extracted from a reading of the four gospels. An example of this extraction would be regarding the quoted words of Jesus as authentic, but not the descriptions of him, or alternatively by accepting any statements in agreement with the Qur'an. Thirdly, the terms might denote the canonical texts themselves, or at least the great majority of the text, the focus then turning to the issue of correct interpretation. In the present work examples of all three of these positions will be encountered, and readers should be alert to these differences.

1.2.4 Previous Discussions

Given the apparent importance and complexity of Muslim views of the Bible to interreligious relations, the topic has generated relatively little secondary scholarship. The first treatment, in the late nineteenth century, was Steinschneider's cataloguing of much Jewish, Christian and Muslim literature written in Arabic by adherents of one of these faiths in response to another.[53] The Hungarian pioneer of non-Muslim study of Islam, Ignaz Goldziher (d. 1921) contributed, while the first to write in English on Muslim treatment of the Bible appears to be Hart-

53 Moritz Steinschneider, *Polemische und Apologetische Literatur in Arabische Sprache* (Leipzig 1877, reprinted Hildesheim: Georg Olms, 1966).

wig Hirschfeld.[54] Both Goldziher and Hirschfeld criticise the lack of historical evidence for traditional Muslim views of the corruption of the Bible. Goldziher states that the charge of falsification is "without concrete data", while Hirschfeld remarks that the accusation is "not historical, but dictated by a combination of dogma and *odium theologicum.*"[55] In ensuing decades there is almost no writing directly focussing on our subject.[56] However, the last seventy years have brought change, unsurprisingly in view of the greater level of contacts between Muslims and non-Muslims.[57] In addition to studies of use, corruption and possible mutual

54 Ignaz Goldziher, "Über Muhammadanische Polemik gegen Ahl al-Kitāb," *ZDMG* 32 (1878): 341–87; Hartwig Hirschfeld, "Mohammedan Criticism of the Bible," *JQR* (1900–01): 222–40.
55 Goldziher, "Polemik," 348; Hirschfeld, "Criticism", 234.
56 The exception is Ignazio di Matteo, "Il 'Taḥrīf' od alterazione della Bibbia secondo i Musulmani," *Bessarione* 26 (1922), 64–111, 223–60; see abbreviated translation by M. Ananikian, "*Tahrif* or the Alteration of the Bible According to the Moslems," *MW* 14 (1924): 61–84.
57 Specialised studies will be mentioned in the course of this book. Useful treatments raising some core issues include, in chronological order, William Montgomery Watt, "The Early Development of the Muslim Attitude to the Bible," *TGUOS* 16 (1957): 50–62, reprinted in his *Early Islam* (Edinburgh: EUP, 1990): 77–85; Ernest Hahn and Ghiyathuddin Adelphi, *The Integrity of the Bible According to the Qur'an and Hadith* (Hyderabad: Henry Martyn Institute of Islamic Studies, 1977); R.G. Khoury, "Quelques réflexions sur les citations de la Bible dans les premières générations islamiques du premier et du deuxième siècles de l'hégire," *BEO* 29 (1977), 269–78; Jean-Marie Gaudeul and Robert Caspar, "Textes de la tradition musulmane concernant le *taḥrīf* (falsification) des écritures," *Islamochristiana* 6 (1980): 61–104; Hava Lazarus-Yafeh, *Intertwined Worlds* (Princeton: PUP, 1992); Jane McAuliffe, "The Qur'anic Context of Muslim Biblical Scholarship," *ICMR* 7 (1996): 141–55; Martin Accad, *The Gospels in the Muslim and Christian Exegetical Discourse from the Eighth to the Fourteenth Century* (Oxford: unpublished D.Phil thesis, 2001); Accad, "The Gospels in the Muslim Discourse of the Ninth to the Fourteenth Centuries: an exegetical inventorial table (part I)," *ICMR* 14 (2003), 67–91, Part II, 205–20, Part III, 337–52, Part IV, 459–79; Accad, *Sacred Misinterpretation: Reaching Across the Christian-Muslim Divide* (Grand Rapids, MI: Eerdmans, 2019); and Camilla Adang and Sabine Schmidtke, *Muslim Perceptions and Receptions of the Bible: Texts and Studies* (Atlanta, GA: Lockwood Press, 2019), which gathers previously published studies by these two authors, many of which are referred to in the ensuing discussion. Two more general treatments are Jean-Marie Gaudeul, *Encounters and Clashes*, 2 vols., (Rome: PISAI, 2000 edn.), who discusses and translates some of the significant texts; and Colin Chapman, *The Bible Through Muslim Eyes and a Christian Response* (Cambridge: Grove Books, 2008), one of a series of short works aimed at Christian leaders outside the academy. Survey articles also provide coverage. There are two relevant chapters in David Thomas, ed., *The Routledge Handbook of Christian–Muslim Relations* (Abingdon: Routledge, 2018): David Bertaina, "Early Muslim Attitudes to the Bible," 98–106, and Martin Whittingham, "Muslims and the Bible," 269–278. David Waines, "The Bible in Muslim–Christian Encounters," in *The New Cambridge History of the Bible, vol 2, From 600–1450*, eds. Richard Marsden and Ann Matter (Cambridge: CUP, 2012), 638–55, explores the topic while ranging more broadly through Muslim–Christian theological debates. See also recent reference works: Gordon Nickel,

influences, there are also explorations of the parallel roles which scripture plays within Islam and other faiths.[58] Stepping back to gain a wider perspective, there are also reflections on reading another's scripture.[59]

1.2.5 Design of the book

Chapter 2 outlines Qur'anic references to previous scriptures. It then analyses how early commentators on the Qur'an treated these references, both the positive verses and those more negative. A separate discussion of the Qur'anic abrogation of Biblical texts is also included. Chapter 3 deals with the extensive material found in hadith and biographical literature. Chapter 4 presents a wide range of different encounters with the Bible, drawing on many types of writing, before finally in Chapter 5 the focus narrows to some key figures who helped to bring about a major change in attitudes.

The question of response deserves comment. The story told here involves many criticisms of the Biblical texts, to which Jews, Christians and others might want to give responses or be provided with them. It goes without saying that there is a vast amount of published analysis of any given Biblical passage, much of which might be relevant to Muslim comments on those same passages. However, thorough discussion of the Biblical passages mentioned in this volume, and their possible linguistic, cultural or theological background would produce a book unmanageable in size and scope. I will refer on occasion in the notes to Biblical scholarship of particular interest, but would emphasise here that such

---

"Qur'anic and Islamic Interpretation of the Bible," *The Oxford Encyclopaedia of Biblical Interpretation*, ed. Steven McKenzie, vol. 2 (Oxford: OUP, 2013),167–176; and David Thomas, "Gospel, Muslim Conception of," in: *EI3*, consulted online on 03 July 2019, http://dx.doi.org/10.1163/1573-3912_ei3_COM_27508.

58 See for example Daniella Talmon-Heller, "Reciting the Qur'an and Reading the Torah: Muslim and Jewish Attitudes and Practices in a Comparative Historical Perspective," *Religion Compass* 6/8 (2012): 369–380; Talmon-Heller, "Scriptures as Holy Objects: Preliminary Comparative Remarks on the Qur'ān and the Torah in the Medieval Middle East," *IHIW* 4 (2016): 210–244; David Friedenreich, "Holiness and Impurity in the Torah and the Quran: Differences within a Common Typology," *CIS* 6 (2010): 5–22.

59 See James Robinson, "Reading Other People Reading Other People's Scripture: the Influence of Religious Polemic on Jewish Biblical Exegesis," *ELN* 50 (2012), 77–78; David Vishanoff, "Other People's Scriptures: Mythical Texts of Imagined Communities," *Numen* 61 (2014): 329–33. Another example of the growing interest in responses to the scriptures of another community is the project *The European Qur'an. Islamic scriptures in European Culture and Religion 1150–1850.* See https://euqu.eu

references represent only a starting point for serious exploration. I shall assume that readers sufficiently interested can seek out relevant literature discussing particular Biblical passages.

The first four centuries of Muslim discussions of the Bible are fundamental in establishing the framework for later treatments of the topic, though they do not entirely limit or define those treatments. We begin this exploration of Muslim discussions by turning to the Qur'an and its early interpreters.

2 Views of the Bible in the Qur'an and Earliest Commentaries

2.1 Introduction

"The Qur'an sets the stage for the sustained ambivalence towards the Bible that characterises all subsequent Islamic literatures."[1] This stage-setting comes about through the Qur'an's including both positive and negative verses about the previous scriptures of Jews and Christians. Many Qur'anic verses address the status of previous scriptures,[2] the majority implying a positive view of some form of scripture revealed to Jews and Christians. A smaller group of verses is more negative, and these statements need careful analysis to determine what kind of corruption or alteration is in view. The negative verses are highly relevant to the question of how early the idea arose that the Bible is textually corrupted. This question is distinct from whether specific Qur'anic teachings contradict specific Biblical teachings, for example over the divinity of Jesus. I shall first discuss important Qur'anic terms for the previous scriptures, after which three commentaries are used to illustrate the history of interpretation of both positive and negative verses.[3] Muqātil ibn Sulaymān (d.c.150 – 158/ c.767 – 775) is the first extant commentator to treat every verse in sequence, in the manner of later commentaries. Abū Ja'far al-Ṭabarī (d. 310/923) is widely regarded as the greatest compiler of exegetical traditions up to his time. His commentary should be seen as part of an ongoing debate rather than, as it often has been, as the summation of early exegetical opinion.[4] Nevertheless, he preserves an important range of views. In addition to these two Sunni commentators, al-Qummī (late 3rd/9th century) is an important figure in the early Shia commentary tradition.[5]

1 Walid Saleh, "The Hebrew Bible in Islam," in *The Cambridge Companion to the Hebrew Bible/ Old Testament*, eds. Stephen Chapman and Marvin Sweeney (Cambridge: CUP, 2016), 413.
2 See Appendix for a full listing.
3 Full references to the commentaries are given below.
4 Walid Saleh, "Re-reading al-Ṭabarī through al-Māturīdī: New light on the third century hijrī," *JQS* 18 (2016): 180 – 209, provides an important corrective to treating al-Ṭabarī as a neutral data bank of earlier tradition, showing instead that he made choices to promote particular views.
5 See Meir Bar-Asher, *Scripture and Exegesis in Early Imāmī Shiism*, IPTS 37 (Leiden: Brill, 1999).

https://doi.org/10.1515/9783110335880-005

2.2 Qur'anic Terms

Several Qur'anic terms recur throughout the unfolding history of Muslim views of the Bible. The Qur'anic concept of other scriptures appears to follow the Qur'an's concept of itself, namely a scripture sent down from God to a prophet without any human involvement.[6]

2.2.1 *Tawrāt*

Tawrāt occurs eighteen times in the Qur'an, and seems to be derived, perhaps indirectly, from the Hebrew *Torah.*[7] It describes a scripture given to Moses (Q25:35), which was "sent down" from God (Q5:44). The Qur'anic term *Tawrāt* is often taken to denote the Pentateuch, or first five books, associated with Moses, though it is later used by Muslims to signify the whole of the Hebrew Bible. Jewish tradition refers to the Written Torah (the Pentateuch) and the Oral Torah (the Midrash and Talmud) and Islamic tradition does not necessarily distinguish these. In subsequent chapters, particularly Chapter 3 on Muslim tradition literature, an invocation that "it says in the *Tawrāt*" may refer to either.

2.2.2 *Zabūr*

Zabūr, denoting a scripture revealed to David, occurs three times in the Qur'an.[8] The reference in Q21:105 is regarded as the only Biblical quotation in the Qur'an: "The earth – My righteous servants will inherit it" (cf. Psalm 37:9, 11, 29, which are very close though not identical in wording to Q21:105). This verse has been described as "central in understanding the meaning of history to early Muslims"

---

6 But if references to the term "Qur'an" in the Qur'an are better understood as a reference to oral recitation than to a fixed written scripture then some flexibility in the application of this template may be in order, a matter beyond our present scope. See William Graham, "The Earliest Meaning of 'Qur'ān,'" in *The Qur'an: Style and Contents* ed. Andrew Rippin (Aldershot: Ashgate, 2001), 361–77, first printed in *Die Welt des Islams* 23–24 (1984): 101–39.

7 Adang, Camilla, "Torah," in: *EQ* 5. Cf. Arthur Jeffery, *The Foreign Vocabulary of the Qur'an* (Baroda: Oriental Institute, 1938), 95–96. An alternative proposal of a Syriac derivation occurs in Christoph Luxenberg, *The Syro-Aramaic Reading of the Qur'an*, (Berlin: Hans Schiler, 2007), 85–88; see the detailed assessment of Luxenberg's method by Daniel King, "A Christian Qur'ān? A Study in the Syriac Background to the Language of the Qur'ān as Presented in the Work of Christoph Luxenberg," *JLARC* 3 (2009): 44–71.

8 Q 4:163; 17:55; 21:105. For discussion of the term see Jeffery, *Foreign Vocabulary*, 148–49.

since it presents – or has been so interpreted – as linking the acquisition of land and authority to righteousness and correct belief.[9] The plural *zubur* is also used to denote scriptures in general.[10]

2.2.3 *Injīl*

The Qur'an mentions the term *Injīl* twelve times, in nine of which it occurs alongside the *Tawrāt*.[11] The word most probably derives from the Greek for gospel or good news, "*euangélion*," through the Ethiopian *wangēl*.[12] What exactly is the referent of the term *Injīl?* As with the *Tawrāt* and *Zabūr*, the Qur'an regards it as the scripture sent down to a prophet, in this case Jesus; Q5:46 and 57:27 state explicitly that, "We gave him the Gospel." Traditional Christian understanding of the term "gospel," by contrast, is that the word refers either to the message about Jesus, or to one of four canonical New Testament books aiming to encapsulate that message. The Qur'an also assumes that a text which it calls the *Injīl* was available to the Christians contemporary to Muhammad, and that this text could serve as a reliable source for their judgments (Q5:47, 7:157). Whether, and to what extent, these verses refer to what Christians understand to be the four gospels is an important question, to which Muslim answers have varied.[13]

---

9 Walid Saleh, "The Psalms in the Qur'an and in the Islamic Religious Imagination," in *The Oxford Handbook of the Psalms*, ed. William Brown (Oxford: OUP, 2014), 284. For more on this linkage of land, righteousness and conquest see also Caterina Bori, " 'All We Know is What we Have Been Told': Reflections on Emigration and Land as Divine Heritage in the Qur'ān," in *The Coming of the Comforter: When, Where and to Whom?: Studies on the Rise of Islam and Various Other Topics in Memory of John Wansbrough*, eds. Carlos Segovia and Basil Lourié (Piscataway, NJ: Gorgias Press, 2012): 303–40.

10 Q3:184, 16:44, 26:196, 35:25, 54:43, 52.

11 The *Tawrāt* and *Injīl* are mentioned together in Q3:3, 48, 65; 5:46, 47, 66, 68, 110; 7:157; 9:111; 48:29; 57:27. The term *Injīl* occurs alone in 5:46, 47, and 57:27.

12 Jeffery, *Foreign Vocabulary*, 71–72. Some attempts were made in the early centuries to produce Arabic etymologies for both *Tawrāt* and *Injīl*. Various writers, including the renowned thinker Fakhr al-dīn al-Rāzī (d. 606/1209), dismiss these attempts, viewing the words as clearly derived from other languages; see Rippin, Andrew, "Foreign Vocabulary", in: *EQ* 2.

13 For an exploration of some Muslim discussions of the meaning and content of "*Injīl*," see Martin Whittingham, 'What is the 'Gospel' mentioned in the Qur'an?' *CMCS Research Briefings* 6 (2016), 3–6; consulted online 12 May 2020, https://www.cmcsoxford.org.uk/s/Research-Briefing-Spring-2016.pdf

The Qur'an always refers to a single *Injīl*, rather than gospels in the plural. This has provoked speculation that the historical origins of this reference to a single "gospel" have their roots in the views of Marcion (d.160), Tatian (d.c.180) or Mani (d.c.274). All three wanted to restore a singular "gospel".[14] There is however, no clear consensus on why the term *Injīl* in the Qur'an is always singular. It could also be because the original Christian usage was to refer to a gospel in the singular, as in the phrase "the gospel according to Mark".

What does the Qur'an say about the *Injīl?* Apart from affirming that it was a scripture given to Jesus, we are told that the *Injīl* mentions Muhammad (Q7:157, see also Q61:6). The *Injīl* contains guidance and light (Q5:46), and the "People of the Gospel" should judge by it (Q5:47). Like the *Tawrāt* and the Qur'an, the *Injīl* is said to promise that believers who sacrifice their wealth and lives to fight for God will be rewarded with Paradise (Q9:111). The *Injīl* is also described as likening the believer to a seed which grows strong and tall (Q48:29). Overall, the Qur'an gives little indication of the content of the *Injīl*, and the points mentioned above show some degree of departure from the New Testament gospels.

2.2.4 Other Terms for Previous Scriptures

In addition to the named scriptures – *Tawrāt, Zabūr* and *Injīl* – other references to scriptural material occur, most notably to the "*kitāb*". Commonly translated as "book", this term has multiple referents, including the Qur'an, and sometimes previous scriptures, as in the phrase "the people of the book".[15] The *kitāb* is also something that is inherited, though several verses (Q7:169, 35:32, 42:14) make clear that inheriting it does not guarantee a response of faith. So the statement that the Children of Israel inherit the *kitāb* (Q40:53) is not necessarily an affirmation of their faithfulness.

The term *ṣuḥuf*, usually translated as "scrolls" or "pages", also refers to previous scriptures. It occurs in the phrase "the former pages" (Q20:133), and in a

14 Jan van Reeth, "L'Évangile du Prophète," in *Acta Orientalia Belgica (Subsidia III): Al-Kitāb: La Sacralité du texte dans le monde de l'islam* (Leuven: Belgian Society for Oriental Studies, 2004): 155–74.

15 See Nickel, *Narratives of Tampering in the Earliest Commentaries on the Qur'ān*, HCMR 13 (Leiden: Brill, 2011), 42–44. Daniel Madigan, *The Qur'an's Self-Image: Writing and authority in Islam's scripture* (Princeton: PUP, 2001) challenges the notion that "*kitāb*" can be assumed to refer to a written book or codex with fixed limits, indicating instead that it signifies an "intertwining of oral and written" (212). On the diversity of understandings of *kitāb* in early exegesis see Herbert Berg, "Ṭabarī's Exegesis of the Qur'ānic Term *al-Kitāb*," *JAAR* 63 (1995): 761–74.

reference to the "pages of Abraham and Moses" (Q87:19).[16] One also reads of parchments or papyrus (*qarāṭīs*) (Q6:91), given to Moses, *raqq*, "parchment" (Q52:1–3) and tablets (*alwāḥ*), also given to Moses (Q7:145, 150, 154).[17] In addition Moses is described (Q2:53) as being given *al-furqān* (which can be translated here as "the criterion"), also said to be given to both Moses and Aaron in Q21:48.[18] Many general references to material which has been previously revealed also occur.

2.3 Positive verses

Most Qur'anic references to previous scriptures assume some kind of positive attitude. The phrase "some kind of positive attitude" is deliberately broad in implication, covering various interpretive possibilities. These apparently positive verses are listed in full in the Appendix, but some of the more important can be reviewed here. Of course, believers of any tradition usually relate to their scriptures through a history of interpretation, so a bare listing of verses alone cannot convey the range of understandings of these texts.

Anyone reading or hearing the Qur'an in its canonical order finds an affirmation of the previous scriptures almost immediately. Q2:4 describes one of the attributes of the godfearing (*al-muttaqūn*) as those who believe in "what was sent down before you". Jesus states, "And (I come) confirming what was before me of the Torah and to make permitted to you some things that were forbidden to you (before)" (Q3:50). Jews and Christians were given the "illuminating Book" (*al-kitāb al-munīr*, Q3:184, 35:25), though what this phrase refers to is not made clear. Believers are exhorted to believe in "the book [*kitab*] which he revealed be-

16 It is possible that *ṣuḥuf* may convey the term "apocalypse" as well as scroll, and thus the reference to the scrolls of Abraham and Moses may refer to the extra–Biblical texts, *Apocalypse of Abraham* and *Apocalypse of Moses*. On the linguistic background to this see Alexander Kulik, "Genre Without a Name: Was there a Hebrew term for 'Apocalypse'?," *JSJ* 40 (2009), 548; on issues of similar content between the Qur'an and these apocalypses see Geneviève Gobillot, "Qur'an and Torah: the Foundations of intertextuality," in *A History of Jewish-Muslim Relations: From the origins to the present day*, eds. Abdelwahab Meddeb and Benjamin Stora, (Princeton: PUP, 2013), 611–21.

17 Nickel, *Tampering*, 45–46.

18 *Furqān* can also refer to the Qur'an itself. "Criterion" here denotes something which separates, for example separating good from bad, or believers from unbelievers. The understanding of *furqān* is much debated; see Walid Saleh, "A Piecemeal Qur'ān: *Furqān* and its Meaning in Classical Islam and in Modern Qur'ānic Studies," *JSAI* 42 (2015), 31–71.

fore" (Q4:136). The *Tawrāt* contains the judgment of God (*ḥukm Allah*) and is guidance and light (Q5:43–44).

In Q5:48, the Quran is described as *muhaymin*, often understood as indicating that it safeguards or protects the previous scriptures.[19] Muhammad, if in doubt, is encouraged to ask those who received the *kitāb* previously (Q10:94 – and see the interpretations of this verse explored later in this chapter).

The theme of continuity with the past is prominent. John the Baptist is urged to "hold fast the Book!" (Q19:12). The message given to Muhammad is said to be "in the scriptures of those of old" (*zubur al-awwalīn:* Q26:196). The jinn, Qur'anic good and evil spirits, affirm that the Qur'an confirms the previous scriptures (Q46:30).

The Qur'an states that the*Tawrāt* is still important for Jews, and the *Injīl* for Christians (Q5:66, 68). Q2:285 is a core statement of faith, emphasising that Muhammad and the believers should believe in "God, and His angels, and His books (*kutub*), and His messengers", a similar statement occurring at Q4:136.

In addition to these explicit references to previous scriptures, there are two identical statements about the words of God, "No one can change His words" (*la mubaddil li-kalimātihi*) (Q6:115, 18:27).

Themes arising from these positive verses include the continuity of the Qur'an with previous teaching and the Qur'an's importance in confirming previous scriptures. Hence the seventh century forms of these earlier scriptures seem to possess ongoing validity – at least in part. This leads in turn to the Jews being at fault for rejecting Muhammad's message, since they already have access to the truth about him in their own scriptures.

2.4 Negative verses

There are twenty-four verses, all occurring in Suras 2–7, which are negative about the previous scriptures, or, more often, about how the followers of those scriptures interpret them. The relevant Arabic verbal roots relating to alteration and concealment of scripture have been discussed by Nickel, who gives an indication of their range of meanings. These include *labasa* (to confound or con-

19 The meaning of *muhaymin* is debated; see Munim Sirry, " 'Compete With One Another in Good Works': Exegesis of Qur'an Verse 5:48 and Contemporary Muslim Discourses on Religious Pluralism," *ICMR* 20 (2009), 425.

fuse), *katama* (to conceal), *baddala* (to substitute), *ḥarrafa* (to alter, or tamper with), *lawā* (to twist) and *nasiya* (to forget).[20]

Perhaps the most prominent verses are Q2:75, 4:46, 5:13 and 5:41, all using the verb *ḥarrafa*, "to alter", or "to corrupt", from which is derived the important though non-Qur'anic term "*taḥrīf*"'(alteration, often understood in this context as corruption).[21] Q2:75 states of the Jews that, "a group of them has already heard the word of God, (and) then altered it after they had understood it – and they know (they have done this)". Q4:46, 5:13 and 5:41 all refer to the Jews altering words from their positions. Q4:46 and 5:13 feature the identical phrase "alter words from their positions" (*yuḥarrifūna al-kalim 'an mawāḍihi*), while Q5:41 is almost identical, substituting the phrase "*min ba'di*" in place of " *'an*".

The term *taḥrīf* has become the most well-known term for alteration or corruption of the Bible, and the issue of what *taḥrīf* might mean, either textual or interpretative distortion, has proven an ongoing issue in Islamic thought. A surface reading of Qur'anic verses on alteration would indicate that what is described is opposition to Muhammad by specific Jews, consisting of either concealing, or occasionally textually altering, the meaning of certain key passages from their scripture. These passages are often thought to concern Muhammad himself. Christians are not implicated in these accusations, even though the Qur'an criticises their doctrines far more than it criticises Jewish beliefs, owing primarily to the dispute with Christians over the identity of Jesus.

2.5 Early Qur'an Commentary

Understanding the Qur'an need not depend entirely on reading commentaries. Reading the text without regard for traditional views can sometimes point to different interpretations, and the question of how best to approach the Qur'an is a live debate.[22] But the commentary tradition is important in indicating how texts were received by particular communities, what traditions were in circulation, and why certain ideas became prominent. It is this historical focus – tracing

20 Nickel, *Tampering*, 50–64.
21 Nickel, *Tampering*, 57–59, summarises Qur'anic discussions of this term.
22 See on this Bori, " 'All We Know'"; and note the role of commentaries in sometimes concealing rather than illuminating, as highlighted by Saleh, "A Piecemeal Qur'ān".

some early Muslim understandings of verses about the previous scriptures – which is in view here.[23]

2.5.1 Commentary on Positive Verses

Given the large number of positive verses, often making similar points, this discussion will draw on a selection of the more striking passages as discussed by the three commentators mentioned above, Muqātil b. Sulaymān, al-Ṭabarī and al-Qummī.

2.5.1.1 Muqātil b. Sulaymān

Muqātil b. Sulaymān was born in Balkh, in present-day northern Afghanistan, and died in Basra (southern Iraq) in 150/767. His importance lies partly in the early date of his works, one of which is his *Commentary* (*Tafsīr*), the earliest extant complete Qur'an commentary. His views inform a wide range of later exegetes, including al-Ṭabarī, who borrows from him without naming him.[24] Three elements of Muqātil's approach are noteworthy in his comments on verses seen as positive about the previous scriptures.[25]

First, he narrows the application of verses which make apparently broad positive statements. Q5:43–48 is the longest positive passage, with Q5:43 mentioning "The Torah, containing the judgment of God." Muqātil states that this refers specifically to the issues of stoning for the married man and woman and to retaliation for murder.[26] Later in his commentary on these six verses, he refers to stoning, and the mission of Muhammad, as the referent, and later, stoning and the description of Muhammad. At the close of this discussion he turns to Q5:47,

---

23 For an introduction to early Qur'an commentaries discussing Christians and Christianity see Claude Gilliot, "Christians and Christianity in Islamic Exegesis.", In *CMR*, 1, 31–56.

24 Saleh, "Rereading al-Ṭabarī", 188–91, on al-Ṭabarī's borrowing from Muqātil. Negative views of Muqātil are often assumed to be because of his reliance on Jewish and Christian traditions, but may more accurately be linked to his use of written sources and lack of use of chains of transmission; see Lyall Armstrong, *The* Quṣṣāṣ *of Early Islam*, IHC 139 (Leiden: Brill, 2017), 97–110.

25 See *Tafsīr Muqātil bin Sulaymān*, 3 vols., (Beirut: Dār al-kutub al-'ilmiyyah, 2003). On Muqātil's commentary, see Nicolai Sinai, "The Qur'anic Commentary of Muqātil b. Sulaymān and the Evolution of Early *Tafsīr* Literature," in Tafsīr *and Islamic Intellectual History: Exploring the Boundaries of a Genre*, eds. Andreas Görke and Johanna Pink (Oxford: OUP, in association with the Institute of Ismaili Studies, 2014), 113–43.

26 Muqātil, *Tafsīr*, I: 301.

which appeals to the People of the Gospel to judge by the Gospel. Muqātil states that this refers specifically to judgment about forgiveness regarding a killer, or someone who injures another or strikes them. Similar comments are made in relation to Q5:66, while the exhortation to Jews and Christians in Q5:68 to observe their scriptures is said to concern "the matter of Muhammad."[27] Regarding Q11:17, the role of the *Tawrāt* as a model and a mercy for those who believe in it is said to refer to the "People of the Tawrāt" who believe in the Qur'an.[28]

Muqātil's brief comment on Q6:115 also narrows the application of an apparently broad verse. He interprets the phrase, "No one can change His words" as meaning that, "there is no alteration (*tabdīl*) concerning his statement about the victory (*naṣr*) of Muhammad."[29] Regarding the same statement in Q18:27 Muqātil is less specific, writing that it means, "No alteration (*taḥwīl*) regarding his statement, because his statement is his mention of truth, so God warned his Prophet against adding to it or taking from it" – in the next Qur'anic phrase, "You will find no refuge other than him."[30] In neither comment does he refer to the previous scriptures, but we will see below that al-Ṭabarī moves closer towards making this connection.

Muqātil's second emphasis in discussing apparently positive verses is criticism of the People of the Book. Q2:285, stating that every believer believes in God's books, plural, prompts him to comment that the People of the Book are at fault for only believing in some of these books. Jews reject the *Injīl* and the Qur'an, and Christians reject the Qur'an, whereas Muslims accept *Tawrāt*, *Injīl* and Qur'an.[31]

Thirdly, Muqātil defends the status of Muhammad. Q10:94, addressing Muhammad, states, "If you are in doubt about what We have sent down to you, ask those who have been reciting the Book before you." Muqātil writes that the people to ask are ʿAbd Allāh b. Salām and his companions, in other words Jews who had accepted Islam. By being specific in this way Muqātil diverts the interpretation away from a more general reference to the People of the Book and towards an exhortation to consult those who have converted to Islam.[32] In a hadith Muhammad's response to the encouragement to ask others

27 Muqātil, *Tafsīr*, 1: 312.
28 Muqātil, *Tafsīr*, 2: 113.
29 Muqātil, *Tafsīr*, 1: 327.
30 Muqātil, *Tafsīr*, 2: 286.
31 Muqātil, *Tafsīr*, I: 153.
32 For more on ʿAbd Allāh b. Salām see Chapter 3, below.

if in doubt is, "I do not doubt and I do not ask."[33] For Muqātil the phrase, "If you are in doubt" is a rhetorical device to draw out a statement about this lack of doubt in Muhammad.[34] So, to summarise, in his exegesis of these positive verses, Muqātil limits their application, criticises the People of the Book, and defends the status of Muhammad.

2.5.1.2 Al-Ṭabarī

Abū Ja'far Muḥammad ibn Jarīr al-Ṭabarī was born in Tabaristan, in present-day northern Iran, in 224/839, and died in Baghdad, the intellectual capital of the Islamic world of the time, in 310/923. His commentary draws together a huge number of exegetical reports, not always in harmony, with the author sometimes indicating his own preference or opinion, sometimes not.[35] Though spending much of his life in 9th10th century Baghdad, the centre of intellectual exchanges between members of the three monotheistic faiths, al-Ṭabarī held the unusual view that Jews and Christians should be expelled from Muslim lands, unless they were needed.[36]

Al-Ṭabarī's exegesis of Q2:4 indicates his overall approach. Those who are god-fearing (*muttaqūn*, Q2:1) are described in Q2:4 as those, "who believe in what has been sent down to you, and what was sent down before you." Al-Ṭabarī makes clear that only those who believe in the previous scriptures and – crucially – also believe in what was revealed to Muhammad can be described as god-fearing.[37] This is a pattern repeated elsewhere. Where people are exhorted

---

33 'Abd al-Razzāq al-Ṣan'ānī, *Al-Muṣannaf*, vol. 6, (Beirut: al-Majlis al-'Ilmī, 1972), 125–26, no. 10211. This hadith is not found in the six canonical Sunni collections.

34 Muqātil, *Tafsīr*, II: 104.

35 Al-Ṭabarī, *Jāmi' al-bayān 'an ta'wīl al-Qur'ān*, ed. M. and A. Shākir, 16 vols., (Cairo: Dār al-ma'ārif, 1955). References throughout the present study are taken from this edition unless otherwise stated. Literature on al-Ṭabari is very extensive; as background to the current study see Abdelmajid Charfi, "Christianity in the Qur'an Commentary of Ṭabarī," *Islamochristiana* 6 (1980): 105–48, and Claude Gilliot, "Ṭabarī et les chrétiens Taġlibites," in *Annales du Département des études arabes, Université Saint–Joseph, Beyrouth. In Memoriam Jean Maurice Fiey 1914–1995*, 1991–92 (1996): 145–59.

36 Seth Ward, "A Fragment from an Unknown Work by al-Ṭabarī on the Tradition 'Expel the Jews and Christians from the Arabian Peninsula (and the Lands of Islam)'," *BSOAS* 53 (1990): 407–420.

37 Al-Ṭabarī, *Tafsīr* 1: 244–45; translated in John Cooper, *The Commentary on the Qur'an by Abū Ja'far Muḥammad bin Jarīr al-Ṭabarī*, vol. 1 (Oxford: OUP, 1987), 101. No further volumes of this series were produced, making it the only English translation of al-Ṭabarī's commentary available in book form.

to have faith in the *Tawrāt*, *Injīl*, and also what was sent down to them through Muhammad (e. g. Q2:285, 5:66 and 68), the emphasis is on the importance of accepting all the revelations, including the revelation to Muhammad, this last being the decisive issue. So, as in Muqātil, apparent Qur'anic affirmation of previous scripture as part of divine revelation is used to criticise the People of the Book for not believing in revelation to Muhammad.

On Q5:44 al-Ṭabarī includes several reports explaining the meaning of the exhortation to judge by what God sent down in the *Tawrāt*. What was sent down can refer to the ordinances (*ḥudūd*) of God, or to an explanation of a quarrel about someone killed in battle, or to the issue of stoning for adultery.[38]

Q5:44 terms those who do not judge by what God sent down in the previous scriptures "disbelievers" (*kāfirūn*). But what is the nature of their unbelief? One explanation given by al-Ṭabarī is that this refers to Jews who altered (*ḥarrafū*) the Book of God and changed (*baddalū*) his judgment. These terms will be more prominent in the discussion of negative verses about the previous scriptures, discussed below. Here the nature of the tampering is not clear.[39]

At Q5:46 al-Ṭabarī offers some explanation as to how to regard the *Injīl*, since it contains "guidance and light."[40] The *Injīl* explains what the people are ignorant of regarding the judgment of God in the time of Jesus. It also reveals to Jesus what was sent down before him from God, in particular regarding what is permitted or forbidden. Clearly this is a concept of the "Gospel" very much shaped by Muslim ideas.

Al-Ṭabarī also discusses at some length the meaning of *muhaymin* in Q5:48. As noted above, this is a term describing the Qur'an, and he understands it as denoting protector or guardian over the previous scriptures.[41] Yet despite this guardianship it appears that the scriptures do differ in certain ways. So al-Ṭabarī addresses an obvious question. Can a believer obey all the revealed scriptures if they differ from one another, and if some abrogate others? This question is raised implicitly by many Qur'anic verses, and is voiced by al-Ṭabarī in discussing Q5:66. This verse states regarding the People of the Book, "Had they observed the Torah and the Gospel, and what was sent down to them from their Lord, they would indeed have eaten from (what was) above them and from (what was) beneath their feet". The answer to how to accept all scriptures despite their differences is that though believers may differ over certain laws, "they are

38 Al-Ṭabarī, *Tafsīr* 10: 345–46.
39 Al-Ṭabarī, *Tafsīr* 10: 346.
40 Al-Ṭabarī, *Tafsīr* 10: 383.
41 See footnote 19 above.

in agreement (*muttafiqa*) concerning the matter of faith in the messengers of God, and trust in what came through him from God."[42] This harmonization of the content of different scriptures clearly operates at a very broad level, and is aimed at pointing out the shortcomings in the faith of Jews and Christians.

Al-Ṭabarī's discussion of Q10:94 raises the question of whether Muhammad could have been subject to doubt.[43] As already noted, the verse reads, "If you [Muhammad] are in doubt about what We have sent down to you, ask those who have been reciting the Book before you." As for whom Muhammad should consult, al-Ṭabarī, like Muqātil, cites various traditions interpreting the verse as encouraging Muhammad to ask those from the People of the Book who have put their faith in him, such as 'Abd Allah b. Salām. However, he also cites one tradition advising consulting the People of the Book in general, not just those who believe in Muhammad. As to the issue of doubt, al-Ṭabarī cites traditions affirming that Muhammad did not doubt and did not ask questions of others as a result. Responding to the objection that the verse indicates the contrary, al-Ṭabarī states that this is a form of address to Muhammad which should be understood as a theoretical question indicating a negative answer, along the lines of "if you are in doubt (though of course you are not…)." Al-Ṭabarī compares this to a master saying to his slave, "if you are my slave, then obey me," or a father saying to his son, "if you are my son, then honour me." The answer to these questions should be obvious. Likewise here – so real doubt is not in view.

In much of this material al-Ṭabarī presents interpretations resembling those of Muqātil, along with other avenues of exploration such as how to accept all scriptures even though they differ. The steadfast focus on Muhammad and the primacy of Islam are, unsurprisingly, centre stage.

2.5.1.3 Al-Qummī

'Alī bin Ibrāhīm al-Qummī was an important early Shia Qur'an commentator, who lived, as his name indicates, in the Persian city of Qom (Arabic "Qumm"). His exact dates are unknown, but he is thought to have lived during the time of the lesser occultation of the Twelfth Imam (from c. 261/874 into the fourth /tenth century).[44] His commentary does not discuss every verse of the Qur'an, and I shall discuss below only passages where something new or significant is

42 Al-Ṭabarī, *Tafsīr*, 10:462.
43 Al-Ṭabarī, *Tafsīr* 15:200 – 03.
44 Meir Bar-Asher, *Scripture and Exegesis*, 34.

added to the preceding discussion, while sometimes noting silences on passages others treat as worthy of comment.

On Q2:4 al-Qummī has nothing specific to say about the need for the god-fearing to accept all revealed scriptures. However, he comments on Q2:6 in a way relevant to the same issue.[45] Q2:6 states, "Surely those who disbelieve – (it is) the same for them whether you warn them or do not warn them. They will not believe." Al-Qummī states that this verse was sent down concerning the Jews and Christians, to whom God had sent the description of Muhammad in the *Tawrāt*, *Zabūr* and *Injīl*. In support of this he quotes Q48:29 as confirming that the description of Muhammad is in these scriptures. So as in our earlier examples, al-Qummī's commentary here concentrates not on the significance of believing in the previous scriptures, but on how it is essential to believe in all the scriptures, including the Qur'an. Jews and Christians are therefore in the wrong.

Al-Qummī says nothing about the reference to believing in "books" in Q2:285. He has little to say on Q5:43–48 and omits Q5:46–47 altogether. He explains that Q5:45, detailing aspects of the law of retaliation ("the eye for the eye…") in the *Tawrāt*,[46] is abrogated by Q2:178, which states, "The (law of) retaliation is prescribed for you in (the case of) those who have been killed: the free man for the free man, the slave for the slave, and the female for the female". Al-Qummī's point here is that the law of retaliation is now "prescribed for you", that is Muslims, removing any need to rely on its revelation to Jews. He is thereby seeking to put distance between the Qur'an and the *Tawrāt*.[47]

On Q5:66, apparently exhorting the People of the Book to base themselves on their own scriptures, al-Qummī's emphasis is on the final phrase, "Some of them are a moderate community". This moderate community is described as Jews who accept Islam, again highlighting that the previous scriptures alone are not enough for acceptable faith. Q6:91–92 affirms the *Tawrāt* as "a light and a guidance," but also criticises the Jews for hiding some of it from other people. Al-Qummī identifies the hidden material as information about the Messenger.[48]

A very interesting turn is taken in his discussion of Q10:94 (" If you [Muhammad] are in doubt about what We have sent down to you, ask those who have been reciting the Book before you.") Rather than regarding "those who have

45 Al-Qummī, *Tafsīr al-Qummī* (Najaf: Maktabat al-Hudā, 1967), 1: 32–33.
46 Cf. Exod 21:24, Lev 24:20, Deut 19:21.
47 Al-Qummī, *Tafsīr*, 1: 169.
48 Al-Qummī, *Tafsīr*, 1: 210.

been reading the Book before you" as the People of the Book, al-Qummī identifies them as "the prophets". He interprets the verse as a reference to an experience during Muhammad's Night Journey, where he is understood to be taken, either spiritually or physically, from Mecca to Jerusalem and from there up to Heaven.[49] Al-Qummī recounts Muhammad's reaction to perceiving in Heaven the nobility and important standing with God of 'Alī, later to be fourth Caliph and the focus of intense Shia devotion.[50] Understanding the true nature of 'Alī's greatness causes Muhammad to have some form of doubt. In al-Qummī's interpretation, the verse therefore exhorts Muhammad, if he has doubt about his own role because of 'Alī's greatness, to consult those (the prophets) who also had 'Alī's greatness revealed in their own scriptures. The implication is that consulting previous prophets would bring Muhammad reassurance of his own high standing alongside that of 'Alī.[51] So the role of the previous scriptures here is to confirm the greatness of 'Alī and also of Muhammad.

Reflecting on all three commentators, apparently positive verses about previous scriptures are generally employed in the service of supporting Islamic claims, in particular the centrality of Muhammad's prophethood. Commentators also use the verses to criticise those Jews and Christians who do not complete their faith by believing in the Qur'an, and thus displease God.

2.5.2 Commentary on Negative Verses

The question "Does the Qur'an teach that the text of the previous scriptures is corrupted?" might appear simple. But it is important to distinguish accusations levelled at particular groups in particular places from the broader charge that the Qur'an supports Biblical corruption as a general phenomenon.[52] The following

---

49 See Christiane Gruber and Frederick Colby, eds., *The Prophet's Ascension: Cross-Cultural Encounters with the Islamic Mi'raj Tales* (Bloomington, IN: Indiana University Press, 2010).

50 Al-Qummī, *Tafsīr*, 1: 316–17.

51 The passage is translated and analysed in Bar-Asher, *Scripture*, 225–232, who emphasizes Muhammad's envy of 'Alī. For a different translation and interpretation of this passage, altering Muhammad's reaction from envy to doubt, see Shahab Ahmed, Review of Bar-Asher, *JAOS* 123 (2003), 183–85.

52 This distinction is not made in, for example, Shari Lowin, "Revision and Alteration," in: *EQ* 4. Similarly Rainer Brunner, "Dispute," 439, in summing up Shī'ite perspectives on the Qur'an, comments, "And as – according to a well-known tradition backed by the Qur'an – both the Torah and the Gospel had been forged, there remained little doubt that the Qur'an had suffered the same fate." Brunner refers the reader to Q2:75, 4:46, 5:13, 5:41; see also Samuel Behloul, "The Testimony of Reason and Historical Reality: Ibn Ḥazm's Refutation of Christian-

discussion aims to shed light on this issue, drawing on the same three exegetes discussed above.[53]

2.5.2.1 Muqātil b. Sulaymān

Muqātil's discussion of possible corruption can be divided into verses of alteration, verses of concealment, and verses about other categories.[54] Turning first to alteration, his treatment of Q2:75 features a long story about seventy leaders associated with Moses, who hear the voice of God. Some of these subsequently alter their report of what God said.[55]

Three verses, Q4:46, 5:13 and 5:41 all feature the phrase, "they alter words from their positions." Muqātil takes this to mean from their places in the *Tawrāt*. In the first two of these verses, he records that it is the description of Muhammad which the Jews have altered in some way. Q5:13 also concerns the Jews breaking their covenant with God. For Muqātil, this act of unfaithfulness centres on Jews denying knowledge of Muhammad which they possessed in the *Tawrāt*.[56]

In Q5:41, altering words is about the commandment to stone the adulterer. So the commandment of stoning and the description of Muhammad are the key elements which have been altered.

Turning secondly to acts of concealment, there are many references, mainly using words derived from the root *katama*. Most of these concern, once again,

---

ity," in *Ibn Ḥazm: the Life and Works of a Controversial Thinker*, eds. Maribel Fierro, Camilla Adang and Sabine Schmidtke (Leiden: Brill, 2013), 457. The distinction between a localised as opposed to general accusation is evident, however, in John Burton, "The Corruption of the Scriptures," *Occasional Papers of the School of 'Abbāsid Studies* 4 (1992), 95–106; W. Montgomery Watt, "The Early Development of the Muslim Attitude to the Bible,"; Mahmoud Ayoub, " 'Uzayr in the Qur'an and Muslim Tradition," in *Studies in Islamic and Judaic Traditions*, eds. William Brinner and Stephen Ricks (Atlanta: Scholars' Press, 1986), 5. Cf. the discussion in Nickel, *Tampering*, 6–8.

53 Nickel, *Tampering*, 67–116, discusses the treatment of negative verses by Muqātil, and also by al-Ṭabarī (117–64). On al-Ṭabarī see also Burton, "Corruption".

54 This division is used in the detailed treatment by Nickel, *Tampering*, 73–116.

55 Muqātil, *Tafsīr*, 1: 57–58; for a summary see Nickel, *Tampering*, 74. There are distant echoes here of the Biblical book of Numbers 11:16–30.

56 The idea of the covenant-breaking of the Children of Israel is sometimes related by later exegetes to the covenant of the prophets in Q3:81. In this verse former prophets accept their responsibility to affirm and support the message of a subsequent prophet. Some exegetes regard the oath-taking in Q3:81 as also taken by the Children of Israel in general, not just the prophets, making the subsequent unfaithfulness of the Jews all the more reprehensible. See Jacob Lassner, "The Covenant of the Prophets: Muslim Texts, Jewish Subtexts," *AJSR* 15 (1990): 207–38.

concealing information about Muhammad.[57] In Q2:146 information about the Ka'ba, the centre of ritual devotion in Mecca, is said to be concealed.[58] In Q4:37 information about Muhammad is said to be concealed by the Jewish leaders, and some manuscripts of Muqātil's commentary say that they "erased (*maḥā*) it from the *Tawrāt*." This would be a clear indication of belief in textual alteration, albeit attributable to the specific Jewish leaders in question.[59]

Two other key verses in regard to textual corruption are Q2:79 and Q3:78. On Q2:79 Muqātil states that "those who write the Book with their (own) hands" refers to Jewish leaders who erase the description of Muhammad and replace it with something else.[60] On Q3:78 he likewise posits a process of erasure and replacement, which seems surprising given that the verse states that among the Jews exists, "a group of them who twist their tongues with the book", indicating verbal misreporting rather than textual alteration.[61]

So Muqātil seems to consider that the Jews had access to a basically sound text with information about Muhammad sufficient to condemn their lack of response. Jewish action was localised in the first/seventh century, involving mainly concealment, but occasionally some erasure of words. Muqātil does not discuss whether these various types of interference with the *Tawrāt* spread to the wider Jewish community beyond the Ḥijāz, the area of the Arabian Peninsula encompassing Mecca and Medina.

2.5.2.2 Al-Ṭabarī

Al-Ṭabarī provides many reports relating to alteration of the previous scriptures, but his own view is not easy to discern. Sometimes he is clear that the meaning of the verb *ḥarrafū* is about alteration of meaning and interpretation (*ma'nā* and *ta'wīl*). He offers this as a clear statement in relation to the exegesis of Q2:75.[62] He indicates likewise at Q4:46 that the verb "*yuḥarrifūna*" ("they alter") refers to changes of meaning and interpretation, again using the terms *ma'nā* and *ta'wīl*.[63]

57 On concealment see Nickel, *Tampering*, 88–96.
58 Muqātil, *Tafsīr*, 1: 84–86.
59 Muqātil, *Tafsīr*, 1:229. See Nickel, *Tampering*, 94–95, who implies that the reference to erasing might be a later insertion into Muqātil's text in commenting, "That the exegete would interpret 'conceal' with 'erase' is unusual, and... seems out of place" (95). The reference to erasing is included in the edition used in the present study.
60 See Muqātil, *Tafsīr* 1: 59; cf. Nickel, *Tampering*, 101.
61 Muqātil, *Tafsīr*, 1:178.
62 Al-Ṭabarī, *Tafsīr*, 2: 248.
63 Al-Ṭabarī, *Tafsīr*, 8: 430.

However, elsewhere al-Ṭabarī indicates something more than wrong interpretation. On Q2:79 he notes that "some Jews wrote a book in line with their own interpretations, departing from what God sent down to his prophet Moses."[64]

On Q3:78, a verse stating that the Jews twist their tongues (*yalūna*), he includes a report stating that this means that the Jews invented something (*ibtada'ū*) and added to the text (*yazīdūna*).[65] On Q5:13 he states that what the Jews wrote was "not what God sent down to their prophet."[66]

Why he presents this diversity of views is uncertain, as is his own definitive position. Adang proposes that al-Ṭabarī considered that two versions of the Torah were in circulation. One was genuine, as restored by Ezra, according to *4 Ezra*, on which al-Ṭabarī relied.[67] A second version was a corrupted Torah written by rabbis, and which Jews mistook for the genuine text.[68] Nickel, taking a different approach, argues that "the obstinacy of the Jews was a reigning narrative theme in the mind of the exegetes."[69] This obstinacy relates primarily to Jewish rejection of knowledge of Muhammad. But since this obstinacy requires a deliberate rejection of knowledge already possessed, then the "reigning narrative theme" likewise requires a largely intact Torah to deliver this knowledge, and this theme therefore outweighs ideas about acts of textual corruption. As often with al-Ṭabarī, it is perhaps impossible to discern his exact position on the topic of corruption; indeed, perhaps he did not have an "exact" position, but was content to present a plurality of ideas.

2.5.2.3 Al-Qummī

Al-Qummī passes over several of the negative verses discussed above without comment, or in some cases without comment on the phrases relevant to this study.[70] As noted previously, Q2:75 states of the Jews that, "a group of them has already heard the word of God, (and) then altered it after they had understood it". Al-Qummī writes that certain Jews used to test the Muslims concerning what was in the *Tawrāt* about the description of the Messenger of God and his

64 Al-Ṭabarī, *Tafsīr*, 2: 270.
65 Al-Ṭabarī, *Tafsīr*, 6: 536.
66 Al-Ṭabarī, *Tafsīr*, 10: 129.
67 See Whittingham, "Ezra," 259–60. For more on the significance of *4 Ezra*, see Chapter 5.
68 Adang, *Muslim Writers*, 231.
69 Nickel, *Tampering*, 212.
70 Q2:146, 4:37, 46, 5:41.

Companions.[71] More distinctively Shī'ite is his commentary on Q5:13, "they alter words from their positions." Al-Qummī relates this to 'Alī, whom he terms, "The Commander of the Faithful." The verse, he states, is about, "the removal of the Commander of the Faithful from his position. The indicator of that is the statement (*kalima*) of the Commander of the Faithful, peace be upon him, 'He established it as a statement everlasting in its effect', meaning the Imamate."[72] So Jews here have removed from their scripture a reference to 'Alī's establishment of the Imamate from their Scripture, a cardinal point of Twelver Shia belief. This echoes early Shia views (discussed in Chapter 1) that Sunnis had, like the Jews mentioned here, also removed references to 'Alī from the Qur'an. So here it is 'Alī, not Muhammad, who is being in some way concealed. But the focus in al-Qummī's discussion of Q5:13 on Jews removing from their scripture a central figure in the commentator's own tradition parallels Sunni commentaries' focus on Jewish concealment or removal from the text of reference to Muhammad.

2.5.3 Conclusion

On the more affirmative verses about previous scripture, the commentators' discussion removes any positive implications from these verses. Some of the exegetical discussion narrows the content affirmed by the previous scriptures to their reference to affirmation of Muhammad, or the issue of stoning. The commentators' affirmation of Muslim concerns and narrowing of application to exclude what might otherwise be assumed to be in view – in this case Biblical scripture in general – is a pattern also found in exegetical discussion of another important Qur'anic category, "the People of the Book". In much traditional Muslim exegesis this phrase is interpreted as referring to those amongst the Jews and Christians who believed in Muhammad and his message, not to Jews and Christians in general. "Delimitation and specification clearly control the emerging depiction."[73] Likewise, our survey indicates, regarding references to previous scriptures.

Secondly, verses apparently affirming belief in the previous scriptures along with the Qur'an are used to criticise any who do not believe in all these scriptures, with belief in the Qur'an becoming the central focus. Thirdly, al-Qummī in-

71 Al-Qummī, *Tafsīr*, 1: 50.
72 Al-Qummī, *Tafsīr*, 2: 163–64.
73 Jane Dammen McAuliffe, *Qur'anic Christians: an Analysis of Classical and Modern Exegesis* (Cambridge: CUP, 1991), 287.

troduces particular Shīʿite concerns which depart from the interests of his Sunni counterparts.

Overall, it can be said that discussion of these verses affirms aspects of Islam, without exploring the issues raised by any possible ongoing validity of the previous scriptures.

Turning to discussion of the negative verses, it appears that both the Qur'an and the earliest commentaries seem to assume a broadly authentic text, and that teaching about wholesale corruption enters at a later stage. Instead, references to corruption have their own specific meanings, and usually refer to particular incidents presumed to have occurred in Medina, and only rarely involving any alteration of the text, even in a local setting. This is reinforced by the findings of this survey of exegesis on important Qur'anic verses, which shows that resisting the information about Muhammad is the key error of the People of the Book, and that this is the meaning behind acts of concealment or deception regarding scripture.[74] The presumed presence in the previous scriptures of this core of information about Muhammad, and about true religion, helps to explain why the great majority of verses about these scriptures are positive.

The following chapters will, amongst other things, illuminate in what ways the question of corruption developed. But the key story regarding the previous scriptures in early commentaries is not about faulty texts but about Jewish and Christian failure or refusal to recognize what had been revealed to them in texts which the Qur'an affirms.

2.6 Excursus: The Question of Abrogation: Does the Qur'an Abrogate the Bible?

2.6.1 Introduction

In broad terms abrogation (*naskh*) refers to the cancelling of one passage of scripture by another. A common view of the Bible in modern Muslim thought is that it is abrogated, in whole or part, by the coming of the Qur'an. After exploring the concept of abrogation I will discuss the related concept of supersession, which appears to be a more suitable category for understanding Muslim views of the Bible.

Muslim thinking on abrogation can be divided into two types. External ab rogation involves the cancellation of all or part of one scripture by another

74 Cf. Nickel, *Tampering*, 222.

later scripture, such as the abrogation of the Bible by the Qur'an. Internal abrogation involves the cancellation of one part of a scripture by another part of that same scripture, so in the context of Islam the replacement of one Qur'anic ruling by another one, understood to have been revealed later. Internal abrogation can occur even if the text of the first ruling remains in the Qur'anic text.

Supersession, however, is the more general notion that one religion has replaced another. The obvious implication of this is that part or all of the scripture of the previous faith is likewise superseded. While abrogation has a long history in classical and modern Islamic discussion, we begin by looking briefly at the Qur'an itself, in isolation from later interpretations, before turning to those interpretations.

2.6.2 Abrogation in the Qur'an

The two most famous Qur'anic verses used to discuss abrogation are Q 2:106 and 16:101. Q 2:106 states, "Whatever verse We cancel or cause to be forgotten, We bring a better (one) than it, or (one) similar to it. Do you not know that God is powerful over everything?" Q16:101 reads, "When We exchange a verse in place of (another) verse – and God knows what He sends down – they say, 'You are only a forger!' No! But most of them do not know (anything)." These two verses are central to Muslim arguments about abrogation. But do they concern the Bible? Muslim scholarship has from earliest times taken these verses to teach internal abrogation.[75] But in more recent years, as will be discussed in volume 2 of the present study, it has become more common to use these verses to support the abrogation of the Bible.

An alternative view of Q2:106 and 16:101 is presented by Burton. He argues that even though internal abrogation was taken to be the message of these verses for centuries, this was mistaken, and they in fact teach a form of external abrogation. This external abrogation is not to be understood as wholesale cancellation of one or both Biblical testaments by the Qur'an. Rather, it is abrogation of certain Biblical laws by new Qur'anic laws, and that explains why both 2:106 and 16:101 occur before lengthy introductions of new laws in the

75 The earliest extant work devoted entirely to abrogation is by Abū 'Ubayd (d. c.224/838). See John Burton, ed., *Abū 'Ubaid al-Qāsim b. Sallām's* K. al-nāsikh wa'l-mansūkh *(MS. Istanbul, Topkapi, Ahmet III A 143)* (Cambridge: E.J.W. Gibb Memorial Trust, 1987). Note also the concept of "emergence" (*badā'*), or "the advent of a divine decree which changes a previous divine decree in response to new circumstances"; see Amir-Moezzi, Mohammad Ali, "Badā'", in: *EI3*, consulted online on 08 May 2020 <http://dx.doi.org/10.1163/1573-3912_ei3_COM_25083.

Qur'an.[76] This is argued on various grounds. First, the changeable nature of divine laws over time is certainly an idea taught in the Qur'an. For example, Q7:157 states that God, through Muhammad, is in the process of changing what is lawful and unlawful in certain respects. Secondly, actual changes in laws are clearly embodied in the text of the Qur'an, for example the change in the direction of prayer from Jerusalem to Mecca in Q2:143–44. Thirdly, Q2:105 is clearly referring to a context of non-believers not wishing to see anything good sent down, implying that new revelation is in fact imminent. The case is not conclusive, but plausible.[77]

2.6.3 Abrogation in Classical Scholarship

Early Muslim scholars' technical treatment of abrogation is concerned with internal abrogation. This takes various forms, a core idea of abrogation being that one verse is understood to be substituted by another which has been revealed later in time. The earliest discussion of this occurs in al-Shāfiʿī's *Epistle* (*al-Risāla*), and al-Shāfiʿī cites the two Qur'anic verses which became pivotal to treatment of abrogation, Q2:106 and Q16:101.[78] The literature discusses verses which abrogate others and those which are abrogated (*al-nāsikh wa'l-mansūkh*).

Interestingly, Muslim discussions of internal abrogation do not raise the issue of positive verses about the previous scriptures being abrogated by negative verses. This is despite the fact that all the negative verses occur in Suras 2–7, traditionally regarded as Medinan and therefore late, thereby being well-placed to act as abrogating texts.

In sum, early Muslim writers on abrogation as a technical subject do not focus on the abrogation of previous scriptures. Instead the focus in discussion of previous faiths is on the phenomenon of supersession.[79]

76 John Burton, *The Sources of Islamic Law*, 165–183.
77 See the review of Burton by David Powers, *JRAS* Third series, vol. 2 (1992), 437.
78 Arabic text and English translation in Al-Shāfiʿī, *The Epistle on Legal Theory*, edited and translated by Joseph Lowry (New York: NYUP, 2013), 82 (Arabic), 83 (English).
79 A point recognized by Camilla Adang, *Muslim Writers on Judaism and the Hebrew Bible* (Leiden: Brill, 1996), chapter 6, "The Abrogation of the Mosaic Law," 192–222; and see 194.

2.6.4 Supersession

The belief that previous faiths are superseded by Islam, and therefore also their scriptures, was assumed in early Islam. This comes to be termed 'abrogation' in a non-technical sense separate from the discussions about internal Qur'anic abrogation. Instead of Q2:106 or 16:101, the foundation of supersessionism is hadiths used to interpret Q3:19 and 3:85. Q3:19 states, "Surely the religion with God is Islam." Similarly, Q3:85 states, "Whoever desires a religion other than Islam, it will not be accepted from him, and in the Hereafter he will be one of the losers." Since Arabic does not use capital letters it is possible to translate the Arabic term *islām* in both of these verses in its wider meaning of "submission", rather than as a reference to "Islam", understood as the developed religion identified by that name. But Muslims typically find in these verses evidence that Islam supplants other faiths.

One example, literally set in stone, is carved into the Dome of the Rock in Jerusalem. Supersession appears to be one of the aims behind the Qur'anic quotations found in the inscriptions here, inscribed by the order of Caliph 'Abd al-Malik in 72/691. These inscriptions focus on themes setting Islam apart from its monotheistic predecessor faiths, and Q3:19 features amongst them.[80]

Sometimes supersession and internal Qur'anic abrogation become intertwined. There is discussion over whether Q3:85 abrogates Q2:62, an optimistic verse regarding the eternal prospects of members of other faiths. It states, "Surely those who believe, and those who are Jews, and the Christians, and the Sabians – whoever believes in God and the Last Day, and does righteousness – they have their reward with their Lord. (There will be) no fear on them, nor will they sorrow." Al-Ṭabarī cites a hadith stating that this verse is abrogated by Q3:85. He rejects this view, advocating instead the theory that God all along instituted stages of revelation whereby a faith had salvific value until the next messenger brought a new dispensation. Thus, according to al-Ṭabarī, God did not affirm being Christian or Jewish in Q2:62, and then abrogate this in Q3:85. Instead, the beginning of revelation to Muhammad saw the break point whereby being

---

80 See Christel Kessler, " 'Abd Al-Malik's Inscription on the Dome of the Rock: a reconsideration," in *Journal of the Royal Asiatic Society of Great Britain and Ireland* 1 (1970), 12, whose article includes the Arabic text of all the inscriptions; for an English translation see Estelle Whelan, "Forgotten Witness: Evidence for the Early Codification of the Qur'ān," *JAOS* 118 (1998): 1–14; for translation of Q3:19 see p. 4. For an overview of discussions of the overall purpose of the Dome of the Rock see Milka Levy-Rubin, "Why was the Dome of the Rock Built? A New Perspective on a Long–discussed Question," *BSOAS* 80 (2017): 441–64.

Christian or Jewish was no longer valid. For al-Ṭabarī, Christianity is superseded, but not because of supposed internal Qur'anic abrogation of Q2:62 by 3:85.[81]

2.6.5 Abrogation of law

The earliest extant argument for the abrogation of Jewish laws is by al-Naẓẓām (d. 231/846). He argues that what God decreed through Moses could be annulled by later divine decrees. This is because what Moses conveys is good only because God decrees it to be good. The goodness of a decree is not intrinsic to it and for that reason the decree can be altered.[82]

The principal of divine leniency is important in relation to abrogation of laws. Ibn Qutayba interprets the reference in Q 2:106 to God bringing "a better (one) than it, or (one) similar to it," to mean that God brings something easier. In other words, God abrogates a harder law by introducing an easier one.[83] Maghen has shown the extent to which the same notion of replacing what is hard with something easier also applies to the Qur'an's abrogation of prior Jewish laws, and that this is central to defining Islamic identity in relation to Judaism.[84] So Jewish law can be presented by Muslims as uniquely burdensome, in contrast to the alleviation brought by God through Islam.

2.6.6 The Bible and Internal Qur'anic Abrogation

There are two further issues connecting the Bible with the phenomenon of internal Qur'anic abrogation. First, in support of the view that abrogation within the Qur'an was possible in principle, Muslims commonly cited cases of supposed internal abrogation within the Bible, such as the wide permission to eat most things given to Noah, followed by the more restrictive food laws given to Moses.[85]

---

81 Al-Ṭabarī, *Tafsīr*, 2:143–56; see Jane Dammen McAuliffe, *Qur'anic Christians* (Cambridge: CUP, 1991), 111, 118–19.

82 The translation and Arabic text of al-Naẓẓām's (untitled) treatise are found in Arthur Tritton, "'Debate' Between a Muslim and a Jew," *IS* 1 (1962), 61.

83 Ibn Qutayba, *Kitāb Ta'wīl mukhtalif al-ḥadīth* (Cairo: Maktabat al-Kulliyāt al-Azhariyya, 1966), 195; and see Adang, *Muslim Writers*, 197.

84 Ze'ev Maghen, *After Hardship Cometh Ease: The Jews as Backdrop for Muslim Moderation* ZGKIO 17 (Berlin: Walter de Gruyter, 2006), 12.

85 Sabine Schmidtke, "Abū al-Ḥusayn al-Baṣrī on the Torah and its Abrogation," *Mélanges de l'université Saint Joseph* 61 (2008), 566–67.

Secondly, the authority of the previous scriptures can be invoked to clarify an issue related to internal Qur'anic abrogation. The penalty of stoning for adultery, a part of Islamic law, is not found in the Qur'an, which stipulates flogging (Q24:2). But most Muslims writing on this regarded a supposed verse on stoning to have been removed from the Qur'anic text, an instance of the abrogation of the text but not the ruling it conveys.[86]

2.6.7 Conclusion

The role of the previous scriptures in discussions of abrogation and supersession is multi-faceted. Sometimes the previous scriptures are seen as superseded. On other occasions they are seen as providing justification for the belief in internal abrogation. The previous scriptures can also be caught up in discussions about the laws of a previous community being abrogated. It is plausible to consider that defending the integrity of the Qur'an against non-Muslim accusations that it is self-contradictory, and hence subject to alteration (*taḥrīf*), lies in the background of these discussions.[87] That said, the drive to find internal coherence would be natural to any believer in their sacred text, even without the possible challenges from those of other faiths. The main point here is twofold. The previous scriptures were not, in the early centuries of Islam, seen as abrogated because of the principal verses on abrogation, Q2:106 and Q16:101. Yet this did not save them from being set aside in practice, as Q3:19, Q3:85 and more general arguments for the supremacy of Islam were used to show that the previous scriptures were superseded along with the faiths they underpinned.

Perhaps the Ḥanafī jurist Abū Bakr al-Jaṣṣās (d.370/981) captures the situation best. "Some of the later authors who were not of the people of *fiqh* claimed that there is no abrogation in the law of our Prophet Muhammad, and that everything which mentions *naskh* means only the *naskh* of the laws of the preceding prophets, such as the Sabbath and prayer to the east and west." Al-Jaṣṣāṣ regards this dismissal of internal Qur'anic abrogation as a sin committed by those lacking technical legal knowledge. At the same time he regards as self-evi-

86 See for example a hadith in the collection of al-Bukhārī, *Kitāb al-Manāqib* (*The Book of Virtues*), no. 3635, which affirms the penalty of stoning on the basis of its occurrence in the *Tawrāt*.
87 As suggested by Andrew Rippin, "The Exegetical Literature of Abrogation: form and content," in *Studies in Islamic and Middle Eastern Texts and Traditions in Memory of Norman Calder*, eds. Gerald Hawting, Jawid Mojaddedi and Alexander Samely (Oxford: OUP, 2000), 224.

dent the general abrogation of the "laws of the preceding prophets".[88] This is a process I prefer to describe as supersession. While the English term "abrogation" can be confused with the less technical implications of supersession, another way of putting it is that the Arabic term *naskh* in fact covers both.[89]

---

88 Abū Bakr al-Jaṣṣās, *Aḥkām al-Qur'ān*, vol. 1 (Constantinople: Dār al-Khilāfah al-ʿAlīyah: Maṭbaʿat al-Awqāf al-Islāmīyah, 1335AH), 59.
89 So Andrew Rippin, "Abrogation,", in: EI3, consulted online on 03 July 2019, http://dx.doi.org/10.1163/1573-3912_ei3_COM_0104

3 Hadith and Biographical Literature

3.1 Hadith and Biographical Literature

3.1.1 Understanding Hadith and Biographical Literature

This chapter will draw on two types of literature. One is known as hadith ("report") literature, the other *sīra* ("biography", literally "way", denoting conduct).[1] Hadith literature is the body of reports understood to preserve a record of what Muhammad said, did, and implicitly condoned, and a brief introduction is in order here. In Sunni Islam such literature also preserves some material from his Companions. (On Shia reports see below). A typical report would include the chain of transmitters, for example, "A said that B said that C said that D said that Muhammad said….", where A is the latest in time, and D the closest to Muhammad (or sometimes a Companion of Muhammad). In Sunni Islam six collections in particular came to be regarded as canonical, through a drawn-out process taking several centuries. Each collection was gathered by an individual compiler in the second/ninth century and consists of several thousand reports. These are the collections of al-Bukhārī (d. 256/870), Muslim (d.261/875), al-Tirmidhī (d.279/892), Ibn Māja (d. 273/886), Abu Dāwūd (d. 275/888) and al-Nasā'ī (d. 303/915).[2] Such works base their reliability on the chain of transmitters (the *isnād*), which connects the most recent transmitter of the report back through a list of individuals to Muhammad or one of his Companions. A small

1 The Arabic term "ḥadīth" has become sufficiently common in English usage not to be given full transliteration here. The English plural "hadiths" is used rather than the Arabic "*aḥādīth*".
2 There are various editions of these six collections, and all are now also translated into English, including at www.sunnah.com (Arabic text and English translations). For the Arabic-English parallel text editions, from which references are taken here, see *Ṣaḥīḥ al-Bukhārī* (Riyadh: Darussalam, 1997), *Ṣaḥīḥ Muslim* (Riyadh: Darussalam, 2007), *Jāmi' al-Tirmidhī* (Riyadh: Darussalam, 2007), *Sunan Ibn Mājah* (Riyadh: Darussalam, 2007), *Sunan Abū Dāwūd* (Riyadh: Darussalam, 2008), *Sunan al-Nasā'ī* (Riyadh: Darussalam, 2007). Numbering systems in different published editions can vary. Other works will also be cited in the course of the present chapter. On the canonization process relating to the most highly regarded collections, those of al-Bukhārī and Muslim, see Jonathan Brown, *The Canonization of al-Bukhārī and Muslim: the Formation and Function of the Sunni Ḥadīth Canon*, IHC 69 (Leiden: Brill, 2007). See also Stijn Aerts, "Canon and Canonisation of Ḥadīth,", in: *EI3*, consulted online on 03 July 2019, http://dx.doi.org/10.1163/1573-3912_ei3_COM_27570 On other hadith collections see Muhammad Abd al-Rauf, "Hadith Literature – 1: The Development of the Science of Hadith," in *The Cambridge History of Arabic Literature*, vol. 10, eds. A.F.L. Beeston, T.M. Johnstone, R.B.Serjeant, G.R. Smith (Cambridge: CUP: 1983–), 271–88.

https://doi.org/10.1515/9783110335880-006

number of earlier collections also exist such as *The Categorized* (*Al-Muṣannaf*) of ʻAbd al-Razzāq al-Ṣanʻānī (d.211/826).[3] For Sunnis, the early jurist al-Shāfiʻī (d. 204/820) established the view of the Hadith as a second form of revelation, distinct from the Qur'an, in which the meaning, though not the exact wording, was revelatory.[4]

The Hadith literature of Twelver Shia Muslims presents reports about the twelve greatly revered Imams, as well as about Muhammad.[5] The four most important Shia collections, which came to be regarded as canonical, are those by al-Kulaynī (d. 329/941), Ibn Bābawayh (d. 381/991), and two by al-Ṭūsī (d. 460/1067).[6]

Early renunciant literature, focussing on ascetic approaches to gaining knowledge of God, is also based on reports, but drawn from a wider pool of reporters. I shall treat this literature separately in Chapter 4.[7]

---

3 ʻAbd al-Razzāq al-Ṣanʻānī, *Al-Muṣannaf*, 11 vols. (Beirut: al-Majlis al-ʻIlmī, 1972). See also Harald Motzki, "The Muṣannaf of ʻAbd al-Razzāq al-Ṣanʻānī as a Source of Authentic Aḥādīth of the First Century A.H.," *JNES* 50 (1991): 1–21.

4 See al-Shāfiʻi, *Al-Risāla*, ed. and trans. Lowry, *The Epistle*, 76–80 (Arabic), 77–81 (English). For discussion of the authority of hadiths in early Islam see Aisha Musa, *Hadith as Scripture* (New York, N.Y.: Palgrave Macmillan, 2008).

5 On Shia hadith collections, see Etan Kohlberg, "Shīʻī Ḥadīth," in *The Cambridge Companion to Arabic Literature*, vol. 12, ed. A.F.L. Beeston, T.M. Johnstone, R.B.Serjeant, G.R. Smith (Cambridge: CUP, 1983–): 299–307; and Ron Buckley, "On the Origins of Shīʻi Ḥadīth," *MW* 88 (1998): 165–184. The Ismāʻīlī Shia tradition placed less emphasis on hadith collections. The only collection is Qāḍī al-Nuʻmān (d. 363/974), *Daʻāʼim al-islām* (*The Pillars of Islam*), vol. 1 (Cairo: Dār al-Maʻārif, 1963), which mentions the previous scriptures only at 1:84.

6 Muḥammad al-Kulaynī, *Al-Kāfī* (*The Sufficient*) (Qom: Dār al-Ḥadīth, 1429/2008); Muḥammad Ibn Bābawayh, *Man lā yaḥḍuruhu al-faqīh (Whoever does not have a jurist present)* (Beirut: Dār Ṣaʻb, 1981); Muḥammad al-Ṭūsī, *Tahdhīb al-aḥkām* (*The Refinement of the Laws)* (Tehran: Dār al-Kutub al-Islāmiyah, 1390/1970–71); idem, *al-Istibsār* (*The Reflection*) (Tehran: Dār al-Kutub al-Islāmī, 1405/1984). These collections were compiled in Baghdad in the period leading up to and under the rule of the Shia Buwayhid dynasty (r. 334–447/945–1055 in Baghdad), despite all the collectors originating from present-day Iran. On the differences between these different works see Robert Gleave "Between *Ḥadīth* and *Fiqh:* the 'Canonical' Imāmī Collections of *Akhbār*," *ILS* 8 (2001), 350–82. On the Buwayhids see John Donohue, *The Buwayhid Dynasty in Iraq 334H./945 to 403H./1012: Shaping Institutions for the Future*, IHC 44 (Leiden: Brill, 2003). The largest collection of traditions (by either Sunnis or Shia) was compiled much later, between 1694–1698 CE by the Shia scholar al-Majlisī (d. 1110/1699), entitled *Biḥār al-anwār* (*Oceans of Lights*), 44 vols., (Beirut: Dār al-Taʻārūf li'l-Maṭbūʻāt, 2001). This preserves thousands of traditions from earlier lost works. *Oceans of Lights*, while important, was compiled in the late 17th century and will not be utilised here.

7 On early renunciants as also transmitters of hadiths, see Christopher Melchert, "Early Renunciants as Ḥadīth Transmitters," *MW* 92 (2002): 407–18.

Biographical literature is related to hadith literature, since it often builds its narrative through linking individual reports into a coherent whole. Many reports used in biographical literature are known as "*khabar*", denoting a historical report recounting events, rather than the more sacred associations of the term "hadith". The earliest extant biography of Muhammad is the *Biography of the Messenger of God* (*Sīra Rasūl Allāh*) by Ibn Isḥāq (d.c. 155/ c.767), the main focus of biographical discussion in what follows. This work is extant in an edited version by Ibn Hishām (d. 218/833), but some additional parts cut out by Ibn Hishām's hand are also recoverable thanks to quotations preserved in other works.[8] Ibn Isḥāq's work presents a grand vision seeking to integrate the emergence of Islam with earlier divine purposes expressed through previous prophets. Early biography is not uniform, however. Ibn Isḥāq's work contrasts with *The Expeditions* (*Kitāb al-Maghāzī*) by Ma'mar ibn Rāshid (d.154/770), the other extant biographical work on Muhammad from this period, which demonstrates no such interest in exploring pre-Islamic events.[9]

There is no attempt here to resolve the complex questions over the dating of individual hadiths. Whether or not they can be traced back to Muhammad and his Companions, their importance lies in recording attitudes and influences prevalent in some early Muslim communities. How early is uncertain. My interest here is primarily the purpose behind the circulation of traditions with links to the Biblical texts.[10]

Reports attested by many transmitters independently at the earliest stage are classed as *mutawātir* ("recurrently transmitted"). Precisely how many transmitters are required for this status is regarded as unknown.[11] *Mutawātir* reports

---

8 Arabic text of Ibn Isḥāq in 'Abd al-Malik Ibn Hishām, *Das Leben Muhammeds*, ed. Ferdinand Wüstenfeld (Göttingen: Dieterichschse Universitäts–Buchhandlung, 1859–60); translated Alfred Guillaume, *The Life of Muhammad* (New Delhi: OUP, 1955). For discussion of the formation of *sīra* literature, and its authors as compilers and reshapers of tradition, see Andreas Görke, "Authorship in the *Sīra* Literature," in *Concepts of Authorship in Pre–Modern Arabic Texts*, eds. Lale Behzadi and Jaakko Hämeen-Antilla (Bamberg: University of Bamberg Press, 2015): 63–92; see also Görke, "The Relationship Between Maghāzī and Ḥadīth in early Islamic Scholarship," *BSOAS* 74 (2011): 171–85.

9 See Ma'mar ibn Rāshid *The Expeditions: an Early Biography of Muḥammad*, ed. and trans. Sean Anthony, LAL (New York: New York University Press, 2014).

10 Conflicting conclusions on the dating of hadiths often depend on the priority given to differing underlying assumptions; see Harald Motzki, "Dating Muslim Traditions: a Survey," *Arabica* 52 (2005): 204–53, and Herbert Berg, The *Development of Exegesis in Early Islam* (Richmond: Curzon, 2000), 6–64.

11 See Martin Whittingham, "How Could So Many Christians be Wrong? The Role of *Tawātur* (Recurrent Transmission of Reports) in Understanding Muslim Views of the Crucifixion," *ICMR* 19 (2008): 167–78.

are regarded as the most reliable, the Qur'an being the supreme example of a set of such reports. *Mutawātir* transmission deserves mention since a common criticism of the Bible in Muslim apologetic works is that it is does not meet this high standard of transmission. Yet although the category of *mutawātir* transmission stems from hadith and legal circles, it is not used to criticise the Bible in hadith literature itself, as we shall see.[12] In fact there is little agreement amongst Muslim writers over which reports are *mutawātir*, beyond the text of the Qur'an, but the category becomes a frequent criticism wielded against Biblical texts.

3.1.2 Attitudes to Jews and Christians in Hadith Literature

Attitudes to the scriptures of a community are inevitably linked to attitudes to the community itself. Jews and Christians are often treated together in the hadith literature, as "People of the Book," but some distinctions can also be drawn, with attitudes to Jews in reports being generally hostile. Jews have lost their chosen status, supplanted by the Muslims, because of their idolatry, rebellion and divisions, and are often a model of evil. They refuse to believe in Muhammad despite the Torah's testimony about him, on account of jealousy.[13] Nonetheless, attitudes to Hebrew scripture can be more positive than the portrayal of Jews themselves, which is unsurprising as the Qur'an itself portrays the *Tawrāt* more positively than Jews.

While Christianity in tradition literature is seen as "a dangerous theological opponent", attitudes to Christians as people range from hostility to respect.[14] Attitudes to the New Testament in the Hadith reflect these varied attitudes towards Christians, rather than adopting a single stance.

---

12 On the relevance of *mutawātir* transmission for criticisms of the Bible, see Whittingham, "How Could So Many?"

13 Uri Rubin, *Between Bible and Qur'ān: the Children of Israel and the Islamic Self–Image* (Princeton: The Darwin Press, 1999), 234; Georges Vajda, "Juifs et musulmanes selon le Hadit," *JA* 229 (1937), 124–25.

14 See David Cook, "Christians and Christianity in ḥadīth works before 900,", introductory essay in: *CMR*, 1: 73–82; see also R. Marston Speight, "Christians in the Hadith Literature," in *Islamic Interpretations of Christianity* ed. Lloyd Ridgeon (Richmond: Curzon, 2001): 30–53; and Speight, "Attitudes Towards Christians as Revealed In the *Musnad* of al-Ṭayālisī," *MW* 63 (1973): 249–68.

3.1.3 Some Important Individuals

Hadiths associate particular individuals with transmitting information from previous scriptures. Although the term *Isrā'īliyyāt* was not used until the mid-tenth century CE, the names of these figures can be seen as associated with this type of reporting, since they bring Jewish and Christian stories into Islamic discourse.[15] Ka'b b. al-Aḥbār (d.32/652), a Yemenite Jew who converted to Islam, is the earliest prominent source of Jewish traditions. Little firm information about his life is known, but his name recurs frequently in traditions citing "the *Tawrāt*"' or ideas associated with it. Ka'b is also linked to many traditions related to the second Caliph 'Umar (r. 13–23/ 634–44), discussed later in this chapter.[16] Another prominent early convert from Judaism was 'Abd Allāh b. Salām (d. 43/663–4).[17]

Wahb b. Munabbih (d.110/728), a Yemeni of Persian origin, was a generation younger. He is reported as having had considerable knowledge of the New Testament, and some of the Old, and is often quoted by later writers including al-Ṭabarī, al-Mas'ūdī and al-Tha'labī.[18] Of the three, Wahb is the most prominent source of traditions said to originate from the previous monotheistic faiths.

However, determining the precise roles that these individuals actually played is not straightforward. The material associated with Wahb's name, for example, is very diverse, and it seems implausible that his references would have swung between close renderings of Biblical material and looser material, often depending on non-biblical works like the sixth century Syriac Christian work *The Cave of Treasures.*[19] It appears more likely that, whatever material originally came from Wahb, he and the others also became symbolic links explaining or justifying why material was absorbed into Islamic circles by, for example, "simple osmosis," as Jews and Christians converted to Islam over time.[20] The key later

15 Armstrong, *Quṣṣāṣ*, 92–97, notes that the people described below should not automatically be linked with the notion of unreliable story–tellers, as has often been the case.

16 See M. Schmitz, "Ka'b al-Aḥbār,", in:*EI2*, consulted online on 03 July 2019, http://dx.doi.org/10.1163/1573–3912_islam_SIM_3734, and on his conversion, Moshe Perlmann, "Another Ka'b al-Aḥbār Story," *JQR* 45 (1954): 48–51.

17 Ibn Isḥāq, in Ibn Hishām, *Das Leben*, 353–54; trans. Guillaume, *Life*, 240–41. See also Michael Lecker, "'Abdallāh b. Salām,", in:EI3, consulted online on 03 July 2019, http://dx.doi.org/10.1163/1573–3912_ei3_COM_24690.

18 See Raif Khoury, *Wahb b. Munabbih*, 2 vols., (Wiesbaden: Otto Harrassowitz, 1972). See I: 214–221 on Wahb and biblical sources; also Alfred–Louis de Prémare, "Wahb B. Munabbih, une figure singulière du premier Islam," *Annales. Histoire, Science Sociales* 60 (2005): 531–549.

19 Michael Pregill, "Isrā'iliyyāt, Myth, and Pseudepigraphy: Wahb b. Munabbih and the Early Islamic Versions of the Fall of Adam and Eve," *JSAI* 34 (2008): 246.

20 Pregill, "Wahb," 237. This point echoes many observations of Tannous, *Medieval Middle East.*

transmitters of material linked to the name of Wahb were all early 'Abbāsid writers, a period when under the new dynasty, Muslims "sought to articulate a more rigid sense of their own identity vis-à-vis other monotheistic communities."[21] In short, anchoring material from diffuse Jewish and Christian sources to these three names imparted respectability to it. Given the number of early converts who would have been Jews and Christians originally, it seems unlikely that only three bridging figures would have formed the dominant route for Jewish and Christian material to enter Islamic discourse.[22]

3.2 Attitudes to Biblical Material

Different attitudes towards reading or reciting Biblical texts exist in tradition literature, ranging from acceptance through neutrality to rejection.[23] As I explore these three categories of response, it will be evident that some hadiths are referring to a notional or general idea of previous scripture, rather than engaging with a specific text or texts.

3.2.1 Acceptance

Accepting some concept of the previous scripture is required as an article of Muslim faith, as previously seen in Q2:4. Some versions of the Hadith of Gabriel, so named because the "man" who questions Muhammad turns out to be the Angel Gabriel, include the following. "A man came to him and said: 'O Messenger of Allāh, what is Imān (faith)?' He said: 'To believe in Allāh, His Angels, His Books, His Messengers and the meeting with Him, and to believe in the Final Resurrection."[24] This reference to God's 'books' relates to Q2:285 and 4:136, which make similar statements.

---

21 Pregill, "Wahb," 240. These key disseminators were 'Abd al-Razzāq al-Ṣan'ānī, Ibn Hishām, 'Abd al-Mun'im al-Idrīsī and Ibn Qutayba; see Pregill, "Wahb," 256.

22 Nabia Abbott, "Wahb B. Munabbih: a Review Article," *JNES* 36 (1977), 112, who is generally more positive about the contribution of Wahb, mentions "the large extent of legendary and fictional materials attributed to these three men" over time.

23 Indeed, sometimes a single hadith on this issue is itself interpreted in widely differing ways; see M.J. Kister, "*Ḥaddithū 'an banī isrā'ila wa–lā ḥaraja:* a Study of an Early Tradition," *IOS* 2 (1972): 215–239, from which the translation is taken; see also reprint in idem, *Studies in Jāhiliyya and Early Islam* (London: Variorum, 1980).

24 Ibn Mājah, *Sunan*, vol. 1, *Kitāb al-Sunna* (The Book of the Sunna), no. 64. Some versions of this hadith use the singular "book" rather than "books", thereby removing any implication of

Another tradition states that the Jews and Christians could have benefited from possessing the *Tawrāt* and *Injīl*, if only they had made good use of them, recalling Q5:66.[25] There is also discussion amongst some Muslim authorities over accepting therapeutic incantations from Jews who used their own scripture to bring about healing for sick Muslims. Some seemed to accept this.[26] In addition the penalty for adultery as stoning was found in the Torah by Muhammad.[27]

Some items of information not found in the extant Hebrew scriptures are attributed to the *Tawrāt*. For example, Jesus will be buried next to Muhammad.[28] God answers prayers every Friday.[29] Al-Nasā'ī records a prayer of David, said to come from the *Tawrāt*, which Muhammad used to recite after finishing his prayer.[30] One well-known tradition states, "Narrate from the Children of Israel, and there is no prohibition". This likely refers to Jewish traditions which extend beyond the Biblical text to the oral Torah, but it indicates, or could justify, a certain openness to Jewish material.[31]

This seeming acceptance of previous scriptures can be interpreted in different ways. One reading is that in early Islam religious boundaries were in practice porous.[32] But there are other interpretations, for example that even when leaders or others did sharply distinguish between different faiths, there were also occasions when such acceptance was useful to the Muslim community or to Muhammad. This usefulness is explored later in the present chapter.

3.2.2 Neutrality

Traditions can also be neutral or even cautious about the previous scriptures. A central assumption is that narrating stories from previous scriptures is allowed for the purpose of information or interest, but that any laws found in such scrip-

previous scriptures. See Muslim, *Ṣaḥīḥ*, vol. 1, *Kitāb al-Īmān* (The Book of Faith), which has both versions; no. 1 for "books", no. 5 for "book."

25 Al-Tirmidhī, *Jāmi'*, vol. 5, *Abwāb al-'Ilm* (Chapters on Knowledge), no. 2653.

26 See the discussion in Uri Rubin, "Muḥammad the Exorcist: Aspects of Islamic–Jewish Polemics," *JSAI* 30 (2005), 107.

27 Al-Bukhārī, *Ṣaḥīḥ*, vol. 4, *Kitāb al-Manāqib* (*The Book of Virtues*), no. 3635.

28 Al-Tirmidhī, *Jāmi'*, vol. 6, *Kitāb al-Manāqib* (*The Book of Virtues*), no. 3617.

29 Al-Nasā'ī, *Sunan*, vol. 2, *Kitāb al-Jum'a* (*The Book of Congregational Prayer*), no. 1433.

30 Al-Nasā'ī, *Sunan*, vol. 2, *Kitāb al-Sahw* (*The Book of Forgetfulness*), no. 1347.

31 This is found in many collections, including two reports in al-Ṣan'ānī, *Al-Muṣannaf*, 6: 109–110. See also Kister, "*Wa–lā ḥaraja*."

32 As argued by Fred Donner, *Muhammad and the Believers* (Cambridge, MA: Harvard University Press, 2010), and Jack Tannous, *Medieval Middle East*.

tures are abrogated unless confirmed by the Qur'an.[33] "The People of the scripture used to recite the Torah in Hebrew and explain it in Arabic to the Muslims. On that Allah's apostle said, 'Do not believe the people of the scripture or disbelieve them, but say, 'We believe in Allah and what is revealed to us'" (Q2:136).[34] This is typically understood as designed to guide Muslims away from accepting any possible falsehoods, while also protecting them from rejecting divine truth.

In addition, the previous scriptures are not comparable to the Qur'an. A common affirmation is that God has never before revealed anything like Sura *al-Fātiḥa*, the opening sura of the Qur'an.[35]

The previous scriptures are also replaced. One hadith reports that Muhammad said, "I was given the seven long surahs instead of the Torah, the surahs of a hundred verses instead of the Gospel, the Repeated Ones instead of the Psalms, and I was given the short surahs as a special favour."[36] This reflects in part an awareness of the significance of opening blocks of previous scriptures – the Torah as the first section of the Hebrew Bible, the Gospels as the first section of the New Testament – and so highlights how Muhammad has received revelation of equal significance.

3.2.3 Negative Views

Negativity here denotes an overall attitude towards previous scriptures, rather than charges of possible scriptural falsification, discussed later in this chapter. The most notable hadith, expressing not just disapproval but anger at the reading of the previous scriptures, circulated widely in various slightly different versions. One of these versions can be found in one of the earliest collections of hadiths, the *Muṣannaf* of the Yemeni traditionist Abd al-Razzāq al-Ṣan'ānī (d. 211/826). The report recounts how Muhammad finds 'Umar al-Khaṭṭāb, the future caliph, reading a section of the Torah. Muhammad's face colours with anger, and he chastises 'Umar.[37] In a second version also given by al-Ṣan'ānī, it is stated that

33 See for example Kister, "*Wa–lā ḥaraja*," 220.

34 Al-Bukhārī, *Ṣaḥīḥ*, vol. 9, *Kitāb al-Tawḥīd* (*The Book of Divine Unity*), no. 7541. Qur'an translation here follows that provided in the translation of the *Ṣaḥīḥ*.

35 Al-Tirmidhī, *Jāmi'*, vol. 9, *Kitāb al-Amthāl* (*The Book of Parables*), no. 2875.

36 See Abū 'Ubayd, *Faḍā'il al-Qur'ān* (*The Merits of the Qur'an*) (Beirut: Dār al-Kutub al-'Ilmiyya, 1991), 120; cf. Dmitry Frolov, "The Problem of the 'Seven Long' Sūrahs," in *Studies in Arabic and Islam: Proceedings of the 19th Congress, Union Européenne des Arabisants et Islamisants, Halle 1998*, eds. Stefan Leder, Hilary Kilpatrick et al, (Leuven: Peeters, 2002): 193–203, esp. 194.

37 'Abd al-Razzāq al-Ṣan'ānī, *Al-Muṣannaf*, 6: 112–13 (no. 10163).

if Moses were alive, the people would follow him and turn away from Muhammad.[38] In other versions it is reported that if Moses were alive he would follow Muhammad. Interestingly, a similar story is reported by al-Ṣanʿānī regarding Ḥafṣa, wife of Muhammad, reading stories about Joseph (Yūsuf). Again Muhammad's face colours with anger, and he states that if Joseph were alive the people would follow him and reject Muhammad.[39]

There is then a range of responses to previous scriptures in hadith literature. The Iberian scholar Ibn ʻAbd al-Barr (d.463/1070), from the end of the period covered in this volume, reflects this range in his chapter on reading and transmitting texts from Jews and Christians. The hadiths he cites are all cautious, questioning the need to consult previous scriptures while not dismissing them out of hand. The final report in the chapter reads, "If you know that it is the *Tawrāt* which God sent down to Moses son of ʻImran then read it by night and by day".[40] In other words, if you know that you are reading from the genuine original scriptures, then your reading is acceptable. Since Ibn ʻAbd al-Barr would most likely have regarded certainty over this question as unattainable, this leaves the matter open and unresolved.

3.2.4 Twelver Shia Views

The early centuries of Shia Islam saw greater use of Israelite motifs and themes than occurred in Sunnism. Furthermore, so great is the sense of identification with previous prophets that Shia sources produce "the main flow of Judaeo-Christian motifs" into early Muslim literature.[41] However, this trend was also resisted by others within Shi'ism who stressed the Arab origins of their faith.[42] The Shia sense of being marginalised or oppressed for righteousness' sake also led to

38 Al-Ṣanʿānī, *Al-Muṣannaf*, 6:113 (no. 10164).

39 Al-Ṣanʿānī, *Al-Muṣannaf*, 6:113–14 (no. 10165). For further instances of this frame story in hadith literature see Avraham Hakim, "Muḥammad's Authority and Leadership Reestablished: The Prophet and ʻUmar b. al-Khaṭṭāb," *RHR* 226 (2009): 189–92.

40 Ibn ʻAbd al-Barr (d.463/1070), *Jāmiʿ Bayān al-ʿilm wa faḍlihi* (*Exposition of Knowledge and its Merits*) (Beirut: Dār al-Kutub al-ʿIlmiyya, 2000), 299–302, in a chapter entitled, "Summary regarding reading the books of the People of the Book and transmitting from them" (*Mukhtaṣar fī muṭālaʿa kutub ahl al-kitāb wa'l-riwāya ʿanhum*).

41 Uri Rubin, "Prophets and Progenitors in the Early Shīʿa Tradition," *JSAI* (1979), 55.

42 Rubin, "Progenitors," *passim*.

an identification with a hadith stating that, "things will happen to my community similar to what happened to the Children of Israel".[43]

This tension over drawing on Biblical predecessors can be seen in two early and competing trends in using the past to validate the Imams. One tendency used Biblical and Judaeo-Christian motifs to establish the role of the Imams, emphasising "The Light of God" (*nūr Allah*), which was passed on via Israelite prophets to Muhammad, then 'Alī. The other trend drew on Arab genealogy, resisting or removing the focus on biblical prophets. This uses "The Light of Muhammad" (*nūr muḥammad*), passed on via Ishmael to the Arab progenitors of Muhammad, as the key source and proof of divine inspiration and affirmation.[44]

There is little negativity in Shia sources about the previous scriptures. Instead, the emphasis is on these scriptures as sources of self-validation. A Shia tradition on corruption will be mentioned in the next section on *taḥrīf*, but this seems to be a solitary example and is not drawn from the four canonical Shia hadith collections.

References to *Tawrāt*, *Zabūr* or *Injīl* in the four main Shia collections yield a variety of interesting items. There is affirmation of the *Injīl*, and an echo of its content, in the statement, "It is written in the *Injīl:* Do not seek knowledge which you do not put into practice, but put into practice what you know. Knowledge, if it was not put into practice by someone, his companion did not advance except to unbelief, so he did not advance".[45] There is also the affirmation that the *Tawrāt* was sent down on the 7th of the month of Ramadan, the *Injīl* on the 13th Ramadan, the *Zabūr* on the 18th and the *Furqān* (the Qur'an) on the 23rd.[46]

There are several traditions stating, "It is written in the *Tawrāt*". For example, "O Moses, withhold your anger from whomever I give you authority over, and

43 Quoted by Uri Rubin, "Apocalypse and Authority in Islamic Tradition: the Emergence of the Twelve Leaders," *Al-Qanṭara* 18 (1997), 38, from Ibn Shahrāshūb, *Manāqib āl Abi Ṭālib* (*The Virtues of the Family of Abū Ṭālib*). Ibn Shahrashub's text was unavailable to me.

44 Ibn Isḥāq, in portions of his biography preserved by al-Ṭabarī but cut out by Ibn Hishām, reflects some of this reliance on the transmission down the line of Israelite prophets, on which more below. See also Rubin, "Progenitors," 41, 65.

45 Al-Kulaynī, *Al-Kāfī*, vol. 1, *Kitāb Faḍl al-'Ilm* (*The Book of the Merit of Knowledge*), chapter 13, no. 114. The emphasis on acting on the knowledge you possess finds parallels both in gospel material and in the Letter of James; see Matt 7:24–27 and Jas 1:22–25.

46 Al-Kulaynī, *Al-Kāfī*, vol. 4,*Tatimma Kitāb al-Īmān wa'l-Kufr* (*The Complement to the Book of Faith and Unbelief*), chapter 13, no. 3574. This view is also found in Sunni thought; see for example al-Suyūṭī, *Itqān fī 'ulūm al-Qur'ān* (*The Perfect Guide to the Sciences of the Qur'an*), vol. 1 (Beirut: Dār Iḥyā al-'Ulūm, 1987), 120.

I will avert my anger from you."[47] There is also reference to the phrase "it is written in the *Tawrāt* which was not changed (*lam tughayyar*)."[48] This could be read as an affirmation of the whole *Tawrāt*, or (more probably) as a statement that at least the part being cited is part of the genuine *Tawrāt*. Furthermore, 'Alī swears an oath on the *Tawrāt* before a Jew.[49]

A distinctive of Shia thought is belief in an item known as *al-Jafr*, traditionally understood as two skin containers containing a variety of books, including the previous scriptures. These were inherited by 'Alī from Muhammad and handed down to subsequent Imams. "With me is the white jafr... In it are the Psalms of David, the Torah of Moses, the Gospel of Jesus, the Books of Abraham, the laws that explain the lawful and the unlawful and the *Musḥaf* of Fatima".[50]

The Bible can be cited as a supporting authority. Sunni Muslims sometimes label Twelver Shī'a as "*rāfiḍa*" or rejecter/ dissenter, for their rejection of the first three caliphs. The sixth Imam Ja'far al-Ṣādiq is reported as saying that, rather than being a term of abuse, this term is actually about rejection of evil, is a commendation of the Shia, and is used in this way in both Biblical testaments.[51]

It appears that within Shia hadiths explicit rejection of Biblical texts is absent. The sense of being an often-persecuted minority provides one explanation for the appropriation of biblically-related material which relates to this theme. Another reason is the capacity of the Bible for attestation of the Imams.

3.2.5 *Taḥrīf*

The concept of Biblical corruption is commonly divided into corruption of the text itself, or corruption of interpretations of the text. There are very few hadiths stating that the Biblical text itself has been altered deliberately and where this charge occurs, a different issue is actually the main point of the report.

---

47 Al-Kulaynī, *Al-Kāfī*, vol. 3, *Kitāb al-Īmān wa'l-Kufr* (*The Book of Faith and Unbelief*), chapter 121, no. 2537.

48 Al-Kulaynī, *Al-Kāfī*, vol. 4, *Tatimma Kitāb al-Īmān wa'l-Kufr* (*The Complement to the Book of Faith and Unbelief*), chapter 21, no. 3192.

49 Al-Kulaynī, *Al-Kāfī*, vol. 14, *Kitāb al-Īmān wa'l-Nudhūr wa'l-Kaffārāt* (*The Book of Faith and Oaths and Expiations*), chapter 15, no. 14753.

50 Al-Kulaynī, *al-Kāfī*, vol. 1, *Kitāb al-Ḥujja* (The Book of Proof), no. 639, ch. 40; and see Etan Kohlberg, "Authoritative Scriptures in Early Imāmī Shī'ism," in *Les Retours aux Écritures: fondamentalismes présents et passes*, eds. Évelyne Patlagean and Alain le Boulluec (Louvain: Peeters, 1993): 295–312; and Liyakat Takim, "The Ten Commandments and the Tablets in Shī'ī and Sunnī Tafsīr Literature: a comparative perspective," in *MW* 101, (2011): 94–109, esp. 101–105.

51 Etan Kohlberg, "The Term '*Rāfiḍa*' in Imāmī Shī'ī Usage," *JAOS* 99 (1979): 677–679.

3.2.5.1 Textual Corruption

A Shia source records one of the clearest accusations that the New Testament Gospels are not the original gospel. *The Choice Reports of al-Riḍā* (*'Uyūn akhbār al-Riḍā*), is a work focussed on the merits of the eighth imam, Imam Reza or al-Riḍā (d.203/818). It is compiled by Ibn Bābawayh (d. 380/991), already encountered as collector of one of the foundational works of Shia hadith.[52] In the report an exchange between Imam al-Riḍā and an unnamed Christian leader, the Catholicos, portrays the Imam as bringing the Catholicos to the point of admitting that the gospel writers lied. This clearly seems to assume textual *taḥrīf.*[53] However, this is highly unusual in the context of Shia attitudes to the previous scriptures as evidenced in hadith literature, and occurs as part of a narrative exalting the great wisdom and knowledge of the Imam more generally. As Thomas notes, the historicity of this encounter is questionable, and the ready admission of the Catholicos that his own tradition is based on falsehood seems too easy, "little more than a literary device" to emphasise the exalted status of the eighth Imam.[54]

Similarly there is very little in the Sunni hadith literature on the accusation of corrupting the previous scriptures textually. The interpretation of the few hadiths which discuss corruption resembles the discussion in the previous chapter on interpreting Qur'anic charges of corruption. Though the traditions may have been taken subsequently as straightforward assertions of widespread textual corruption, the hadith reports themselves do not necessarily claim this. To my knowledge only three traditions relate to textual corruption.

One example, from the collection of al-Bukhārī, involves a quotation from Q2:79:

Ibn 'Abbās said, "O Assembly of Muslims! How do you ask the people of the Scriptures, though your Book which was revealed to His Prophet is the most re-

---

52 Although this report is not in one of the four principal collections of Shia hadith, I include it since it is narrated by Ibn Bābawayh, one of the three collectors of Shia hadith, in *'Uyūn akhbār al-Riḍā* (Qom: Chāpkhānah-I Dār al-'Ilm, 1377AH/1958), 163.

53 Ibn Babawayh *'Uyūn akhbār al-Riḍā*, 163. This passage also occurs in his *Kitab al-Tawḥīd*, from which it is translated by David Thomas, "Two Muslim-Christian Debates from the Early Shī'ite Tradition," *JSS* 33 (1988): 53–80 (65–75 for translation). For a complete translation of *Kitab al-Tawḥīd* see *The Book of Divine Unity*, tr. Ali Adam, ed. Michael Mumisa and Mahmood Dhalla (Birmingham: AMI Press, 2013); see 507–30 for the relevant passage. See also David Wasserstein, "The 'Majlis of al-Riḍā': A Religious debate in the court of the Caliph al-Ma'mūn as represented in a Shī'ī hagiographical work about the Eighth Imām 'Alī ibn Mūsā al-Riḍā," in *The Majlis: Interreligious Encounters in Medieval Islam*, ed. Hava Lazarus-Yafeh (Wiesbaden: Harrassowitz, 1999): 108–119.

54 Thomas, "Two Muslim-Christian Debates,", 75.

cent information from Allāh and you recite it, that has not been distorted? Allāh has informed you that the people of the Scriptures distorted and changed what was revealed to them, with their own hands and they said: 'This is from Allāh,' in order to get some worldly benefit thereby' [Q2:79]." Ibn 'Abbās added, "Isn't the knowledge revealed to you sufficient to prevent you from asking them? By Allāh, I have never seen any one of them asking you about what has been revealed to you."[55]

In its original context the Qur'anic verse cited here is an accusation against a particular group, though the charge is often extended to cover all the People of the Book.

A second report is from the *Musnad* (*The Supported*) of Aḥmad Ibn Ḥanbal (d. 241/855), and is the only prominent Sunni hadith report which mentions Christians (*al-naṣāra*) corrupting scripture. When Mu'ādh sees Christians bowing to their leaders, he says to Muhammad that it would be more suitable for Muslims to greet Muhammad this way. But Muhammad rejects bowing as a greeting, saying that, "They lied about their prophets just as they corrupted (*ḥarrafū*) their scripture."[56] This report could legitimately be interpreted either as a comment only intended to criticise a specific group, or a more generalised condemnation.

The third hadith indicating textual corruption is found in the collection of al-Nasā'ī. It aims at explaining the Qur'anic call to the people of the Gospel to judge by the Gospel (Q5:47). The Qur'anic verse concludes, "Whoever does not judge by what God has sent down, those – they are the wicked". The hadith in question narrates the story of unidentified kings who fail to "judge by what God has sent down". Instead, they "altered" ("*baddalū*"") the *Tawrāt* and *Injīl*.[57] More faithful people challenged these deceiving kings, and when these faithful ones are threatened with the choice of death or giving up reading the scripture except for the parts altered by the kings, they ask for a third option, permission to live elsewhere, some becoming monks (the hadith cites Q57:27 on sincere but misguided monasticism). When only a few of those living elsewhere were left, Muhammad appears, and they believe in him. Here we see a clear distinction between true believers in the *Tawrāt* and *Injīl*, whose goodness is shown in their recognition of Muhammad when he appears, and those who alter the scripture, fail to respond to Muhammad's call and stray from truth. The idea of scriptural

55 Al-Bukhārī, *Ṣaḥīḥ*, vol. 3, *Kitāb al-Shahādāt* (*The Book of Witnesses*), no. 2685.
56 Aḥmad ibn Hanbal, *Musnad*, ed. S. al-Arna'ūt, vol. 32 (Beirut: al-Risalah, 1999/1460), 149 (no. 19404). Al-Arna'ūt notes that one manuscript has the term *ḥarraqū* (they burned) rather than *ḥarrafū*. I am grateful to Belal Abo al-Abbas for drawing my attention to this reference.
57 Al-Nasā'ī, *Sunan*, vol. 6, *Kitāb Ādāb al-Quḍā* (*The Book of the Etiquette of Judges*), no. 5402.

corruption is a sub-plot to the central idea, the importance of belief in Muhammad.

This hadith is an example of a broader theme that true believers among Christians and Jews will recognise the truth of Islam. For example, a hadith of al-Bukhārī concerns three types of people who will receive a double reward. One of them is "a believer from the people of the Scriptures who has been a believer and then he believes in the Prophet."[58]

There are some reports not found in canonical hadith texts indicating textual corruption, some associated with Ka'b b. al-Aḥbār. He is reported as stating that, "The *Tawrāt* ended with Q17:111, 'Praise (be) to God who has not taken a son'."[59] This particular tradition is of course double-edged, citing the authority of one previous scripture, the Torah, in order to refute Jesus' divine sonship, a central doctrine of the New Testament. In Muslim perspective the original *Injīl* could not have taught such a false doctrine, so the refutation is of Christian failure to preserve or rightly interpret the *Injīl*. There are also accounts of Ka'b's conversion, conflicting in many details, which tell of texts revealing the truth of Islam being cut out of the Torah.[60]

Turning to the treatment of textual corruption in biographical literature, the *Sīra* of Ibn Isḥāq yields limited but notable material. The book can be understood as written for the 'Abbāsid Caliph al-Manṣūr (r.136–158/754–775) to stress the continuity of the Muslims (understand equally here the 'Abbāsids) with previous prophetic history.[61] More will be said on this continuity below. Ibn Isḥāq applies the term "Paraclete" from John's Gospel to Muhammad, an important indication for how early this claim about the meaning of Paraclete was circulating, and discussed further below. He appears to have deliberately altered some of his Biblical quotations, so that the reports he had received were rendered more clearly in

58 Al-Bukhārī, *Ṣaḥīḥ*, vol. 4, *Kitāb al-Jihād* (*The Book of Striving*), no. 3011, adapted. While technically *jihād* means "striving", the translation of the Darussalam edition, "Fighting for Allāh's cause" is also legitimate here since all the hadith reports which al-Bukhārī includes are related to military activity

59 Abū Nu'aym, *Ḥilyat al-Awliyā'* (*The Adornment of the Friends of God*) vol. 6, (Cairo: Maktabat al-Khānjī: Maktabat al-Sa'āda, 1932–38), 30; see Christopher Melchert, "Quotations of Extra-Qur'ānic Scripture in Early Renunciant Literature," in *Islam and Globalisation: Historical and Contemporary Perspectives. Proceedings of the 25th Congress of L'Union Européenne des Arabisants et Islamisants*, ed. Agostino Cilardo (Leuven: Peeters, 2013), 101. Many Muslim scholars realised that not all that was labelled as "from the Tawrat" was in fact so (Kister, "*Wa-lā ḥaraja*," 229).

60 See Moshe Perlmann, "A Legendary Story of Ka'b al-Aḥbār's Conversion to Islam," in *The Joshua Starr Memorial Volume* (New York: Conference on Jewish Relations, 1953), 85–99; and Perlmann, "Another Ka'b al-Aḥbār Story," *JQR* 45 (1954), 48–51.

61 Lassner, "Covenant of the Prophets," 209.

agreement with Islamic views of what the true *Injīl* must have said.[62] For example, three times the phrase "my father" is altered to read "the Lord, al-Rabb" so as to eliminate the notion of Jesus as Son of God the Father. If so, this indicates that Ibn Isḥāq, or his sources, accepted the idea that the Gospel of John needed correcting since it had strayed from the original message. The alternative, that Ibn Isḥāq simply misquotes the gospel text, perhaps because of relying on orally transmitted reports, is less likely given the persistent pattern of de-Christianisation in his gospel quotations. It is unclear whether Ibn Isḥāq thought that once so corrected, the Bible provided basically reliable information, including about Muhammad. So these alterations could be taken either as an indication of Ibn Isḥāq's scepticism about the original text, or conversely regarded more positively, as a sign that he thought it was essentially reliable if brought into line with the truth through minor adjustments.

3.2.5.2 Corruption of interpretation

Just as tradition literature contains few references to textual corruption of the Bible, it likewise provides few references to the issue of corrupt Biblical interpretation (*taḥrīf al-ma'nā* or *taḥrīf ma'nawī*). Al-Bukhārī adds a note between hadiths in the section of his hadith collection entitled "The Book of Divine Unity" (*Kitab al-tawḥīd*). Here he quotes Ibn 'Abbās, Muhammad's cousin and one of his Companions, as commenting on the term "*yuḥarrifūna*"' (here best translated as "they alter.") Referring to Q4:46, which uses this term, Ibn 'Abbās is reported as explaining *yuḥarrifūna* by saying, "but no one removes an utterance from one of the books of God. But they altered it: they interpreted it according to the wrong interpretation".[63] This concerns Q4:46, which specifically accuses some Jews of taking words out of their context. The statement appears to conflict with Ibn 'Abbās' other statement in the hadith quoted above and involving Q2:79, which states that at least some Jews corrupted the text. The two statements could be reconciled if the accusation related to Q2:79 was

62 See Ibn Isḥāq, in Ibn Hishām, *Das Leben*, 149–50; trans. Guillaume, *Life*, 103–04. For a valuable analysis see Sidney Griffith, "Arguing from Scripture: The Bible in the Christian/Muslim Encounter in the Middle Ages," in *Scripture and Pluralism: Reading the Bible in the religiously plural worlds of the Middle Ages and Renaissance*, eds. Thomas Heffernan and Thomas Burman, SHCT (Leiden: Brill, 2005): 29–58; on the Paraclete passages see 36–45.
63 Al-Bukhārī, *Ṣaḥīḥ*, vol. 9, *Kitāb al-Tawḥīd* (*The Book of Divine Unity*), comment before hadith no. 7553, my translation. The translators of the Darussalam edition leave this comment untranslated.

regarded as only describing a specific group of Jews, rather than as a general statement.

Another hadith making the accusation of corrupt interpretation is recorded by al-Dārimī (d. 255/869) in his *Sunan*, one of the collections not included in the canonical six collections but included in the most prominent nine. "They have corrupted (*ḥarrafū*) the scripture through their interpretation (*tafsīr*)."[64]

In sum, Biblical corruption of either text or interpretation barely features in hadith and *sīra* literature. Despite the great prominence of this theme in more recent centuries, tradition literature actually yields more regarding use of the Bible.

3.3 Using the Bible

Hadith and biographical literature uses the Bible to strengthen support for a number of key Muslim figures and events. The most prominent is of course Muhammad, but the role of the Muslims in history, the Caliph ʿUmar and the early conquests also feature. Exploring the possible background to these hadiths involves delving into areas of early Islamic history where much is contested. In what follows, the aim is to note important debates rather than attempting to resolve them.

Use of the Bible implies interaction with Jews and Christians, either as sources of information or as targets of intended persuasion. Opinion remains divided over how much can be known about the presence of Jews and Christians in the Hijaz.[65] While some regard retrieving reliable data as impossible, given the dearth of contemporary sources, others consider that we can reconstruct much information about, for example, the Jews of Medina at the time of Muhammad.[66]

64 Al-Dārimī, *Sunan al-Dārimī*, vol. 1 (Beirut: Dar al-Kitab al-ʿArabi, 1987), 169. These reports are not numbered, but the report cited here is the last in the section of assorted introductory topics before the commencement of the first "Book," on "Purity" (*Ṭahāra*).

65 For an overview of the presence of Christianity in the Arabian peninsula more broadly, around the time of the rise of Islam, see Suleiman Mourad, "Christianity in Arabia: an Overview (4th–9th Centuries CE)," in *The Syriac Writers of Qatar in the Seventh Century*, eds. Mario Kozah, Abdulrahim Abu-Husayn, Saif Shaheen al-Murikhi, Haya al-Thani (Piscataway, NJ: Gorgias Press, 2014): 37–60.

66 Michael Lecker is the most eminent recent optimist about reconstructing aspects of Muhammad's Medina through highly detailed combing of sources. See his *Muslims, Jews and Pagans*, IHC 13 (Leiden: Brill, 1995), and many articles. For thoughtful discussion of the complex issues involved, see the reviews of Lecker by Chase Robinson, *JRAS* 7 (1997): 129–31, and Robert Hoy-

Note that the presence of Jewish narratives from outside the canonical Hebrew text is much more common in the Hadith literature than the use of canonical texts, but these non-canonical narratives lie outside our focus here.[67]

3.3.1 Attestation of Muhammad

Ibn Isḥāq's *Sīra* originally began with a section, known as the *Book of the Beginning* (*Kitāb al-Mubtada'*) which drew partly on Biblical tradition, and even more on Jewish and Christian extra-Biblical tradition. This was cut by his subsequent editor, Ibn Hishām. Ibn Isḥāq's omitted text can be partially recovered only from other versions, such as the recension of Ibn Bukayr and the many reports from Ibn Isḥāq preserved in the history of al-Ṭabarī.[68] Ibn Hishām comments that "I shall begin this book with Ismā'īl son of Ibrāhīm and mention those of his offspring who were the ancestors of God's apostle ... omitting some of the things which Ibn Isḥāq has recorded in this book in which there is no mention of the apostle and about which the Quran says nothing." Ibn Hishām also omits, "things which it is disgraceful to discuss; matters which would distress certain

land, *BSOAS* 61 (1998): 129 – 31. No consensus exists over how much knowledge of the religious situation of Muhammad's Medina can be recovered.

67 Samuel Rosenblatt, "Rabbinic Legends in Hadith," *MW* 35 (1945): 237 – 52. This Jewish material might have been available via Christian, as well as Jewish, sources; see Sebastian Brock, "Jewish Traditions in Syriac Sources," *JJS* 30 (1979): 212 – 32. Early contact with Jews may be a source, if one follows Lecker's optimistic view of the historical reliability of reports, as exemplified in his "Zayd b. Thābit, 'A Jew with Two Sidelocks': Judaism and literacy in pre–Islamic Medina (Yathrib)," *JNES* 56 (1997): 259 – 73.

68 It is unclear whether Ibn Isḥāq's work ever existed in one definitive form, as it was transmitted in different versions via dictation to students; see Chase Robinson, "Islamic Historical Writing, Eighth Through the Tenth Centuries," in *The Oxford History of Historical Writing: Volume 2: 400 – 1400*, eds. Sarah Foot and Chase Robinson (Oxford: OUP, 2012), 252. The version of Ibn Hishām is based on the transmission of al-Bakkā'ī. For information on published fragments of the recension of Ibn Isḥāq by Yūnus ibn Bukayr (d.199/815) see Michael Lecker, "Notes About Censorship and Self–Censorship in the Biography of the Prophet Muhammad," *Al-Qanṭara* 35 (2014): 233 – 54. Gordon Newby, *The Making of the Last Prophet* (Columbia: University of South Carolina Press, 1989) attempts a reconstruction of *Kitāb al-Mubtadā'*, in English translation, using quotations preserved in other works. For important questions over how accurately the text of Ibn Isḥāq can be recovered, and a critique of Newby's work, see Lawrence Conrad, "Recovering Lost Texts: Some methodological issues," *JAOS* 113 (1993): 258 – 263. Ibn Isḥāq's work is in three sections, the other two being *The Book of the Call* (*Kitāb al-Mab'ath*) and *The Book of Raids* (*Kitāb al-Maghāzī*).

people."[69] It is not surprising that in this broad-ranging cull, aimed at training the gaze on Muhammad himself, Biblical material has largely fallen by the wayside. Yet Ibn Hishām preserves the famous identification of the Paraclete, referred to in John's Gospel (John 14:16, 26; 15:26; 16:7) with Muhammad. This is explicable because although this is a Biblical reference, it is taken by Ibn Isḥāq to be a reference to Muhammad, the person at the heart of Ibn Hishām's concerns. Ibn Isḥāq in his *Sīra* preserves a Christian Palestinian Aramaic translation of "*paráklētos*" (Paraclete) as "*mnḥmn*", a unique rendering compared with later Arabic translations drawn from Greek or Syriac. Of four different recensions of Ibn Isḥāq's work, mostly incomplete, it is only the version used by Ibn Hishām which preserves the reference to the Paraclete.[70]

An example of the biblical material cut out by Ibn Hishām is a report found in Ibn Bukayr's version of Ibn Isḥāq stating that Muhammad's description is found in the *Tawrāt*. "His name is *al-Mutawakkil* ("the one who trusts," [in God]). He is not harsh or rough; nor does he walk proudly in the streets. He is given the keys that by him God may make blind eyes see, and deaf ears hear, and set straight crooked tongues so that they bear witness that there is no god but Allah alone without associate. He will help and defend the oppressed."[71] This passage contains various resemblances to Isaiah 42:2–7. The application to Muhammad parallels the application of Isaiah 42 to Jesus (Matt 12:15–21).

Ibn Isḥāq's *Book of the Beginning* (*Kitāb al-Mubtada'*) gives an account of previous prophets from creation up to the time of Muhammad. The purpose of this first, pre-Islamic section of his biography is to show that Muhammad and the Muslims are integrated into the grand sweep of divine and Biblical history – in fact, they are the climax of it. Ibn Ishaq's *Sīra*, in its original and complete form, can thus be seen as the first of the Muslim universal histories, which begin

69 Ibn Hishām, Introduction to Ibn Isḥāq's *Sīra*, *Das Leben*, 4; trans. Guillaume, *Life*, 691.

70 Sean Anthony, "Muḥammad, Menaḥem, and the Paraclete: New Light on Ibn Isḥāq's (d.150/767) Arabic version of John 15:23–16:1," *BSOAS* 79 (2016): 255–78. On the four recensions, and the use by Ibn Hishām of the recension of al-Bakkā'ī, which includes the Paraclete passage, see 274. The first suggestion that Muhammad's identity as the Paraclete can be confirmed by linking the epithet Aḥmad ("praised one") in Q61:6 to a (mis)reading of *paráklētos* as *periklutos* ("renowned" or perhaps "praised one"), comes from Ludovicco Marracci (d.1700), a Catholic priest and professor of Arabic; see Anthony, "Muḥammad," 274. For discussion of the Paraclete in the Gospel of John in relation to Qur'anic statements that Jesus predicts the coming of Muhammad see Timo Güzelmansur, ed., *Hat Jesus Muhammad angekündigt? Der Paraklet des Johannesevangeliums und seine koranische Bedeutung* (Regensburg: Verlag Friedrich Pustet, 2012).

71 Alfred Guillaume, *New Light on the Life of Muhammad* (Manchester: MUP, 1960), 32. Guillaume surveys a manuscript of Ibn Bukayr's report of the lectures of Ibn Isḥāq.

not with Muhammad but at creation.[72] Ibn Hishām's editorial cuts have obscured Ibn Ishaq's role in the development of these histories, so that the genre of universal history is more commonly associated, for example, with names such as Ibn Ḥabīb, al-Yaʿqūbī and al-Ṭabarī.[73] In such histories it can be argued that the Bible is a shaping influence, providing the grand narrative into which Muslim writers sought to fit Islam.[74] Some uncertainty is however justified over whether Ibn Isḥāq himself is responsible for more direct Biblical quotations preserved in al-Ṭabarī's reports linked to his name. For example, there is some evidence that the long quotation from Numbers 13–14, cut by Ibn Hishām but attributed by al-Ṭabarī to Ibn Isḥāq, may have entered the *Sīra* text subsequent to Ibn Isḥāq himself.[75]

Moving beyond the *sīra* literature, Biblically-linked attestations of Muhammad and his community occur in hadiths. However, in early hadith works focussed specifically on proofs of prophethood, there is no material drawing on Biblical verses used to support Muhammad's prophethood. Proofs consist instead of Muhammad's miracles, or portents of nature.[76] Subsequent works of hadith which focussed on proofs of prophethood began to include Biblical verses. A notable example is *Proofs of Prophethood* (*Dalāʾil al-nubuwwa*) by al-Bayhaqī (d. 458/1066), who collects reports drawing both on recognisable Biblical text

---

72 As noted in passing by Hayrettin Yücesoy, "Ancient Imperial Heritage and Islamic Universal History: al-Dīnawarī's Secular Perspective," *JGH* 2 (2007), 138, n.7.

73 These histories are discussed in Chapter 4. For an argument that Ibn Ḥabīb (d. 245/860) is formative in introducing Biblical elements into Muslim historical writings, see Abed El-Rahman Tayyara, "Ibn Ḥabīb's *Kitāb al-Muḥabbar* and its Place in Early Islamic Historical Writing," *JIS* 29 (2018): 392–416. It is arguable that Ibn Isḥāq precedes him by around a century.

74 Various Biblical parallels to elements of the sira literature have been claimed. For example it is argued that Ibn Isḥāq's universal history not only links Islam to Biblical events, but in its conception and design is actually modelled on the Biblical history from Genesis to 2 Kings. Both the Biblical version and that of Ibn Isḥāq have a programmatic speech at the structural centre of the story: Moses' restatement of the law in Deuteronomy, paralleled by Muhammad's "Farewell Sermon". See Peter Wright, "Critical Approaches to the 'Farewell Khutba' in Ibn Ishaq's Life of the Prophet," *CIS* 6 (2010): 217–49. See also Rubin, The *Eye of the Beholder: the Life of Muhammad as Viewed by the Early Muslims: a Textual Analysis* (Princeton: Darwin Press, 1995), on Moses as a model for Muhammad.

75 For this evidence see Ronny Vollandt, *Arabic Versions of the Pentateuch* (Leiden: Brill, 2015): 103–05. Less sceptical is Joseph Witztum, "Ibn Isḥāq and the Pentateuch in Arabic," *JSAI* 40 (2013): 1–71.

76 See Mareike Koertner, *"We Have Made Clear the Signs": Dalāʾil al-Nubuwa* [sic] – *Proofs of Prophecy in Early Hadith* (Unpublished Ph.D. thesis, University of Yale, 2014), and Koertner, "*Dalāʾil al-Nubuwwa* Literature as Part of the Medieval Scholarly Discourse on Prophecy," *Der Islam* 95 (2018): 91–109.

and other material.[77] The first six of al-Bayhaqī's eleven hadiths are in fact variants of the report mentioned above in which Muhammad is given attributes associated with a messianic figure in Isaiah 42, including not being coarse, nor shouting in the streets. These motifs, associated with messiahship, gradually lose the messianic association in Islamic literature and thus become seen as actual descriptions of Muhammad's behaviour.

Al-Bayhaqī then offers traditions of a different kind mentioning revelation to previous prophets, but which are not grounded in the extant Biblical texts. The connecting theme in these reports is the affirmation of Muhammad and his followers by pre-Islamic texts. For example, a long tradition is reported about Moses finding in the *Tawrāt* a community with various good traits, which he asks to be his community. God replies that this is the community of Muhammad. Next, David receives in the *Zabūr* information predicting the merits of Muhammad and his community. A further tradition describes a codex (*muṣḥaf*) of the Book of Daniel being found by Daniel's dead body. The main point of this tradition is the fact that the bodies of prophets do not decay in the grave, information relevant to perceptions of Muhammad even though he is not named. Throughout these traditions the theme of previous scriptures predicting Muhammad, his community, and truth about them, is the dominant note.

Another possible reference to previous scriptures occurs in the Muslim accounts of Muhammad's encounter with the monk Baḥīra.[78] There are multiple and varying traditions about the young Muhammad, on a trade journey to Syria with his family, encountering a monk who recognises his prophetic status even before the start of his mission. Baḥīra possesses an ancient book containing a reference to a new prophet. The association of an old book and a monk implies scripture, though the reference is not explicit, while the Baḥīra stories are obviously related to the theme of the previous faiths attesting to the new prophet.[79]

77 Al-Bayhaqī, *Dalā'il al-Nubuwwa*, vol. 1, (Beirut: Dār al-kutub al-'arabiyya, 1985), 373–383. The relevant chapter is entitled "The Character of the Messenger of God in the *Tawrāt* and the *Injīl* and the *Zabūr* and other books, and the character of his community."

78 See Barbara Roggema, *The Legend of Sergius Baḥīrā: Eastern Christian apologetics and apocalyptic in response to Islam*, HCMR 9 (Leiden: Brill, 2009), 37–60; and Roggema, "Baḥīrā", in: *EI3*, consulted online on 03 July 2019, http://dx.doi.org/10.1163/1573-3912_ei3_COM_23570.

79 Roggema, *Legend*, 38.

3.3.2 Establishing the role of the Muslims in God's purposes

Support for Muhammad's prophethood should not be seen as occurring only via references to Muhammad himself. All Muslim accounts of previous prophets function as a form of attestation of Muhammad, since they provide the setting into which the climactic jewel, Muhammad, is placed. For this reason the early Muslim self-image as a people chosen by God was presented not as a new development, but rather, "reflected a divine global scheme in which Islam had played the pivotal role since the very beginning of human history".[80] Connecting Muhammad to the lineage of previous (and Biblical) prophets was important as the Qur'an affirms that prophecy is passed down through Abraham and his descendants (Q 29:27).

The focus here is on the roles of Abraham and in particular Ishmael, with brief comment on the group known as Arab prophets. Abraham is a key figure in Muslim self-understanding, being seen as the prototypical monotheist, whom the Qur'an terms the first Muslim (Q2:131)[81] and neither a Jew nor a Christian (Q3:65). Through Ishmael he is regarded as the ancestor of Muhammad (on which more below). Yet traditions about Abraham rarely involve episodes from the Biblical book of Genesis (see Genesis 12–25). Abraham's depiction in Islam can be divided into three geographic areas, Babylon, al-Shām (modern Syria, Lebanon, Jordan and Israel/ Palestine) and Arabia.[82] His life in al-Shām, which includes Canaan, the centre of attention of Abraham's Biblical portrayal, is minimised in Muslim sources. Much more emphasis is given to his exploits either in Babylon, centred on opposition to idols, or in Arabia, focussed on building the Ka'ba with Ishmael, and also involving the potential sacrifice of his son, named in early sources variously as Ishmael or Isaac, and often transferred to an Arabian setting.[83] The complex Muslim elaboration of the figure of Abraham may

---

80 Uri Rubin, "Islamic Retellings of Biblical History," 299. Tony Maalouf, *Arabs in the Shadow of Israel: the unfolding of God's prophetic plan for Ishmael's line* (Grand Rapids, MI: Kregel, 2003) explores the Arabs' role in Biblical narratives.

81 Or "submitter", if "*muslim*" here is understood in its broader sense.

82 Shosh Ben-Ari, "The Stories About Abraham in Islam: a Geographical Approach," *Arabica* 54 (2007): 526–53.

83 Peter Webb, "Pre-Islamic al-Shām in Classical Arabic Literature: Spatial Narratives and History-Telling," *SI* 110 (2015): 135–64, esp. 161–64. On the sacrifice of Abraham's son see Suliman Bashear, "Abraham's Sacrifice of his Son and Related Issues," *Der Islam* 67 (1990): 243–77, and Norman Calder, "From Midrash to Scripture: The Sacrifice of Abraham in early Islamic Tradition," in *The Formation of the Classical Islamic World* (Aldershot: Ashgate Variorum, 1999): 81–108.

be explained by interaction with conquered Jews and Christians.[84] But his importance lies not only in being the prototypical monotheist, but in linking Muhammad and the Arabs genealogically to Adam and thus to the whole unfolding of divine purposes. This brings us to the role of Ishmael.

In integrating Biblical figures such as Ishmael into 7th century Arabia, genealogy becomes important. Analysing early Muslim genealogies is complex, since they were often developed and adapted to meet the needs of the present, not primarily accurately to represent the past.[85] Ishmael is a figure both Biblical (see Genesis 16–25) and also prominent in Muslim constructions of the Arab past. Although he is commonly associated with Arabs and Muslims the Qur'an gives him a minor role, and never links him to Arabness.[86] (There is recent debate over whether the term "Arabs" is meaningful in the pre-Islamic period, but it is used here while discussion continues).[87]

Some uncertainty over Ishmael's links to 'Arabness' is understandable since while hadiths promote the connection between Arab identity and Israelite history, the Qur'an is more ambivalent about it.[88] The Qur'an does not link Muhammad or Arabs to Ishmael genealogically, and it has been argued that Ishmael be-

---

84 Gerald Hawting, "The Religion of Abraham and Islam," in *Abraham, the Nations and the Hagarites: Jewish, Christian and Islamic Perspectives on kinship with Abraham*, eds. Martin Goodman, George van Kooten and Jacques van Ruiten (Leiden: Brill, 2010), 477–501. See also Shari Lowin, *The Making of a Forefather: Abraham in Islamic and Jewish Exegetical Narratives*, IHC 65 (Leiden: Brill, 2006).

85 See Peter Webb, *Imagining the Arabs* (Edinburgh: EUP, 2016) for extensive discussion of the use of genealogy; also Michael Macdonald, "Ancient Arabia and the Written Word," *Proceedings of the Seminar for Arabian Studies* 40, Supplement: The Development of Arabic as a Written Language (2010): 22, on Arab genealogies in an oral culture.

86 For a summary account of the twelve Qur'anic references to Ishmael see Reuven Firestone, "Ishmael," in: *EQ* 2.

87 For doubts about the use of the term 'Arab' before the rise of Islam see Webb, *Imagining*. In response, see Robert Hoyland, "Reflections on the Identity of the Arabian Conquerors of the Seventh–Century Middle East," *Al-ʿUṣūr al-Wusṭā* 25 (2017): 113–40. On Arabs and Christianity in the pre–Islamic period, and including the association of "Ishmaelite" and "Arab", see Greg Fisher et al, "Arabs and Christianity" in Greg Fisher, ed., *Arabs and Empires before Islam* (Oxford: OUP, 2015), 276–372.

88 Sometimes Israelite history and Arab identity are separated. Israelite monotheism is portrayed as the foundation and precursor of Islam, for example in Q4:163, while the Quraysh and Bedouin are presented negatively in Qur'anic perspective. Conversely, Q14:35–41 associates Abraham and Ishmael with the Kaʿba. See Rubin, "Retellings," 312.

comes particularly important to Muslims in the process of constructing a new pan-Arab identity which is retrojected into pre-Islamic history.[89]

Before turning from the Qur'anic Ishmael to Ishmael in the Hadith, the identification of Arabs as descendants of Ishmael, and thus of Abraham, needs probing. There is no clear association of Arabs with "Ishmaelites" in the Bible, the terms occurring separately.[90] But Jewish pre-Islamic sources identify Ishmael as an ancestor of the Arabs. *The Book of Jubilees* is a retelling of the events of the Book of Genesis with much altered detail, probably from the second century BC. Referring to the sons of Ishmael and also of Keturah, wife of Abraham, it states, "They mixed with one another and were called Arabs and Ishmaelites."[91] *The Antiquities of the Jews* by Josephus (d.100 CE) also make this connection. Josephus writes of circumcision, "The Arabs defer the ceremony to the thirteenth year, because *Ishmael, the founder of their race*, born of Abraham's concubine, was circumcised at that age" (emphasis added).[92]

But when exactly Arabs *themselves* began to uphold their identity as descendants of Ishmael and therefore of Abraham is less clear.[93] Since the connection of Ishmael to the Arabs was circulating in Jewish and Christian sources prior to the rise of Islam, it is possible that the Arabs' own adoption of this genealogical link between Arabs and Ishmael comes from their encounters with Jews and

---

89 Webb, *Imagining*, 212–13. On emphasising Arabness see also Tayeb el-Hibri, *Parable and Politics in Early Islamic History* (New York: Columbia University Press, 2010), 84–88, who draws attention to the way in which early 'Abbāsid sources stress Caliph 'Umar's specifically Arab identity.

90 Israel Eph'al, " 'Ishmael' and 'Arabs': a transformation of ethnological terms," *JNES* 35 (1976), 228. Eph'al traces how the two terms of his title began life separately, but eventually became interchangeable.

91 Originally written in Hebrew, of which passages were found among the Dead Sea Scrolls, full versions of the text are preserved in Ge'ez (Ethiopic). For the Ethiopic text see James VanderKam, ed., *The Book of Jubilees: a critical text*, CSCOSA 88 (Leuven: Peeters, 1989), 114 [section xx:13]; trans. James VanderKam, *The Book of Jubilees*, CSCO 511 (Leuven: Peeters, 1989), 119.

92 Josephus, *Antiquities*, Book I, trans. H. Thackeray, LCL 242 (Cambridge, MA: Harvard University Press, 1998), 106 (Greek), 107 (English). The connection of Ishmael to the Arabs crops up again in the third century, in the work of the church father Origen and others, and in the fifth century with Sozomenus, Bishop of Gaza; see Millar, "Hagar," 40–42. On the effect on Christian thought of Christians linking Arabs with Ishmaelites see David Grafton, '"The Arabs" in the Ecclesiastical Historians of the 4th/5th centuries: Effects on Contemporary Christian–Muslim Relations," *Het Teologiese Studies* 64 (2008), 177–92, and Calvin Kendall, "Bede and Islam," in *Bede and the Future* eds. Peter Darby and Faith Wallis (Farnham: Ashgate, 2014): 93–114. On Rabbinic portrayals of Ishmael see Carol Bakhos, *Ishmael on the Border: Rabbinic Portrayals of the First Arab*, JHMR (Albany, N.Y.: SUNY Press, 2006).

93 Webb, *Imagining*, 212–221.

Christians, either in the pre-Islamic period or later.[94] However, it is also possible that the early non-Muslim sources are representing what those living in Arabia thought of themselves.[95]

It is in hadith and biographical literature that Ishmael's significance grows. The extant version of Ibn Isḥāq's life of Muhammad begins with a genealogy linking Muhammad to Adam through Ishmael and Abraham, via ʻAdnān. Both ʻAdnān, the traditional ancestor of the Northern Arabs,[96] and Qaḥtān, traditional ancestor of the South Arabians, were related by Muslim sources to Biblical figures. ʻAdnān is understood to be a descendant of Ishmael, albeit with varying and unclear links between the two.[97] A hadith warns against tracing Muhammad's line beyond a certain ancestor, but it is unclear whether this is ʻAdnān or his son Maʻadd.[98] Qaḥṭān, ancestor of the South Arabians, is equated with Joktan son of Eber (See Genesis 10:25).[99]

Ibn Isḥāq gives Ishmael an Arab wife, al-Sayyida bint Muḍāḍ,[100] and one or other of Ishmael's first two sons, Nebaioth and Kedar (Genesis 25:13) is sometimes regarded as an ancestor of Muhammad. There is no overall consensus in Muslim sources on the identity of the figures connecting Muhammad and Ishmael, but the reality of this link, and thus Muhammad's link to Abraham and Adam, was upheld by all. So Muhammad, crucially, is portrayed as a descendant of Abraham via Ishmael and is thus integrated into primordial, and also global history.[101] Ishmael is also closely associated with the sanctity of Mecca, through its being promoted as the site of Abraham's call to sacrifice his son, where that son is identified as Ishmael rather than Isaac[102] as well as through the Qur'an's reference to Ishmael helping his father build the Kaʻba (Q2:127).

---

94 For discussion of relevant themes, see Webb, *Imagining, passim*; Hawting, "Religion of Abraham," 491.

95 For a succinct overview of complex data on this theme see Fisher (ed.) *Arabs and Empires*, 367–72.

96 Ibn Isḥāq, in Ibn Hishām, *Das Leben*, 3; trans. Guillaume, *Life*, 3.

97 Eva Orthmann, "ʻAdnān," in: *EI3*, consulted online on 03 July 2019, http://dx.doi.org/10.1163/1573-3912_ei3_COM_24770.

98 Al-Ṭabarī, *Ta'rīkh*, 1112, and cited by Tayyara, "Ibn Ḥabīb," 412–13.

99 Webb, *Imagining*, 213–14, discusses the linking of Qaḥṭān and Ishmael to Yemenis. The claim that Qaḥṭān is an Arabicized from of Joktan is described as 'phonologically hazardous' by A. Fischer and A. Irvine, "Ḳaḥṭān," in Fischer, A. and Irvine, A.K., "Ḳaḥṭān," in: *EI2*, consulted online on 08 May 2020, http://dx.doi.org/10.1163/1573-3912_islam_SIM_3790.

100 Al-Ṭabarī, *Ta'rīkh*, 351–2; cf. Rubin, "Retellings," 305.

101 Rubin, "Retellings," 306–07.

102 Bashear, "Abraham's Sacrifice."

The events narrated in Genesis 21, in which Hagar and Ishmael wander in the desert of Beersheba, are transferred by Islamic tradition to Arabia, even though Ishmael is not seen by Muslim sources as an indigenous Arab.[103] However, Ishmael was not so important to a distinctively Arab identity, once that identity had been constructed, and his importance, and his own identity as father of the Arabs, subsequently fade from view. There is "a decoupling of Arabness" from Ishmael, seen in the fact that he is not named amongst accounts of 'Arab' prophets named in later sources.

The idea of Arab prophets, first used by the historian Ibn Ḥabīb (d.245/859), did not include Ishmael.[104] Hūd, Ṣāliḥ, Shu'ayb and Muhammad are the only Qur'anic prophets not mentioned in the Bible by name, but, like Muhammad, Hūd, Ṣāliḥ and Shu'ayb are however also linked to Biblical figures.[105] Ibn Isḥāq records a tradition (preserved in al-Ṭabarī's *History*), stating that Hūd is to be identified with Eber, mentioned in Genesis 10:24.[106] Ṣāliḥ is given a genealogy linking him to Noah through Shem, while Shu'ayb is often identified with the Midianite Jethro, father-in-law of Moses or understood to be Jethro's uncle (see Exod 3:1, 4:18, 18:1–12).[107]

Ibn Isḥāq introduces various links between perceived Arab predecessors and the genealogies recorded in Genesis 10. Lud, a son of Shem (Genesis 10:22), is without sons in the Biblical account, but is said by Ibn Isḥaq to have fathered Ṭasm and 'Imlīq (Amalek), ancestor of the Amalekites,[108] and al-Arqam, who was "king of the Hijaz". Aram, another son of Shem (Genesis 10:22) has descendants including the people of 'Ād and Thamūd, mentioned in the Qur'an.[109] But

103 Rubin, 'Retellings', 304.

104 Ibn Ḥabīb, *Kitāb al-Muḥabbar* (Hyderabad: Maṭba'at Jām'iyat Dā'irat al-Ma'ārif al-'Uthmāniyya, 1942), 131–32, cf. Webb, *Imagining*, 217–18. For more on the prophets seen as Arab, see Brannon Wheeler, "Arab prophets of the Qur'an and Bible," *JQS* 8 (2006): 24–57. Abraham is sometimes also included.

105 Hūd in the Qur'an is found at Q 7:65–72, 11:50–60, 26:123–40, 46:21–6. For Ṣāliḥ see Q7:73–9; 11:61–8; 26:141–59; 27:45–53; 54:23–31; 91:11–15). On Shu'ayb see Q7:85–93; 11:84–95; 26:176–91; 29:36–7.

106 Al-Ṭabarī, *Ta'rikh*, 231; cf. Rubin, "Retellings," 303. See also Roberto Tottoli, "Hūd", in: EI3, consulted online on 03 July 2019, http://dx.doi.org/10.1163/1573-3912_ei3_COM_30532.

107 See Andrew Rippin, "Ṣāliḥ", in:*EI2*, consulted online on 03 July 2019, http://dx.doi.org/10.1163/1573-3912_islam_SIM_6536 and Rippin, "Shu'ayb", in: *EI2*, consulted online on 08 May 2020 http://dx.doi.org/10.1163/1573-3912_islam_SIM_6972.

108 See Georges Vajda, "'Amālīḳ", in *EI2*, consulted online on 03 July 2019, http://dx.doi.org/10.1163/1573-3912_islam_SIM_0576, who makes the connection to Genesis 10 explicit, unlike Roberto Tottoli, "'Amālīq", in: *EI3*, consulted online on 03 July 2019, http://dx.doi.org/10.1163/1573-3912_ei3_COM_22870.

109 For references see Rubin, "Retellings," 303.

the standing of ʿĀd and Thamūd as Arab peoples was disputed. They are never called Arab in the Qur'an, and were incorporated by Yemenis into their presumed ancestry when they were themselves seeking to assert their Arab identity.[110] But, as previously noted, by the time Ibn Isḥāq was writing, the ʿAbbāsids were seeking to strengthen the perceived relationship of Islam and their own dynasty to prior prophetic history.

What is clear is that Ibn Isḥāq gathers biblically-related material, and also adds to Biblical genealogies, so as to emphasise the connection of the Muslims to God's purposes as worked out through Abraham and Ishmael.[111] Writing after the first century of Islamic conquest, Ibn Isḥāq represents a move to locate Arab predecessors of the Muslims within Biblical history. He seeks to portray these Arabian figures not as peripheral to divine purposes, but as always having been part of them. This purpose of Ibn Isḥāq would seem to be related to the support of the ʿAbbāsid Caliph al-Manṣūr and his political project of legitimising the new dynasty after its violent overthrow of the Umayyads.[112]

3.3.3 The Role of ʿUmar

The second caliph ʿUmar (r. 13–23/634–44) is depicted as a fundamental figure in the formation of early Islam, associated with religious zeal and conquest.[113] We have already seen that he features in the story of Muslim perceptions of the Bible, in the report of Muhammad becoming angry at his reading a sheet of the *Tawrāt*.[114] However, there are other reports invoking the previous scriptures – in a variety of ways – where ʿUmar emerges more positively.

110 Webb, Imagining, 116, 213–15.

111 Cf. discussion above on divided Shia views over the competing roles of Arab or Biblical heritage in their self-understanding.

112 See Antoine Borrut, *Entre Mémoire et Pouvoir: l'espace Syrien sous les derniers Omeyyades et les premiers Abbassides (v. 72–193/ 692–809)* (Leiden: Brill, 2011), 82–83.

113 An interpretation of accounts of ʿUmar's life noting the connections of these accounts to the concerns of ninth century ʿAbbāsid Iraq is given by el-Hibri, *Parable and Politics*, 77–121, and el-Hibri, "ʿUmar b. al-Khaṭṭāb and the ʿAbbāsids," *JAOS* 136 (2016): 763–83.

114 On shifting attitudes to ʿUmar, promoting him as ideal leader, partly in the image of Moses, then demoting him so as to prioritise Muhammad, see Avraham Hakim, "Context: ʿUmar b. al-Khaṭṭāb," in *The Blackwell Companion to the Qur'ān*, ed. Andrew Rippin (Oxford: Blackwell, 2006): 205–20. The report about ʿUmar reading a sheet of the Tawrāt, when set alongside more positive traditions, seems to reflect this tension. See also Hakim, "Muḥammad's Authority and Leadership."

First, Biblical warrant is offered for ‘Umar's role as conqueror. A learned hermit of Dayr ‘Udas identifies ‘Umar as the future conqueror of al-Shām. He identifies him after recognising his description as given in the previous scriptures. This reported prediction dovetails with ‘Umar's role as conqueror of Jerusalem at some point shortly after 13/634.[115] The report echoes accounts of the monk Baḥīra's identification of Muhammad as the future prophet, mentioned above, also related to a description read beforehand.[116]

Secondly, ‘Umar's death was said to have been predicted in the *Tawrāt*. Ka‘b b. al-Aḥbār tells ‘Umar to appoint his successor, for he is going to die within three days, information Ka‘b has acquired from the Torah.[117] The idea that ‘Umar's death is predicted in previous scripture emphasises the importance of ‘Umar; even his death was divinely foretold. However, there is a different account in the earliest of the Arab biographical dictionaries, the *Kitāb al-Ṭabaqāt al-kabīr* (*The Great Book of Generations*) by Ibn Sa‘d (d. 230/845).[118] Ka‘b's prediction of ‘Umar's death as given by Ibn Sa‘d includes a longer anecdote which aims to separate ‘Umar from the Biblical background. Ka‘b tells of an unnamed Israelite king who, when told by an unnamed prophet that he will die within three days, pleads for an extension to his life. God instructs the prophet to tell the king that his prayer has been granted and he will live longer. This clearly echoes the interaction of King Hezekiah of Judah and the prophet Isaiah depicted in the Biblical books 2 Kings and Isaiah.[119] But when Ka‘b is portrayed as holding out to the stabbed ‘Umar the option of prayer for longer life which God will certainly answer, ‘Umar rejects this, saying, ‘O Allah, take me to You neither powerless nor blamed’. ‘Umar will not take the path of weakness implicitly here associated with the action of the Israelite king. Hence the different reports of Ka‘b's statements regarding ‘Umar's death can be taken in two different ways. In the first, they seem to buttress the role of the Torah. But in Ibn Sa‘d the opposite is true. Israelite weakness is primarily a foil to ‘Umar's inner strength.

---

115 See Heribert Busse, “Omar's Image as the Conqueror of Jerusalem,” *JSAI* 8 (1986): 149–68.

116 Al-Dīnawarī (d. c. 940), *al-Mujālasa wa jawāhir al-‘ilm* (Beirut: Dār Ibn Ḥazm, 1998), 5:175–77, al-Iṣfahānī (d. 961), *al-Diyārāt* (London: Riyād al-Rayyis li'l-kutub wa'l-nashr, 1991), 118–120; see Avraham Hakim, “The Biblical Annunciation made to ‘Umar b. al-Khaṭṭab,” *JSAI* 42 (2015): 130–31.

117 Avraham Hakim, “The Death of an Ideal Leader: Predictions and premonitions,” *JAOS* 126 (2006), 2.

118 Ibn Sa‘d, *al-Ṭabaqāt al-kubrā*, 9 vols., (Beirut: Dār Sādir, 1957–58): 3:354; trans. from Ibn Sa‘d, *The Companions of Badr*, tr. Aisha Bewley (London: TaHa, 2013), 276.

119 See 2 Kings 20:1–7 and Isaiah 38:1–6.

Thirdly, some descriptions of 'Umar have messianic overtones. In one tradition Ka'b describes 'Umar as an iron horn (*qarn min ḥadīd*), a messianic image found in the Biblical book of Micah 4:13. It is possible that later Muslims did not recognise the original messianic overtones of this description.[120] Likewise the title "*al-fārūq*," often associated with 'Umar, is usually understood by Muslims as "one who distinguishes right from wrong." However, some traditions indicate that it signifies "redeemer," and was first given to 'Umar by Jews, or converts to Islam from Judaism. This was because of his conquest of Jerusalem, seen as a deliverance of the city and of the Jewish people from Christian Byzantine rule.[121] The portrayal of 'Umar's conquests as messianic can be related to traditions portraying the anti-Byzantine campaign and the conquest of Jerusalem and al-Shām as a Jewish-Arab messianic movement, to which we now turn.

3.3.4 Legitimisation of conquest

There has been much recent discussion of what to call the events typically termed the "Islamic Conquests" or "Arab Conquests". Can the term "Islamic" be applied to such an early period when the developed Islamic tradition was arguably not fully formed? And was the term "Arab" part of the self-identity of those involved?[122] Whatever the ideal terminology for the conquests, the focus here is on portrayals of elements in these conquests which draw on Biblical ideas or terms. As Sizgorich puts it, "When the momentum of the conquest had slackened after c.750 CE… the Arab communities newly settled in the conquered lands of Syria and Mesopotamia found that they had a lot of explaining to do."[123] It may be that the following traditions form one small part of that explanatory process. This would be unsurprising, given the complex processes in-

120 This description of 'Umar is recorded by Abū Nu'aym, Nu'aym b. Ḥammād, and Aḥmad ibn Hanbal; see Hakim, "Annunciation,"139 ff. Hakim's broad statement, 145, that, "Early Muslim scholars had access to the Old Testament, where they may have found Micah's prophecy," begs a number of questions tackled by the present work.

121 Found in Ibn Sa 'd, Ibn Shahba, al-Balādhūrī and al-Ṭabarī; see Suliman Bashear, "The Title 'Fārūq', and its Association with 'Umar I," *SI* 72 (1990), 69. For the report see Ibn Sa'd, *al-Ṭabaqāt*, 3:270; cf. the discussion in Bashear "Title", 66–68 for discussion and other sources. The portrayal of 'Umar as redeemer is mentioned by Patricia Crone and Michael Cook, *Hagarism* (Cambridge: CUP, 1977), 5.

122 See Fred Donner, "Talking About Islam's Origins," *BSOAS* 81 (2018): 1–23, and bibliography therein, and cf. Webb, *Imagining.*

123 Thomas Sizgorich, "Narrative and Community in Islamic Late Antiquity," *Past and Present* No. 185 (November 2004): 9.

volved in identity formation and the accompanying need to work out relationships of the newly emerging identity to elements of existing societies and structures.[124]

There are indications that the conquest of al-Shām under 'Umar and the wider anti-Byzantine campaign were portrayed as a joint Arab-Jewish messianic movement. Whether the conquest actually had elements of such a movement is a separate question beyond our scope; the portrayal is the focus here. In this portrayal a messianic redeemer, an obviously Biblical theme, will cast off the yoke of Byzantine rule.[125] Ka'b b. al-Aḥbār is the key figure in the occurrence of such reports. Applying the motif of the Biblical Exodus and the conquest of Canaan to the conquest of al-Shām is seen in a tradition in which Ka'b gives a quotation said to be from the *Tawrāt* predicting the conquest of Palestine. "This land, in which the Children of Israel dwelt, will be conquered by God at the hand of a man of the righteous."[126] The appeal to the "*Tawrāt*'" shows an attempt to legitimise conquest as part of divine plans foretold in previous scripture.

Ka'b b. al-Aḥbār also locates the prediction of the building of the Dome of the Rock in the *Tawrāt*.[127] Nor was the Biblical legitimation of conquest limited to sites in al-Shām. The conquest of Constantinople, a long-held dream of Muslim rulers since the first attempts in the 660's CE, is predicted in language echoing Ezekiel's prophecies about the fall of Tyre (Ezekiel 26–27).[128] In a variety of ways, the aim is to use Jewish messianic hopes to enhance justification for the anti-Byzantine campaign.

124 Sizgorich, "Narrative and Community," explores some of these processes in relation to drawing on symbols from the surrounding milieu.

125 Rubin, *Bible and Qur'an*, 5, 30. On the limited extant evidence for actual Jewish attitudes to the Muslim conquest of Jerusalem, see Stefan Leder, "The Attitude of the Population, especially the Jews, towards the Arab–Islamic Conquest of Bilād al-Shām and the Question of their Role Therein," *Die Welt des Orients* 18 (1987): 64–71. On Jewish Messianic thought and its expectation of this–worldly change, see Lawrence Schiffman, "Messianism and Apocalyticism in Rabbinic Texts," in *The Cambridge History of Judaism*, ed. Steven Katz (Cambridge: CUP, 1990): 4:1053–1072.

126 Rubin, *Bible and Qur'an*, 14. Rubin argues that this quotation uses words blending Qur'anic and biblical ideas, drawing on Q48:29 and other Qur'anic elements, with elements of *Isaiah* 42 to portray Muhammad and his followers. The biblical elements of this quotation from "The Torah" are less prominent than Rubin indicates.

127 Rubin, *Bible and Quran*, 19–20. See the discussion of possible Jewish views of earliest Islam as a hopeful messianic development, in relation to the Temple Mount, by Guy Stroumsa, *The Making of the Abrahamic Religions in Late Antiquity*, OSAR (Oxford: OUP, 2015), 73–85. Discussion of reasons for building of the Dome of the Rock is plentiful; see Milka Levy-Rubin, "Why was the Dome of the Rock Built?"

128 See Rubin, *Bible and Qur'an*, 20–23.

There are also echoes of the idea of the portrayal of Islam as a Jewish-Arab messianic movement in non-Muslim sources, though the significance of these accounts as a record of actual events, as opposed to perceptions, is unclear. Jewish messianic movements grew in the seventh century, fuelled by the Persian defeat of the Byzantines and restoration of Jerusalem to Jewish control from 614–617. This was shortly followed by the Arab conquests, all leading to a period of turbulent hope for an upturn in Jewish fortunes.[129] An eighth-century Jewish work, The *Secrets of Rabbi Simon ben Yoḥai*, regards the kingdom of Ishmael as a source of deliverance from Christian domination.[130] The *Doctrina Jacobi*, a Greek Christian anti-Jewish work (dated either to the 630s/40s or 670s) sees such a messianic movement more negatively.[131] The Armenian writer associated with the name Sebeos, writing in the 660's, also regards Islam as involving Arab-Jewish collaboration over conquest of land.[132] So Muslim traditions reflecting Jewish-Arab messianism find some parallels in non-Muslim sources.[133] A possible context for invoking the *Tawrāt* in support of the conquest of al-Shām is that of a new community of emigrants and conquerors understanding themselves, or portraying themselves, as divinely mandated, in order to help legiti-

129 See Sean Anthony, "Who was the Shepherd of Damascus? The Enigma of Jewish and Messianist Responses to the Islamic Conquests in Marwānid Syria and Mesopotamia," in *The Lineaments of Islam: Studies in Honor of Fred McGraw Donner*, ed. Paul Cobb, IHC 95 (Leiden: Brill, 2012): 21–59.

130 See Robert Hoyland, *Seeing Islam as Others Saw it* (Princeton: Darwin Press, 1997), 526–27, who translates the relevant passage. A full English translation by John Reeves of *The Secrets of Rabbi Simon ben Yoḥai* is available at https://pages.uncc.edu/john-reeves/research-projects/trajectories-in-near-eastern-apocalyptic/nistarot-secrets-of-r-shimon-b-yohai-2/ (accessed 31.1.2019), along with publication details of the Hebrew text.

131 See Sean Anthony, "Muḥammad, the Keys to Paradise, and the Doctrina Iacobi: a Late Antique puzzle," *Der Islam* 91 (2014): 243–65. See also Hoyland, *Seeing Islam*, 526–31.

132 Robert Hoyland, "Sebeos, the Jews and the Rise of Islam," *SMJR* 2 (1995): 89–102; translation of the relevant passage on 89. Hoyland argues for taking the chronicle of Sebeos seriously as preserving genuine information about early Islam.

133 There have been other examples of Jews and Arabs jointly following a messianic figure (though this provides no proof of seventh century events, of course). The Jewish philosopher Maimonides (d.1204) condemns a purported harbinger of the Messiah in Yemen who was followed by both Jews and Arabs; for the Hebrew text see Alexander Marx, "The Correspondence Between the Rabbis of Southern France and Maimonides about Astrology," *HUCA* 3 (1926): 350–51; English translation of the passage in A. Halkin and B. Cohen (edited and translated) *Moses Maimonides' Epistle to Yemen; the Arabic original and three Hebrew versions* (New York: The American Academy for Jewish Research, 1952), note 19 (where they cite the Hebrew text as 50–51 in Marx). For a nineteenth century example connecting Jewish and Muslim messianic ideas see Bat-Zion Eraqi Klorman, "Muslim Supporters of Jewish Messiahs in Yemen," *MES* 29 (1993): 714–25.

mate their rule. A developed theology or ideology is not necessary for military conquest, but it can be more useful for the subsequent justification of ongoing rule of conquered land.[134]

The idea of conquest of the Promised Land is also extended in some traditions to the conquest of the Ḥijāz. Biblical elements in this effort to assert the centrality of the Ḥijāz include not only portraying the land of the Ḥijāz itself as part of the Promised Land, but also depicting Arabian sanctuaries as places visited by Moses, Jonah, Elijah and Jesus.[135] Hence conquering the Ḥijāz and removing unbelievers becomes part of fulfilling Biblical prophecy about the Promised Land, while elevating the status of Mecca. This association of Mecca with the Promised Land seems to reflect the concern of Medinan writers in particular (of whom Ibn Isḥāq was one), to emphasise the centrality of Muhammad's Arabian heritage over against the Umayyad focus on Palestine and Syria. Various traditions indicate rivalry between Palestine and the Ḥijāz, and between Jerusalem and Mecca, as cultic centres in early Islam.[136]

3.3.5 Apocalyptic Literature

Apocalyptic is another theme in tradition literature which makes reference to Biblical predecessors. Apocalyptic reports occur either in separate hadiths scattered in more general collections, or in works devoted specifically to the subject. These reports purport to describe events immediately preceding the end of time and should not be confused with eschatological literature, which describes events once the final day actually arrives.

This material did not emerge in a vacuum; as Cook notes, "Islam was heir to a vast apocalyptic tradition handed down from the classical world," which in-

134 Tannous, *Medieval Middle East*, 308. This notion of divinely mandated conquerors spreading out in unspecified directions in fact fits the Qur'anic material on emigration (*hijra*) if it is gathered and read without the framework of the exegetical tradition; see Caterina Bori, " 'All We Know." See also along similar lines, Stephen Shoemaker, *The Death of a Prophet: the End of Muhammad's Life and the Beginnings of Islam*, DRLAR (Philadelphia: University of Pennsylvania Press, 2012).

135 Rubin, *Between Bible and Qur'an*, 37–46.

136 It has even been argued that the Umayyad focus on al-Shām, and Jerusalem as cultic centre, was not a deviation from the original focus on Mecca, but was the prevailing position in early Islam until the assertion of Ḥijāzī prominence gradually grew in the second century AH. Suliman Bashear, "Qur'ān 2:114 and Jerusalem," *BSOAS* 52 (1989): 215–238; Bashear, "Abraham's Sacrifice of his Son and Related Issues," *Der Islam* 67 (1990): 243–277.

cluded Zoroastrian, Jewish and Christian texts.[137] The earliest complete Muslim work which gathers together apocalyptic traditions is *The Book of Tribulations* (*Kitāb al-Fitan*) by Nu'aym b. Ḥammād al-Marwazī (d. 228/843).[138] He preserves many traditions absent from what became the Sunni canonical collections, works which diminish the sense of apocalyptic tension which seems to have circulated in the first two centuries of Islam.[139] Part of the significance of this literature is in indicating the fears amongst a community riven by violence and uprisings in its early centuries.[140]

Apocalyptic traditions referring to the Bible amount to an interesting though relatively minor element in Nu'aym's work. I counted nineteen such traditions in a collection of nearly 2,000.[141] Amongst the reports mentioning previous scriptures, Ka'b b. al-Aḥbār predicts the annihilation of the Arabs following civil wars. He recognises a specific road when he sees it, saying, "I found its description in the books of the Israelites."[142] Another report states, "I find in the *Tawrāt* that this community will have twelve lords." This stems from an idea in Genesis 17:20, stating that Ishmael will father twelve princes, as the very next tradition listed by Nu'aym makes clear. Here Ka'b states, "God Most High gave to Ishmael from his loins twelve righteous leaders, the best of them were Abū Bakr, 'Umar and 'Uthmān."[143] The apocalyptic element is contained in the prediction that they will fall to fighting one another. There is also a tradition in which Ka'b adds that this prediction of twelve leaders, after which he lists caliphs, is stated in the Torah.[144] This tradition of twelve leaders went though many adaptations as different groups, including Shī'ite ones, deployed it for their own purposes.[145]

---

137 David Cook, *Studies in Muslim Apocalyptic*, SLAEI 21 (Princeton: Darwin Press, 2002), 2.

138 Nu'aym b. Ḥammād, *Kitāb al-Fitan* (Mecca: Maktabat al-Tijārīyah, n.d.); English translation by David Cook, *The Book of Tribulations: The Syrian Muslim Apocalyptic Tradition*, ESAE (Edinburgh: EUP, 2017).

139 Cook, *Studies*, 32.

140 Sandra Campbell, "It must be the end of time: Apocalyptic Aḥādīth as a record of the Islamic Community's Reactions to the Turbulent First Centuries," *ME* 4 (1998): 178–87.

141 Yücesoy's remark that, "biblical materials constitute a frequent source of many Muslim prophecies," seems overstated, at least in relation to Nu'aym, as do his regular references to, for example, an "interconfessional dimension". Rather, these references to previous scripture, and the echoes of Biblical themes, are enlisted in the cause of Muslim concerns. Hayrettin Yücesoy, *Messianic Beliefs and Imperial Politics in Medieval Islam: the 'Abbāsid Caliphate in the Ninth Century* (Columbia SC: University of South Carolina Press, 2009), 138.

142 Nu'aym b. Ḥammād, *Kitāb al-Fitan*, 31; trans. Cook, *Tribulations*, 20.

143 Nu'aym b. Ḥammād, *Kitāb al-Fitan*, 52; trans. Cook, *Tribulations*, 41. A longer version from Ka'b also appears at *Kitāb al-Fitan*, 64; trans. Cook, *Tribulations*, 50.

144 Nu'aym b. Ḥammād, *Kitāb al-Fitan*, 113; trans. Cook, *Tribulations*, 98.

Three times the Caliph ʿUmar is referred to as an "iron horn," which, as noted in the previous discussion of ʿUmar, is a title with originally messianic overtones drawn from the Biblical book of Micah. Furthermore, in the apocalyptic battles against the Byzantines, the Mahdi will retrieve the Ark of the Covenant (cf Exod 31:7 and many other references) and find the previous scriptures therein.[146]

As with all the material presented in this section on using the Bible, it is important not to overstate the importance of Biblical material. It is one of many strands woven into the voluminous hadith literature, but woven in a purposeful way, here recording a desire to explain events in the light of a past more distant than the 1st/7th century emergence of Islam.

3.4 Biblical elements in Hadith Literature

Some Hadith reports are strongly reminiscent of Biblical passages, and there are several possible interpretations of this phenomenon. The reports in question could be the result of borrowings from previous scriptures, either from written texts or via oral transmission. These could then be retrospectively associated with Muhammad. Secondly, Muhammad could have made the statements attributed to him, but after hearing them from Jews or Christians. Thirdly, from a Muslim viewpoint, they could be some form of divine inspiration, since in Muslim perspective the previous scriptures, at least in their original form, were inspired by God, and therefore contain truths which Muhammad could also plausibly have received and uttered. This would conform with the view that God's various revelations can be expected to be in agreement.

3.4.1 Old Testament

Most occurrences or echoes of the Old Testament in tradition literature involve predictions of Muhammad, or indirect attestation of Muhammad via discussion of previous prophets, as discussed above. However, a number of other instances deserve comment.

---

145 See Uri Rubin, "Apocalypse and Authority in Islamic Tradition: the Emergence of the Twelve Leaders," *Al-Qanṭara* 18 (1997): 11–42.

146 Nuʿaym b. Ḥammād, *Kitāb al-Fitan*, 220–21; trans. Cook, *Tribulations*, 203–04.

Sometimes statements occur in hadiths which merely suggest a Biblical background. Prayers can be formed from Biblical material, such as one prayer combining elements of Psalms 51 and 103. This prayer is associated with soldiers asking God for forgiveness, before going to fight the Byzantines, and reads, "O God, make the distance between me and my sins the same distance as between the east and the west...".[147]

Occasionally an important Biblical idea is found in a hadith, without the Biblical connection being made explicit. For example, the idea that God creates human beings in his image (cf. Gen 1:27) is echoed in some hadiths, image being rendered by *ṣūra*. This can occur in a short version, "God created Adam in his image." A longer version warns against hitting someone's face. "When any of you fights with his brother, he should avoid his face, as God created Adam in his own image".[148] This idea of humans bearing the divine image generated some controversy, reflecting Muslim unease over implying some resemblance between humankind and God. One argument was therefore that the phrase "his image" should refer to Adam's image, not God's, such that the tradition states merely that humanity is made in humanity's image. But Ibn Qutayba pointed out that this was scarcely meaningful.[149]

An example of a miracle resembling a Hebrew Bible passage is when Muhammad restores the flow of milk to the ewe of Umm Maʻbad. This recalls Elijah's miraculous supply of oil to the widow of Zarephath (1 Kings 17: 9–16).[150] However, where a miracle of Muhammad resembles a Biblical episode this is more typically linked to the New Testament, as will be seen shortly.

The call of Muhammad as narrated by Ibn Isḥāq provides another Biblical echo. It resembles the call of Isaiah (40:6), and the Arabic and Hebrew texts are closely related. Muhammad is told to recite or read (*iqra'*), and replies

147 See Ibn Bishrān (d.1039), *Amalī*, 249 (no. 573), as quoted in David Cook, "New Testament Citations," 192.

148 Muslim, *Saḥīḥ*, vol. 6, *Kitāb al-Birr* (*The Book of Righteousness*), no. 6655.

149 See Christopher Melchert, "'God Created Adam in His Image'," *JQS* 13 (2011): 113–24. Ibn Qutayba, *Ta'wīl Mukhtalif al-Ḥadīth*, (*The Book of Interpreting Disputed Traditions*) (Cairo: Maktabat al-Kulliyāt al-Azhariya, 1966), 217–9. See also W. Montgomery Watt, "Created in his Image," *TGUOS* 18 (1961): 38–49, and more readily available, Watt, *Islam and the Integration of Society* (London: Routledge and Kegan Paul, 1961), 223–26. For a Qur'an-centred reflection on this theme see Stefan Schreiner, *Die Jüdische Bibel in Islamischer Auslegung, TSMEMJ 27* (Tübingen: Mohr Siebeck, 2012), 19–31.

150 Al-Ṭabarī, *Ta'rīkh*, 2407–08, trans. Ella Landau-Tasseron as *The History of al-Ṭabarī vol. XXXIII: Biographies of the Prophet's Companions and their Successors*, (Albany, N.Y.: SUNY Press, 1998), 138. Nabia Abbott, "Wahb b. Munabbih: a Review Article," *JNES* 36 (1977), 110, draws attention to this similarity.

"what shall I read?" (*mā aqra'*)." Likewise a voice cries out to Isaiah to "proclaim" (*qerā*). He replies, "what shall I proclaim?" (*māh 'eqrā*).[151]

The complex question of when parallels indicate influence also emerges in biographical traditions about Muhammad which resemble the Biblical and post-biblical narratives of David. Canonical Biblical material which parallels Muslim material about David include both men participating as youths in a major incident with an important enemy, both leaving town in a hurry at night to avoid danger, both fleeing to a cave, both demonstrating mildness and perspicacity, and parallels also in their relations with women.[152] Connections between Muhammad's marriage to Zaynab and David's to Bathsheba, along with a range of other Biblical echoes, have also been the subject of recent study.[153]

3.4.2 New Testament

The Gospel of Matthew is the New Testament book most recognisable in hadiths, for reasons shortly to be discussed.[154] Yet Muslim traditions about Jesus often parallel apocryphal gospels or collections of wisdom sayings more than they resemble canonical gospel material.[155] For that reason, presentations of Jesus can depart markedly from the New Testament, such as Ibn 'Asākir's presentation of Jesus as an austere ascetic.[156] In fact, hadith literature resembling the Gospels

---

151 See Anthony, "Paraclete,", 273; cf Ibn Isḥāq, in Ibn Hishām, *Das Leben*, 152–53; trans. Guillaume, Life, 106. The translation of Ibn Isḥāq given above follows that of Guillaume rather than Anthony.

152 Ze'ev Maghen, "Davidic Motifs in the Biography of Muḥammad," *JSAI* 35 (2008): 91–139, quoted from 92. See also Maghen, "Intertwined Triangles: Remarks on the relationship between two prophetic scandals," *JSAI* 33 (2007): 17–92.

153 David Powers, *Zayd: the Little Known Story of Muḥammad's Adopted Son* (Philadelphia: University of Pennsylvania Press, 2014). See also his *Muhammad is not the Father of any of your Men* (Philadelphia: University of Pennsylvania Press, 2009). See the cautious review of Powers, *Zayd*, by Sean Anthony, *RQR* 1 (2015): 1–5 (online pagination).

154 Ignaz Goldziher, "The Ḥadīth and the New Testament," in *Muslim Studies*, vol 2, trans. C.R. Barber and S.M. Stern (London: George Allen and Unwin, 1971): 346–62, from which the division of biography, teachings and phrases used here is taken; Cook, "Citations"; and the collection of Jesus' sayings edited and translated by Tarif Khalidi, *The Muslim Jesus: Sayings and Stories in Islamic Literature* (Cambridge, Mass.: Harvard University Press, 2001); cf. Cook, "Citations", 206–218, for a list of 59 hadiths which draw on New Testament texts, all but five of which are from the Gospels.

155 Cook, "Citations," 186–87.

156 Suleiman Mourad, "Jesus According to Ibn 'Asākir," in *Ibn 'Asākir and Early Islamic History*, ed. James Lindsay, SLAEI 20 (Princeton: The Darwin Press, 2001), 39–41.

rearranges Gospel material in unfamiliar ways. Elements of the Gospels appear like pieces of a mosaic which have been separated from their original setting and re-assembled to create a different picture.

3.4.2.1 Biography

Biographical traditions about Muhammad which echo the New Testament include descriptions of miracles of multiplication of food and water, and also of healing. Muhammad miraculously provides water or food, echoing Jesus' multiplication of bread and fish to feed 5,000 men along with their families.[157] Such traditions portray Muhammad in a way more akin to the Jesus of the Gospels. By contrast hadiths about Jesus tend to focus on his asceticism, or his role in the end times, and his role in comparison with Muhammad, generally omitting reference to his healing miracles, his crucifixion and resurrection, these last two having no part in Muslim beliefs about Jesus. So when comparing Muhammad in the hadith with Jesus in the hadith it is Muhammad who more closely resembles the Jesus of the Gospels.[158]

3.4.2.2 Teaching

One category of hadith, numbering a few hundred reports, is known as *ḥadīth qudsī* (pl. *aḥādīth qudsiyya*) or divine saying. The term denotes "a direct-discourse statement ascribed to God."[159] A small proportion of these resemble Biblical phrases, one commonly occurring example being "I have prepared for My righteous worshippers what no eye has seen, no ear has heard, and no human heart has conceived." This strongly resembles the Pauline Epistle 1 Corinthians 2:9.[160]

---

157 Al-Bukhārī, *Ṣaḥīḥ*, vol. 4, *Kitāb al-Manāqib* (*The Book of Virtues of the Prophet*), nos. 3579, 3581.

158 One event associated with the lead-up to the crucifixion does however occur. Al-Ṭabarī and others preserve Jesus' prediction in the gospels of his being betrayed before the cock-crow is completed. Al-Ṭabarī, *Annales*, I: 736; cf. Roberto Tottoli, "At Cock-crow: Some Muslim Traditions about the Rooster," *Der Islam* 76 (1999), 147.

159 William Graham, "Ḥadīth qudsī", in: *EI3*, consulted online on 08 May 2020 http://dx.doi.org/10.1163/1573-3912_ei3_COM_30166.

160 This hadith occurs in four of the six canonical sunni hadith collections. It is quoted here from al-Tirmidhī, *Jāmiʿ*, vol. 5, *Abwāb Tafsīr al-Qur'ān* (*Chapters on Exegesis of the Qur'an*), no. 3198. See also Davide Tacchini, "Paul the Forgerer: Classical and modern radical views of the Apostle of Tarsus," *Islamochristiana* 34 (2008): 129–47. The hadith also occurs in works dedicated to *ḥadīth qudsī*. See for example Ibn al-ʿArabī, *Mishkāt al-Anwār*, quoted from Ibn al-

Another tradition, though not a *ḥadīth qudsī, occurs* in the collection of al-Bukhārī and recalls 1 Corinthians 12:25. Believers are described as merciful and loving, "resembling one body, so that, if any part of the body is not well then the whole body shares the sleeplessness and fever with it."[161]

A further example is the hadith recorded by Muslim stating that God says "I fell sick and you did not visit me". When asked when this happened, he says "Did you not know that my slave so-and-so was sick and you did not visit him?" The hadith continues similarly regarding those who are hungry or thirsty, the whole hadith strongly recalling Matthew 25:36, except for its exclusion of Jesus.[162]

Echoes of the Gospels can affirm the truth of Islam. So, when a woman cries out, 'Blessed is the womb which carried you and the breast which suckled you' (cf Luke 11:27), Jesus replies, 'No, but blessed is he who reads the Qur'an and follows its [teachings]'.[163]

Alongside apparent use and adaptation of the New Testament, there is also occasional opposition to Christian teaching. For example, al-Damīrī records a report that Aḥmad b. Ḥanbal rejects the idea that if a person's eye causes them to sin they should pluck it out (Matt 5:29). This was "perhaps permitted by the law of the Israelites and of those who were before us (Christians). Rather do we ask God for pardon, and afterwards take care to avoid the sin."[164]

The Sermon on the Mount (Matt 5–7) is a popular New Testament source in hadith literature.[165] A version of the prayer known as the Lord's Prayer, part of the Sermon, (Matt 6:9–13) can be found in the hadith collection of Abū Da'ūd, within "The Book of Medicine". Here the prayer, in altered but recognisable form, is offered as a healing incantation. A similar prayer also occurs in al-Tanūkhī's *The Book of Comfort After Misfortune* (*Kitab al-Faraj ba'da al-shid-*

'Arabī, *Divine Sayings: 101 Ḥadīth Qudsī*, trans. Stephen Hirtenstein and Martin Notcutt (Oxford: Anqa Publishing, 2004), 21; cf the discussion of this and other examples in James Robson, "The Material of Tradition II," *MW* 41 (1951): 261–67 (264). For a discussion of the possible influence on this hadith of early Arabic Bible translations and the *Arabic Apocryphal Gospel of John*, see Claire Clivaz and Sara Schulthess, "On the Source and Rewriting of 1 Corinthians 2:9 in Christian, Jewish and Islamic Traditions (*1Clem* 34.8, *GosJud* 47.10–13; a *ḥadīth qudsī*)," *NTS* 61 (2015): 183–200 (194–98).

161 Al-Bukhārī, *Ṣaḥīḥ*, vol. 8, *Kitāb al-Ādāb* (*The Book of Etiquette*), no. 6011.

162 Muslim, *Ṣaḥīḥ*, vol. 6, *Kitāb al-Birr* (*The Book of Righteousness*), no. 6556.

163 Mourad, "12th century," 41.

164 Al-Damīrī, quoted by Goldziher, *Muslim Studies*, 2: 359–60.

165 See for example Cook, "Citations," 192–93.

da.)[166] Another part of the Sermon, (Matt 6:3), seems to lie behind a commendation of practising generosity in secret, so that, "the left hand does not know what the right hand has given".[167]

Why does Matthew's gospel predominate in tradition literature? In addition to the fact that the Sermon on the Mount's apparently legal or ethical content is more readily recognisable to Muslims as being scripture, this preference for Matthew has also been attributed to his emphasis on the coming of the Kingdom of Heaven to earth.[168] But to my knowledge no Muslim literature addresses the apparent preference for Matthew.

Patterns of occurrence of Gospel material are not simple or predictable. For example, in the *History of Damascus* by Ibn 'Asākir (d. 571/1176), which includes a great deal of hadith material, the section on the disciples preserves a great deal of the Sermon on the Mount. This has prompted the suggestion that this material comes from a document based on an early translation of Matthew's Gospel into Arabic, provisionally dated to the early/mid 2nd/8th century.[169] But Ibn 'Asākir's treatment of Jesus has far less connection to the Biblical text, serving other agendas related to the author's own place and time.[170] Another striking report of the words of Jesus himself, which includes parts of the Sermon on the Mount mingled with other sayings loosely resembling it, is found in *The Masterpieces of Minds* (*Tuḥaf al-'uqūl*) by the Shi'ite traditionist Ibn Shu'ba al-Ḥarrānī (d. c. 4th/10th century).[171]

Looking beyond the Sermon on the Mount, but keeping Matthew's Gospel in view, the words of Jesus, or something similar to them, can be attributed to Muhammad, but refracted to reflect Muslim concerns. A striking example is the parable of the workers in the vineyard, a hadith with clear connections to Matt 20:1–16. Matthew portrays Jesus emphasising that the workers who arrive towards the end of the day (the Gentiles) will receive the same reward as

166 Abū Dāwūd, Sunan, vol.4, *Kitāb al-Ṭibb* (*The Book of Medicine*), no. 3892. Al-Tanūkhī, *Kitāb al-faraj ba'da al-shidda* (*The Book of Comfort after Misfortune*), vol. 5 (Beirut: Dār Ṣādir, 1978), 130, and cited by Cook, "Citations", 196.

167 Al-Bukhārī, *Ṣaḥīḥ*, vol. 2, *Kitāb al-Zakāt* (*The Book of Obligatory Alms*), no. 1423.

168 Cook, "Citations," 204.

169 See Cook, "Citations," 200–06 for discussion, and 218–223 for a translation of Ibn 'Asākir's section.

170 Suleiman Mourad, "Jesus According to Ibn 'Asākir," in *Ibn 'Asākir and Early Islamic History* ed. James Lindsay (Princeton: Darwin Press, 2001), 24–43; Mourad, "A Twelfth Century Muslim Biography of Jesus," *ICMR* 7 (1996): 39–45.

171 Ibn Shu'ba al-Ḥarrāni, *Tuḥaf al-'Uqūl* (Tehran: Maktabat al-Ṣadūq, 1376/ 1956–57), 501; trans. Badr Shahin as *Tuhaf al-Uqoul* [sic]: *The Masterpieces of the Mind* (Qom: Ansariyan, 2000), 452.

those who arrived earlier (the Jews). Al-Bukhārī records Muhammad depicting the Muslims as the last workers of the day. For their shorter spell of work they receive not merely the same pay, but in fact more than the earlier workers, said to be the Jews and Christians.[172] It is possible that the form of this hadith is also influenced by Rabbinic literature, where a version occurs stressing the favour shown to a community, in this case the Jews.[173] The exact lines of influence are probably irretrievable, as the hadith, in various versions, blends elements of the Gospel and rabbinic versions.

3.5 Conclusion

In weighing up continuity with previous revelation alongside opposition to it, hadith and biographical literature tip the scales in favour of continuity. This is either in the form of Biblical echoes in the content of Hadith, or through appeal to the *Tawrāt* in a more generalised form as a point of reference. The implications of this apparent openness to appealing to the authority of the Bible, its motifs, or even its text are hard to gauge. It might strengthen arguments for indistinct boundaries in the identity of early "believers."[174] It is probably equally related to so many early Muslims being converts from Jewish and Christian communities, and that their knowledge of their scriptures inevitably coloured the nature of early Muslim discourses without necessarily indicating a single or unified purpose in so doing. I am not convinced that we have to depict early Muslims as either part of a wider movement of "believers," as Donner argues, or that all of them were clearly thought-through converts with a sense of their distinct Muslim identity. Individuals would have varied in their self-understanding, with some clearly having permeable boundaries to their faith identity. The apparent openness to Biblical material can be attributed to one of two factors. First, some Muslims might have held the view that the previous scriptures extant in 1st/7th and 2nd/8th centuries really did preserve a measure of genuine revelation from God. Alternatively, use of the Bible might arise primarily from the desire to give added profundity or pedigree to the relatively newly established Muslim faith.

172 Al-Bukhārī, *Ṣaḥīḥ*, vol. 9, *Kitāb al-Tawḥīd* (*The Book of Divine Unity*), no. 7467. Ze'ev Maghen, *After Hardship Cometh Ease*, 79–80, links this to the wider theme of God's favour and leniency to the Muslim community in comparison with the Jews (see the discussion of abrogation in Chapter 2 for more on this theme).
173 See Marston Speight, "A Versatile *mathal:* 'the man who hired laborers," *ICMR* 14 (2004): 91–98.
174 As Donner, *Muhammad and the Believers.*

As for comparing Sunni and Shia responses, both are similar in drawing on Biblical elements primarily to support their own positions. In the case of Sunnis this is not necessarily support for their own distinctives, over against those of the Shia. This is to be expected as the bigger, more powerful group in any such division has less need to assert its validity in relation to a weaker, smaller grouping. Shia sources, by contrast, use the Bible to reinforce the truth of Shi'ism specifically.

There were various possible reasons behind using the Bible. Such usage could plausibly function as proofs for non-Muslims of the divine mandate of Islam, or as reinforcing the validity of that mandate for new and other Muslims, to strengthen their adherence to the faith. The general tenor of many of the references to the previous scriptures indicates the perception – or the desire to project the perception – of a shared history with Jewish and Christian tradition, broadly defined. As for the echoes of Biblical content, this is most likely attributed to the circulation of many different elements of tradition, sometimes transposed from one figure to another, notably from Jesus to Muhammad. The idea of similarity is emphasised, namely that the Muslim faith, its Prophet, and its significance all stand in a sequence of divinely ordained events. Continuity with what has preceded, rather than a break from it, is the dominant note.

The almost total lack of traditions about textual corruption of the Bible is striking. Hadith and biographical literature provide only a wafer-thin basis for ideas about this form of *taḥrīf*. This might indicate the relative lack of focus on the issue in the 2nd/8th century, and perhaps the 1st/7th, depending on differing views of the dating of hadiths. Setting the issue of Biblical corruption in broader historical perspective will be part of the task of the next chapter.

4 Engaging on Many Fronts: Other Writings from the Early Centuries

4.1 Introduction

Looking beyond the Qur'an, hadith and biographical literature, a wide variety of other genres comes into view. Some of the works encountered here make use of the Bible in support of Islam, while others explore the issue of Biblical corruption (*taḥrīf*). This chapter will begin with literature emphasising use of the Bible more than corruption of it. As the chapter progresses there will be a gradual shift to voices criticising the Bible, though they may still use it. The interweaving of use and criticism, sometimes within the same texts, means that this gradual shift is preferable to trying to separate starkly the two approaches. Indeed, at times an instance of using the Bible can also incorporate criticism of the text. Beginning with use of the Bible is fitting since at this stage in the development of Islam Biblical texts were extensively used and less harshly criticised than in subsequent centuries.[1] I conclude the present chapter with views from outside the fold of Islam, drawing evidence of Muslim views from non-Muslim sources.

The twin foci of use and criticism of the Bible can be illustrated by people famous for other works. Abu 'Ubayd al-Qāsim b. Sallām (d.224/838), already encountered in the discussion of abrogation in Chapter 1, wrote *The Book of Sermons and Exhortations* (*Kitāb al-Khuṭab wa'l-mawā'iẓ*), containing many traces of Biblical knowledge. He attributes the following saying to Jesus: "Pious action (*iḥsān*) is not doing good to whoever does good to you; that is repayment for good deeds. But pious action is doing good to the one who does evil to you'.[2] In addition, the words of Jesus are sometimes attributed to someone else. The famous early ascetic Ḥasan al-Baṣrī (d. 110/728) is reported as saying, "Son of Adam, you see the minute particle in the eye of your friend, but ignore the shaft in your eyes".[3]

As for criticism, one of the most renowned of Arabic literary figures, al-Jāḥiẓ (d. 255/869) wrote a *Refutation of the Christians* (*Al-Radd 'alā al-naṣārā*). In this

1 The major change occurring in the 4th–5th/11th century is explored in Chapter 5.

2 Abu 'Ubayd al-Qāsim b. Sallām, *Kitāb al-Khuṭāb wa'l-mawā'iẓ* (Cairo: Maktabat al-Thaqāfa wa'l-Dīnīya, 1986), 156; cf. Matt 5:43–48.

3 One of a number of Jesus sayings from various sources later attributed to al-Ḥasan al-Baṣrī; see Ibn al-Mubārak, *Kitāb al-Zuhd* (Beirut: Mu'assassat al-risāla, 1971), 69–70, no. 211; this and other transferred sayings are noted by Suleiman Mourad, *Early Islam Between Myth and History*, IPTS 62 (Leiden: Brill, 2006), 80, from which the translation is taken. Cf. Matt 7:3.

https://doi.org/10.1515/9783110335880-007

he criticises the gospels as unreliable, but does not emphasise the point, being more concerned about the place of Christians in society.[4] The corruption of the Bible is assumed yet, perhaps surprisingly, only briefly mentioned, while the doctrines of the Trinity and the divinity of Jesus gain more attention.[5]

4.2 Proofs of Prophethood

Literature on the proofs or signs of prophecy became a particular focus with the rise of the 'Abbāsid dynasty around 132/750, and its need both to rebut Jewish and Christian challenges to Muhammad and to boost its legitimacy with the Islamic community. Judaism and Christianity had not themselves devoted particular energy to prophethood as a category prior to the rise of Islam.[6] But in their newly built power base of Baghdad the 'Abbāsids found large numbers of Jews and Christians keen to dispute the truth claims of Islam. Proofs of prophecy literature originated amongst hadith scholars, as Koertner has recently demonstrated, and while proof motifs could occur as part of broader works of theological disputation (*kalām*), texts dedicated solely to the theme of proofs of Muhammad also arose. Within this "proofs" literature Biblical proofs of the prophethood of Muhammad were a regular feature.[7]

The earliest extant collection of Biblical proofs for the prophethood of Muhammad occurs in a letter sent on behalf of the Caliph Hārūn al-Rashīd (r. 170–193/786–809) to the Byzantine Emperor Constantine VI (r. 780–797). It was written by Ibn al-Layth (d.c. 203–204/819), and its date (c. 179–180/795–796) sheds light on a very early stage of the Muslim use of Biblical proofs. This date can be established since the addressee, Constantine VI, was deposed

4 Al-Jāḥiẓ, *Al-Radd 'alā al-naṣārā*, Arabic text in Joshua Finkel, ed., *Three Essays of Abū 'Othmān 'Amr ibn Baḥr al-Jāḥiẓ (d. 869)* (Cairo: Salafyah Press, 1926), 24; English translation in Charles Fletcher, *Anti-Christian Polemic in Early Islam: A Translation and Analysis of Abū 'Uthmān 'Amr B. Baḥr al-Jāḥiẓ's Risāla: Radd 'alā al-Naṣārā (A Reply to the Christians)* (Unpublished M.A. thesis, McGill University, Montreal, 2002), 79. Fletcher translates the whole text, incorporating the partial translation previously produced in Joshua Finkel, "A *Risāla* of al-Jāḥiẓ," *JAOS* 47 (1927): 311–34.

5 David Thomas, "The Bible in Early Muslim Anti-Christian Polemic," 29 and passim.

6 Sarah Stroumsa, "The Signs of Prophecy: The Emergence and Early Development of a Theme in Arabic Theological Literature," *HTR* 78 (1985): 101–14.

7 See Koertner, "*Dalā'il al-nubuwwa* Literature," 91–109; Adang, *Muslim Writers*, 139–191; Lazarus-Yafeh, *Intertwined Worlds*, 75–110.

after this time.[8] The occasion of the letter is to persuade the Byzantines to resume paying tribute, which had ceased in 168/785, threatening them with the resumption of hostilities if payment is not forthcoming.[9] The letter also summons Constantine to Islam, including by using Q3:64, the verse referring to coming to a word "common between us and you" and which has been the centre of the modern Muslim initiative "A Common Word."[10]

Ibn al-Layth may be using a collection of Biblical verses gathered for purposes of argument, rather than a complete Bible. His use of the Old Testament is more extensive than use of the New, which is much more fragmentary, drawing mainly on John's Gospel. Some arguments occur which become standard features of Biblical proofs of Muhammad, such as the view that the Biblical Paraclete is a prediction of Muhammad, though in this passage the Biblical references to God as father and testimony to Jesus are omitted, presumably deliberately.[11] There is a brief reference to two riders in Isa 21:6–7 as representing Jesus and Muhammad, since Muhammad is the only prophet since Moses to ride a camel. This passage is discussed below in relation to its longer treatment by Ibn Qutayba.[12] Ibn al-Layth includes another motif also found in Ibn Qutayba, the sword and the chaining up of God's enemies, found in Psalm 149. For Ibn al-Layth, it must be Muhammad who fulfills such a passage since only he used force to destroy unbelief and idolatry. Predictions of Muhammad based on Isaiah 42 include the messianic description, discussed in the previous chapter on hadith, saying that he does not raise his voice in the streets.[13] Two passages from Deuteronomy (both famous in later Biblical proofs of Muhammad) also occur. Deuteronomy 33:2 states that God will come from Sinai, arise from Seir, and become manifest from Mount Paran. These three places are connected by Ibn al-Layth with the giving of the *Tawrāt* to Moses, the *Injīl* to Jesus, and the

---

8 See Barbara Roggema, "Ibn al-Layth," in: *CMR*, 1:347–53. The text of the letter is published in several editions, and cited here from A.Z. Ṣafwat (ed.) *Jamharat rasā'il al-'Arab fī 'uṣūr al-'arabiyya al-zāhira*, vol.3. (Cairo: Mustafā al-Bābī al-Ḥalabī, 1937), 252–324; French translation, along with Arabic text, in Hadi Eid, *Lettre du Calife Hārūn al-Rašīd à l'Empereur Constantin VI* (Paris: Cariscript, 1992). See also D.M. Dunlop, "A Letter of Hārūn ar-Rashīd to the Emperor Constantine VI", in *In Memoriam Paul Kahle*, eds. Matthew Black and Georg Fohrer (Berlin: A. Töpelmann, 1968): 106–15; Ryan Schaffner, *The Bible Through a Qur'ānic Filter: Scripture Falsification* (Taḥrīf) *in 8th- and 9th- century Muslim Disputational Literature*, (Unpublished Ph.D. thesis, Ohio State University, 2016): 298–304.

9 Dunlop, "A Letter", discusses the historical background.

10 Ibn al-Layth, *Risāla*, 253. For the modern initiative see www.acommonword.com

11 Ibn al-Layth, *Risāla*, 309; cf. Schaffner, *The Bible*, 303–04.

12 Ibn al-Layth, *Risāla*, 309.

13 For the passages relating to both Psalm 149 and Isa 42, see Ibn al-Layth, *Risāla*, 311.

Qur'an to Muhammad. The statement that God will raise up another like Moses from among his brothers (Deut 18:18) is likewise cited.[14] All of the passages mentioned above become standard in later expositions of the Biblical proofs of Muhammad's prophethood.

In addition to proofs of Muhammad's prophethood, Ibn al-Layth also quotes the Bible to oppose the divinity of Jesus. He quotes John 14:28, in which he alters Jesus going to the "Father" to his going to "God." He also quotes John 20:17, the most frequently used verse by Muslims denying Jesus' divinity, and the opening line of the Lord's Prayer (Matt 6:9).[15] More unusual is Ibn al-Layth's quoting the New Testament to urge Constantine VI to peace (Matt 5:39–41) and to have mercy on his people, by avoiding war through accepting the Caliph's demand (Matt 5:7–9, approx).[16]

It is difficult to gauge Ibn al-Layth's attitude to Biblical corruption. He describes the scriptures in general as preserved (*maḥfūẓa*). But this could be a tactical appeal to a textual authority recognised by the Byzantine ruler, rather than an actual affirmation of the Biblical text (which, as noted above, Ibn al-Layth adjusts to fit Islamic thinking regarding the Paraclete). He makes no explicit criticism of the text of the Bible, but the significance of this remains unclear.

Following this diplomatic epistle, in which a brief defense of Muhammad's prophethood is embedded in a much longer work, the first extant work specifically devoted to proofs of prophethood is *The Book of Religion and Empire* (*Kitāb al-Dīn wa'l-dawla*) by Ibn Rabbān 'Alī al-Ṭabarī (d.c.860).[17] Another early work is *The Proofs of Prophethood* (*Dalā'il al-nubuwwa*) by Ibn Qutayba (d. 276/889). Some of Ibn Rabbān's quotations are very close to those of Ibn al-Layth though it is unclear whether there is any direct influence.[18]

Ibn Rabbān 'Alī al-Ṭabarī was a doctor at the caliph's court in Samarra in present-day Iraq, during the period when the 'Abbāsid capital was moved away from Baghdad (221–279/836–892). He converted from Christianity to Islam late in life.[19] Around half of the *Book of Religion and Empire*, chapters 9

14 Ibn al-Layth, *Risāla*, 312–13.

15 Ibn al-Layth, *Risāla*, 306, 313. On John 20:17 see Martin Accad, "The Ultimate Proof-Text: the Interpretation of John 20.17 in Muslim–Christian Dialogue (Second/Eighth–Eighth/Fourteenth Centuries)," in *Christians at the Heart of Islamic Rule: Church Life and Scholarship in 'Abbāsid Iraq*, ed. David Thomas (Leiden: Brill, 2003): 199–214.

16 Ibn al-Layth, *Risāla*, 318, 322.

17 For the Arabic text and parallel English translation of *The Book of Religion and Empire* see Rifaat Ebied and David Thomas, eds., *The Polemical Works of 'Alī al-Ṭabarī*, HCMR 27 (Leiden: Brill, 2016).

18 Adang, *Muslim Writers*, 148.

19 See David Thomas, "'Alī al-Ṭabarī," in *CMR*, 1:669–74.

and 10, uses Biblical material, most likely an Arabic translation popular amongst Arabic-speaking Christians, translated from an East Syriac version.[20] Chapter 9 argues a specific point, that the promises given to Abraham in Genesis about Ishmael are fulfilled in Muhammad, and that it was therefore essential for Muhammad to come in order for these Biblical passages to be fulfilled.[21] Chapter 10 presents at length Biblical predictions of Muhammad and the rise of Islam from Psalms, Isaiah, Hosea, Micah, Habakkuk, Zephaniah, Zechariah, Jeremiah, Ezekiel and Daniel.[22] In addition to texts such as Deuteronomy 18 and 33, already noted in relation to Ibn al-Layth, Ibn Rabbān draws on texts relating to God bestowing power and victory on his servant,[23] and a host of verses from Isaiah which refer to praise, and which Ibn Rabbān takes to be references related to the name Muhammad (which can mean "the praised one"). The desert, Mecca ("the ends of the earth", Isa 24:16–18), and the use of force are also seen as predictions of Islam. For Ibn Rabbān, the temple of Ezekiel (40–47) refers to Mecca, while the 'Abbāsid dynasty which Ibn Rabbān served is the fourth beast of Daniel (cf. Dan 7). On turning to the New Testament he first discusses the Paraclete as a prediction of Muhammad. He also finds further reference to Mecca ("the house of God", cf 1 Pet 4:17), justification for using the sword (Luke 22:35–36), and discusses Jesus bringing changes to Old Testament laws (hence justifying changes brought in turn by Muhammad).[24]

On two related points Ibn Rabbān is ambiguous. In mentioning the issue of corruption he indicates that this is brought about by translators and scribes. His reluctance to attack the Biblical text directly is understandable in a work basing its own plausibility on using the Bible. Secondly, on the crucifixion, he stresses

---

20 Vollandt, *Versions*, 67, 91–96.

21 Ebied And Thomas, eds., *Polemical works*, 326–39. Ibn Rabbān argues that Genesis' description of Ishmael as a wild ass (Gen 16:12) is a positive description, referring to his daring and also strength to "protect his lineage and safeguard his liberty" (337). Some Biblical exegetes had made a similar argument; see Maalouf's discussion of the Biblical Ishmael in his *Arabs in the Shadow*, 69–71.

22 See Ebied and Thomas, eds., *Polemical Works*, 340–473.

23 Ebied and Thomas, eds., *Polemical Works*, 347, drawing on Psalm 72.

24 His wide range of interpretations have been labelled as "eccentric" and "unprecedented" by his modern co-translator. See David Thomas, " 'Alī Ibn Rabbān al-Ṭabarī: A Convert's Assessment of his Former Faith," in *Christians and Muslims in Dialogue in the Islamic Orient of the Middle Ages*, ed. Martin Tamcke (Beirut: Orient Institut, 2007), 155. Ibn Rabbān's Biblical predictions of Mecca focus mainly, though not exclusively, on Isaiah and the theme of nations bowing down in recognition. A full list comprises Ps 72 (347), Isa 24:16–18 (361), Isa 54:11–14 (375), Isa 60:1–7 (379–80), Isa 49:16–21 (385), Isa 49:22–23 (387), Isa 62:10–12 (391), Mic 4:1–2 (395), Ezek 40–47 (409), 1 Pet 4:17 (429), Gal 4:22–26 (433).

Jesus' foreknowledge of events, but does not say what those events were. This is an attempt to solve the dilemma of either affirming the crucifixion, against Muslim dogma, or of denying it, and thereby undermining the reliability of one of his main supports, the gospels.[25]

The influence of the *Book of Religion and Empire* seems to have been limited at the time (though it was used by Ibn Qutayba; see below). A few verses were used in other works, but it is possible that its use of the Bible was seen as weak. However, the Muʿtazilite Abū al-Ḥusayn al-Baṣri (d.436/1045) used the work in *The Finest of Proofs* (*Kitāb Ghurar al-adilla*). Al-Baṣrī's text, now lost, directly influences work by other writers, including the famous Sunni thinker Fakhr al-Dīn al-Rāzī (d.606/1209).[26] Ironically, however, Ibn Rabbān's work is the most popular early source used in modern defenses of the prophethood of Muhammad, whereas our next author, Ibn Qutayba, after proving influential on this topic in the centuries following his death, is now largely ignored.[27]

Ibn Qutayba (d. 276/889) was a Baghdad *qāḍī* (judge) from the Ḥanbalite school of thought, though he also spent around twenty years in legal service in Dīnawar in northern Iran.[28] His work may have some links to that of Ibn Rabbān, since both seem to have been drawing on pre-existing material using the Bible. This is indicated by the similarities in some of their material, but differences elsewhere, as if they were both using other sources no longer extant.[29] In addition texts among the Zaydi Shia of Iran also indicate that other sources were also available.[30]

Ibn Qutayba employs the Bible in several works, often paraphrasing rather than quoting exactly. The focus here is on his *Proofs of Prophethood* (*Dalāʾil al-nubuwwa,* also known as *Aʿlām al-nubuwwa*) which until recently was thought to

---

25 See Ebied and Thomas, eds., *Polemical Works*, 441–43.

26 Sabine Schmidtke, "Abū al-Ḥusayn al-Baṣrī and his Transmission of Biblical Materials from *Kitāb al-Dīn wa-al-Dawla* by Ibn Rabban Al-Ṭabarī: The Evidence from Fakhr al-Dīn al-Rāzī's *Mafātīḥ al-ghayb,*" *ICMR* 20 (2009): 105–118. Fakhr al-Dīn al-Rāzī will feature in Volume 2 of the present study.

27 Keating, "The Paraclete and the Integrity of Scripture," in *Theological Issues*, 19.

28 For an account of Ibn Qutayba's life and works see Joseph Lowry, "Ibn Qutaybah (828–889)," in *Arabic Literary Culture, 500–925*, eds. Shawkat Toorawa and Michael Cooperson, DLB 311 (Detroit: Thomson Gale, 2005): 172–83.

29 Ebied and Thomas, *Polemical Works*, 189–90.

30 See Sabine Schmidtke, "Biblical Predictions of the Prophet Muhammad among the Zaydis of Iran," *Arabica* 59 (2012): 218–66. On Zaydism see Wilferd Madelung, "Zaydiyya", in: *EI2*, consulted online on 03 July 2019, http://dx.doi.org/10.1163/1573-3912_islam_COM_1385.

be preserved only through partial quotations by Ibn al-Jawzī and others.[31] Ibn Qutayba in *Proofs* draws on Genesis, Deuteronomy, Habakkuk, and extensively from Isaiah and the Psalms. His accurate quotations come only from Genesis, probably indicating that this text was the only one fully available to him. Other passages, (or perhaps also his Genesis quotations), were most likely taken from an anthology of Biblical texts.[32] Either way, the Syriac Peshitta translation underlies whatever Arabic version Ibn Qutayba used.[33] Ibn Qutayba's quotations and paraphrases seek Biblical references to Muhammad and also to the city of Mecca. He quotes a number of passages in *Proofs* which become standard reference points for Muslim proofs of Muhammad in the following centuries such as Deut 18:15 and 18. Both these verses refer to God raising up a prophet like Moses from among the Israelites' brothers.[34]

Another notable example is Isaiah 21:6–7, a text referring to "riders on donkeys, riders on camels." Ibn Qutayba, like Ibn al-Layth and Ibn Rabbān, interprets this as a prediction of the coming of Jesus, on a donkey, and Muhammad,

---

31 Lowry, "Ibn Qutaybah," makes no mention of *Dalā'il*. For Ibn Qutayba's text see Ibn al-Jawzī, *Al-Wafā' bi aḥwāl al-muṣṭafā* (*The Complete Account of the Characteristics of the Chosen One*) (Cairo: Dār al-Kutub al-ḥadītha, 1966), 61–73; and now also the reproduction of a manuscript version from Damascus in Sabine Schmidtke, "The Muslim Reception of Biblical Materials: Ibn Qutayba and his A*'lām al-nubuwwa*," *ICMR* 22 (2011): 249–74. English translation of Ibn Qutayba's Old Testament material, from a different edition of al-Jawzī, can be found in Adang, *Muslim Writers*, 267–77. Vollandt, *Versions*, 95–102, discusses Ibn Qutayba's partial reliance on Ibn Rabbān for Biblical material. For broader discussion of Ibn Qutayba's use of the Bible in a range of his works see Gérard Lecomte, "Les citations de l'Ancien et du Nouveau Testament dans l'œuvre d'Ibn Qutayba," *Arabica* 5 (1958): 34–46. Other works by Ibn Qutayba are discussed later in the present chapter.

32 Adang, *Muslim Writers*, 112.

33 For extensive evidence of Ibn Qutayba favouring readings from the Peshitta, see Albert Isteero, *'Abdullāh Muslim Ibn Qutayba's Biblical Quotations and Their Source: an Inquiry into the Earliest Existing Arabic Bible Translations* (unpublished Ph.D. thesis, Johns Hopkins University, 1991).

34 Ibn Qutayba, *Dalā'il*, in Ibn al-Jawzī, *Al-Wafā'*, 63; trans. Adang, *Muslim Writers*, 269; cf 'Ali al-Ṭabarī, in Ebied and Thomas, *Polemical Works*, 341. For a discussion of pre-Islamic interpretation of the passages in Deuteronomy 18:15, 18, see Julie Robb, *The Prophet Like Moses: its Jewish Context and Use in the Early Christian Tradition* (unpublished Ph.D. thesis, King's College, London, 2003). For a Karaite Jewish rejoinder to Muslim use of the passage see Daniel Frank, *Search Scripture Well: Karaite Exegetes and the Origins of the Jewish Bible Commentary in the Islamic East*, EJM 29 (Leiden: Brill, 2004): 234–47. The term "brothers" is sometimes translated by other phrases in English, such as "your own people" (NRSV). But the discussion of the identity of "brothers" became a source of contention, since Muslim texts often regard this as referring to Ishmaelites, rather than Israelites.

on a camel.[35] There is no evidence that this passage was regarded as messianic in Jewish or Christian exegesis prior to the rise of Islam, indicating that this is a distinctively Muslim interpretation. It must have circulated relatively early in Muslim-Christian discussion, since it is rejected by Patriarch Timothy of the Assyrian Church of the East (r. 780 – 823) in his dialogue with Caliph al-Mahdī (r. 158 – 169/775 – 785) as early as c.782 – 83. In fact several records cite Ibn Isḥāq as the source.[36] The immediate Biblical context of Isaiah 21:1 – 10 announces the fall of Babylon, with no particular emphasis on the identity of the messengers arriving on animals to bring this news.

In discussing Isaiah 21:6 – 7 Ibn Qutayba takes up the theme of the forceful overthrow of idolatry.

> The one riding the ass is taken by us and by the Christians to be the Messiah. Now, if the one on the ass is the Messiah, then why should not the man riding the camel be Muhammad, for did not the destruction of Babylon and its graven idols occur at his hands? Not by the Messiah, for there continued to be in the region of Babylon kings who worshipped idols from the days of Abraham onwards. And is not the Prophet better known for his riding a camel than the Messiah for riding an ass?[37]

Ibn Rabbān likewise states that idolatry was not purged from Babylon, "until the Prophet (may God bless him and give him peace) appeared and ended their power, and destroyed the housings of their idols and fires, and brought them into the faith willy-nilly."[38] It is interesting that the subsequent popularity of this interpretation of Isaiah 21:6 – 7, promoted by Ibn Qutayba and others, is re-

---

35 Ibn Qutayba, *Dalā'il*, in Ibn al-Jawzī, *al-Wafā'*, 66 – 67; trans. Adang, *Muslim Writers*, 272. Cf. Ibn Rabbān, *Polemical Works*, 354 – 59.

36 On the originality of the Muslim interpretation see John Reeves, "The Muslim Appropriation of a Biblical Text: the Messianic Dimensions of Isa 21:6 – 7," in *Shaping the Middle East. Jews, Christians and Muslims in an Age of Transition 400 – 800 C.E.*, eds. Kenneth Holum and Hayim Lapin (Bethesda, Maryland: University Press of Maryland, 2011): 218. For Timothy's refutation see *Timotheus I, Ostsyrischer Patriarch: Disputation mit den Kalifen al-Mahdi*, German translation by Martin Heimgartner (Leuven: Peeters, 2011), 39 – 40, sections 8.23 – 8.39, keyed to same sections in *Timotheus I, Ostsyrischer Patriarch: Disputation mit den Kalifen al-Mahdi*, Syriac text, ed. Heimgartner (Leuven: Peeters, 2011). An English translation from the Arabic version of Timothy's dialogue is available in "The Dialogue of Patriarch Timothy I and the Caliph al-Mahdi," in *The Early Christian-Muslim Dialogue: a Collection of Documents from the First Three Islamic Centuries (632 – 900 A.D.). Translations With Commentary*, ed. N.A. Newman (Hatfield, PA: Interdisciplinary Biblical Research Institute, 1993), 195 – 96. On Ibn Isḥāq as the source see Suliman Bashear, "Riding Beasts on Divine Missions: An Examination of the Ass and Camel Traditions" *JSS* 37 (1991): 37 – 75.

37 Ibn Qutayba, in al-Jawzī, *al-Wafā'*, 66 – 67; trans. Adang, *Muslim Writers*, 272.

38 Ebied and Thomas, *Polemical Works*, 358 (Arabic), 359 (English).

flected in its being the subject of one of the very first artistic depictions showing Muhammad's face. This occurs in an illustrated manuscript of al-Bīrūnī's *Chronology of Ancient Nations.*[39]

The emphasis on the use of force to bring about God's triumph over false belief, as a proof that the Biblical passage in view predicts Muhammad, also occurs elsewhere in Ibn Qutayba's biblical proofs. He cites several Psalms in similar vein, quoting Psalm 149 in full. His version of verses 6–8 reads as follows. "May they magnify God with resounding voices, and may two-edged swords be in their hands, so that they may take vengeance [for God] on the nations which do not worship him, binding their kings with chains and their nobles with fetters."[40]

Ibn Qutayba then asks, "Now, which is the nation whose swords are two-edged, if not the Arabs, and who is the one to wreak vengeance on the nations that do not worship him, and who among the prophets is the one who was sent with the sword if not his prophet?"[41] The forceful overthrow of unbelieving regimes is one of the signs that Muhammad and his mission are from God. This motif, along with references to camels, the desert and praise, to name some of the most prominent, form the foundation of interpretations finding Muhammad in the Bible. Vollandt has shown that Ibn Qutayba borrowed his Pentateuch quotations in *Proofs of Prophethood* from Ibn Rabbān's *Book of Religion and Empire*, unlike the quotations found in his other works, discussed shortly.[42]

Ibn Qutayba never levels the charge of textual corruption against the Old Testament, though he twice uses the term *taḥrīf* to describe false interpretations by the People of the Book.[43] However, he does mention textual corruption in his

---

39 The illustration occurs in an Ilkhanid manuscript dated from 1307–08 of al-Bīrūnī's *Al-Āthār al-bāqiya 'an al-qurūn al-khāliya* (*Chronology of Ancient Nations*), originally written around the year 1000. The image can be found on a variety of websites. On the illustrated manuscript see Robert Hillenbrand, "The Edinburgh Biruni Manuscript: a Mirror of its Time?"*JRAS*, Series 3, 26 (2016): 171–99, who calls the Biblical interpretation under discussion "improbably eccentric" (187); see also Hillenbrand, "Images of Muhammad in al-Biruni's Chronology of Ancient Nations" in *Persian Painting from the Mongols to the Qajars: Studies in Honour of Basil W. Robinson*, ed. Robert Hillenbrand (London: I.B. Tauris in association with the Centre of Middle Eastern Studies, Cambridge, 2000): 129–46. On the use of Isaiah more generally see also Jean-Louis Déclais, *Un Récit musulmane sur Isaïe* (Paris: Cerf, 2001).

40 Ibn Qutayba, *Dalā'il*, in al-Jawzī, 65; my translation. Cf. trans. Adang, *Muslim Writers*, 271.

41 Ibn Qutayba, *Dalā'il*, in al-Jawzī, 65; trans. Adang, *Muslim writers*, 271.

42 Vollandt, *Versions*, 97–102. Ibn Qutayba in his other Biblical quotations clearly uses an Arabic translation from Syriac which Vollandt terms ArabSyr1. Like other authors in this study, Ibn Qutayba adjusts his quotations to fit with Islamic beliefs where necessary; see Vollandt, *Versions*, 102.

43 Ibn Qutayba, *Dalā'il*, in al-Jawzī, 62, 64; trans. Adang, *Muslim writers*, 268, 270.

discussion of the New Testament. One of these occasions is over the question of the name of Muhammad occurring in the Bible. He paraphrases Jesus' statement about John the Baptist in Matt 11:11–15, including Matthew's statement that "If you are willing to accept it, he is Elijah who is to come" (Matt 11:14, referring back to Malachi 4:5). He comments that the name of Muhammad is not actually missing since "It stipulated that Aḥmad would come, so they changed (*ghayyarū*) the name, just as God, may He be exalted, says: 'They alter words from their positions." (cf Q5:41).[44]

Ibn Qutayba's other New Testament discussion implying textual *taḥrīf* concerns the Paraclete in John's Gospel. He comments that different verses about the Paraclete seem to differ, a puzzle explained by the fact that those who transmitted the *Injīl* from Jesus are numerous. He is nevertheless convinced that the Paraclete must be a reference to Muhammad.[45]

Ibn Qutayba's historical work, *The Book of Noteworthy Information* (*Kitāb al-Ma'ārif*), is discussed later in this chapter in the treatment of historical works. Brief comment on his other works drawing on the Bible can however be included here.[46] The first of these relates to his concern in *Proofs* to strengthen trust in Muhammad. His aim in *The Book of Interpreting Disputed Traditions* (*Kitāb Ta'wīl mukhtalif al-ḥadīth*) is to allay anxiety about alleged contradictions in the Hadith literature. Ibn Qutayba asserts the soundness of the gospel passages he quotes, a logical move since he uses the Biblical texts to underpin his defence of the hadith.[47] This contrasts with his brief accusation of Christian alteration, discussed above in relation to his *Proofs*.

Ibn Qutayba's approach to non-Islamic sources is summed up in the introduction to his *Choice Narratives* (*'Uyūn al-akhbār*). This is a work providing morsels of knowledge of religious and non-religious topics for those in official roles or otherwise prominent. The introduction includes the striking statement – quoted at the outset of the present study – of his openness to gathering materials from diverse places.

Returning to "Proofs of Prophethood" literature, writers more famous for other works composed passages reproducing the verses offered in earlier centuries.[48] As to why the Bible offered an attractive option amongst the different pos-

44 Ibn Qutayba, *Dalā'il*, in al-Jawzī, *Al-Wafā'*, 68; cf Adang, *Muslim Writers*, 225.

45 Ibn Qutayba, *Dalā'il*, in al-Jawzī, *Al-Wafā'*, 67.

46 See Lecomte, "Les citations," 34–46.

47 Ibn Qutayba, *Kitāb Ta'wīl mukhtalif al-ḥadīth*, 213, referring to "*al-Injīl al-Ṣaḥīḥ*" or "the sound/trustworthy Gospel."

48 For example, al-Māwardī (d. 449/1058), author of the famous *Ordinances of Government* (*al-Aḥkām al-Sulṭāniyya*) on the theory of the caliphate, produced a *Book of the Proofs of Prophecy*

sible ways of proving Muhammad's prophethood, the fact that early Muslims were surrounded by large populations of Jews and Christians is an obvious factor. The Qur'an's positive statements about previous scriptures must also have prompted some writers at least to seek proof of this in the extant scriptures, along with the Qur'anic statements Q7:157 and 61:6 which create the expectation of finding Muhammad in the Bible.

4.3 Historical Writing

Early Muslim historical writings have prompted much debate over their reliability regarding both the earliest stages of the rise of Islam and also pre-Islamic history. This is because of the distance in time between the writers and the events they present. These controversies need not detain us here, since the focus is on the narrative which writers sought to present and how Biblical material served their purposes. The underlying aim of these histories is often to help to bolster the 'Abbāsid dynasty and its linkage to God's call and purposes following the upheavals of the 'Abbāsid Revolution in the early 130's/late 740's, and the continuing political instability in the first 'Abbāsid century. We are often subject as readers to an 'Abbāsid perspective on the Umayyad period and earlier decades.[49]

Robinson notes that historical reports were presented in three broad forms, biography, prosopography and chronography (annalistic chronicles progressing through time up to the period of the writer).[50] Having looked at biography through the lens of Ibn Isḥāq in the previous chapter, the focus here is on chronicles, including universal histories which present Islam as the culmination of a historical narrative beginning at creation. With creation as the start point and with such a concern for divine purposes, Biblical texts were an obvious place to turn for assistance.[51]

The following broadly chronological account charts the engagement of some of the early historical writers with Biblical material. Abū Ja'far Ibn Ḥabīb (d. 245/

(*Kitāb al-A'lām al-nubuwwa*) including a chapter on Biblical proofs. See Sabine Schmidtke, "The Muslim Reception of the Bible: Al-Māwardī and his *Kitāb A'lām al-nubuwwa*," in *Le Sacre Scritture e le Loro Interpretazioni*, eds. Carmela Baffioni, Anna Passoni Dell'Acqua et al (Milan/Rome: Veneranda Biblioteca Ambrosiana, 2016): 1–27. Biblical passages continue to be part of "Proofs of Prophethood" literature right up to the present time.

49 See for example Borrut, *Entre mémoire et pouvoir*, 79–108.

50 Robinson, "Islamic Historical Writing," 238–266.

51 Not all universal histories were equally focused on prophetic history, though they may have used it. See Yücesoy, "Ancient Imperial Heritage," 135–55.

860), from Baghdad, was the author of the earliest extant historical work incorporating Biblical information about previous prophets (the earliest historical work if we discount Ibn Isḥāq, as discussed in Chapter 3). Ibn Ḥabīb's, *The Perfected* (*Kitāb al-Muḥabbar*) concentrates mainly on pre-Islamic and Islamic genealogies and history. But it "ties the history of the Arabs into that of the Jews," by drawing on the accounts of time spans between different individuals found in Genesis 5:4–32 and 11:10–26.[52] In this it resembles Ibn Isḥāq's *Sīra*, which, as noted in the previous chapter, can be seen in some ways as the very first extant universal history, attempting to set the rise of Islam in the context of previous prophetic history from creation onwards. Ibn Ḥabīb narrates an account linking the Biblical prophet Jeremiah to Ma'add, the key Arab predecessor named in accounts of Muhammad's lineage. Jeremiah rescues Ma'add from the Babylonian king Nebuchadnezzar. According to Biblical history it was this king who took the Jews into exile (see 2 Kings 25, Jeremiah 52) in the early sixth century BCE. In this way Ibn Ḥabīb interweaves Muslim and Biblical concerns.[53]

This interest in depicting universal history is not present in another early work, the *History* (*Ta'rīkh*) of Khalīfa b. Khayyāṭ (d.c. 240/854–855), a native of Basra and close contemporary of Ibn Ḥabīb. However, it would be too simple to assume that he therefore had no interest in previous prophets and their background. Khalīfa b. Khayyāṭ demonstrates interest in previous prophets in hadiths associated with him, but in his *History* focusses instead on matters of politics and administration, not in connecting early Islamic history to Biblical history.[54] This reminds us that early works of history need to be read with an awareness of their individual purpose, where it can be determined, not as a simple indicator of the personal interests of the author.

---

52 Ibn Ḥabīb, *Kitāb al-Muḥabbar*, 1–5. Quotation from Julia Bray, "Lists and Memory: Ibn Qutayba and Muḥammad b. Ḥabīb," in *Culture and Memory in Medieval Islam: essays in honour of Wilferd Madelung*, eds. Farhad Daftary and Josef Meri (London: I.B. Tauris, 2003), 222. See also Abed El-Rahman Tayyara, "Ibn Ḥabīb's *Kitāb al-Muḥabbar* and its Place in Early Islamic Historical Writing," *JIS* 29 (2018): 392–416; and Ilse Lichtenstädter, "Muḥammad Ibn Ḥabīb and his *Kitāb al-Muḥabbar*," *Journal of the Royal Asiatic Society of Great Britain and Ireland* 1 (1939): 1–27, and Lichtenstädter, "Muḥammad b. Ḥabīb", in: *EI2*, consulted online on 03 July 2019 <http://dx.doi.org/10.1163/1573–3912_islam_SIM_5350.

53 Ibn Ḥabīb, *Kitāb al-Muḥabbar*, 6–7.

54 Tobias Andersson, *Early Sunni Historiography: a Study of the* Tārīkh *of Khalīfa b. Khayyāṭ*. IHC 157 (Leiden: Brill, 2018): 197. See Khalīfa b. Khayyāṭ, *Ta'rīkh* (Damascus: Dār al-Qalam, 1977); partial English translation by Carl Wurtzel, with Robert Hoyland, *Khalifa b Khayyat's History on the Umayyad Dynasty (660–750)*, TTH 63 (Liverpool: Liverpool University Press, 2015).

Ibn Qutayba also drew on the Bible in his historical compendium, *The Book of Noteworthy Information* (*Kitāb al-Ma'ārif*). This work has Ibn Ḥabīb's *The Perfected* as a partial prototype.[55] However, *The Book of Noteworthy Information* does not seek to be a comprehensive work of history, but presents accounts of Biblical history amongst its compilation of brief items of historical information. Ibn Qutayba gathered these items to educate those who needed them (or whom Ibn Qutayba felt needed them) in order to be able converse knowledgeably when associating with rulers, nobles and scholars. He makes explicit his hope that readers should in fact memorise the material.[56] Here, as elsewhere, Ibn Qutayba's only genuine quotations from the Hebrew Bible come from Genesis, with which he begins the work. This, and his exclusion of anything related to the Exodus stories, implies his ignorance of much of the Pentateuch.[57] One striking example of his use of Genesis is his identification of Isaac as the intended sacrifice of Abraham.[58] When it comes to the New Testament, Ibn Qutayba has detailed knowledge, but is capable of carefully adjusting the information he provides. For example, he omits any mention of the Holy Spirit from involvement in the conception of Jesus when drawing on Matt 1:18–21, presumably to downplay any Trinitarian overtones.[59]

On a lighter note, Ibn Qutayba used the Biblical text for one of his tests for his target audience of readers whom he hoped to educate in the art of knowledgeable conversation. After asking which of Adam's sons had offspring, Cain or Abel, Ibn Qutayba points out that the correct answer is neither, since it was Adam's third son, Seth. This test is a memory training exercise, since he has already given the information previously.[60]

The Twelver Shia writer al-Ya'qūbī (d.c. 293/905 or later) was born in Baghdad, but was active in Khurasan (North East Iran) and Egypt, among other places. His *History* (*Ta'rīkh*) is in two parts. He deals first with pre-Islamic history, including Biblical coverage from creation to Jesus, followed by the history of Islam up to 259/872–73.[61] He provides accounts which for a Muslim writer of

---

55 Bray, "Lists and Memory," 225. Ibn Qutayba, *Kitāb al-Ma'ārif* (Cairo: Maṭba'at Dār al-Kutub, 1960).

56 Ibn Qutayba, *Kitāb al-Ma'ārif*, 6–7.

57 Adang, *Muslim Writers*, 112–13.

58 Ibn Qutayba, *Kitāb al-Ma'ārif*, 35–38. Cf. Bashear, "Abraham's Sacrifice of his Son."

59 Ibn Qutayba, *Kitāb al-Ma'ārif*, 53, as noted by Accad, *Gospels*, 209.

60 Ibn Qutayba, *Kitāb al-Ma'ārif*, 25, and cf. Bray, "Lists and Memory," 212.

61 Aḥmad b. Abī Ya'qūb b. Ja'far b. Wahb b. Wāḍiḥ al-'Abbasī, now known as al-Ya'qūbī, *Ta'rīkh*, published as *Ibn Wāḍiḥ qui dicitur al-Ya'qūbī, Historiae*, ed. M. Houtsma, 2 vols., (Leiden: Brill, 1883), and in other editions. For a complete English translation see Matthew Gordon, Chase Robinson, Everett Rowson and Michael Fishbein, eds., *The Works of Ibn Wāḍiḥ al-Ya'qūbī: an English*

this period stay unusually close to the Biblical texts, especially for his narrative of Jesus. He makes minor adjustments to the gospel text at times, but even records the crucifixion, though adding that the gospel writers who record this are, "those who differ over all the meanings." This implies some form of error, even if only corruption of interpretation.[62] Al-Ya'qūbī then quotes Q4:157, the key Qur'anic verse normally understood to deny the crucifixion, presumably as an affirmation for his readers that the Qur'an is the ultimate judge of such controversial points. He also interprets the Gospel of John's reference to the Paraclete as a reference to a prophet, by implication Muhammad – though this reading of al-Ya'qūbī's text can now be plausibly questioned on the basis of a different manuscript. He may not have intended a reference to a prophet after all.[63] Despite al-Ya'qūbī's Shia identity it is hard to discern any distinctively Shia influence on his treatment of these matters.

Al-Ya'qūbī's accounts of Old Testament narratives are more confused, and he seems regularly to have relied on oral reports which he sought out from Jews or Christians.[64] But his overall aim, even if only partly fulfilled, seems to have been to provide a sober account of history with minimal intrusion of either his own commentary or of Islamicized versions of Biblical events. It is hard to assess why his work had almost no influence on later writers. It could be his unusually extensive use of the Bible, or his Shia identity.

By contrast, al-Ya'qūbī's more famous Sunni near contemporary, al-Ṭabarī (d. 310/ 923), whose Qur'anic exegesis was discussed in Chapter 2, offers much

Translation, 3 vols., IHC 152 (Leiden: Brill, 2017). The section on the Old Testament from Joshua to the end of the Exile is also translated by R.Y. Ebied and L.R. Wickham, "Al-Ya'ḳūbī's Account of the Israelite Prophets and Kings," *JNES* 29 (1970): 80–98. See also Camilla Adang, *Muslim Writers*, passim. On New Testament narratives, the chapter on Jesus is also translated by Dwight Donaldson, "Al-Ya'qūbī's Chapter About Jesus Christ," *The Macdonald Presentation Volume* (no editor) (Princeton: 1933): 89–105; see also Sidney Griffith, "The Gospel, the Qur'ān, and the presentation of Jesus in al-Ya'qūbī's *Ta'rīkh'*," in *Bible and Qur'an*, ed. John Reeves, 133–60. On the Shia identity of al-Ya'qūbī see Sean Anthony, "Was Ibn Wāḍiḥ al-Ya'qūbī a Shi'ite Historian? The State of the Question," *Al-'Uṣūr al-Wusṭa* 24 (2016): 15–41.

62 Al-Ya'qūbī, *Ta'rīkh*, 1:88; The translation here is my own; cf. Gordon et al (eds.), *Works*, 1: 341, and Donaldson, "Chapter," 103. Accad, *Gospels*, 213, draws attention to al-Ya'qūbī's avoidance of anthropomorphism by altering "every word from the mouth of God" to "the word [*kalima*] of God" in Matt 4:4 (al-Ya'qūbī, *Ta'rikh*, 1:76).

63 Al-Ya'qūbī, *Ta'rikh*, 1: 84, trans. Gordon et al, *Works*, 339, trans. Donaldson, "Chapter," 100. Gordon et al, *Works*, 339, fn. 327 note that an alternative reading for "*nabiyyan*" (a prophet) is given in the Manchester manuscript which they compare with the one used in Houtsma's edition. The Manchester manuscript reads "*abadan*" (forever) which corresponds with the Biblical text (John 14:16). So no Islamic interpretation may be in view here.

64 Ebied and Wickham, "Account," 82.

less direct engagement with Biblical sources. In his monumental *History* he traces events from creation to 303/915–16, the first five books of which involve Biblical events. However, he relied for Biblically-related material on Muslim traditions, for example those attached to the name of Wahb b. Munabbih.[65] This is unsurprising – though not inevitable – given his profound immersion in the fields of Islamic law and hadith literature, a dimension of his career often forgotten since so much of his legal work no longer survives. An unusual example of a relatively close Biblical quotation by al-Ṭabarī, which he cites from Ibn Isḥāq, is Genesis 4:9–16, concerning Cain and Abel.[66] As noted in Chapter 3, al-Ṭabarī is a valuable source for some of the material which Ibn Hishām cut from Ibn Isḥāq's biography of Muhammad. It is known that al-Ṭabarī studied in Rayy with a teacher known as a transmitter of the first lost section of Ibn Isḥāq's work, *The Book of the Beginning* (*Kitāb al-Mubtada'*).[67]

For Biblically-related information, al-Ṭabarī typically draws on traditions which can be traced to non-canonical Jewish and Christian works. For example, al-Ṭabarī's treatment of Isaiah is filtered through several layers of transmission. Al-Ṭabarī cites Ibn Isḥāq on Isaiah, from Wahb b. Munabbih. But his account seems to derive ultimately from an account of Isaiah found in *Ben Sira* 48:17–25.[68] *The Wisdom of Ben Sira* is a Hellenistic Jewish work completed in Hebrew by around 175BCE. While not included in Jewish or Protestant canons, it is included as one of the Deutero-canonical works or "Apocrypha" printed between the two testaments in Roman Catholic and Orthodox Bibles, sometimes being named *Ecclesiasticus*. *Ben Sira* circulated in Syriac, in Christian circles, from at

65 Al-Ṭabarī's *History* is published as *Annales quos scripsit Abu Djafar ibn Djarir at-Tabari*, ed. M. de Goeje et al (Leiden: Brill, 1879–1901). This work is produced in several volumes but uses continuous pagination throughout. Pagination rather than volume number will be used in references below as the volume numbering system varies. The work is translated into English in 39 individually titled volumes (Albany, N.Y.: SUNY Press, 1989–). See also Hugh Kennedy, ed., *Al-Ṭabarī: a Medieval Muslim Historian and his Work*, SLAEI 15 (Princeton: Darwin Press, 2008), amongst many resources on al-Ṭabarī.

66 Al-Ṭabarī, *Annales* 140 ff; trans. Franz Rosenthal, *The History of al-Ṭabarī, vol. I: General Introduction and from Creation to the Flood* (Albany, N.Y. SUNY Press, 1989), 310 ff. Whether this quotation can actually be traced to Ibn Isḥāq remains an open question; see the discussion in Witztum, "Ibn Isḥāq". Vollandt, *Versions*, 104–05, raises questions indicating that the Biblical passages could be later insertions into a recension of Ibn Isḥāq.

67 Chase Robinson, "Al-Ṭabarī (839–923)," in *Arabic Literary Culture, 500–925*, eds. Michael Cooperson and Shawkat Toorawa, DLB 311 (Detroit: Thomson Gale, 2005), 340. The teacher was Aḥmad ibn Ḥammad al-Dulabī.

68 Al-Ṭabarī, *Annales*, 638–45; translation in *The History of Al-Ṭabarī, vol. IV, The Ancient Kingdoms*, trans. Moshe Perlmann (Albany, N.Y.: SUNY Press, 1987), 36–42. On the influence of *Ben Sira* see Déclais, *Un Récit musulman sur Isaïe*, 60–61.

least c.300CE onwards, meaning that it would have been available to Christians, as well as Jews, in the milieu of the early Muslims.[69] The short account of Isaiah in *Ben Sira* mentions two themes. One is Isaiah's involvement in God driving away Sennacherib's army, the second his prophecy about the healing of the sick and despairing King Hezekiah. These two themes, amplified with some Biblical detail from the tradition reported by Ibn Isḥāq, are the foci of al-Ṭabarī's account.[70]

On the question of using Muslim traditions, rather than the Biblical text itself, to provide information related to Biblical narratives, al-Ṭabarī has been said "to have tipped the scales in favour of that material, and against greater respect for the original sources".[71] However, we have already seen that some of the more Biblically-inspired material in Ibn Isḥāq is only preserved for us by al-Ṭabarī, since Ibn Hishām cut much of it out of his recension.[72] So while al-Ṭabarī reduces this material he does not exclude it to the extent of Ibn Hishām. It seems that al-Ṭabarī is willing to grant space to information ultimately drawn from Biblical or non-canonical wells, but he is content to receive the water from buckets provided by Islamic sources such as Ibn Isḥāq. Either he regarded the water as thus guaranteed clean, or he simply lacked the curiosity of an al-Ya'qūbī to search outside the bounds of Muslim sources.[73]

Two widely-travelled writers follow next. The first, an acquaintance of al-Ṭabarī, is Abū'l-Ḥasan al-Mas'ūdī (d. 345/956), a Shia writer born in Baghdad who is a renowned figure of Arabic literature. He did not share al-Ṭabarī's relative lack of curiosity about other traditions. In his two extant works, *The Meadows of Gold* (*Murūj al-dhahab*) and *The Book of Indication and General View*

69 See Robert Owens, "The Early Syriac Text of Ben Sira in the Demonstrations of Aphrahat," *JSS* 34 (1989): 39–75.

70 A further example of al-Ṭabarī drawing from traditions related to non-canonical Jewish and Christian works can be seen in his account of Ezra's restoration of the Torah, which has clear links to *4 Ezra*. See Whittingham, "Ezra as Corrupter of the Torah?," 259–60, and cf. chapter 2 above.

71 Franz Rosenthal, "The Influence of the Biblical Tradition on Muslim Historiography," in *Historians of the Middle East*, ed. Peter Holt and Bernard Lewis (London: OUP, 1962), 42.

72 A point made by Ulrika Mårtensson, "Discourse and Historical Analysis: The Case of al-Ṭabarī's History of the Messengers and the Kings," *JIS* 16 (2005): 318, whose article (287–331) interprets al-Ṭabarī's concern with covenant as a symbol expressing his concerns with upholding 'Abbāsid power. See likewise Mårtensson, "Bund und Land in muslimischer Rezeption: Biblische Kategorien in Ṭabarī's Geschichtswerk," *Judaica* 62 (2006): 289–308.

73 McAuliffe, "Prediction and Prefiguration," 130, argues that while not citing Biblical texts, al-Ṭabarī is using Biblical models in constructing his biography of Muhammad, including themes of prediction, maternity, birth, infancy narrative, all of which echo his life of Jesus, given earlier in his *History*.

(*Kitāb al-Tanbīh wa'l-ishrāf*) he ranges over history, geography and religious traditions, amongst other topics.[74] Though well-known for his interest in other faiths, al-Mas'ūdī engages with the Bible itself as one of many sources often mixed together freely and fleetingly. He was aware of different translations of the Hebrew Bible, and knew the Jewish translator Sa'adya Gaon personally.[75] He appears not to have levelled the charge of textual corruption at the Bible, only of distorted understanding.[76]

Little is known of the life of the second widely-travelled writer, Abū Naṣr al-Maqdisī, who wrote his theologically-oriented *Creation and History* (*Kitāb al-bad' wa'l-ta'rīkh*) around 355/966.[77] This gives brief and usually unremarkable treatment of Jewish and Christian thought. Taking his account of Jesus by way of illustration, this is based largely on the Qur'an, with other non-canonical traditions used to add detail. There is very little which is shaped by the New Testament gospels. He is, however, prepared to record the view of some Muslim exegetes of Q4:157, concerned with the crucifixion of Jesus (or not, as most Muslims would think). Al-Maqdisī records, rather than recommends, the view that Jesus died bodily and his spirit was raised to life. But the very presence in his account of some form of Jesus' death reflects a consideration for issues provoked by the prominence of the death of Jesus in the New Testament and ensuing Christian belief. Needless to say, al-Maqdisī need not have consulted the gospels directly to engage with this view.[78]

Al-Maqdisī's view of Biblical unreliablity is noteworthy. He adopts the story of Ezra being involved in producing a new, distorted Torah, a story shaped by responses to *4 Ezra* . According to al-Maqdisī Ezra hands over the miraculously

74 Al-Mas'ūdī, *Murūj al-dhahab*, published as Maçoudi, *Les Prairies D'Or*, Arabic text and French translation, Barbier de Meynard and Pavet de Courteille (Paris: L'Imprimerie Impériale, 1861–77); Al-Mas'ūdī, *Kitāb al-Tanbīh wa'l-ishrāf* (Leiden: Brill, 1894). A partial English translation of *The Meadows of Gold* is available: Paul Lunde and Caroline Stone, *The Meadows of Gold: the 'Abbāsids* (London: Kegan Paul International, 1989). See also Adang, *Muslim Writers*, 44–48 and discussions throughout the book for al-Mas'ūdī's treatment of Judaism and the Hebrew Bible.

75 Ahmad Shboul, *Al-Mas'ūdī and his World* (London: Ithaca Press, 1979), 96–102.

76 Al-Mas'ūdī, in *Les Prairies D'Or*, 2: 551, and cf. Adang, *Muslim Writers*, 232.

77 See Adang, *Muslim Writers*, 48–50 and discussions throughout the book, especially 126–31.

78 For the account of Jesus see al-Maqdisī, *al-Bad' wa'l-tar'īkh*, ed. and trans. Clément Huart (Paris: Leroux, 1899–1919), 118–27 (Arabic), 122–31 (French). For reference to Jesus' death, see 126 (Arabic), 130 (French).

restored Torah which he had received from God to a disciple who subsequently distorted it, a variant on the notion of Ezra himself being responsible.[79]

Ḥamza al-Iṣfahānī (d. 350–360/961–971) was briefly a student of al-Ṭabarī during the first of al-Iṣfahānī's visits to Baghdad, though he spent most of his life in his native Isfahan, Iran. His *History of the Years of the Kings of the Earth and of the Prophets* (*Ta'rīkh sinī mulūk al-arḍ wa'l-anbiyā'*) includes a chapter on the history of the Israelites, and demonstrates more openness to non-Muslim sources than does al-Ṭabarī.[80] However, he appears to have relied on excerpts from the Bible, rather than consulting the actual text.[81] Al-Iṣfahānī is aware of differences between the Hebrew, Samaritan and Greek Torahs, but does not turn this into an accusation of deliberate corruption.[82] Intriguingly, however, his omission of any references to the Book of Esther are most likely deliberate. Isfahan had a Jewish community (so he would have seen the celebrations of the festival of Purim, based on Esther), he states that he had Jewish informants, and yet he omits Esther from his list of Hebrew Biblical books.[83] The motivation for this omission, if such it be, remains unknown.

Abū Rayḥān al-Bīrūnī (d. 440/1048), the renowned historian of science and of India, refers to al-Iṣfahānī on various occasions in his *Chronology of Ancient Nations* (*Al-Āthār al-bāqiya 'an al-qurūn al-khāliya*).[84] He comments on differences of chonology between Jewish, Samaritan and Septuagint versions, yet his frustration sounds like that of the historian in search of information rather than the polemicist. "Now if such is the diversity of opinions, as we have described, and if there is no possibility of distinguishing – by means of analogy

---

79 On *4 Ezra* see Chapter 5. Al-Maqdisī, *al-Bad' wa'l-ta'rīkh*, 29–30 (Arabic), 32 (French). See the discussion in Adang, *Muslim Writers*, 233–34. The possible role of disciples of Ezra is also found in the work of al-Juwaynī; see below Chapter 5.

80 Ḥamza al-Iṣfahānī, *Ta'rīkh sinī mulūk al-arḍ wa'l-anbiyā'* (Beirut: Dār Maktabat al-Ḥayāt, 1961), 76–82. For an English translation of the relevant chapter, see Camilla Adang, "The Chronology of the Israelites According to Ḥamza al-Iṣfahānī," *JSAI* 32 (2006): 286–310. Note that Adang's edition, from the same publisher as cited above, uses different pagination for the chapter in view, though not for the reference to scriptures, below.

81 Adang, "Chronology," 301–02.

82 Al-Iṣfahānī, *Ta'rīkh*, 11; cf. Adang, "Chronology," 290.

83 As noted by Adam Silverstein, *Veiling Esther, Unveiling her Story: the Reception of a Biblical Book in Islamic Lands*, Oxford Studies in the Abrahamic Religions (Oxford: OUP, 2018), 41–42.

84 Al-Bīrūnī, *Al-Āthār al-bāqiya 'an al-qurūn al-khāliya*, ed. Eduard Sachau (Leipzig: Brockhaus, 1878); trans. Sachau, *Chronology of Ancient Nations* (London: William Allen, 1879). The English translation is reprinted identically in *Theology, Ethics and Metaphysics: Royal Asiatic Society Classics of Islam. Volume III: The Chronology of Ancient Nations* (London: RoutledgeCurzon, 2003). On al-Bīrūnī see Adang, *Muslim Writers*, 54–59, and discussions throughout the book, especially 131–33.

– between truth and fiction, where is the student to search for exact information?"[85] His desire for orderly data is also in evidence as he wrestles with the genealogies of Matthew and Luke in their gospels.[86] Alongside his more searching and individual enquiries, he also incorporates, in what had become a standard pattern, some of the most familiar Biblical passages seen as predictions of Muhammad, encountered earlier in the present chapter.[87]

In sum, these histories reveal varied reasons for consulting the Bible. One reason could be the scholar's appetite for complete information, but another is the desire to link Islamic history to earlier Jewish and Christian history, seen as part of God's preparation for Islam. Topics included chronology of Biblical time periods or accounts of prophets' lives. While some, notably Ibn Qutayba and al-Ya'qūbī, consult the Bible directly, others rely on intermediary sources, and it is not clear whether that is for lack of access or of desire. Al-Ṭabarī, a giant in the fields of Qur'an commentary and history, is a minor figure in the direct use of Biblical texts, though Biblical material leaks into his *History* through his knowledge of Ibn Isḥāq's reports on previous prophets.

The most interesting development evident from this survey is the interweaving of Islamic history with pre-Islamic events. This emerged under the 'Abbāsids, and it seems likely that the aim was to underpin the 'Abbāsid claims to a universal faith following their ascent to power. By the time of the later writers mentioned above, treating the lives of Biblical figures as part of Islamic history would have been taken for granted. This follows the seeds sown by Ibn Isḥāq, and the wide distribution his reports would have received owing to the huge success of al-Ṭabarī's work which incorporated them. It seems as if Ibn Hishām ultimately failed in his attempt to remove Biblical elements from Muslim accounts, but perhaps he need not have worried. The spread of these elements was not designed to rival or undermine Islam, but on the contrary to support it.

4.4 Ismā'īlī Use of the Bible

Ismā'īlī Islam is a branch of Shia Islam which departs from the majority Twelver Shia belief in twelve imams. Ismā'īlīs believe that Twelvers recognised the wrong

---

85 Al-Bīrūnī, *Al-Āthār*, 21–22; *Chronology of Ancient Nations*, 25. The Septuagint, often referred to as LXX, is a Greek translation of the Hebrew Bible widely used by Greek-speaking Jews, and by Christians in the early centuries of the church. See Siegfried Kreuzer (ed.), *Introduction to the Septuagint*, trans. David Brenner and Peter Altmann (Baylor University Press: Waco, TX, 2019).
86 Al-Bīrūnī, *Al-Āthār*, 22; *Chronology*, 25–6.
87 Isa 21:6–9, Deut 18:18, 33:2; see al-Bīrūnī, *Al-Āthār* 19; *Chronology*, 22–23.

son of the sixth Imam, Ja'far al-Ṣāḍiq, as his successor, contending that Ismā'īl should have been recognised rather than Mūsā al-Kāẓim. Ismā'īlīs held power at the time of the Fāṭimids, an Ismā'īlī dynasty which ruled from Cairo (with interruptions) from 358–567/969–1171, following a period of rule in North Africa from 297/909. Today Ismā'īlīs are most prominently represented by followers of the Aga Khan, descendants of one branch of a further split within Ismā'īlism.[88]

Ismā'īlī texts in this early period demonstrate a level of engagement with the Bible unusual amongst Muslim writers. This can be explained by the fact that Ismā'īlī thought stresses the underlying unity of all revelations, Qur'anic and pre-Qur'anic. History unfolds in a series of cycles, each introduced by the coming of a prophet, who is succeeded by a legatee (*waṣī*), who reveals the secret interpretation of the prophet's law. Seven imams follow each prophet, their role being to transmit this secret teaching.

4.4.1 Iranians

Early Ismā'īlī thinkers engaging with the Bible can be divided into Iranians and Fāṭimids. Amongst Iranians, Abū Ḥātim al-Rāzī (d.c.322/933–34), whose name indicates his origins in Rayy, on the outskirts of modern Tehran, was a prominent missionary, or *dā'ī*, for the Ismā'īlī cause. He used the Bible in *The Signs of Prophethood* (*A'lām al-nubuwwa*), in which he opposes the religious scepticism of an opponent, Abū Bakr al-Rāzī (known in medieval Europe as the physician Rhazes).[89] Abū Ḥātim quotes from seventeen Old Testament and seven New Testament books, giving generally accurate renditions of Biblical verses. A degree of mild paraphrase can occur, as in his version of Malachi 1:8 as "Why do you offer to me every lame and one-eyed beast?"[90] Similarly, from the New Testament he alters John 12:36 to "Believe in the light in order to become sons of God," rather than ending with "sons of light." These minor adjustments seem to

---

88 For an accessible introduction to Ismā'īlī groups and ideas, see Diana Steigerwald, 'Ismā'īlī *Ta'wīl*' in Andrew Rippin (ed.), *The Blackwell Companion to the Qur'ān* (Oxford: Blackwell, 2006): 386–400. See also the works of Farhad Daftary, including *The Ismā'īlīs: Their History and Doctrines* (Cambridge: CUP, 1992). For attitudes to Christians during the early Fāṭimid period see R. Marston Speight, "Muslim Attitudes toward Christians in the Maghrib during the Fāṭimid Period, 297/909–358/969," in *Christian-Muslim Encounters*, eds. Yvonne Yazbeck Haddad and Wadi Haddad (Gainesville: University of Florida Press, 1995): 180–93.

89 Abū Ḥātim al-Rāzī, *The Proofs of Prophecy*, Arabic text with English translation by Tarif Khalidi, METI (Provo, Utah: Brigham Young University Press, 2011).

90 Abū Ḥātim al-Rāzī, *Proofs*, 87.

have no theological significance, unlike some of the changes discussed already (and see below on al-Rassī). Immediately after his alteration of John 12:36 he quotes John 20:17 accurately.[91]

How do these Biblical quotations contribute to Abū Ḥātim's aim of opposing the scepticism of Abū Bakr al-Rāzī? Abū Ḥātim stresses the underlying unity of all the prophets' messages in order to counter Abū Bakr al-Rāzī's argument that the existence of contradictory messages from different prophets proves that prophecy is nonsense. For example, Abū Ḥātim's discussion of the crucifixion argues, from both the Gospels and the Qur'an, that Jesus did in fact die bodily, although not in his spirit. Accordingly, "the claim advanced by the heretic that the Qur'ān contradicts the Gospel in this respect is false."[92] Such an approach is highly unusual in Muslim texts, but Abū Ḥātim shared it with other Ismā'īlī thinkers, including al-Sijistānī and Ja'far ibn Manṣūr al-Yaman, discussed below.[93] However other biblical quotations from Abū Ḥātim provide a more familiar diet, such as the section on Biblical proofs of Muhammad, or the view that Christians believe in the divinity of Jesus only because of wrongly interpreting their own gospels.[94]

Another Iranian, Abū Ya'qūb al-Sijistānī (d. after 361/971) quotes in his *Book of Wellsprings* (*Kitāb al-yanābī'*) an adapted version of Matt 25:31–46. In Matthew's gospel this is a Christocentric passage in which Jesus, named as the Son of Man, judges people at the end of time according to how they treated the poor and needy. It includes the phrase, "just as you did it to one of the least of those who are members of my family, you did it to me" (Matt 25:40). Al-Sijistānī replaces "the Son of Man" with "the Lord", so as to displace the Christocentric element of the text, much like the version found in the hadith collection of Muslim.[95] However, unlike in both Matthew's gospel and the hadith, al-Sijistānī alters the quotation to state that "all that you have done for *yourselves*, you have done for me" (emphasis added). This change in focus towards all that you have done for yourselves, not for "one of the least of those who are members

---

91 Abū Ḥātim al-Rāzī, *Proofs*, 119.
92 Abū Ḥātim al-Rāzī, *Proofs*, 125.
93 See Todd Lawson, *The Crucifixion and the Qur'an* (Oxford: Oneworld, 2009), 81–85.
94 Abū Ḥātim al-Rāzī, *Proofs*, 142–144, 118.
95 Al-Sijistānī, *Kitāb al-Yanābī'* in *Trilogie Ismaélienne*, ed. Henry Corbin (Tehran: Département d'Iranologie de l'Institut francoiranien, 1961), 88 (Arabic section); complete translation in Paul Walker, *The Wellsprings of Wisdom* (Salt Lake City: University of Utah Press, 1994). For the quotation see Walker, 105. Cf. also the occurrence of this Biblical verse in *Ṣaḥīḥ Muslim*, vol. 6, no. 6556, discussed in Chapter 3, above.

of my family", would appear to turn the message of altruism in the gospel passage into a call for selfishness. But al-Sijistānī is reading the passage in the context of Gnostic theories of the soul which shaped Ismā'īlī thought. In this scheme the figure of judgment who voices these words is not "the Son of Man," as in Matt 25:31, but the "universal soul" of this world, the demiurge or spiritual Adam. This figure needs individual souls' help in order to rise back to a spiritual level from which he had fallen. When individual souls elevate their own spiritual state, they simultaneously help the Universal Soul.[96] Reading a gospel text through an Ismā'īlī lens like this indicates how Gnostic ideas are used to shape that lens.

4.4.2 The Fāṭimids

The Fāṭimids also produced interpretations of both Biblical testaments. It has been argued that they did so not to reach out to Jews or Christians, but to affirm the legitimacy of their own teaching, using non-Qur'anic scriptural sources to imbue believers with the sense that they had access to secret knowledge unknown to other Muslims. A striking example is Ja'far ibn Manṣūr al-Yaman (d.c. 349/960?) who composed an interpretation of the story of Judah and Tamar (on which see Gen 38) in his *Secrets of the Speakers* (*Asrār al-nuṭaqā'*) – "speakers" here denoting prophets. He did so to polemicize against Twelver Shī'ites and other Muslims, rather than to reach Jews with his message, as becomes clear from his equating the unrighteous acts of Judah in the passage with the acts of corrupt (non Ismā'īlī) Muslim jurists.[97]

Another leading Fāṭimid missionary, Ḥamīd al-dīn al-Kirmānī (d. after 411/1020), may even have known some Hebrew and Syriac, though the extent of this knowledge is difficult to gauge from his quotations using these languages.[98]

96 Al-Sijistānī, *Kitāb al-yanābī'*, 88; trans. Walker, *Wellsprings*, 105, and see the discussion of this passage in Henry Corbin, *Cyclical Time and Ismaili Gnosis* (London: Kegan Paul International, 1983), 162–165.

97 Ja'far ibn Manṣūr al-Yaman, *Sarā'ir wa'l-asrār al-nuṭaqā'*, ed. M. Ghālib (Beirut: Dār al-Andalus, 1984), 150–52; see discussion in David Hollenberg, "Disrobing Judges with Veiled Truths: an Early Ismā'īlī Torah Interpretation (*ta'wīl*) in service of the Fātimid mission," *Religion* 33 (2003): 127–45; for English translation of Ja'far's story of Judah and Tamar see 135–37; see also David Hollenberg, *Beyond the Qur'an* (Columbia, SC: University of South Carolina Press, 2016), especially chapter 5, "The Torah's Imams," 100–25.

98 See the discussion in Paul Walker, *Master of the Age: an Islamic Treatise on the Necessity of the Imamate* (London: I.B. Tauris, 2007), 24–26, 32–34. Walker provides the Arabic text and English translation of al-Kirmānī's *Lights illuminating the Proof of the Imamate* (*al-Maṣābīḥ fī ithbāt*

Born in Kirmān in Eastern Iran, he was brought to Cairo, where he used the Bible, amongst other sources, in support of the prophethood of Muhammad, quoting lines in Hebrew and Syriac which approximate Biblical verses.[99] Interestingly, Kraus records the text of Biblical quotations by al-Kirmānī mentioned in a later Ismāʿīlī text, in support of the Fāṭimid caliph al-Ḥākim (r.386–411/996–1021). Al-Kirmānī finds references to al-Ḥākim in Zech 9:9 and Isa 11:4, and in Dan 12:12, where he adapts the wording.[100]

So it seems that Ismāʿīlī engagement with the Bible shares with Sunni texts the underlying aim of self-affirmation. The concerns of the Ismāʿīlī system – spiritual hierarchies, the unity of all revelations, and in some cases support for the Fāṭimids – are different to typical Sunni concerns. But the impulse to adopt the Bible to prove the truth of one's beliefs remains.

4.4.3 The Brethren of Purity

The *Epistles of the Brethren of Purity* (*Rasāʾil Ikhwān al-Ṣafāʾ*), is a work of 52 epistles commonly associated with a circle of thinkers in Basra around 370/980. They appear to be Ismāʿīlīs, though they do not describe themselves as such, never even mentioning their names. The Brethren of Purity combined their Islamic framework with knowledge from ancient Greek, Indian and Persian learning, along with references to the Bible. It now seems that the epistles were circulating in some form earlier than the third/tenth century, and the precise origins of the works will probably remain obscure.[101] To what extent their thought can be fully identified with Ismāʿīlī thought is difficult to determine.

---

al-imāma). See also Paul Kraus, "Hebräische und syrische Zitate in ismāʿīlitischen Schriften," *Der Islam* 19 (1930): 243–63, and Daniel De Smet and Jan Van Reeth, "Les Citations Bibliques dans l'oeuvre du *Dāʿī* Ismaélien Ḥamīd ad-dīn al-Kirmānī," in *Law, Christianity and Modernism in Islamic Society: Proceedings of the Eighteenth Congress of* Union Européenne des Arabisants et Islamisants *held at the Katholieke Universiteit Leuven (September 3–September 9, 1996)*, eds. U. Vermeulen and J. Van Reeth (Leuven: Uitgeverij Peeters, 1998): 147–160

99 For the use of Hebrew and Syriac, see Walker, *Master*, 63–64 (Arabic pagination), 94–96 (English pagination).

100 See Kraus, "Zitate," 252–57. Al-Ḥākim has become famous for his destruction of the Church of the Holy Sepulchre in Jerusalem (and other churches), an act to which the Crusades are in part a response. On the state of mind of al-Ḥākim, often assumed to be highly unstable, see Jennifer Pruitt, "Method in Madness: Recontextualizing the Destruction of Churches in the Fatimid Era," *Muqarnas* 30 (2013): 119–39.

101 *Rasāʾil Ikhwān al-Ṣafāʾ* (Beirut: Dār Ṣādir, 1957), from which references are taken. A major series gradually producing Arabic critical editions and complete English translations of individ-

The Brethren of Purity place the previous scriptures on a level virtually akin to the Qur'an, referring to "the revealed books brought by the prophets – upon them the grace of God – such as the Torah, the Gospel, the Furqan [i.e. the Qur'an], and other prophetic books whose meanings come from revelation".[102] This theoretical support for the parity of scriptures is borne out by references to them, and perhaps most surprisingly their affirmation of the bodily crucifixion of Jesus.[103] Both of these features recall the approach of Abū Ḥātim al-Rāzī discussed above, in seeking to harmonize elements of different scriptures where possible.

4.5 Qur'anic Exegesis

Qur'anic commentaries are known as works of *tafsīr* (literally, "explanation"). Since the Qur'an mentions many figures who also occur in the Bible, it is unsurprising that commentators sometimes draw on Biblical background in their exposition of particular Qur'anic passages. In the early centuries there is some openness to Biblical background, though, as seen below, some reshaping of Biblical material is operative. The treatment of David and his repentance in Sura *Ṣād* (38:21–25) provides a valuable case-study, as this passage raises questions for commentators for which the Biblical texts provide some clear but also potentially controversial solutions. It is therefore informative to see how far Qur'anic exegetes used the Bible in addressing whether David committed a sin, in apparent contravention of the doctrine of the sinlessness of prophets (*'iṣma*). Secondly, if so, what was that sin? The Qur'anic passage is short enough to be quoted in full.

Has the story of the dispute come to you? When they climbed over the wall of the place of prayer, when they entered upon David, and he was terrified of them, but they said, 'Do not fear! (We are) two disputants: one of us has acted oppressively toward the other. So judge between us in truth, and do not be unjust, and guide us to the right path. Surely this (man) is my brother. He has nine-

---

ual epistles is underway from the Institute of Ismaili Studies, London. See Nader El-Bizri (ed.) *The* Ikhwān al-Ṣafā' *and their* Rasā'il: *an introduction* (Oxford: OUP 2008), and translations of the *Epistles* in this series. On the *Epistles*, see Godefroid de Callataÿ, *Ikhwān al-Ṣafā': A Brotherhood of Idealists on the Fringe of Orthodox Islam*, MMW (Oxford: Oneworld, 2005), and Yves Marquet, "Les Iḫwan al-Ṣafā' et le Christianisme," *Islamochristiana* 8 (1982): 129–58, especially 141–42.

102 Epistle 45, in *Rasā'il*, 4:42; translation from de Callataÿ, *Brotherhood*, 84.

103 Epistle 44, in *Rasā'il*, 4:31. The passage on the crucifixion is translated in Lawson, *The* Crucifixion, 86.

ty-nine ewes and I have (only) one ewe. He said, "Give her into my charge," and he overcame me in the argument.' He said, 'Certainly he has done you evil in asking for your ewe (in addition) to his ewes. Surely many (business) partners indeed act oppressively toward one another, except those who believe and do righteous deeds – but few they are.' And David guessed that We had (somehow) tested him, so he asked his Lord for forgiveness, and fell down, bowing, and turned (in repentance). So We forgave him that. Surely he has intimacy with Us and a good (place of) return.

This passage has echoes, albeit brief and compressed, of the Biblical 2 Sam 12:1–15. In this Biblical text the prophet Nathan challenges David over his deliberately arranging the death of Uriah in battle following David's adultery with Bathsheba, the wife of Uriah. Nathan tells David a parable about injustice involving a rich man taking the only ewe lamb belonging to a poor man. Nathan then makes the application explicit in telling David that he was the man who took what did not belong to him, a reference to Uriah's wife. The Qur'anic passage, by contrast, makes no mention of wives, nor of why David had been tested or needed to repent. For this reason it is ripe for explanation or elaboration by commentators.

Muqātil b. Sulaymān, discussed in Chapter 2, makes clear in his commentary that David sinned, and that his sin was arranging to send Uriah (Udriyā) to the front of the battle lines so as to ensure his death. This is clear from the reference to David's repentance (*tawba*).[104] However, David does not commit adultery with Uriah's wife, only having relations with her after marrying her following Uriah's death.[105] It is likely that Muqātil gained his information from reports combining written Biblical and midrashic elements. Given the apparent lack of Arabic Bible translations in his lifetime (see Chapter 1 above) it is far less likely that he accessed the written text directly, though he may have had it recounted to him

104 Muqātil b. Sulayman, *Tafsīr*, vol. 3, (Beirut: Dār al-Kutub al-'Ilmiyya, 2003), 116. For the whole account see Muqātil, *Tafsīr*, 3: 115–17; English translation in Khaleel Mohammed, *David in the Muslim Tradition: The Bathsheba Affair* (Lanham, MD: Lexington Books, 2014), 43–45, with occasional omissions. Gordon Nickel, "Muqātil on Zayd and Zaynab," in *Islamic Studies Today: Essays in Honor of Andrew Rippin*, eds. Majid Daneshgar and Walid Saleh (Leiden: Brill, 2017): 43–61, while rightly drawing out differences between the acknowledgement of David's sin in Biblical and *tafsīr* material, underplays the acknowledgement by Muqātil of at least some sin on David's part.

105 This adaptation of material originally deriving from the written Torah is augmented by motifs also occurring in Jewish midrash. These include David's desire to be tested by God, and his attempt to capture a bird and in so doing seeing Bathsheba. See *Babylonian Talmud*, Tractate Sanhedrin, 107a.

by Jews and/or Christians, or by Muslims who had converted from that background.

The open acknowledgement that David sinned in arranging the death of Uriah, while simultaneously eliminating any mention of his adultery, is a pattern followed by other early commentators. The most detailed account is given by Hūd b. Muḥakkam (d.c. 290/903), an Ibāḍī Muslim exegete whose work *Commentary on the Book of God the Almighty* (*Tafsīr Kitāb Allāh al-'Azīz*) has only recently received attention. His belonging to the Ibāḍīs, a small minority group within Islam who are neither Sunni nor Shia, may have contributed to his subsequent neglect by Sunni authors.[106] In a long exposition of the five Qur'anic verses he explains how David desired that the husband (Uriah, though he is not named here) should die as a martyr, so that he could then marry his wife.

Al-Ṭabarī likewise draws on the Biblical background to the Qur'anic verses, with the same affirmation of David's sin yet elimination of any mention of adultery.[107] It is important to note that while al-Ṭabarī is seen as a bastion of orthodoxy, Muqātil b. Sulaymān, as noted previously, has been criticised for his reliance on Jewish and Christian traditions. Yet both al-Ṭabarī and Muqātil are here drawing on such traditions, and a more accurate explanation for criticisms of Muqātil in early sources lies in his use of written sources and lack of use of chains of transmission.[108]

This openness in commentaries to the idea of David sinning is gradually reduced as time progresses. In fact a clear trajectory of attitudes to David's possible adultery with Bathsheba can be traced in Islamic literature if one steps outside the genre of commentaries and begins with open acknowledgements of David's adultery in early versions of the little-known Muslim Psalms of

---

106 Hūd b. Muḥakkam, *Tafsīr Kitāb Allāh al-'Azīz*, (*The Commentary on the Book of God the Almighty*), vol. 4 (Beirut: Dār al-Gharb al-islāmī, 1990), 11–14. English translation in Mohammed, *David*, 45–48. Mohammed omits without comment Hūd's discussion of Qur'anic readings on p. 45, cf. Hūd, *Tafsīr* 4:12, line 1. See also Claude Gilliot, "Le Commentaire coranique de Hūd B. Muḥakkam/Muḥkim," *Arabica* 44 (1997): 179–233. On Ibāḍī Muslims see Tadeusz Lewicki, "Al-ibāḍiyya", in:*EI2*, consulted online on 03 July 2019, http://dx.doi.org/10.1163/1573-3912_islam_COM_0307.

107 Al-Ṭabarī, *Tafsīr*, vol. 10 (Beirut: Dār al-Kutub al-'Ilmiyah, 1999), 565–75; for discussion of the treatment by al-Ṭabarī see Anthony Johns, "David and Bathsheba: a Case Study in the Exegesis of Qur'anic Story-telling," *MIDEO* 19 (1989): 225–66. On al-Ṭabarī and a range of other commentators see Jean-Louis Déclais, *David raconté par le musulmanes* (Paris: Cerf, 1991). Al-Ṭabarī also provides several reports about David and his sin in arranging the death of Uriah in his *History*. See *Annales*, 564–70, trans. William Brinner in *The History of Al-Ṭabarī, vol. III: The Children of Israel* (Albany, NY: SUNY Press, 1991), 145–50.

108 See Armstrong, *Quṣṣāṣ*, 97–110.

David.[109] The trajectory can then be traced from open acknowledgement to a more muted recognition of David's sin as being only the arranging of Uriah's death, until ideas of his sin are minimised or removed completely, as will be discussed in Volume 2 of this study.[110]

4.6 Tales of the Prophets (*Qiṣaṣ al-Anbiyā'*)

The Islamic literature known as Tales of the Prophets (*qiṣaṣ al-anbiyā'*) is a genre established by the ninth century, in both Sunni and Shia traditions.[111] The tales provide instructive and entertaining stories about a variety of figures, some of them found in the Bible as well as the Qur'an. For this reason the Bible was one source for fleshing out these portraits, but less so than might be expected. Before exploring a notable Sunni example of the literature, note that the purpose of *qiṣaṣ* traditions in Shia writings is different. The main concern of reports of previous prophets here was to affirm Shia beliefs, by indicating connections between the lives of previous prophets and the events and persons central to Shi'-ism, such as Noah being seen as a type or forerunner of 'Alī. However, there appears to be no reference to canonical Biblical texts in the Shia tales.[112] This is unsurprising since the particularly strong Shī'ite emphasis on the infallibility ('*iṣma*) of prophets and imams often conflicts with the Bible's openness about the failings or sins of its prominent figures (with the obvious exception of Jesus).[113]

The most famous Sunni example of *qiṣaṣ* literature is by Abū Isḥāq al-Tha'-labī (d.427/1035), entitled *The Finest (literally 'brides') of Sessions concerning the Tales of the Prophets* (*'Arā'is al-majālis fī qiṣaṣ al-anbiyā'*).[114] This offers stories

109 On the rewritten Psalms of David see Vishanoff, "Images of David."

110 A major new exploration of the use of the Bible in *tafsīr* literature is Samuel Ross, *The Biblical Turn in Modern Qur'an Commentary* (Unpublished Ph.d thesis, Yale University, 2018). This work surveys the prevalence (or lack thereof) of direct use of the Bible in pre-modern commentaries, as background for discussion of the greater use of the Bible ("the Biblical turn") in the last two centuries.

111 For this date, and a valuable discussion of the genre more generally, see Roberto Tottoli, *Biblical Prophets in the Qur'an and Muslim Literature* (Richmond: Curzon, 2002), 146 and *passim.*

112 Etan Kohlberg, "Some Shī'ī views of the Antediluvian World," *SI* 52 (1980): 41–66.

113 On the gradual emergence of the doctrine of infallibility of prophets, and its likely absorption into Sunnism from Shia ideas see Gerald Hawting, "The Development of the Doctrine of the Infallibility (*'iṣma*) of Prophets and the Interpretation of Qur'ān 8:67–69," *JSAI* 39 (2012): 141–63.

114 Abū Isḥāq al-Tha'labī, *'Arā'is al-majālis fī qiṣaṣ al-anbiyā'* (Cairo: Sharikat Maktabat wa Maṭba 'at Muṣṭafā al-Bābī al-Ḥalabī, 1954); trans. William Brinner, *'Arā'is al-majālis fī qiṣaṣ al-*

about three categories of prophets. Some are mentioned in the Bible but not the Qur'an, though they do occur in other Islamic literature, such as Isaiah, discussed below. Others occur in the Qur'an but not the Bible, such as Shu'ayb and Ṣāliḥ. The third group occur in both Bible and Qur'an, such as Adam, Abraham, Joseph, David, Solomon and Jesus. The stories are works of literary entertainment before they are theological. Biblical passages occur, or more often are paraphrased or suggested, but these are often overshadowed by extensive material from hadith and Jewish midrash. Three examples indicate the level of engagement with the Bible. These concern the Ten Commandments, Isaiah and Jesus.

Al-Tha'labī discusses the Biblical Decalogue or Ten Commandments (Exod 20:1–17), but, like other Muslim writers of this period, engages not with the actual text of Exodus, but with Qur'anic passages which recall it.[115] He has in view here Q17:22–39, the closest Qur'anic passage to the Exodus list of commandments. After giving a paraphrase of the Qur'anic passage, he states, "These are the words of the Ten Commandments. God gave them in their entirety to the Prophet Muḥammad in eighteen ayas".[116] So the Qur'an is seen as incorporating the Biblical text, thereby removing the need to consult Exodus directly.

Secondly, al-Tha'labī discusses Isaiah, drawing heavily on the account of al-Ṭabarī with its focus on the defeat of Sennacherib and the healing of King Hezekiah (discussed in section 4.3 above). The tale of Isaiah is presented as part of the fulfilment of Q17:4–8, with which the Isaiah section opens. The account finishes with Isaiah predicting the coming of one named Aḥmad, a reference to Muhammad, the passage including the use of Isaiah 42 already noted in the present work. So the account of Isaiah begins and ends with quotation from the Qur'an, and Isaiah is clearly serving Muslim purposes here, although much of his story concerns Israelite history. There are passages echoing text from the Biblical

---

anbiyā' or 'Lives of the Prophets' as recounted by Abū Isḥaq Aḥmad ibn Muḥammad ibn Ibrāhīm al-Tha'labī, SAL (Leiden: Brill, 2002). On this work see M.O. Klar, *Interpreting al-Tha'labī's Tales of the Prophets: Temptation, Responsibility and Loss* (Abingdon: Routledge, 2009).

115 Al-Tha'labī, *'Arā'is*, 204–08; Brinner, *Lives*, 337–38. In addition to Q17:22–39, Q 6:152–4 is also cited. On the Ten Commandments in Muslim writings, see Sebastian Günther, "*O People of the Scripture! Come to a Word Common to You and Us* (Q.3:64): The Ten Commandments and the Qur'an," *JQS* 9 (2007): 28–58; William Brinner, "An Islamic Decalogue," in William Brinner and Stephen Ricks (eds.) *Studies in Islamic and Judaic Traditions* vol I (Atlanta: Scholars Press, 1986): 67–84.

116 Günther, '*O People of the Scripture*', 33, who correctly translates "eighteen," cf. Brinner, *Lives*, 338, who translates as "ten."

Isaiah, such as Isa 5:1–2, and these are presented to enrich the narrative portrayal of the figure of Isaiah.[117]

Jesus receives extensive treatment from al-Thaʿlabī, much of it drawn from the Qur'an or a rich range of stories with no links to the New Testament. The closest passage to the canonical gospels is an account of the crucifixion and events leading up to it. This passage telescopes Biblical details such as the exhortation to the disciples to pray when they sleep and Jesus predicting a denial before the cock crows three times, all into a presentation of the Last Supper. This meal also features Jesus washing the disciples hands (not feet). The crucifixion is based on a standard Muslim substitution theory where the likeness of Jesus is cast upon Judas. Nevertheless, the account intriguingly adds that, "God caused Jesus to die for three hours, then He raised him up to Heaven."[118]

In sum, al-Thaʿlabī usually sidelines Biblical material in favour of other sources. The treatment of Jesus offers glimpses of a different approach, an approach seen more regularly in some examples of Renunciant literature.

4.7 Renunciant Literature

An interesting partial contrast to this tendency to sideline actual Biblical material in favour of other traditions can be seen in early renunciant literature. Renunciation (*zuhd*), which focussed on the renunciation of worldly pleasure and the pursuit of knowledge of God, was the seedbed from which grew Sufism, usually equated with Islamic mysticism.[119] This literature makes some use of Jesus in particular as the model ascetic. Two significant early works are the *Book of Renunciation* (*Kitāb al-Zuhd*) by Ibn al-Mubārak (d. 181/797), and *The Book of Renunciation* by Aḥmad ibn Ḥanbal (d. 241/855).[120] Tarif Khalidi has

117 See al-Thaʿlabī, *ʿArāʾis*, 329–33 on Isaiah; Brinner, *Lives*, 549–57.

118 See al-Thaʿlabī, *Arāʾis*, 400–01; Brinner, *Lives*, 670–71.

119 Differing views of whether Sufism can be equated with mysticism can be surveyed by reading both Christopher Melchert, "Origins and Early Sufism," in *The Cambridge Companion to Sufism*, ed. Lloyd Ridgeon (Cambridge: CUP, 2014), 3–23 (in favour) and Lloyd Ridgeon, "Mysticism in Medieval Sufism," in Ridgeon, ed., *The Cambridge Companion to Sufism*, 125–49 (against).

120 Ibn al-Mubārak, *Kitāb al-Zuhd* (Beirut: Mu'assassat al-Risālah, n.d.). Aḥmad ibn Ḥanbal, *Kitāb al-Zuhd*, 2 vols. (Alexandria: Dār al-Fikr al-Jāmiʿī, 1980); for the chapter on Jesus see 176–203. On Ibn al-Mubārak see Feryal Salem, *The Emergence of Early Sufi Piety and Sunni Scholasticism: Abdulllāh b. al-Mubārak and the Formation of Sunni Identity in the Second Islamic Century, IHC 125* (Leiden: Brill, 2017), esp. Chapter 4 (105–38) for his work on renunciation. On Aḥmad ibn Ḥanbal see Christopher Melchert, "Aḥmad ibn Ḥanbal's Book of Renunciation," *Der Islam* 85 (2011): 345–59.

gathered many Jesus sayings together in a chronological survey beginning with statements from these two works, and for convenience his survey can be used to give a flavour of their use of material clearly related to New Testament texts.[121] The means of transmission of such material is, as with many other early texts, unclear, and depended as much on oral transmission as written.

My reading of Khalidi's collection yields 45 sayings of Jesus with clear connections to Biblical material, out of 303 in total.[122] It is notable that these Biblically-influenced sayings are more prominent in earlier works, with echoes of the New Testament dwindling as the collection progresses chronologically. Of these 45 sayings, 21 come from the two authors named above, with four from Ibn al-Mubārak and seventeen from Aḥmad ibn Ḥanbal.[123] The first is an admonition not to reveal when you are fasting, from Ibn al-Mubārak's *Book of Renunciation*.[124] Amongst those from Aḥmad ibn Ḥanbal there is a reference to treasure in heaven,[125] and to doing good to those who harm you.[126] An adulterer (male, in this case) should be stoned only by someone who has not committed the same sin (cf. John 8).[127] Be kind to those who are not kind to you, and also turn the other cheek.[128] These statements clearly emphasise Jesus as ethical teacher and model, and are sometimes at pains deliberately to remove any indications of his divinity. A stark example of this is an account of Jesus being tempted by Satan with the offer of bread, and being invited to jump from his place and receive the protection of the angels. Jesus replies, "God ordered me not to put myself to the test, for I do not know whether he will save me or not."[129]

As noted, the directly Biblical content of such material declines as the centuries progress. This could be because many converts turned to Islam in the early stages of the faith and brought Biblical and related knowledge with them. This scenario presupposes clear distinctions between the identity of each faith. An al-

121 Tarif Khalidi, *The Muslim Jesus* (Cambridge MA: Harvard University Press, 2001).
122 Sometimes there is a distant echo of a Biblical text which is debatable as a meaningful connection to the Biblical material. Readers might therefore arrive at slightly different figures depending on what they deem a meaningful connection.
123 Salem, *Emergence*, 135, notes that Ibn al-Mubārak is more resistant than Aḥmad ibn Ḥanbal to drawing on traditions from Jews and Christians, for reasons she does not explain beyond saying that it was "an internal development based on how Muslims interpreted their traditions." I would explain it as the personal preference of the compilers.
124 Ibn al-Mubārak, *Zuhd*, 48–49; cf. Khalidi, *Jesus*, 53.
125 Aḥmad ibn Ḥanbal, *Zuhd*, 1:179; cf. Khalidi, *Jesus*, 71.
126 Aḥmad ibn Ḥanbal, *Zuhd*, 1:180; cf. Khalidi, *Jesus*, 73.
127 Aḥmad ibn Ḥanbal, *Zuhd*, 1:186–87; cf. Khalidi, *Jesus*, 82.
128 Aḥmad ibn Ḥanbal, *Zuhd*, 1:191; cf. Khalidi, *Jesus*, 88–89.
129 Ahmad ibn Ḥanbal, *Zuhd*, 1:179; cf. Khalidi, *Jesus*, 72. Cf. Matt 4:5–7.

ternative explanation is that this literature points to a time "when religious lines were less definite" and "Islam was still incompletely disengaged from other monotheisms and scriptures other than the Qur'an had considerable authority."[130] The wider issues of the emergence of the Islamic tradition cannot detain us here, but the issue of other scriptures having "authority" is interesting. This would bear out the appeals to previous scripture in hadiths (see Chapter 3), as well as other evidence already set forth in the present chapter. Perhaps "authority" should be softened to "presence" or "traction." That is, the idea of the previous scriptures had a certain value or weight as extra support for a view, as long as nothing was used which contradicted the Qur'an.

4.8 Disputation (*Kalām*)

Kalām is the term used for Muslim theological writing, and means "speech" or "disputation."[131] In the ninth century two authors stand out for their detailed engagement with the Bible, their works arising respectively from Egypt and 'Abbāsid Iraq.

The first of these authors is al-Qāsim ibn Ibrāhīm al-Rassī (d. 246/860), an adherent of a minority group within Shī'ism, the Zaydis.[132] He wrote the earliest *kalām* work devoted to the refutation of Christianity, *The Book of Refutation of the Christians (Kitāb Radd 'alā al-naṣārā).* Born in Medina, he also spent time in Egypt from 815–826, where more frequent encounters with Christians most likely prompted his refutation.

Al-Rassī's *Refutation* is unusual in including a reworked version of Matthew's Gospel, chapters 2–8. He clearly seems to have an Arabic text of Matthew in front of him, of unknown provenance, but makes deliberate changes to bring

130 Melchert, "Quotations of Extra-Qur'ānic Scripture," 105, 107.

131 See Alexander Treiger, "Origins of Kalām," in *The Oxford Handbook of Islamic Theology*, ed. Sabine Schmidtke (Oxford: OUP, 2016): 27–43.

132 The text of al-Rassī's *Refutation* is available in various editions. References in what follows are to the text of the *Kitāb Radd 'alā al-naṣārā* in Ignazio di Matteo, "Confutazione contro i Cristiani dello Zaydita al-Qāsim b. Ibrāhīm," *RSO* 9 (1921–23), 301–64; see also 'Abd al-Karīm Jadabān, *Majmū' kutub wa rasā'il li'l-Imām al-Qāsim ibn Ibrāhīm al-Rassī*, vol.1, (Ṣan'ā': Dār al-Ḥikmah al-Yamāniyah, 2001), 387–442. For background on al-Rassī see Wilferd Madelung, *Der Imam al-Qāsim ibn Ibrāhīm and die Glaubenslehre der Zaiditen*, ZGKIO 1 (Berlin: Walter de Gruyter, 1965). Much of Schaffner's recent doctoral thesis is devoted to al-Rassī's attitude to the Bible; see Schaffner, *The Bible Through a Qur'anic Filter*, 77–294. On the Zaydi Shia see Wilferd Madelung, "Zaydiyya", in: *EI2*, consulted online on 03 July 2019, http://dx.doi.org/10.1163/1573-3912_islam_COM_1385.

the text into line with Qur'anic norms. After outlining the key features of al-Rassī's work some consideration is given to why he produced this unusual text.

Al-Rassī makes explicit criticisms of Christian scriptural interpretations along with implicit criticisms of the text itself. These implicit criticisms emerge, as seen below, from his regular alterations to the text so as to bring it into greater conformity with Islamic beliefs. His criticisms of interpretation centre on familial language, particularly the terms "Father" and "Son". These should be interpreted metaphorically, he argues, and understood more broadly than Christian doctrine asserts. Al-Rassī emphasises that Jesus is sometimes called the son of someone other than God, while others are called God's children. Both of these undermine the Christian claim that Jesus' sonship is unique.[133]

Opinions differ on whether al-Rassī himself composed his reworked translation of Matthew's Gospel, chapters 2–8 (in rhymed prose) or whether he borrowed and adapted it from existing Christian models.[134] Implicit criticisms of the canonical text of Matthew are plentiful if judged by the number of alterations al-Rassī makes. He replaces or cuts all seventeen references to God as "Father", sometimes inserting "God" or "Lord".[135] Jesus is the "pure one" (*ṣafī*) rather than "Son."[136] Some passages are cut, their content suggesting that they are too close to affirming a unique divine status for Jesus. These include Jesus' baptism and his teaching on lust and divorce.[137] Most of Jesus' miracles are likewise omitted from al-Rassī's version of Matthew. It is clear that these changes are not due to carelessness or similar factors but follow a clear pattern of seeking to remove the divine element of Jesus' identity.

What can be said of al-Rassī's purpose and intended audience? One suggestion is that al-Rassī's Islamicised reworking of Matthew reflects an understanding of "previous scriptures as having been written for their [Muslims'] particular benefit."[138] This view presumes that al-Rassī considered the extant version of

133 Al-Rassī, *Radd*, 321.

134 Thomas, "Early Muslim anti-Christian Polemic,", 34, and Wilferd Madelung, "Al-Qāsim Ibn Ibrāhīm al-Rassī and Christian Theology," *Aram* 3 (1991), 43, attribute this section to al-Rassī. Samir Khalil Samir, 'Une adaptation arabe musulmane en prose rimée des Évangiles (IXe s.)' in *Graeco-Latina et Orientalia. Studia in honorem Angeli Urbani heptagenarii*, eds. Samir Khalil Samir and Juan Pedro Monferrer-Sala (Cordoba: CNERU-CEDRAC, 2013): 295–325, argues that rhymed prose translations of the Gospels can be found in various Christian works of this period, from which al-Rassī borrows.

135 Schaffner, *Disputational Literature*, 264.

136 Al-Rassī, *Radd*, 324–25. See also Accad, *Misinterpretation*, 207–210, on al-Rassī's alterations.

137 Schaffner, *Disputational Literature*, 268.

138 Thomas, "The Bible in Early Muslim anti-Christian Polemic," *ICMR* 7 (1996), 36.

Matthew as consisting mainly of genuine parts of the *Injīl* originally sent down to Jesus, and that al-Rassī's own alterations are designed to rectify the proportion of the text which has become corrupted. Whether al-Rassī regarded Matthew's gospel in this relatively positive way is a possibility that cannot be ruled out on current evidence. However, al-Rassī may have had the more pragmatic intent of using the Biblical text to reinforce the truth of Islam, without necessarily endorsing all the parts which he preserved unaltered. In other words, such parts were Islamically acceptable, but not necessarily fully endorsed as scripture by al-Rassī. To borrow a phrase given by Sidney Griffith in a different context, "religious accuracy, and hence scriptural accuracy... would have been measured by the Qur'ān's teachings, and not by Christian manuscripts in Greek, Syriac, or Arabic."[139]

What benefit al-Rassī saw in this part of his *Refutation* is unclear. Egypt would still have been a majority Christian population in late second/ early ninth century, so there would be a clear impulse for a Muslim leader to respond to or refute Christianity. Mikhail describes Islamization in part as "the interpretive strategies that facilitated the adoption and (re)framing of pre-Islamic ideals, views and monuments, synchronizing them with Islamic history, legends and beliefs."[140] Perhaps al-Rassī's reworking of Matthew can be included as an example of this synchronisation of pre-Islamic elements with Islam, though his ultimate motives remain obscure. However, his criticism of Christian character in the *Refutation* makes it unlikely that the work was designed primarily for Christian consumption.[141]

Al-Rassī's text seems to align with the approach found in the Sunni hadith collections discussed in Chapter 2, and which were being compiled in the course of his lifetime. They too usually use the Bible in support of Islam, rather than criticising it. Likewise hadiths sometimes also adjust the text to make it fit for purpose. But recalling the often general or paraphrased echoes of the Bible in hadith literature reminds us, by contrast, that al-Rassī's engagement with the Biblical text was much more detailed.

Like al-Rassī, Ibn Rabbān, discussed earlier in this chapter in relation to Proofs of Prophethood literature, wrote a *Refutation of the Christians* (*al-Radd*

---

139 Sidney Griffith, "The Gospel in Arabic," 140. He writes this in relation to the work of Ibn Isḥāq.

140 See Maged Mikhail, *From Byzantine to Islamic Egypt: Religion, Identity and Politics after the Arab Conquest* (London: I.B. Tauris, 2014), 107, and more generally for background to Egypt in this period.

141 Al-Rassī, *Radd*, 320–21.

'alā'l-naṣārā). This work shows the same tendency as al-Rassī to use the Bible but with minor alterations.[142] These alterations, as with al-Rassī, focus on eliminating any reference to divine status for Jesus, as is evident in his quotations from John 6:38–39 and Matt 3:17. Ibn Rabbān also flatly denies that John 5:31 can be correct, a verse in which Jesus says that if he testified about himself then his testimony would not be valid. "But such words about himself are not appropriate for Christ."[143] These brief examples show Ibn Rabbān pushing at the boundaries of his method of using rather than criticising the Biblical text. Occasionally he feels the need to step outside those boundaries, though without drawing attention to the fact that he is doing so, and without making explicit charges of corruption, even where his words imply it.[144]

Moving from works of refutation to the treatment of Christianity in the earliest systematic theological treatises by Muslims, such treatises show limited engagement with the Bible.[145] *The Book of Divine Unity* (*Kitāb al-Tawḥīd*) by al-Māturīdī (d.333/944), from Samarqand in Central Asia, makes only modest use of the Bible, since this and similar treatises are more concerned with theological concepts. But the Bible is used in refuting claims to the unique status of Jesus based on his miracles. Al-Māturīdī likens Jesus' miracles to those of Ezekiel, Moses, Elisha and Elijah.[146]

Al-Bāqillānī (d.403/1013), active in Shiraz and Baghdad, had practical as well as literary debate with Christians. He was sent to Constantinople in 371/981 to negotiate over border fortresses with the Byzantine Emperor Basil II, where he debated Christian theologians. Like al-Māturīdī, al-Bāqillānī's *Introduction* (*Kitāb al-Tamhīd*) makes only limited use of the Bible. He deploys it to

---

142 Ebied and Thomas, eds., *Polemical Works*, 62–169, provides the Arabic text with parallel English translation.

143 Ebied and Thomas, *Polemical Works*, 84 (Arabic), 85 (English).

144 Another convert from Christianity, al-Ḥasan ibn Ayyūb (third/tenth century, exact dates unknown) drew on Ibn Rabbān's work amongst others in order to refute Christianity, with a similar approach to the Bible. See David Thomas, "Al-Ḥasan ibn Ayyūb," in: *CMR*, 2:510–513, and Clint Hackenburg, *Voices of the Converted: Christian Apostate Literature in Medieval Islam* (Unpublished Ph.D thesis, Ohio State University, 2015), 231–266 on al-Ḥasan ibn Ayyūb's treatment of the Bible.

145 See David Thomas, *Christian Doctrines in Islamic Theology*, HCMR 10 (Leiden: Brill, 2008). This work provides parallel-text translations of the sections on Christianity by its chosen authors, who include al-Māturīdī and also 'Abd al-Jabbār, discussed in Chapter 5, below.

146 Thomas, *Christian Doctrines*, 102–05. See also David Thomas, "The Miracles of Jesus in Early Islamic Polemic," *JSS* 39 (1994): 221–43, who discusses how the tradition of comparing miracles developed over time. On al-Māturīdī more broadly, see Ulrich Rudolph, *Al-Māturīdī and the Development of Sunnī Theology in Samarqand*, IHC 100 (Leiden: Brill, 2012).

compare the miracles and other actions of Jesus with those of other prophets. In so doing he refers to the canonical text, while also paraphrasing or occasionally inventing statements he claims to be Biblical.[147]

This survey of *kalām* literature demonstrates a clear focus on the truth of Islam, with the status of Jesus as a special pre-occupation. The Bible serves, sometimes in adapted form, to reinforce Muslim beliefs, sometimes requiring re-interpretation, or even that its text be subtly altered.

4.9 Law

Legal discussions of actual situations provide the starting point for our exploration of legal works. Separate works of legal theory (*uṣūl al-fiqh*) were produced to provide the underpinnings and justifications for discussions of situations already occurring. However early legal treatises sometimes included introductions or conclusions dealing with matters of theory, with the discipline of *uṣūl al-fiqh* then developing lengthy works in its own right.[148]

Legal discussion of the previous scriptures could lead down unexpected paths. One issue was the recitation of the previous scriptures in ritual prayer. The Māliki jurist Shihāb al-dīn al-Qarāfī (d. 684/1285) narrates an earlier report prohibiting the recitation of the previous scriptures in ritual prayer: "Whoever prays (reciting) the Tawrāh or Injīl or Zabūr, whether he is good at (reciting) the Qur'ān or not, his prayer is invalidated".[149] The same question about using the *Tawrāt* or *Injīl* in ritual prayer angers Aḥmad b. Ḥanbal (d. 241/855), who answers negatively.[150] Why is this apparently unlikely situation addressed at all? Not all legal statements are proof that the practice discussed actually occurred, but some evidence for early instances of Muslims praying in churches is available. It is worth pausing to consider the possible social situations behind

147 Thomas, *Christian Doctrines*, 190–201.

148 See Ahmed El Shamsy, "Bridging the Gap: Two Early Texts of Islamic Legal Theory," *JAOS* 137 (2013), 506.

149 Shihāb al-dīn al-Qarāfī, *Al-Dhakhīra* (*The Stored Treasure*), ed. M. Būkhubzah, 14 vols., (Beirut: Dār al-Gharb al-islāmī, 1994), II:187, reported from the Mālikī Ashhab (d. 203/818). See Christopher Melchert, "Whether to Keep Unbelievers Out of Sacred Zones: a Survey of Medieval Islamic Law," *JSAI* 40 (2013), 177–78. Al-Qarāfī will feature in volume 2 of this study.

150 See Aḥmad ibn Hanbal, *Masā'il al-imām Aḥmad ibn Hanbal, riwāyat Isḥāq ibn Ibrāhīm ibn Hānī al-Nīsābūrī* (*The Questions of Aḥmad ibn Hanbal according to the narration of Isḥāq ibn Ibrāhīm ibn Hānī al-Nīsābūrī*) (Al-Manṣūrah: Dār al-Ta'sīl, Dār al-Mawaddah, 2008), 61, no. 256. For a positive view of the reliability of this work as a reflection of what Aḥmad ibn Hanbal said see Christopher Melchert, *Ahmad ibn Hanbal*, MMW (Oxford: Oneworld, 2006), 69–70.

these and other discussions.[151] It used to be thought that in the immediate aftermath of the conquests, churches were partitioned, with a section being used for Muslim prayer. But it seems more likely that the prevalent pattern was initially to build a mosque, probably on a small scale, somewhere in the compound of a church complex, or adjoining the church.[152] Worship would therefore occur close by, but not in the same building. Yet the physical separation of worship spaces was not necessarily reflected in a clear separation of beliefs. While religious leaders from both faiths attempted to draw clear demarcation lines between those faiths, the enormous non-Muslim majority surrounding small early Muslim communities made some mutual absorption of practices and influences inevitable.[153] Of course, many early Muslims would have previously been adherents of Judaism or Christianity, and may not have sharply distinguished their practices and beliefs, even while transferring their community allegiance to Islam. This is all the more likely given the Qur'an's affirmations of the *Tawrāt* and *Injīl*. So the brief references to prayer using previous scripture probably afford a glimpse of real situations where confessional boundaries were not maintained in the way jurists and others may have desired.

In a discussion on making Jews, Christians or Zoroastrians swear an oath, the question is raised as to whether a Christian may swear "by God who revealed the *Injīl* to Jesus". The answer is negative; they should swear simply by God, and the same applies to the Jew regarding the *Tawrāt*. A certain Ka'b b. Siwār used to swear by God and place the *Injīl* on his head at the altar, but this is also dismissed.[154]

It is important not to overstate the place of previous scriptures in the earliest works of Islamic law. References, where found, can be fleeting, a glimpse of previous scripture amidst lengthy discussion of other matters. Al-Shāfi'ī (d. 204/820) was a hugely influential figure in the formation of Islamic law. In *The Exemplar* (*Kitāb al-Umm*), a long work of positive law, he criticizes his interlocutor at one point for consulting the People of the Book. Only the Qur'an should be consulted, since the People of the Book alter their scripture. He quotes Q2:79 twice and

151 See in relation to this, but without reference to the use of the previous scriptures, Suliman Bashear, "Qibla Musharriqa and Early Muslim Prayer in Churches," *MW* 81 (1991): 267–82.

152 See Mattia Giudetti, *In the Shadow of the Church: the Building of Mosques in Early Medieval Syria*, AAIW 8 (Leiden: Brill, 2016).

153 See Tannous, *Medieval Middle East*, passim.

154 Saḥnūn, *Al-Mudawwana al-Kubrā li Imam Mālik b. Anās*, vol.4, (Beirut: Dār al-kutub al-'ilmiyya, 1994), 56–57. *Al-Mudawwana* (*The Code*) by Saḥnūn (d.240/ 855) collects legal opinions of the early jurist Mālik b. Anās (d.179/795), after whom the Māliki school of jurisprudence is named.

treats the references there to Jews altering the scripture as a general statement forbidding consulting the People of the Book of his own day.[155]

Clear indications of belief in textual corruption of the Bible sometimes occur. A question is recorded as being put to a judge and a legal scholar in the fourth/ninth century regarding how it was possible for Jews and Christians to alter their scriptures whereas God preserved the Qur'an. The reply cites Q15:9, which states that, "Surely We have sent down the Reminder, and surely We are indeed its Watchers." This, it is argued, proves that God himself preserves the Qur'an, whereas the previous scriptures were entrusted to the Jews and Christians (the implication being that they failed in their responsibility to preserve them).[156]

The requirement to believe in God's books, stated in Q2:285, occurs in a question put to the North African jurist al-Qābisī (d. 403/1012). He was asked for a fatwa or legal ruling about whether a Muslim who had cursed the Torah in a dispute with a Jew was a blasphemer.[157] The case was disputed as the accused claimed he had cursed "The Torah of the Jews," which al-Qābisī regarded as a distorted version, not God's original. The distorted version would not deserve the same protection from cursing as the original, sent down from God. This shows both the respect for a theoretical original Tawrāt, and the belief that it had subsequently been textually corrupted.[158]

155 Al-Shāfiʿī, *Kitāb al-umm*, 7 volumes in 4, vol. 6 (Bulāq: Al-Maṭbaʿat al-kubrā al-amīriyya, 1903–08), 129–30. As noted in the discussion of abrogation in Chapter 2, however, the *Tawrāt* became an important reference point for discussion of the penalty of stoning for adultery, the standard Muslim penalty but not found in the Qur'an.

156 Al-Bunnāhī (also al-Nubāhī), *al-Marqaba al-ʿulyā fī man yastaḥiqq al-qaḍāʾ waʾl-futya* (Beirut: Dār al-Kutub al-ʿIlmiyyah, 1995), 52. The legal scholar asked about the Christian scripture was recorded as Ibn Waḍḍāḥ al-Qurṭubī (d.900), on whom see Maribel Fierro, "Ibn Waḍḍāḥ," in *CMR*, 1:834–39, who cites this passage from a different edition. Though al-Bunnāhī died after 798/1389–90, his recording of the questions as dating from the late ninth century CE is of interest, as there seems little reason for this to be fabricated.

157 See Camilla Adang, "A Fourth/Tenth Century Tunisian Muftī on the Sanctity of the Torah of Moses," in *The Intertwined Worlds of Islam: Essays in Memory of Hava Lazarus–Yafeh*, eds. Nahem Ilan et al (Jerusalem: Ben Zvi Institute for the Study of Jewish Communities in the East, 2002): vii–xxxiv. The fatwas indicating al-Qābisī's view are found in Aḥmad al-Wansharīsī (d.915/1508), *Al-Miʿyār al-muʿrib waʾl-jāmiʿ al-mughrib ʿan fatāwī ʿulamāʾ ifrīqiyya waʾl-andalus waʾl-maghrib* (*The Clear Measure and Marvellous Collection of Fatwas of Scholars from North Africa, al-Andalus and the Maghreb*), vol.2, (Beirut: Dār al-Maghrib al-Islāmī, 1981–1983), 362–63 and 525–28.

158 Elsewhere al-Qābisī urged against Muslims being influenced by previous scriptures. This is evident in his opposition to Christians and Jews teaching their books to Muslim children, an opinion implying that this practice occurred in mixed classrooms. The reason given for this prohibition is that Jews and Christians are not trustworthy (*maʾmūn*) regarding their books. This

A practical issue arose over touching the Bible when ritually impure. One view was that the Bible should not be touched by someone in a state of major ritual impurity (*junub*), after sexual intercourse. This is because touching the Qur'an in a state of impurity is forbidden, and the same prohibition might be extended to Biblical scriptures.[159] This implies a high view of the previous scriptures. An opposing view is that the prohibition does not apply since the Bible has been corrupted, and no-one is therefore handling the original, pure scripture. The Shāfiʿī jurist al-Māwardī (d.450/1058) records both views without stating his preference.[160] The possible reasons he gives for permitting the impure person (*muḥdath*) to touch the *Tawrāt* and *Injīl* are that these books are either abrogated (*mansūkha*) or altered (*mubaddila*). The second of these is another occurrence of the belief in textual corruption. It cannot be a reference to errors in interpretation since these would not be relevant to the issue of how much respect should be given to physical copies of the scriptures.

Turning from positive law to works of legal theory, our discussion focusses on Sunni writings. This is because the earliest Shia works of *uṣūl al-fiqh*, dating from the end of the period in view, do not discuss the role of previous scriptures.[161] Works of *uṣūl al-fiqh* were concerned with identifying the correct sources of Islamic law and how they should be used to derive the law. "The law of those who preceded us" (*sharʿ man qablanā)* was one of a number of possible secondary sources of law, and referred to the laws and scriptures of Jews and Christians in particular.[162]

Al-Shāfiʿī (d. 204/820) makes little mention of previous scriptures in his pivotal theoretical work, *The Epistle* (*al-Risāla*) nor does he discuss the issues

could refer either to textual corruption, or perhaps more likely, to unreliable or deliberately deceitful acts of interpretation. See al-Qābisī, *The Detailed Epistle* (*Al-Risāla al-mufaṣṣala*) in Aḥmad al-Ahwānī, *al-Taʿlīm fi raʾy al-Qābisī* (*Teaching According to al-Qābisī*) (Cairo: Dār al-Kutub al-ʿArabīya, 1945), 280, and discussed in Speight, "Muslim Attitudes toward Christians", 185.

159 Avoiding touching the Qur'an in a state of impurity is a ruling elaborated from Q56:79, "No one touches it but the purified."

160 Al-Māwardī, *al-Ḥāwī al-kabīr* (*The Great Compendium*), vol. 1 (Beirut: Dār al-Fikr, 1994), 176.

161 The earliest Shia sources are Sharīf al-Murtaḍā (d. 436/1044), *Al-Dharīʿah ilā uṣūl al-sharīʿa* (*The Means to the Principles of the Law*), 2 vols., (Tehran: Dānishgāh–I Tihran), 1967–70, and Muḥammad ibn Ḥasan al-Ṭūsī (d. 460/1067), *ʿUddat al-uṣūl* (*Equipment for the Principles*) (Qom: Chapkhaneh Setarah, 1417/1997).

162 The reference to law or ʿ*shar* ʿ' can be taken as closely related to scripture, since scriptural revelation is the Islamic understanding of how divine will is revealed. For an overview of attitudes to *sharʿ man qablanā* see Mohammed Hashim Kamali, *Principles of Islamic Jurisprudence*, 3rd edition (Cambridge: Islamic Texts Society, 2003), 306–12.

around "The law of those who preceded us."[163] He does, however, comment on the question of corruption. He refers to the People of the Book "who exchanged His rulings for others." *Aḥkām* is a term referring to legal rulings, rather than scriptural statements themselves. *Baddalū* ("exchanged") is, however, a strong term for alteration or corruption, so something is clearly being textually altered. Al-Shāfiʿī was clearly not seeking an irenic position, since he notes elsewhere of Jews and Christians "How embroiled in lies they are!", a comment likely to bear on his view of Jewish and Christian handling of their scriptures, amongst other matters.[164]

Perhaps the earliest explicit discussion of the role of previous laws is found in a short work entitled *The Book of Parts and Properties* (*Kitāb al-aqsām wa'l-khiṣāl*) by Abū Bakr al-Khaffāf (fl. Early 4th/10th century). Al-Khaffāf states, "Know that the laws of the prophets who were before us are binding on us except in two cases. One is when it is abrogated by our law. The other is when our law mentions it. Incumbent on us is adherence to our law even if it comes earlier in their laws".[165] This indicates that the reason to follow a previous law was if it is affirmed by Islamic law, not because it is independently authoritative for Muslims. There is a theoretically positive attitude in evidence here, but dependent on Islamic validation.

The positive note struck by al-Khaffāf is continued in the first extensive discussion in legal theory of the issue of previous scriptures and laws. The Ḥanafī jurist Abū Bakr al-Jaṣṣāṣ (d. 370/981), in his work *Chapters on Principles* (*Al-Fuṣūl fī uṣūl*) asserts that scriptures and laws (he uses the term "sharīʿa", which I take to cover both scriptures and laws in this context) from previous times are binding on Muslims unless they are abrogated. But they are binding because they become a law for Muhammad. One follows them because of the Qur'an, not because the earlier prophets were sent for the Muslim community. So here again there is a measure of affirmation alongside clear grounds for maintaining the

163 Opinions differ on the relationship of the work of al-Shāfiʿī to later *uṣūl al-fiqh*. For the pivotal role of al-Shafiʿī see Ahmad El Shamsy *The Canonization of Islamic Law: a Social and Intellectual History* (New York: CUP, 2013).; but cf. Joseph Lowry Early *Islamic Legal Theory* (Leiden: Brill, 2007), 359–68. See also David Vishanoff, *The Formation of Islamic Hermeneutics: How Sunni Legal Theorists Imagined a Revealed Law*, AOS 93 (New Haven,CT.: American Oriental Society, 2011).

164 Al-Shafiʿī, *The Epistle on Legal Theory*, ed and translated Joseph Lowry (New York: New York University Press, 2013), 3.

165 The complete Arabic text of *The Book of Parts and Properties* is found in El Shamsy, "Bridging the Gap", 521–36. For this quotation see 530.

centrality of Islamic revelation.[166] Al-Jaṣṣāṣ quotes a number of Qur'anic verses in the course of his discussion, notably verses stating that God revealed true religion to previous prophets, including Noah (Q42:13) and Abraham (Q16:123). Al-Jaṣṣāṣ also quotes verses from Sura 5 (al-Mā'ida) on the *Tawrāt* and *Injīl* being guidance and light, and containing the judgment (*ḥukm*) of God (Q5:43–47). As for the question of textual corruption, al-Jaṣṣāṣ refers to this charge in passing without focussing on it.[167]

Abū Zayd al-Dabūsī (d. 430/1039) was another important Ḥanafī writer of legal theory, and was influenced by al-Jaṣṣāṣ. His name derives from his birthplace of Dabūsiya, between Bukhara and Samarqand in present-day Uzbekistan. His *The Assessment of Proofs in the Principles of Jurisprudence* (*Taqwīm al-adilla fī uṣūl al-fiqh*) became itself an influential work of Ḥanafī legal theory.[168] Al-Dabūsī includes a section on the *shar' man qablana*, in which he takes a positive view of the potential validity of the previous scriptures. He outlines three positions, affirming the third. The first is that the previous scriptures endure for the prophet to whom they are sent, while secondly they are annulled when a subsequent prophet is sent by God. Thirdly, the position he affirms, the previous sharī'a not only endures, but provides a sharī'a for any prophet sent subsequently. Like al-Jaṣṣāṣ, al-Dabūsī appeals for support to a number of Qur'anic verses, including Q3:95 "follow the creed of Abraham the Ḥanīf" and Q5:43, referring to "the Torah, containing the judgment of God." He concludes his discussion with Q5:48, noted above as a frequent reference point.[169]

However, al-Dabūsī and the other jurists discussed here were not advocating regular appeal to the previous scriptures which were extant in their day. The discussion is theoretical, establishing a position of principle rather than of practice, and appealing to the idea of original or uncorrupted scriptures which the Qur'an states that God sent down. Biblical laws may have influenced Muslim discussion, but were not readily cited as an authoritative source. As noted in our earlier discussion of hadith literature, a common position was that the previous scriptures

---

166 Abū Bakr al-Jaṣṣāṣ, *Al-Fuṣūl fī uṣūl*, vol. 3, (Kuwait: Dawlat al-Kuwayt, Wizārat al-awqāf wa'l-shu'ūn al-islāmiyah, al-idārah al-'āmmah li'l-iftā' wa'l-buḥūth al-shar'īyah, 1994), 22–23.
167 Al-Jaṣṣāṣ, *Fuṣūl*, 3:22.
168 Abū Zayd al-Dabūsī, *Taqwīm al-adilla fi uṣūl al-fiqh* (Beirut: Dār al-kutub al-'ilmiyya, 2001). Spelling of his name can involve the letter 'b' in single or double form. See Brannon Wheeler, "Al-Dabūsī", in: *EI3*, consulted online on 03 July 2019, http://dx.doi.org/10.1163/1573-3912_ei3_COM_25771; Murteza Bedir, *The Early Development of Ḥanafī* uṣūl al-fiqh (Unpublished Ph.D. thesis, University of Manchester, 1999), 26–30; Murteza Bedir, "Revelation and Reason: Abū Zayd al-Dabbūsī on Rational Proofs," in *IS* 43 (2004): 227–245.
169 See the discussion in al-Dabūsī, *Taqwīm*, 253–55.

could be searched for narratives about past individuals or other historical information, but not for legal rulings. In fact, in subsequent centuries even the theoretically positive position outlined here would become subject to challenge.

4.10 Philosophers

Abū'l-Ḥasan al-'Āmirī (d.381/992), from the region of Khurasan (in present-day north-eastern Iran), was a noted philosopher who wrote on a variety of topics.[170] His *Exposition on the Merits of Islam* (*Al-I'lām bi manāqib al-Islām*) compares Islam with Judaism, Christianity and other faiths (the faiths listed in Q22:17) in order to show the superiority of Islam.[171] In his *Exposition* al-'Āmirī demonstrates the dual attitude to the Bible often found in Muslim writers, both using but also criticising it.

In keeping with many other writers previously discussed, al-'Āmirī's use of the Bible overshadows his criticism of it. He regards the testimony to Muhammad in the previous scriptures as one of the decisive proofs (*burhān*) about him.[172] First he justifies why these references are indirect, saying that they are designed to distinguish the wise (who discern Muhammad in them) from the foolish, and the diligent from the negligent.[173] Al-'Āmirī then proceeds to quote various verses familiar to those versed in Biblical proofs of Muhammad, including Deuteronomy 18 about a prophet like Moses, and Deuteronomy 33:2 about three prophets arising from Mount Sinai, Mount Seir and Mount Paran.[174] His references are sometimes shortened or adapted, but not for any apparent theological reason. These verses are transmitted in Arabic, from Syriac, states al-'Āmirī, presumably a reference to his immediate sources rather than a definitive statement about the original scriptural languages. A possible source may be Ibn Rabbān's *Book of Religion and Empire*.[175]

---

170 Al-'Āmirī came to be overshadowed in philosophy by the towering figure of Ibn Sīnā, on whom more below.

171 Abū al-Ḥasan al-'Āmirī, *Al-I'lām bi Manāqib al-Islām* (Cairo: Dār al-Kātib al-'Arabī, 1967). For discussion of this work see Paul Heck, "The Crisis of Knowledge in Islam (I): the Case of al-'Āmirī," *Philosophy East and West* 56 (2006): 106–35, esp. 117–123.

172 al-'Āmirī, *Al-I'lām*, 201.

173 Al-'Āmirī, *Al-I'lām*, 202. For the following discussion see 202–08.

174 Al-'Āmirī, *Al-I'lām*, 203.

175 See Ebied and Thomas, *Polemical Works*, 195, for discussion of the possible link to Ibn Rabbān. See the discussion of Proofs of Prophethood literature earlier in the present chapter for more on these verses.

Al-ʿĀmirī goes on to cite John 14:26, referring to the Paraclete. In explaining why Jesus' reference to the spirit of truth who will teach all things must refer to Muhammad, he cites a number of Qur'anic references to the spirit (*rūḥ*).[176] In particular, he contends that the spirit predicted in the gospel is speaking (*nuṭuqiyya*) and holy (*qudusiyya*).

As for his criticisms of the Bible, al-ʿĀmirī makes some general comments about scriptures of all previous faiths. He comments that non-Qur'anic scriptures lack the full authority of Qur'anic commands. Instead, they are similar to "the speech of a wise man, proclaiming his wisdom through his statements and his explanation, and connecting some of those utterances to his lord".[177] On the New Testament gospels, he states that they are subject to false interpretations, and that "they include reports from the Messiah, and what his circumstances entailed for him from his birth to the end of his days, linked to mention of what they heard from his sermons and parables and his praise for God".[178] The verb "include" may indicate a certain caution in endorsing the gospels, though it is hard to be certain of this. Al-ʿĀmirī states that the Book of Acts of the Apostles ("*Barākasīs*," from the Greek name for Acts, *Práxeis*) is written by "Simon the Pure" (rather than by Luke, to whom it is traditionally ascribed). It only includes reports from Jesus' disciples, rather than Jesus himself, an implicit criticism of its unreliability.[179] Moving from implication to direct criticism, al-ʿĀmirī states that Paul's Epistles contain manifest differences from the gospels.[180] So textual corruption of parts of the New Testament is clearly in view. While criticism of the gospels concerns how they are interpreted, the Pauline Epistles contradict them at points.[181]

Ibn Sīnā (d. 428/1037), known in the West as Avicenna, was the foremost philosopher in the Islamic tradition.[182] He makes a single but memorable comment on the Hebrew Bible. Ibn Sīnā regarded scriptural revelation as God's way of communicating truths via imagery to the masses who needed such help, truths which philosophers could discern directly by understanding the reality behind

---

176 Q40:15, 4:171, 2:87, 253, 42:52, 16:102; see Al-ʿĀmirī, *Al-Iʿlām*, 206.

177 Al-ʿĀmirī, *Al-Iʿlām*, 134.

178 Al-ʿĀmirī, *Al-Iʿlām*, 202, 207.

179 Al-ʿĀmirī, *Al-Iʿlām*, 134.

180 Al-ʿĀmirī, *Al-Iʿlām*, 208. This criticism of Paul is elaborated in the work of ʿAbd al-Jabbār, discussed in the next chapter.

181 My understanding of al-ʿĀmirī therefore departs from that of Accad, *Misinterpretation*, 238, who considers that al-ʿĀmirī does not believe there to be any textual corruption of the New Testament.

182 See amongst many studies Dimitri Gutas, *Avicenna and the Aristotelian Tradition*, 2nd edition (Leiden: Brill, 2014).

the image.[183] In seeking to argue that the Qur'an is therefore composed of images which need interpreting (by philosophers) in order to be understood properly, he appeals to the case of the Hebrew Bible to prove his point. He states that while it is clear that the Hebrew scripture is "pure anthropomorphism from beginning to end", that is, describing God in overly human terms, this aspect of the Hebrew Bible cannot be explained by claiming that such images are a result of corruption. "One cannot say that that Book is entirely corrupted (*muḥarraf*), for how can this be the case with a book disseminated through innumerable peoples living in distant lands, with so different ambitions – like Jews and Christians with all their mutual antagonisms?"[184]

The impossibility of enemies conspiring together across vast distances in order to corrupt scripture is an argument previously set out by Christians. But while the idea is not original to Ibn Sīnā, he seems to be the first Muslim to express it, and evidence of Muslim ideas found in non-Muslim sources more generally now requires attention.

4.11 Views from Non-Muslim Sources

Jewish and Christian sources concentrate on responses to the charge of textual corruption, but in diverse ways. While such sources raise the question of whether they fairly represent Muslim views, they also have the advantage of responding to climates of thought which might otherwise remain inaccessible to the modern reader.

183 See Martin Whittingham, *Al-Ghazālī and the Qur'an: One Book Many Meanings* (London: Routledge, 2007), 104–08, on this idea and an illustration from the Light Verse, Q24:35. For more on Ibn Sīnā's approach to the Qur'an, see Daniel De Smet and Meryem Sebti, "Avicenna's Philosophical Approach to the Qur'an in the Light of his '*Tafsīr Sūrat al-Ikhlāṣ*'," *JQS* 11 (2009): 134–48.

184 Ibn Sīnā, *Al-Risāla al-Aḍḥawiyya fi'l-Ma'ād* (literally, *The Immolation Epistle on the Destination*) (Beirut: al-Mu'assasat al-Jāmi'īyyat al-Dirāsāt wa'l-Nashr wa'l-Tawzī', 1984), 102; translation adapted from Fazlur Rahman, *Prophecy in Islam* (London: George Allen and Unwin, 1958), 44. The title refers to an epistle on the destination of the soul, written on the occasion of the Feast of Immolation (*'īd al-aḍḥā*).

4.11.1 Jewish Responses

One response to Muslim criticism of the validity or reliability of the Hebrew Scriptures might be the rise of Karaite Judaism. This movement opposed Rabbanite Judaism by undoing the Rabbanite dual formulation of a written and an oral Torah (the Mishnah and Talmud). Karaism stressed the primacy of the written Torah, and it has been argued that this development, occurring in Arab areas, is a reaction to the Muslim emphasis on the primacy of written scripture. So rather than a rebuttal of specific Muslim charges or arguments over verses, Karaism can be seen as a reshaping of Jewish tradition in response to Muslim views.[185]

More explicit Jewish responses to Islamic challenges are rare in the early centuries. However, the polemical environment of interreligious debates in tenth century Baghdad gave rise to some Jewish works which tackled central issues, such as the alleged abrogation of the Hebrew Bible, and the inimitability of the Qur'an.[186]

4.11.2 Christian Responses

In contrast to the relative paucity of early Jewish responses to Muslim views of the Bible, there were more direct Christian ripostes to the charge of textual corruption. This indicates that it was, at least in the perception of these Christian writers, a standard Muslim assumption. There seems no reason to doubt that this perception was based on Muslim views, even if we lack extensive records of the ways the charge was made. Many though not all Christian texts mention the issue of biblical corruption.[187] The *Disputation of the Monk of Bēt Ḥālē and an*

---

185 Meira Polliack, "Deconstructing the Dual Torah. A Jewish Response to the Muslim Model of Scripture," in *Interpreting Scriptures in Judaism, Christianity and Islam: Overlapping Enquiries*, eds. Mordechai Cohen and Adele Berlin (Cambridge: CUP, 2016): 113–29; Polliack, "The Karaite Inversion of 'Written' and 'Oral' Torah in Relation to Islamic Arch-models of Qur'an and Hadith," *JSQ* 22 (2015): 243–302.

186 David Sklare, "Responses to Islamic Polemics by Jewish Mutakallimūn in the Tenth Century," in *The Majlis. Interreligious Encounters in Medieval Islam*, eds. Hava Lazarus-Yafeh, Mark Cohen, Sasson Somekh, Sidney Griffith (Wiesbaden: Harrassowitz, 1999): 137–61. Sklare examines works by two authors, the Rabbanite Samuel ben Ḥofni and the Karaite Yūsuf al-Baṣīr.

187 I omit from the following discussion the alleged correspondence of figures using the names Leo III and 'Umar II. Recent analysis of the origins of this material has generated many different viewpoints on it, and it adds no new detail to the overall point that Christian texts regularly refuted the charge of textual corruption. See Cecilia Palombo, "The 'correspondence' of Leo III and

Arab Notable, one of the very earliest such texts, perhaps dating from the 720's, does not mention the issue.[188] However, the following chronological survey shows how authors routinely engage with the charge of textual *taḥrīf.*

John of Damascus (d.c.750) was a Melkite/ Byzantine theologian who served as a financial official for the Umayyad dynasty in Damascus. Retreating to the Palestinian monastery of Mar Saba, he wrote treatises in Greek. He provides the first extended discussion of Islam in his *On Heresies* (*De Haerisibus*), the second part of his three-part work *The Fount of Knowledge* (*Pēgē Gnoseōs*). In the context of discussing the divinity of Christ, he writes of Muslims, "And some of them say that we added such things, having allegorized the prophets. But others say that the Jews, hating us, deceived us by writing things as though from the prophets so that we might get led astray."[189]

The charge of textual corruption is also refuted in the Dialogue of Mar Timothy (d.823), Patriarch of the Church of the East, with the Caliph al-Mahdī. This dialogue, dating from c.782 and conducted in Arabic, is preserved by Timothy in his Syriac account given in a letter he wrote to a priest of his church, and extant along with many others of his letters.[190] This work became a famous exemplar of Christian-Muslim exchange.

Theodore bar Koni mentions corruption in the 790's in his Syriac *Book of Commentaries*, otherwise known as the *Scholion* (*Eskolyon*). In his stylised exchange between a Muslim and a Christian, the Muslim states of the New Testament, "I do not adhere to all of it, because there are many things in it that are

'Umar II: traces of an Early Christian Arabic Apologetic Work," *Millennium* 12 (2015): 231–64, who mentions all the leading views on this material.

188 See Sidney Griffith, "Disputing with Islam in Syriac: the Case of the Monk of Bêt Ḥālê and a Muslim Emir," *Hugoye* 3 (2000): 29–54, who gives an account of this as yet unpublished text. For background on Christian writings of this period, see, among others, Sidney Griffith, *The Church in the Shadow of the Mosque* (Princeton: PUP, 2008), and his many other writings listed therein. A brief debate, which may be seventh century, touches on questions of scripture, but the dating is disputed. See Barbara Roggema, "The Debate Between Patriarch John and an Emir of the Mhaggrāyē: a Reconsideration of the Earliest Christian-Muslim Debate," in *Christians and Muslims in Dialogue in the Islamic Orient of the Middle Ages*, ed. Martin Tamcke (Beirut: Orient Institut, 2007): 21–39.

189 For the Greek text and this English translation of the section on Islam from *The Fount of Knowledge* see Peter Schadler, *John of Damascus and Islam: Christian Heresiology and the Intellectual Background to Earliest Christian-Muslim Relations*, HCMR 34 (Leiden: Brill, 2017), 224–25; see also Daniel Sahas, *John of Damascus on Islam* (Leiden: Brill, 1972), 136–37.

190 For the Syriac text and German translation see Timothy I and Martin Heimgartner, *Timotheos I*, sections 10.1–10.25. For an English translation see N.A. Newman, *Dialogue*, 212–15.

falsified. He (i.e. Christ) did not bring them. Others have introduced and intermingled them for the purpose of deception."[191]

The *Apology* of al-Kindī is an anonymous, long and influential work (the author's name is thought to be a pseudonym), dating from around the beginning of the ninth century CE. The *Apology* presents itself as two epistles, by a Muslim and a Christian, each inviting the other to convert, but is thought to be entirely written by a Christian.[192] Al-Kindī does not devote lengthy discussion to the topic of corruption, but towards the end of his work makes a number of clear statements refuting any such charge. He advances the argument, found in other Christian writings and later by the Muslim philosopher Ibn Sīnā, as noted above, that it would be inconceivable for Jews, who are hostile to the truth about Christ, to collaborate with Christians on corrupting the Biblical text.[193]

There is also brief reference to corruption in the work of Theodore Abū Qurrah (d.820), a Melkite follower of John of Damascus and the first Christian theologian to write in Arabic.[194] However, it is with non-Melkite theologians that we find more extensive engagement with the charge of corruption.

Ḥabīb ibn Khidma Abū Rā'iṭa (d.c. 835) was probably an educated lay Jacobite Christian writer from Takrit in modern Iraq.[195] It is possible that he was in

191 Addai Scher, ed., *Theodorus bar Koni. Liber Scholiorum*, vol. 2 (Paris: E Typographeo Reipublicae, 1910–12), 235; French translation, Théodore bar Koni, *Livre Des Scolies li: Mimrè VI–XI*, trans Robert Hespel and René Draguet, CSCO 432 (Louvain: Peeters, 1982), 175. English translation from Sidney Griffith, "The Prophet Muḥammad his Scripture and his Message according to the Christian Apologies in Arabic and Syriac From the First 'Abbāsid Century," in Griffith, *Arabic Christianity in the Monasteries of 9th century Palestine* (Aldershot: Variorum, 1992), 141.

192 Al-Kindī, 'Abd al-Masīḥ ibn Isḥaq, whose work is usually known as the *Apology*. The full title is *Risālat 'Abdallah ibn Ismā'īl al-Hāshimī ilā 'Abd al-Masīḥ ibn Isḥāq al-Kindī yad 'ūhu bihā ilā'l-islām wa-risālat al-Kindī ilā'l-Hāshimī yaruddu bihā 'alayhi wa–yad 'ūhu ilā'l-naṣrāniyya (The Letter of 'Abdallah ibn Ismā'īl al-Hāshimī to 'Abd al-Masīḥ ibn Isḥāq al-Kindī in which he invites him to convert to Islam and the letter of al-Kindī to al-Hāshimī in which he refutes him and invites him to convert to Christianity*). See Bottini, Laura, "al-Kindī, 'Abd al-Masīḥ ibn Isḥāq (pseudonym)", in: CMR, 1:584–97, who gives details of various Arabic editions, including London: SPCK, 1885, used here. An English translation is available in N.A. Newman, ed., *Early Christian–Muslim Dialogue* (Hatfield, Penn: Interdisciplinary Biblical Research Institute, 1993), 382–515, although the existence of variant manuscripts means that the translation does not align exactly with the SPCK publication.

193 Al-Kindī, *Apology*, (London: SPCK, 1985), 138–39, trans. in Newman, 498–99. In this passage al-Kindī also calls on Qur'anic verses in defence of the Bible, including Q10:94.

194 See John Lamoreaux *Theodore Abu Qurrah*, LCE 1 (Provo, UT: Brigham Young University Press, 2005), 215, part of *Refutations of the Saracens by Theodore Abū Qurrah, the Bishop of Haran, As Reported by John the Deacon*, in Lamoreaux, *Theodore Abu Qurrah*, 211–27.

195 The previous assumption that he was a bishop has been replaced by good evidence that he was instead a recognized teacher. See Sandra Tonies Keating, *Defending the People of Truth in*

communication with the writer of the *Apology* of al-Kindī, who includes an abridged passage from Abū Rā'iṭa's *First Epistle on the Holy Trinity* in his work, though this cannot be proven.[196] This epistle, one of several works by Abū Rā'iṭa, tackles the issue of corruption directly, but only briefly, after a much longer discussion of Christian beliefs based on logic. This predominance of logic over scripture can be seen as an indication of the prevalence of the charge of Biblical corruption amongst Muslims at the time. Abū Rā'iṭa chooses to engage primarily on the basis of reason rather than scripture since he seeks ground for debate which both sides can accept. Yet at the same time his decision to include the question of corruption clearly flags the presence of the issue in both his mind and his milieu. He cites a charge, closely based on Qur'anic verses, that Christians have "altered the words from their places" and refutes this by the argument that Jews and Christians did not conspire together. Even if the Jews had deliberately passed on corrupted copies of their scripture to the Christians, then other different (genuine) copies would also be in circulation. Yet this is not what we find; Jews and Christians share the same scripture. His emphasis on the impossibility of Jewish-Christian collaboration means that all the Biblical references he presents on this issue are from the Old Testament, so as to stress the point.[197]

The most extensive treatment of corruption by a Christian from the first two centuries of Islam comes from 'Ammār al-Baṣrī, a close contemporary of Abū Rā'iṭa. He was active in the early to middle decades of the ninth century. His works are better preserved than any record of his life, of which all we know is that he was associated with the East Syrian Christian community and the city of Basra. In two of his works he addresses directly the accusation of the textual corruption of the scriptures, in his case focussing on the gospels, in contrast to Abū Rā'iṭa's use of the Old Testament. In *The Book of the Proof* (*Kitāb al-burhān*) the question of corruption is the fourth of twelve issues discussed. In a longer

the Early Islamic Period. The Christian Apologies of Abū Rā'iṭa, HCMR 4 (Leiden: Brill, 2006), 40–48. See Keating 164–215, for a parallel-text Arabic edition and English translation of *The First Epistle on the Holy Trinity.* See also Keating, "Refuting the Charge of *taḥrīf.* Abū Rā'iṭa (d.ca. 835 CE) and his first *Risāla* on the Holy Trinity" in *Ideas, Images, and Methods of Portrayal. Insights into Classical Arabic Literature and Islam*, ed. Sebastian Günther, IHC 58 (Leiden: Brill, 2005): 41–57.

196 Keating, *Defending*, 161–62.

197 Keating, *Defending*, 206–09.

work, *The Book of Questions and Answers* (*Kitāb al-masā'il wa'l-ajwiba*), twenty pages are devoted to refuting the same charge.[198]

'Ammār focusses on the gospels specifically, but in neither book does he debate specific verses. Instead the arguments in his shorter *Book of the Proof* draw on the historical implausibility of a widespread conspiracy by believers, or of their widespread submission to a ruler or rulers who forced a text on them. A final argument makes very clear that corrupted interpretation is not the topic of discussion, since 'Ammār highlights dissimilarities between the Gospels and the Qur'an to show that corrupted interpretation alone would not produce such differences. In his longer *Book of Questions and Answers* he argues against the charges that the gospels are lax in their teaching, or that corrupted versions were accepted because of the threat of the sword, because of financial inducements, ethnic loyalties, magic which could make signs and wonders appear plausible, or by the persuasion of rulers.

Two other works close this survey. A ninth century CE text (exact date unknown) commonly known as the *Disputation of the Monk Abraham of Tiberias with the Emir* has come down to us in two forms. The shorter Melkite recension devotes a section to refuting the charge of textual corruption, as does an expanded version deriving from the Church of the East.[199] Secondly, the prominent Arab Christian philosopher Yaḥyā b. 'Adī (d.974), from Takrit, also the home town of Abū Rā'iṭa, wrote a short tract against textual corruption of the Bible. He resists the charge of collusion amongst gospel writers by arguing that overly similar gospels would actually indicate collusion more than would minor differences. "If the expressions and meanings and language of the gospels were the same, then it would be possible for one to accuse the evangelists of collusion in writing

198 Both works are published in Michel Hayek, ed., *'Ammar al-Baṣrī: Apologie et Controverses* (Beirut: Dār al-Mashriq, 1977); see *Kitāb al-burhān*, 21–90; on corruption see 41–46. *Kitāb al-masā'il wa'l-ajwiba*, 91–266; on corruption see 128–47. See also Mark Beaumont, "'Ammār al-Baṣrī on the Alleged Corruption of the Gospels" in *The Bible in Arab Christianity*, ed. David Thomas, HCMR 6 (Leiden: Brill, 2007): 241–55; and Sidney Griffith, "'Ammār al-Baṣrī's *Kitāb al-Burhān:* Christian Kalām in the First 'Abbāsid Century" *Mus* 96 (1983): 145–81, esp. 165–68.

199 For the Arabic text and parallel French translation of the shorter version see Giacinto Marcuzzo, *Le Dialogue d'Abraham de Tibériade avec 'Abd al-Raḥmān al-Hāshimī à Jérusalem vers 820* (Rome: Pontificia Universitas Lateranensis, 1986). For the discussion of Biblical corruption see 394–403. For the German translation of the longer ('Beta') version from an Arabic manuscript subsequently lost, see Kurt Vollers, "Das Religionsgespräch von Jerusalem (um 800 D)," in *ZKG* 29 (1908): 29–71, 197–221. For the relevant passage see 62. For background on this text see Mark Swanson, "The Disputation of the monk Ibrāhīm al-Ṭabarānī," in *CMR*, 1:876–881.

them and spreading them through the world, as those who oppose us amongst the sects claim".[200]

The foregoing discussion shows that the accusation of tampering with the Biblical text, not just its interpretation, was an issue of concern for Christian writers in the early centuries of Islam. As far back as John of Damascus, we have records of Christians believing that Muslims suspected or dismissed various texts. The Muslim sources of the specific accusations these writers engage are often not available to us, and the charge would frequently have been delivered in speech, not in words. But the consistency of the Christian concern to refute the charge clearly shows that it circulated freely. The next chapter will witness how this charge came to be powerfully promoted by significant Muslim writers.

4.12 Conclusion

Exploring the many settings in which Muslim authors engaged with the Biblical text has revealed a number of important points. One reason for using the Bible is for proving the validity of the author's own concerns, whether those be the prophethood of Muhammad, the truth of Islam, the validity of the twelve Shia Imams or, in the case of Ismāʿīlī writers, more specific elements of their own belief system such as the harmony of all revelations. Historians draw on Biblical text for information about the Israelite people and their prophet. Qur'anic commentaries also draw on Biblical background, though they do not tend to name the source as the Bible, and are most likely drawing from traditions blending canonical and non-canonical material. The literature of Stories of the Prophets, by contrast, though discussing at length characters who also occur in the Bible, uses very little Biblical narrative except insofar as previous Muslim sources incorporate these. Legal works demonstrate a theoretical acceptance of some role for the previous scriptures, under discussions of "the law of those who came before us" (*sharʿ man qablanā*) but this does not lead to actual engagement with Biblical texts or laws in the formulation of Islamic law. Indeed, works of positive law are either silent or cautious about the use of the previous scriptures.

200 Yaḥyā b. ʿAdī, untitled tract, in *Vingt Traités philosophiques et apologétiques*, ed. Paul Sbath (Cairo: Maktabat H. Frīdrīkh, 1929): 171–72. The Arabic text and an English translation are also available at http://www.tertullian.org/fathers/sbath_16_yahya_ibn_adi_02.htm, accessed 10/10/2018. For background on Yaḥyā b. ʿAdī see Sidney Griffith's introduction to his translation of Yaḥyā b. ʿAdī's *Kitāb tahdhīb al-akhlāq*, translated as *The Reformation of Morals: a parallel English-Arabic Text*, METI (Provo,UT: Brigham Young University Press, 2002), xiii–xlvi.

The issue of textual corruption is not a dominant note, but is often present in the background. Works refuting Christianity use the Bible extensively, but also alter it where needed, providing a form of implicit criticism of the reliability of the text. Only the philosopher Ibn Sīnā addresses the historical or logical problems inherent in exploring the case for geographically widespread corruption, and that only briefly. And yet we cannot entirely affirm the view that corruption was a minor issue at this stage in the development of Islam. It is striking how regularly the idea emerges as one of various concerns voiced by Christian writers in particular when they seek to refute Muslim ideas, even though it is not the central concern.

By the 5th/11th century a complex blend of responses to the Biblical text had developed. There is little sign of exploring the text for its own sake, but the gradual establishment of Islam through conquest, debate and gradual social change is accompanied by clear willingness to draw on the previous scriptures when necessary or convenient. Yet the balance of use and criticism was about to shift.

5 A Tale of Three Critics – and one Apostle

In the 4th–5th/11th century Muslim criticism of the Bible took a new turn.[1] Two writers born in Iran and one from al-Andalus (Islamic Iberia, covering areas of present day Spain and Portugal) focussed on criticising the reliability of the Biblical text, intensifying the element of direct confrontation. These three critics are Qāḍī ʻAbd al-Jabbār (d. 415/1025), Abū Muḥammad Ibn Ḥazm (d. 456/1064) and Abū'l-Ma'ālī al-Juwaynī (d. 478/1085). For whatever reason, it seems that until this period, the Bible, though regarded as a questionable source, was not of sufficient interest in itself to warrant extended critical treatment.[2] The writers discussed in this chapter were significant in changing that situation. After the wide-angle lens of the previous two chapters, the present focus narrows to explore in detail the ideas of these three figures. Because one of them engages with the role of Paul (for Christians, an apostle), this will also be a good stage at which to address Muslim understandings of his influence on the Bible.

5.1 Qāḍī ʻAbd al-Jabbār

5.1.1 Biography and context

Qāḍī ("Judge") ʻAbd al-Jabbār was born around 325/937 in present-day Iran. He rose to become a very wealthy chief judge of Rayy (today a suburb of Tehran) before falling from grace amidst the political intrigues of his day. By his death in 415/1025, he had become the chief exponent of the Mu'tazilī school of rationalist Muslim theology. He responds to Christians past and present, referring to well-known names such as Ḥunayn b. Isḥāq (d. 873), while from his own day he primarily addresses the Assyrian Church of the East, commonly termed Nestorians, the church of Patriarch Timothy, mentioned in Chapter 4. The reason is not hard to fathom, since this was the dominant church in Rayy at the time. There had been a bishop of this church in Rayy since at least 410CE, and the city was elevated to the seat of a Metropolitan around the turn of the ninth century CE.[3]

1 I refer to a long 11th century, since the first work discussed in this chapter was written in 385/995.

2 See Thomas, "The Bible and the Kalām," 184.

3 Gabriel Said Reynolds, *A Muslim Theologian in the Sectarian Milieu: ʻAbd al-Jabbār and the* Critique of Christian Origins, IHC 56 (Leiden: Brill, 2004), 67–74.

https://doi.org/10.1515/9783110335880-008

5.1.2 Works

'Abd al-Jabbār left behind a large number of works on Muslim theology. His major work, *The Summa on Divine Unity and Justice* (*al-Mughnī fi abwāb al-tawḥīd wa'l-'adl*) includes a sustained critique of Christian doctrine.[4] In this, he makes only brief, though fairly dismissive, comment on the status of the Biblical text.[5] Most importantly for our purposes, he composed a critique of Christianity involving an account of the Bible, written in 385/995, the critique forming part of a longer work on the prophethood of Muhammad, *The Confirmation of the Proofs of Prophethood* (*Tathbīt dalā'il al-nubuwwa*).[6]

The Confirmation, another example of the Proofs of Prophethood literature discussed in Chapter 4, rejects the claims of Christianity to be based on the genuine teachings of Christ and on knowledge of his miracles. 'Abd al-Jabbār refutes Christianity's historical basis in order to support the central claim of his work, the prophethood of Muhammad. To write against Christianity was a normal activity for a Mu'tazilī *kalām* scholar.[7] Many aspects of 'Abd al-Jabbār's critique resemble previous Muslim writers, such as his statement that Christians misinterpret metaphorical language about fatherhood and sonship by taking it literally.[8] Likewise he criticises the soundness of the transmission of Christian teachings. But 'Abd al-Jabbār's treatment of the New Testament is unusual in his recounting of a story to explain the corruption he believed had affected it.

---

4 For the Arabic text and an English translation of this section of the *Mughnī*, see David Thomas, *Christian Doctrines in Islamic Theology* (Leiden: Brill, 2008), 225–377.

5 See Thomas, *Christian Doctrines*, 358 (Arabic), 359 (English), and more briefly, 294 (Arabic), 295 (English).

6 'Abd al-Jabbār, *Tathbīt dalā'il al-nubuwwa*, ed. 'Abd al-Karīm 'Uthmān (Beirut: Dār al-'Arabīyah li'l-Ṭibā'ah wa'l-Nashr wa'l-Tawzī', 1966). For the Arabic text and English translation of the section on Christianity see Gabriel Said Reynolds and Samir Khalil Samir, eds.,*The Critique of Christian Origins*, METI (Provo, UT: Brigham Young University Press, 2010). On the biography of 'Abd al-Jabbār, see Gabriel Said Reynolds, "The Rise and Fall of Qāḍī 'Abd al-Jabbār," *IJMES* 37 (2005): 3–18. See also Samuel Stern, " 'Abd al-Jabbār's Account of how Christ's Religion was falsified by the Adoption of Roman Customs," *JTS* 19 (1968): 128–85, and Paul van Koningsveld, "The Islamic Image of Paul and the Origin of the Gospel of Barnabas',"*JSAI* 20 (1996): 200–28.

7 Reynolds, *Milieu*, 28–41.

8 *Critique*, 44.

5.1.3 The Gospels

'Abd al-Jabbār's treatment of the gospels is underpinned by the idea of a Christian conspiracy. The fact that there is no gospel in Hebrew, which he regards as the language spoken by Jesus, "is a plot and a scheme" designed to hide the presence of lies in the gospels the Christians produced.[9] He writes that the gospels are in fact full of lies and contradictions, with "a little in them of the speech of Christ, his commandments, and his works".[10] The main conspiracy involves the disciples' defection to the cause of pagan Rome, as follows.

According to 'Abd al-Jabbār, some early Christians defected to the Romans in order to gain protection from the Jews and ascendancy over them.[11] Other more faithful Christians criticised them strongly for this, a feud resulted, and the faithful Christians refused to let the new movement of defectors to Rome have access to the true *Injīl*. The pro-Roman defectors therefore conspired to produce new, false gospels to replace the *Injīl*. Eighty gospels were composed, then "These were continuously transcribed and abridged until only four Gospels by four individuals remained".[12] In a statement pithily summarising his discussion, 'Abd al-Jabbār writes that, "The Christians became Romans and fell back to the religions of the Romans. You will not find that the Romans became Christians".[13] This explains why Christians do not follow the true teaching of Jesus as found in the Qur'an.

5.1.4 Paul and his Letters

For 'Abd al-Jabbār, one of the key figures entangled with Rome was Paul, whom he regards as a prime example of a defector. "Paul tore himself away from the religion of Christ and entered the religion of the Romans."[14] According to 'Abd al-Jabbār, Paul's motive in this early Christian scheming is rooted in the same character flaw as found in those other Christians who went over to the Romans to oppose the Jews – the desire for power and dominance. Paul "desired leadership and dominion and used every kind of plot to this end."[15] So Paul advocates

9 *Critique*, 95.
10 *Critique*, 97.
11 *Critique*, 93–94.
12 *Critique*, 94.
13 *Critique*, 103.
14 *Critique*, 103.
15 *Critique*, 103.

monogamous marriage, abandons circumcision, declares all foods acceptable to eat, allows believers to marry unbelievers, declares the *Tawrāt* to be evil, all because of his desire to ingratiate himself with the Romans.[16] Even his name reflects conspiracy. "He took the name Paul, which is a Roman name, to win them over."[17] What is more, he was successful. "Now the affair of Paul was significant among the common people and the mob in the land of the Romans. He enamored them through things equivalent to incantations, medicine, sorcery, and magic."[18]

This view of Paul clearly has implications for views of the New Testament. 'Abd al-Jabbār does not focus on the question of whether Paul's letters could be seen as scripture, an unsurprising situation since from his account of Paul as a deceiver it is obviously impossible. In 'Abd al-Jabbār 's view the worthlessness of these letters is perhaps so obvious that his only comment on them occurs in a criticism of Christians' overly positive attitude to them. "When his letters and discourse are read in the church, they stand, venerating and exalting him and his discourse. They do not do this for the Tawrāt... nor during the Gospels."[19]

The wider context of Abd al-Jabbār's writing on Paul is part of a tradition of Muslim views on Paul to be examined shortly.

5.1.5 Use of the Bible

Did 'Abd al-Jabbār read the Bible itself? It seems very likely that the Bible in Arabic would have been available in Rayy, although far less likely in Persian.[20] But there are reasons to think that he drew primarily on compilations of quotations from others rather than using the Biblical text independently, though not all of these indicators are conclusive.[21] For example 'Abd al-Jabbār's language is influenced by Syriac terminology, implying that he was drawing on Christians writing in Arabic but using Syriac names. So Jesus is termed both Yashu' (West Syriac) and 'Isho (East Syriac). Furthermore, when quoting Exod 4:22 in a discussion about the meaning of "son" he adds a non-canonical extra sentence very similar to that added by al-Jāḥiẓ quoting the same verse. This indicates that 'Abd al-Jab-

---

16 *Critiquc*, 100 03.
17 *Critique*, 101.
18 *Critique*, 104.
19 *Critique*, 90.
20 Reynolds, *Milieu*, 196–200, and see Chapter 1 on availability of the Bible.
21 Reynolds in *Critique*, lxivff

bār is almost certainly reliant on al-Jāḥiẓ here.[22] However, gauging his knowledge of the Bible is also complicated by his altering Biblical passages and then quoting them as if they represent the actual Biblical text. For example, when Mary stands at the cross, Jesus stands next to her, and the person who was substituted in Jesus' place (a standard Muslim belief) says to Mary from the cross "this is your son" and to Jesus, "this is your mother." This is a startling re-working of John 19:26–27. In other words, 'Abd al-Jabbār alters the Bible, the very practice for which he criticises the Christians, such that "*taḥrīf* is the accusation and the means to accuse."[23] But this means that an apparently inaccurate Biblical quotation might be a deliberate part of his rhetorical strategy rather than revealing lack of familiarity with the Biblical text.

5.1.6 Influence and Evaluation

The Confirmation is mentioned by such notable figures as Ibn Taymiyya (d. 728/1328) and Ibn Kathīr (d. 774/1373). It is also used by Ibn Qayyim al-Jawziyya (d. 751/1350), and the great Sunni commentator Fakhr al-dīn al-Rāzī (d. 606/1209).[24] 'Abd al-Jabbār's perspective on "the problem of how Christianity arose became a lasting feature of Islamic literature".[25]

What kind of picture does *The Confirmation* paint? It can be argued that Sunni self-legitimation required the identification of figures who were corrupters, regardless of the strength of the historical evidence for labelling certain individuals in that way. Barzegar writes that, "The historical (in)accuracy of Muslim accounts of Paul of Tarsus tells us more about the mythic power of his representation and his role therein as a critical component of Muslim identity formation than they do about the actual person of Paul."[26] The key issue is the need to explain what went wrong with an originally true set of teachings from Jesus, and how large numbers were led astray into historic Christianity. So Paul, initially having no role in Islam, gradually becomes more significant as a means of helping to explain Muslim thought on Christian doctrine and divisions, related to the Qur'anic statement that God causes divisions amongst the Christians because of their disobedience (Q5:14).

22 Reynolds, *Milieu*, 157.
23 Reynolds, *Milieu*, 199.
24 See Reynolds, *Milieu*, 77–79, and Reynolds, *Critique*, lxxiv.
25 Reynolds, *Critique*, lxxiii.
26 Abbas Barzegar, "The Persistence of Heresy: Paul of Tarsus, Ibn Sabā', and Historical Narrative in Sunni Identity Formation," *Numen* 58 (2011), 219. See also van Koningsveld, "Image," 202.

Exploring some other Islamic constructions of the figure of Paul will help to put 'Abd al-Jabbār's discussion in context. Understanding these constructions is important since Christians have traditionally understood Paul to be the divinely inspired author of a significant part of the non-gospel material in the New Testament. So attitudes to Paul are closely linked to attitudes to the New Testament text, even if Muslim writers do not make this connection explicit.

5.2 Excursus: Paul in Classical Islamic and Other Traditions

Muslim writers usually discuss Paul and his errors or plots in relation to Christian doctrines, or to Muslim and Christian ideas of the history of early Christianity. The status of the New Testament is much less frequently discussed. But if Paul is a deceiver, then the reliability of any section of the New Testament associated with him can scarcely even be considered – which is presumably why 'Abd al-Jabbār barely mentions the issue directly. In addition, by writing letters, Paul adopted a genre which to most Muslims seems far removed from what can be considered divine scripture.[27]

Paul as a conspirator is key to understanding early Muslim portrayals of him. But on whose behalf is he conspiring? This question turns out to have a variety of answers.

5.2.1 Paul in the Qur'an

There is no explicit reference to Paul in the Qur'an. However, Q36:13–14 is occasionally interpreted as a reference to Paul. "Strike a parable for them: the companions of the town, when the envoys came to it. When We sent two men to them, and they called them liars, We reinforced (them) with a third. They said, 'Surely we are envoys to you'." The commentator Ibn Kathīr records a tradition that "The names of the first two messengers were Sham'ūn and Yuhanna, and

27 Kenneth Cragg, *Jesus and the Muslim* (Oxford: Oneworld, 1985), 92, comments that the Muslim reader may well be "perplexed and dismayed" by the claim that letters can be scripture. Cragg also offers (210–33) broader reflection on possible Muslim responses to Paul. See on Paul more generally Michael Kuhn, "Early Islamic Perspectives on the Apostle Paul," in Mark Beaumont (ed.) *Arab Christians and the Qur'an from the Origins of Islam to the Medieval Period*, HCMR 35 (Leiden: Brill, 2018), 150–73.

the third was Būlus, and the city was Antioch'.[28] If Paul is referred to in this verse, it is the only trace of him found in the Qur'an.

5.2.2 Paul in Early Islamic Literature

There is likewise no explicit reference to Paul in hadith literature. Instead his profile grows from small beginnings in brief and neutral historical reports. Ibn Isḥāq's *Life of Muhammad*, in the edition of Ibn Hishām, mentions Paul without criticism. He writes, "Those whom Jesus son of Mary sent, both disciples and those who came after them, in the land were: Peter the disciple and Paul with him (Paul belonged to the followers and was not a disciple) to Rome."[29] Al-Ṭabarī records this same tradition, adding that Nero crucified Paul head down in Rome.[30]

But a quite different and more negative tradition of accounts of Paul also exists in Islamic writings. These involve the idea of Paul as conspirator, an idea evident in the work of 'Abd al-Jabbār, as seen above, but predating him by several centuries. One important early narrative of Paul is found in Sayf b. 'Umar al-Tamīmī, *The Book of the Wars of Apostasy and Conquest* (*Kitāb al-Ridda wa'l-futūḥ*).[31] Sayf b. 'Umar died in the period c. 180–193/796–809, according to one account, but virtually nothing is known about him. His fame rests on al-Ṭabarī's choosing him as the main source of his account of the wars of apostasy and

---

28 Ibn Kathīr, *Tafsīr* (Beirut: al-Risala, 2000), 1106, referring to Simon, John and Paul. However, Ibn Kathīr considers it implausible that the the city referred to is Antioch, since, amongst other reasons, Antioch was historically a strong base for Christianity, whereas the Qur'an records the city in question as being destroyed for its unbelief. See *Tafsīr*, 1106–07. By implication, he presumably sees the identification of Paul in this verse as likewise implausible. Ryan Szpiech, 'Preaching Paul to the Moriscos: The *Confusión o Confutación de la Secta Mahomética y del Alcoran* (1515) of "Juan Andres"', *La Corónica* 41 (2012): 317–43, provides an example of the exegetical tradition of linking Paul to Q36:14 being used by a Christian author to vindicate Paul as a genuine messenger of God. Szpiech also notes the origins of this tradition of Paul as one of three messengers to Antioch in the apocryphal *Acts of Peter.*

29 Ibn Isḥāq, in Ibn Hishām, *Das Leben*, 972; trans. Guillaume, *Life*, 653.

30 See al-Ṭabarī, *Ta'rīkh*, 737, 741; trans. Moshe Perlmann, vol. 4, *The Ancient Kingdoms* (Albany, N.Y.: SUNY Press, 1987), 123.

31 See Sayf b. 'Umar al-Tamīmī, *Kitāb al-ridda wa'l-futūḥ* and *Kitāb al-Jamal wa masīr 'Ā'isha wa 'Alī*, ed. Qasim al-Samarrai (Leiden: Smitskamp, 1995); translation in Sean Anthony, "The Composition of Sayf b. 'Umar's Account of King Paul and his Corruption of Ancient Christianity," *Der Islam* 85 (2008): 164–202. See also Sean Anthony, *The Caliph and the Heretic: Ibn Saba' and the Origins of Shī'ism*, IHS 91 (Leiden: Brill, 2012), 66–71, 85, 146, 173.

conquest for his own monumental history.[32] Sayf's narrative is much earlier than most Muslim accounts of Paul.[33] His point in writing about Paul is to warn Muslims to beware of divisive figures who will undermine true religion. Sayf draws a parallel between Paul and Ibn Saba', a Yemenite Jew who converted, or pretended to convert, to Islam and is blamed for introducing extreme Shi'ite views into Islam at the time of 'Alī.[34] Sayf's real concern is the preservation of Islam from corruption. For Sayf, Paul is an important example, a warning from history of a parallel case where true faith did indeed become corrupted. Sayf's message is clear: if it has happened before, when the followers of Jesus let Paul corrupt Jesus' teaching, it must not be allowed to happen again, with Shi'ism corrupting true (i. e. Sunni) Islam.

In Sayf's account Paul's plan is to cause the Christians to be damned. He does this by pretending to convert to Christianity so as to introduce into the Christians' minds a false version of their faith. Sayf writes that "King Paul" says about certain Jews who have decided to follow Jesus:

Indeed, their [Christians] message is appealing, and they [some Jews] have gone to your enemy. They are still acting as the benefactors of the Christians. Soon, they will come riding against you [Jews] with the aid of your enemies unless you pay heed to what I am about to say to you now... Then he pursued them [Christians] with the intent to lead them astray (material in square brackets added).

King Paul, in saying "unless you pay heed to what I am about to say" means here that he will save true Jewish faith by leading Christians astray. Then all the Jews will see more clearly that they should not follow Jesus. An example of the false teaching which Paul intends to introduce is that all foods are regarded as clean. "Everything from the beetle to the elephant is licit".[35] In this way Paul encourages the Christians to abandon Jewish food laws, a step which of course faithful Jews would resist. Paul also teaches that Christians abandon the proper

---

32 However, Sayf is often also regarded as unreliable and there are complaints by other Muslim writers about identifying the transmitters in the reports he uses. While al-Ṭabarī uses other accounts by Sayf, he ignores his account of Paul. See Wilferd Madelung, "Sayf b. 'Umar: *Akhbārī* and Ideological Fiction Writer," in Mohammad Ali Amir-Moezzi, Meir Bar-Asher, Simon Hopkins, eds., *Le Shī'isme Imāmite Quarante ans après: homage à Etan Kohlberg* (Turnhout: Brepols, 2009), 325–37.

33 Sean Anthony, 'Composition,' 196.

34 See Keith Lewinstein, "'Abdallāh b. Saba'", in: *EI3*, consulted online on 08 May 2020 <http://dx.doi.org/10.1163/1573-3912_ei3_COM_24156.

35 Sayf b. 'Umar, *Kitāb al-Ridda*, 133; Anthony, "Composition," 177. On all foods being clean, see Mark 7:14–15.

direction of prayer, the law, and the right to wage military jihad, replacing it with turning the other cheek.[36]

Another motive for Paul to conspire is given in the Qur'an commentary of al-Tha'labī (d. 427/1035). Writing in relation to Q9:31, al-Tha'labī states that Paul concludes that Christianity is true, considers himself damned, and then seeks to consign Christians to hell along with himself by deceiving them. Al-Tha'labī cites a tradition dating back to al-Kalbī (d. 146/763).[37]

So taking power ('Abd al-Jabbār), saving the Jews (Sayf b. 'Umar), and damning the Christians (al-Tha'labī) are three alleged motives for Paul's deception of the Christians. But 'Abd al-Jabbār's account is very different from Sayf's in its details, indicating that he was not using Sayf as a direct source. Instead they are more likely both drawing on a shared basic narrative about Paul as conspirator. Ibn Ḥazm describes the source of these conspiracy theories about Paul as the Jews themselves. According to Ibn Ḥazm, Jews state that their ancestors, "Agreed to bribe the Benjamite Paul – God curse him – and to commission him as declaring the religion of Jesus, to lead astray his [Jesus'] followers, and to bring them to state that he [Jesus] is divine."[38]

Ibn Ḥazm also makes exactly the same comparison as Sayf b. 'Umar. The Jews, as well as successfully corrupting the true teachings of Jesus, also tried the same ploy with Islam, via the Yemenite Jew Ibn Saba'.[39] But why does Ibn Ḥazm attribute the story of Paul the plotter to the Jews?

5.2.3 Paul in Jewish Literature

Complex links between Jewish and Muslim criticisms of Christianity are increasingly recognized. The direction of influence is not always easy to determine, since "arguments which were introduced into the polemical scene quickly became part of the common polemical arsenal and could then circulate and be re-

---

36 Anthony, "Composition," 182. On turning the other cheek, see Matt 5:39.

37 Al-Tha'labī, *Tafsīr al-Tha'labī*, vol. 5 (Beirut: Dār Iḥyā' al-Turāth al-'Arabī, 2002), 33; trans. Reynolds, *Milieu*, 164–65. This tradition is repeated in al-Damīrī, *Ḥayāt al-ḥayawān al-kubrā (The Lives of Animals)*, vol. 2 (Cairo: al-Maṭba'at al-Khayrīyah, 1891),187; trans. Anthony, "Composition," 198–99.

38 Ibn Ḥazm, *Kitāb al-Faṣl fi'l-milal wa'l-ahwā' wa'l-niḥal (The Book of the Distinction regarding Religions, Sects and Heresies)*, 1:246.

39 Ibn Ḥazm, 1: 247; trans Anthony, 'Composition', 194.

cycled."[40] Jewish literature provides an important context within which to read Islamic views of Paul, and therefore as background to Islamic views of those parts of the New Testament writings linked to Paul. Before Jewish theological refutations of Christianity emerged, a very different genre also circulated – a parody of the New Testament gospels and the Book of Acts, known as *Toledot Yeshu.*

5.2.3.1 Toledot Yeshu

The portrayal of Paul as a deceitful schemer occurs in *Toledot Yeshu* (*The Generations of Jesus,* that is, *The Life of Jesus*). There is no entirely fixed text for this collection of stories which form a Jewish anti-gospel, in which Jesus is not born of a virgin, is a charlatan and sorcerer, and whose body is hidden by others, rather than raised to life, after his death on the cross. This parody or polemic, which may now seem the obscure interest of specialists, was for centuries a hugely popular work amongst many Jewish communities, circulating very widely across Europe and the Middle East.[41] The earliest extant manuscripts are medieval, but reflect traditions which are clearly older. The content, date and significance of this work all require comment.

The first reference to *Toledot* as a written composition is by Agobard Bishop of Lyon in France (d. 840), but its material goes back much earlier than that (arguments over its dating are discussed below). It should be seen as a frame story, with varied versions built around a common outline, rather than a fixed text. The original language of *Toledot* seems to have been Aramaic, with versions in Hebrew and Judeo-Arabic and Judeo-Persian also circulating.[42] While its anti-gospel section vilifies Jesus, some manuscripts of *Toledot* also target the New Testa-

---

40 Daniel Lasker and Sarah Stroumsa, *The Polemic of Nestor the Priest: Qiṣṣat Mujādalat al-Usquf and Sefer Nestor Ha-Komer: Introduction, Annotated Translations and Commentary,* vol I (Jerusalem: Ben-Zvi Institute for the Study of Jewish Communities in the East, 1996), 22. *Qiṣṣat Mujādalat al-Usquf* is the earliest Jewish theological refutation of Christianity.

41 Major work has recently been done on *Toledot.* See in particular Michael Meerson and Peter Schäfer, edited and translated, Toledot Yeshu: *The Life Story of Jesus: two volumes and database* (Tübingen: Mohr Siebeck, 2014); and for a collection of studies on *Toledot* see Peter Schäfer, ed., Toledot Yeshu ("*The Life Story of Jesus*") *Revisited.* TSAJ 143 (Tübingen: Mohr Siebeck, 2011). See also Alexandra Cuffel, "Between Epic Entertainment and Polemical Exegesis: Jesus as antihero in *Toledot* Yeshu," in *Medieval Exegesis and Religious Difference: Commentary, Conflict and Community in the Premodern Mediterranean,* ed. Ryan Szpiech (New York: Fordham University Press, 2015): 155–170.

42 Philip Alexander, "The *Toledot Yeshu* in the Context of Jewish–Muslim Debate," in Schäfer, ed., *Toledot Yeshu... Revisited,* 137–58.

ment Book of Acts in an anti-Acts section.[43] In this, Paul is commissioned by other Jewish leaders to conspire against Christians by going to them, pretending to have converted, and introducing false teaching claiming to come from Jesus but not actually doing so. The purpose is to protect Jews from converting to Christianity by making the new faith seem less attractive.

There is a clear resemblance here to the account of Sayf b. ʻUmar. In addition, there is one striking verbal similarity of *Toledot* to Sayf's account of Paul, concerning the abandonment of Jewish food laws. As already noted, Sayf has Paul declare that, "Everything from the beetle to the elephant is licit", while we find in the anti-Acts section of *Toledot* "everything... from a small mosquito to an elephant, which is big, you may spill its blood upon the earth."[44] This, along with the thematic links in the portrayal of Paul, makes some kind of connection between *Toledot* traditions and Sayf likely. But there is also a striking difference. Rather than Paul being portrayed as a wicked deceiver, *Toledot* presents him as a good Jew, plotting to preserve Judaism from this new and pernicious teaching of Jesus.

While *Toledot* may not have directly influenced ʻAbd al-Jabbār, it is highly plausible that it could have influenced Sayf b. ʻUmar, and that its various fluid forms could have influenced other Muslim writers in contact with Jews.[45] This is despite the fact that it is very hostile to Jesus, a markedly non-Islamic position. But what suggests that *Toledot,* or traditions related to it, influenced Sayf, rather than Sayf influencing *Toledot?* This leads us to questions of dating.

As with much in *Toledot*, dating questions remain disputed, with manuscripts ranging from the medieval period to the 19th century. It is agreed that *Toledot* carries some ancient ideas, notably the notion found in the Church Father Tertullian (d. after 220) that a gardener stole the body of Jesus after his burial.[46] It has been argued that the anti-Acts section dates from the 5th century. Others disagree but concede that the anti-Acts section might have circulated at an early date, separately from the anti-gospel narrative.[47]

---

43 See Meerson and Schäfer, *Toledot*, 1: 179–82.

44 Anthony, "Composition," 177; Meerson and Schäfer, eds, *Toledot*, 181.

45 This influence is discussed by Stern, "Account," especially 181–82. See also Anthony, "Composition," 199.

46 Meerson and Schäfer, eds., *Toledot*, 178–79, and see William Horbury, "Tertullian on the Jews in the Light of *De Spectaculis* XXX. 5–6," *JTS* (1972): 455–59.

47 For a fifth century date, see Daniel Stökl Ben Ezra, "An Ancient List of Christian Festivals in 'Toledot Yeshu': Polemics as Indication for Interaction," *HTR* 102 (2009): 481–96; see also John Gager, "Simon Peter, Founder of Christianity or Saviour of Israel?," in Toledot Yeshu... *Revisited*, eds., Schäfer, Meerson and Deutsch, 236–41. For differing views see Meerson and Schäfer, (eds) *Toledot*, 1: 104–10.

If manuscript and internal data are inconclusive, we can ask which community, Muslim or Jewish, is more likely to have generated the motif of Paul as conspirator. The story of Paul deliberately corrupting Christian teaching to protect Judaism fits well as part of Jewish-Christian debate. By contrast, it is unlikely that Sayf or other Muslims would have had any need to generate a story of Paul preserving and protecting Jewish faith. More probably these stories circulated widely as Jewish narratives, first in Aramaic in the Palestinian area, and were then borrowed or absorbed by Sayf b. ʻUmar, quite possible orally.[48] Indeed Sayf's main aim is not to explain Islamic views of Paul. His main aim is to warn against the corruption of Islam by Shīʻite or proto-Shīʻite influences. It seems most likely that Sayf found the stories associated with *Toledot*, or circulating in a similar form, an interesting parallel and illustration of what he really wanted to say, which was "beware the corrupter within the fold."

Sayf's likely borrowing of motifs from non-Muslim sources is the more plausible in view of the wider milieu of late Umayyad and early ʻAbbāsid society. There is strong evidence that the historiographical tradition in this period in the region of Iraq and Syria does not simply borrow isolated details from late antique Christian and Jewish literature. Instead, given that Muslims were still at this stage a small minority of the population, there was "a fundamental and decisive contribution by the community of the vast majority [i.e. Jews and Christians] to the newly emerging literary tradition – including historiography – of the small ruling elite in its midst" (material in square brackets added).[49] This contribution was built at least in part on assimilated converts to Islam and their recent descendants bringing a variety of models and motifs into early Islamic literature. This enabled them "to participate in the shaping of the tradition itself and to contribute major paradigms and techniques as well as a host of details."[50] Interestingly, Sayf b. ʻUmar shows elsewhere his openness to borrowing motifs, such as in his account of the conversion of a Byzantine commander. The story of "Georgius" is clearly modelled on the account of Thomas moving from doubt to faith in John 20:29. The faith of Georgius is said to be especially meritorious as he believed without seeing the things in which he is trusting.[51] So Sayf's borrowing

48 Oral transmission is all the more likely if Alexander, "Context," 143, is correct that the first Arabic translations of *Toledot* occur in the ninth century. The means of transmission of stories to Sayf remains unclear.

49 Lawrence Conrad, "The *Mawālī* and Early Arabic Historiography," in *Patronate and Patronage in Early and Classical Islam*, eds. Monique Bernards and John Nawas, IHC 61 (Leiden: Brill, 2005), 379.

50 Conrad, "*Mawālī*," 380.

51 Conrad, '*Mawālī*', 379.

and reshaping of *Toledot*-related traditions about Paul the conspirator would fit with what he does with the story of Georgius, and would also accord with wider trends in Muslim historical writing in his cultural milieu.

5.2.3.2 Other works

There are other possible Jewish examples of the idea of Paul being the real architect of Christian beliefs. Jewish theological refutation of Christianity begin with Dāwūd al-Muqammiṣ (d.937), notably his *The Book of Urging on to Attack* (*Kitāb al-Ḍarā'a*), parts of which are preserved by the Karaite Jewish writer al-Qirqisānī.[52] Here we read that,

When the Christians could not find in the Gospels any decisive regulations about certain things, they claimed that Paul and Peter -- who is the Jew Abba Saul the Jewish fisherman [sic] – laid down for them laws and regulations found neither in the Gospels nor in the Torah, excepting those concerning Sabbath; and that these two men commanded them to obey these laws, saying that these laws were divulged to them by Jesus.[53]

Al-Muqammiṣ calls Paul Abu Shā'ūl, as does Sayf b. 'Umar.[54] Al-Qirqisānī adds in his own voice, "As for the religion of the Christians which they profess today, it was Paul who introduced and established it".[55] These ninth and tenth century quotations, while too late to have originated the idea of Paul as conspirator which circulated earlier in *Toledot Yeshu* and Sayf b. 'Umar, reflect the varied traditions available in Arabic, which may have influenced later writers such as 'Abd al-Jabbār.[56]

The conspiracy motif, found in *Toledot*, occurs also in the commentary of the French rabbi Rashi (d. 1105) on the Babylonian Talmud. Rashi depicts Paul,

52 Sarah Stroumsa, "Jewish Polemics," 246.

53 Quoted by Ya'qūb al-Qirqisānī, *Kitab al-Anwār wa'l-marāqib* (*The Book of Lights and Watchtowers*) ed. Leon Nemoy, vol.1 (New York: The Alexander Kohut Foundation, 1939–1943), 44; trans. Leon Nemoy, "Al-Qirqisānī's Account of the Jewish Sects and Christianity," *HUCA* 7 (1930): 366–67. Al-Qirqisānī (or a later scribe?) mistakenly attributes Peter's occupation of fisherman to Paul. See also the discussion in Wout Jac. Van Bekkum, "The Karaite Jacob al-Qirqisānī (Tenth Century) on Christianity and the Christians," in *Syriac Polemics*, eds. Wout Jac. Van Bekkum, Jan Willem Drijvers, Alex Klugkist (Leuven: Peeters, 2007): 173–92.

54 Anthony, "Composition," 200, draws attention to this name for Paul found in various Jewish sources.

55 Al-Qirqisānī, *Kitāb al-Marāqib*, 1: 43; trans. Nemoy, "Account," 365.

56 Reynolds and Samir, *Critique*, lxviii, argue that 'Abd al-Jabbār is very likely aware of al-Muqammiṣ through the medium of al-Qirqisānī, who was in close contact with Mu'tazilī thinkers.

along with Peter,[57] as good Jews who deliberately misled the Christians so as to protect the people of Israel. Because Israel was in distress on account of the trickeries of Jesus, Paul and Peter, "Created nonsense for them [the Christians] in order to keep them apart from them [i.e. Israel] and to remove them from Israel. They [Paul and Peter] were not heretics/ converts [to Christianity] for they did everything for the benefit of Israel"[58] (material in square brackets added). Rashi was writing only a few years after Ibn Ḥazm, reflecting perhaps similar traditions to those which led Ibn Ḥazm to attribute the idea of Paul as corrupter to Jews.

5.2.4 Implications

Rashi, like the traditions in *Toledot Yeshu*, wants to reclaim Paul as a good Jew, protecting his people from the threat of conversion. Paul adds new falsehoods to the pernicious message of Jesus so that right-thinking Jews will see that the message is false and not be attracted to it. By contrast, the Muslim sources wish to present Paul as a wicked Jew, taking the pure (Islamic) message of Jesus and corrupting it to damn Christians and/ or save Jews. In both narratives Paul is first and foremost a Jew. Neither the Muslim nor Jewish narratives about Paul are primarily about Christianity or the status of the Bible, though they have major implications for them. For Jews, they are about preserving Jewish faith from threat. For Muslims, they are an example, a warning against letting Islam be corrupted as Christianity was corrupted by Paul. So the threat of Paul is turned into stories about preserving Judaism, and then also about preserving Islam. This is a reminder that, "In the triangular marketplace where Muslims, Christians and Jews set up their doctrinal booths, the arguments brought up in the discussion – both oral and written – served as currency, quickly changing hands. The exact value of a given coin can only be learned if one follows its course from

57 Peter is included along with Paul in many versions of *Toledot*; see John Gager, "Simon Peter, Founder of Christianity or Saviour of Israel?" in Schäfer et al, eds., Toledot Yeshu... *Revisited*, 221–45.

58 From Rashi's commentary on the Babylonian Talmud, *Avodah Zarah 10a*, as translated in Gager, "Simon Peter," 226. Rabbi Shlomo Yitzhaki (1040 – 1105) is known from his Hebrew initials as Rashi; see Avraham Grossman, *Rashi* (Oxford: Littman Library of Jewish Civilization, 2012).

hand to hand."[59] Part of the value of the "coin" of undermining Paul was effectively to dismiss a significant portion of the New Testament text.

5.3 Ibn Ḥazm

5.3.1 Biography and context

Abū Muḥammad Ibn Ḥazm is the most well-known critic of the Biblical text in the classical period of Islam. He was born in 384/994 in Cordoba, Spain, part of the area known to Muslims as al-Andalus.[60] The son of an important official, he was quite possibly from a family relatively recently converted from Christianity.[61] His life was intertwined with the political upheavals of Umayyad Spain, which featured civil war, caliphs installed and deposed, and in 1031 the end of Umayyad rule as the area split into petty kingdoms (known as the *Ṭā'ifa* kingdoms). Ibn Ḥazm withdrew from political life after unsuccessful attempts to be involved in various minor royal courts, his uncompromising views and verbal aggression probably hindering his ability to ingratiate himself into court life.[62]

Ibn Ḥazm's society was, of course, multi-religious. For Jews in particular the 11th century was a time of greater influence, including a cultural efflorescence

59 Sarah Stroumsa, "Jewish Polemics Against Islam and Christianity in the Light of Judaeo-Arabic Texts," in, *Judaeo-Arabic Studies; Proceedings of the Founding Conference of the Society for Judaeo-Arabic Studies*, ed. Norman Golb (Amsterdam: Studies in Muslim-Jewish Relations, 3, 1997), 241.

60 On 11th century al-Andalus see for example David Wasserstein, *The Rise and Fall of the Party–kings: politics and society in Islamic Spain, 1002–1086* (Princeton: PUP, 1985). A valuable resource is Olivia Constable (ed.), *Medieval Iberia: readings from Christian, Muslim and Jewish Sources* (Philadelphia: University of Pennsylvania Press, 1997).

61 Adang, *Muslim Writers*, 60. Scholarship on Ibn Ḥazm is prolific: see, for example, Camilla Adang, Maribel Fierro, Sabine Schmidtke (eds), *Ibn Ḥazm of Cordoba: the life and works of a controversial thinker.* Handbook of Oriental Studies: Section 1, the Near and Middle East, 103 (Leiden: Brill, 2012); Theodore Pulcini, *Exegesis as Polemical Discourse* (Atlanta: Scholars Press, 1998); Samuel–Martin Behloul, *Ibn Ḥazms Evangelienkritik: Eine Methodische Untersuchung*, IPTS 50 (Leiden: Brill, 2002); Daniel Potthast, *Christen und Muslime im Andalus* (Wiesbaden: Harrassowitz, 2013).

62 Bruno Soravia, "A Portrait of the *'Ālim* as a Young Man: the formative years of Ibn Ḥazm, 404/1013–420/1029' in *Controversial Thinker*, eds. Adang et al: 25–49, gives an account of Ibn Ḥazm's early political life.

and some role in these minor courts. So Ibn Ḥazm lived in a politically and religiously shifting situation.[63]

5.3.2 Works

Ibn Ḥazm was a prolific author, and while many of his works are lost, a substantial number survive.[64] The most important work for this study is *The Book of the Distinction regarding Religions, Sects and Heresies* (*Kitāb al-Faṣl fi'l-milal wa'l-ahwā' wa'l-niḥal*).[65] Other relevant texts for the present study include a legal work, a work of dogma, and a refutation of a supposed Jewish criticism of the Qur'an. The legal work, *Precision Regarding the Principles of Rulings* (*al-Iḥkām li-uṣūl al-aḥkām*), includes a section on the sharias of prophets before Muhammad.[66] The work of dogma, *Principles and what is Derived from them* (*al-Uṣūl wa'l-furū'*) was written in 422/1030, and in some ways anticipates the longer criticism of the Bible and of unacceptable groups found in *The Book of the Distinction.*[67] *Principles* includes some Biblical testimonies to Muhammad.[68] Although these Biblical testimonies are subsequently omitted in *The Distinction* Ibn

---

63 On the inter-religious situation in al-Andalus, see, for example, Janina Safran, *Defining Boundaries in al-Andalus: Muslims, Christians and Jews in Islamic Iberia* (Ithaca, N.Y.: Cornell Univ Press, 2013), and Daniel Potthast, *Christen und Muslime.* Wasserstein, *Rise and Fall*, 191–223, gives valuable perspective on the situation of Jews.

64 See J.M. Puerta Vilchez, "Inventory of Ibn Ḥazm's works," in *Controversial Thinker*, eds. Adang et al: 683–760.

65 Ibn Ḥazm, *Kitāb al-Faṣl fi'l-milal wa'l-ahwā' wa'l-niḥal*, 3 vols., Beirut: Dār al-Kutub al-'Ilmiyya, 2007, with many other editions also available. A brief, clear overview of the whole of the *Faṣl*, not just the sections on Judaism and Christianity, which form less than one third of the whole work, is given by Puerta Vilchez, in Adang et al, *Controversial Thinker*, 699–701. James Sweetman, *Islam and Christian Theology*, Part 2 vol. I, 178–262, gives a lengthy summary of the sections on Judaism and Christianity, as does Theodore Pulcini, *Exegesis as Polemical Discourse*, (Atlanta: Scholars' Press, 1998), 57–128. Abdelilah Ljamai, *Ibn Ḥazm et la polémique islamo-chrétienne dans l'histoire de l'Islam* (Leiden: Brill, 2003), 52–71, has shown that Ibn Ḥazm produced a revised manuscript in later life which featured various differences from the printed versions currently in circulation.

66 Ibn Ḥazm, *Al-iḥkām li uṣūl al-aḥkām*, vol. 2 (Cairo: Maṭba'at al-sa'āda, 1345–47/1926–28), 160–87.

67 Adang, *Muslim Writers*, describes *al-Uṣūl wa'l-furū'*, and *al-Radd 'ala Ibn al-Naghrīla* (64–65, 67–69). For dates of these and other works see Ljamai, *Polémique*, 43–79.

68 Ibn Ḥazm, *Al-Uṣūl wa'l-furū'*, ed. M. 'Irāqī, vol. 1 (Cairo: Dār al-Nahḍa al-'Arabiyya, 1978), 187–95. For an English translation of the Old Testament material see Camilla Adang, "Some Hitherto Neglected Biblical Material in the work of Ibn Ḥazm," *Al-Masāq* 5 (1992): 17–28.

Ḥazm does not avoid the topic completely in that work. He defends finding references to Muhammad in the Bible even in a work as critical of the Biblical text as *The Distinction*, stating that God "prevented their hands from distorting whatever He wished to preserve in these two books, to stand as a testimony against them."[69]

The Refutation of Ibn Naghrila (*Al-Radd 'alā Ibn Naghrīla*) is Ibn Ḥazm's rebuttal of a prominent contemporary Jew. Samuel ibn Naghrīla (d.1056) was vizier of Granada, wrote poetry, led armies and became the leader of the Jewish community of al-Andalus.[70] Ibn Ḥazm tells us that aged only 19 he had first met Ibn Naghrīla in 404/1013 and had engaged him in debate. Assuming that Ibn Ḥazm accurately reports the date, this shows how young he developed his desire to oppose Judaism and its scriptures.[71] *The Refutation* will merit further comment after discussion of Ibn Ḥazm's major work of Biblical criticism.

5.3.2.1 The Book of the Distinction (*Kitāb al-Faṣl fi'l-milal wa'l-ahwā' wa'l-niḥal*)

The Distinction includes a fierce attack on the Bible. It occurs as part of more broad-ranging criticism of many groups, including Muslims with whom the author disagrees. Composed and revised between 418/1027 and 450/1058, *The Distinction* is famously insulting and harsh towards opponents, even though Ibn Ḥazm writes elsewhere on the issue of manners in debate.[72] The section of *Distinction* dealing with Jews and Christians originally existed as a separate work,

69 Ibn Ḥazm, *Faṣl*, 1:238.

70 Ibn Ḥazm, *al-Radd 'alā ibn al-naghrīla wa rasā'il ukhrā*, ed. Iḥsān 'Abbas (Cairo: Dār al-'urūba, 1960), 45–81. The date of composition of this work is not known. For a summary of *The Refutation*, see David Powers, "Reading/Misreading One Another's Scriptures: Ibn Ḥazm's Refutation of Ibn Nagrella al-Yahūdī," in *Studies in Islamic and Jewish Traditions*, eds. W. Brinner and S. Ricks, vol. 1 (Atlanta: Scholars' Press, 1986): 109–21. On Ibn Naghrīla's life see David Wasserstein, "Samuel ibn Naghrīla Ha-Nagid and Islamic Historiography in al-Andalus," *Al-Qanṭara* 14 (1993): 109–25.

71 Ibn Ḥazm, *Faṣl*, 1: 178; Ibn Naghrīla is also mentioned at 1: 161–62.

72 See Ibn Ḥazm, *al-Taqrīb li ḥadd al-manṭiq* (*Introduction to the Scope of Logic*) (Beirut: Dār Maktabat al-Ḥayāt, 1959), 197, where he states that one of the reasons for declaring someone defeated in a round of formal debate was their resorting to rudeness. See the translation and discussion of wider issues in Sarah Stroumsa, "Ibn al-Rāwandī's *sū' adab al-mujādala:* the Role of Bad Manners in Medieval Disputations," in *The Majlis: Interreligious Encounters in Medieval Islam*, eds. Hava Lazarus-Yafeh, Mark Cohen, Sasson Somekh, Sidney Griffith (Wiesbaden: Harrassowitz, 1999): 66–83. One predecessor in rudeness is the Jewish work *Qiṣṣat*, mentioned above, which calls the four evangelists "wretches", but no direct connection between this and Ibn Ḥazm need be inferred from this similarity.

Exposition of the Alteration of the Tawrāt and Injīl by Jews and Christians (*Iẓhār tabdīl al-yahūd wa'l-naṣārā li'l-tawrāt wa'l-injīl*). Listed as a separate work in early Muslim sources, *Exposition* no longer exists independently, but has been incorporated into *The Distinction* in a section entitled *Treatise on Obvious Contradictions and Clear Lies* (*Faṣl fi munāqadāt ẓāhira wa takādhib wāḍiḥa*).[73]

One of Ibn Ḥazm's key concerns in this work is deliberately to oppose the more lenient view of some Muslims that Biblical corruption consists only of wrong interpretations, not corrupted text. "We have learned that some Muslims out of ignorance deny the statement that the *Tawrāt* and *Injīl* which the Jews and Christians possess are corrupted. They are led to this by their lack of concern for the words of the Qur'an and the traditions (*sunan*)."[74]

5.3.2.2.1 Ibn Ḥazm and the Old Testament

It appears that for the Old Testament Ibn Ḥazm drew mainly on Sa'adya Gaon's translation in Arabic script, although he sometimes departs from this text, indicating access to other versions, or his own alterations.[75] He concentrates his criticisms on the Pentateuch, though he also writes briefly on Joshua, Psalms, Ezekiel and Isaiah.[76]

Moral and factual errors, and charges of faulty transmission, are the key criticisms levelled against the Old Testament.[77] Ibn Ḥazm is repelled by Biblical criticisms of the prophets, (better termed here "prominent Biblical characters," since Jews and Christians do not see all such figures as prophets). For example, the account of Lot sleeping with his two daughters scandalises Ibn Ḥazm, since such an account contravenes the doctrine of *'iṣma* (protection from sin) of the prophets.[78]

---

73 Ibn Ḥazm, *Faṣl*, 1: 138–367. A partial English translation of some of the material on Judaism is given by N.A. Rifat, *Ibn Ḥazm on Jews and Judaism*, University of Exeter: Unpublished Ph.D. thesis 1988, 435–88. An extensive summary of the material on Judaism and Christianity is given by J.W. Sweetman in his *Islam and Christian Theology*, London: Lutterworth Press, 1955, Part 2, vol. 1: 179–262. Translations given below are my own.

74 Ibn Ḥazm, *Faṣl*, 1: 240.

75 Vollandt, *Arabic Versions*, 106–108, and see discussion of Sa'adya in Chapter 1. Cf Sweetman, *Islam*, 179, and Ernst Algermissen, *Die Pentateuchzitate Ibn Ḥazms: ein Beitrag zur Geschichte der arabischen Bibelübersetzungen*, (University of Münster: dissertation,1933), 84–90.

76 Ibn Ḥazm, *Faṣl*, 1: 229–35.

77 Pulcini, *Exegesis*, 95. The following discussion follows Pulcini's categorization of Ibn Ḥazm's material, 59–95.

78 Ibn Ḥazm, *Faṣl*, 1: 159–61; cf Gen 19:30–38. Ibn Ḥazm discusses *'iṣma* at length in *Faṣl*, 2: 284–322.

In addition he criticises arithmetical, historical and geographical errors. For example, information about rivers in Genesis is wrong.[79] There are also internal contradictions, absurdities and impossibilities, such as Abraham offering the visiting angels milk and meat together, when this is forbidden in the law.[80] (Ibn Ḥazm here ignores the significance of historical sequence in the Bible; Abraham is depicted as living before such laws were given). There are also unsuitable or blasphemous portrayals of God. For example, God is described as a consuming fire (Exod 24:17; Deut 9:3). This is much too physical a description for Ibn Ḥazm, thus demeaning God. He adds that Qur'anic descriptions of God as light (for example Q24:35) are a metaphor for his grace, not a physical phenomenon, and therefore not subject to the same criticism.[81]

The flawed transmission of the Biblical text is a focus of Ibn Ḥazm's attention. Because of the persecution and dispersal of the Jews into exile in Babylon beginning in 597BCE, Ibn Ḥazm argues that it was impossible for the Jews to preserve a reliable copy of the text. He attributes to Ezra the role of re-writing the *Tawrāt* in altered form, and the origins of this portrayal of Ezra deserve comment.[82]

Ezra's role in preserving the Torah was initially seen as positive in Jewish texts. *4 Ezra*, an apocryphal work by an unknown Jewish author from the late first century CE, portrays Ezra as miraculously restoring the Torah after it had been lost following the Exile to Babylon under Nebuchadnezzar.[83] Because of its availability in Arabic translation, *4 Ezra* influenced Muslim writing as early as the 2nd/8th century.[84] Indeed, Muslim traditions explaining the Qur'anic reference (Q9:30) to Jews regarding Ezra as "the son of God" reflect these Jewish views of Ezra's miraculous restoration of the Torah.[85] But Muslim exegetes comment that the error of some Jews was to let their admiration for Ezra because of his restoring the Torah grow into veneration, then worship, thus explaining the reference in Q9:30. As a result of this perceived error, Ezra's positive image in Jewish sources gradually transitions in Muslim perspective into that of a fabrica-

---

79 Ibn Ḥazm, *Faṣl*, 1: 141.
80 Ibn Ḥazm, *Faṣl*, 1: 157.
81 Ibn Ḥazm, *Faṣl*, 1: 185.
82 For a fuller account, see Martin Whittingham, "Ezra as the Corrupter of the Torah? Re-assessing Ibn Ḥazm's role in the long history of an idea', *IHIW* 1 (2013): 253–271. On Ibn Ḥazm's alleged role in spreading the idea of Biblical criticism to Europe, see below, 'Influence'.
83 See Drint, Adriana, *The Mount Sinai Arabic Version of 4 Ezra*, CSCOSAr 48–49, Leuven: Peeters, 1997.
84 Whittingham, "Ezra," 260–61.
85 See Mahmoud Ayoub, " 'Uzayr."

tor of scripture. There is an early, brief reference to Ezra as alterer of the Torah, in the correspondence bearing the names of Byzantine Emperor Leo III (r. 717–41) and Caliph ʿUmar II (r. 99–101/717–20), but which comes from later in the 3rd/9th century,[86] and this view is made much more explicit by Ibn Ḥazm.

One further type of criticism levelled by Ibn Ḥazm is discrepancy between the Septuagint and the Masoretic text of the Hebrew Bible. He states that this occurs, for example, over the recording of numbers, such as the great ages of some of characters mentioned in Genesis.[87]

5.3.2.1.2 Ibn Ḥazm and the New Testament

It is not clear what Arabic version of the New Testament Ibn Ḥazm used – possibly the translation of Isaac Velasquez (Isḥaq ibn Balashk), based on the Old Latin translation and finished in Cordoba in 946, though this is unlikely to have been his only source.[88] Ibn Ḥazm's knowledge is thorough, though he twice refers to the gospels depicting Jesus as drinking honey on the cross, a detail not found in the New Testament gospels, and which I have been unable to trace to other sources.[89]

Ibn Ḥazm mentions the corrupters of the Gospels and other New Testament writings more frequently than he mentions Ezra for the Old Testament. The transmission of the New Testament, deeply flawed in Ibn Ḥazm's view, can be traced back to a small group, namely the gospel writers Matthew, Mark, Luke and John and a handful of others described as "the most deceitful people of creation and the most wicked among them."[90] He regards the transmission history of the New Testament as even weaker than that of the Old Testament, because the Christians were, right from the outset, a small and persecuted minority with no power or stable community to help them to preserve a uniform text.[91] The explanation

86 See Palombo, "The 'correspondence'," for a variety of views on this correspondence. The Christian correspondent assumes that the Muslim charge of a falsified Torah is a reference to Ezra, even though the Muslim correspondent (or the voice portrayed as Muslim) does not mention the name. This indicates a relatively early circulation of the idea. See further, Whittingham, "Ezra."

87 Ibn Ḥazm, *Faṣl*, 1: 257.

88 See Vollandt, *Arabic Versions*, 71–72, and P.S. Van Koningsveld, "Christian-Arabic Manuscripts from the Iberian Peninsula and North Africa: a Historical Interpretation," *Al-Qanṭara* 15 (1994), 425, and more generally for the wider context. Potthast, *Christen und Muslime in Andalus*, 61–88, discusses New Testament versions available in al-Andalus in this period.

89 Ibn Ḥazm, *Faṣl*, 1: 297, 322.

90 Ibn Ḥazm, *Faṣl*, 1: 253.

91 Ibn Ḥazm, *Faṣl*, 1: 253, 341.

of the origins of the flawed text is historical – the beleaguered believing community was incapable of preserving the text from corruption, a situation parallel to the Old Testament. This reflects the Muslim understanding that the Caliph 'Uthmān (r. 23–35/ 644–656) organised the standardization of the Qur'anic text as a centralised government activity. If one follows this top-down model, political weakness helps to explain the development of a flawed text.

In addition to transmission, Ibn Ḥazm criticises the New Testament for discrepancies with Jewish scripture, blasphemy against God, and blasphemy against Jesus by portraying him as a liar, as being subject to Satan and a counterfeit miracle-worker. He also attacks contradictions between and within the gospels, absurdities and falsehoods.[92] Once again an example of each type of criticism will give the flavour of Ibn Ḥazm's writing.

Blasphemy against God can be seen when the Gospel of John grants to the Messiah the right to judge.[93] Blasphemy against Jesus occurs in the account of his temptation – does he submit to Satan willingly, which is unthinkable, or unwillingly, indicating that he is possessed?[94]

The most frequent attacks are on perceived contradictions within and between the Gospels, and on what Ibn Ḥazm sees as absurdities and falsehoods. He spends considerable energy on the question of the genealogies of Jesus given by Matthew and Luke.[95] This is an example of an issue which has also exercised Biblical scholars. Rather different are his points reflecting lack of awareness of Biblical context and language, such as over whether Jesus lay buried for three days, as the Bible states, or two, since it was from Friday to Sunday, which would at that time have been counted as three days.[96]

As another example, did Jesus come to bring fire and the sword, or to save people? These are alternatives which Ibn Ḥazm, unlike the New Testament, sees as mutually exclusive.[97] Ibn Ḥazm castigates as nonsense such beliefs as the union of the believer with Christ, asking if the Father is in the disciples, and vice versa.[98] All this and more causes him regularly to brand the New Testament writers with labels such as "stupid shameless atheists".[99]

92 These categories are taken from the summary given in Pulcini, *Exegesis*, 97–128. See also Sweetman, *Islam*, Part 2, vol I: 181–262.
93 Ibn Ḥazm, *Faṣl*, 1: 322. Cf John 5: 22.
94 Ibn Ḥazm, *Faṣl*, 1: 265.
95 Ibn Ḥazm, *Faṣl*, 1:261–65; cf Matt 1:1–17, Luke 3:23–38.
96 Ibn Ḥazm, *Faṣl*, 1: 282–83; cf Luke 13:32 for an indication of the type of counting in view.
97 Ibn Ḥazm, *Faṣl*, 1: 277–78; cf Matt 10:34, Luke 12:49, John 3:17.
98 Ibn Ḥazm, *Faṣl*, 1: 321.
99 Ibn Ḥazm, *Faṣl*, 1: 322.

5.3.5.1.3 Methods

Two related guiding principles in *The Distinction* are Ibn Ḥazm's concern with logic, and his theory of language. Briefly stated, Ibn Ḥazm believes that the human intellect can determine what is true or false by means of logic. He is in fact an optimist when it comes to human capacity to use reason.[100] Ibn Ḥazm draws attention to logic right at the outset of *The Distinction*, referring the reader to his work on the subject, *The Introduction to the Scope of Logic* (*al-Taqrīb li-ḥadd al-manṭiq*).[101] The role of logic and reason in informing his approach to his polemics emerges in his very first criticism in the section on the gospels. "They have no rationality in them."[102]

Alongside his interest in logic, Ibn Ḥazm is committed to a particular theory of language. He is known as the promoter of an ultimately unsuccessful legal school, the Ẓāhirī, distinguished by a strong attachment to interpreting words at face value, according to the evident meaning (*ẓāhir*). Hence, for Ibn Ḥazm the union of the believer with Christ makes a nonsense of human language, even setting aside other theological objections to the idea. The importance of Ẓāhirī hermeneutics for Ibn Ḥazm is to deny his opponents any escape by means of re-interpretation of terms. In the final passage of his long critique of the gospels he summarises some of the gospels' claims about the Messiah, then states that "Of necessity this demands that they speak of two gods who are definitely different."[103] All this accords with Ibn Ḥazm's concern with logic and reason. Revelation and reason are in harmony, since for him language is a stable and fully adequate vehicle to convey to the human mind what God intends.

Logic, hermeneutics and the type of argumentation designed to confound an opponent are all influences in *The Distinction*. But how original is his Biblical criticism? His comments do not spring from a vacuum, and there are similarities to some Muslim predecessors, including al-Rassī. As for non-Muslim predecessors, questions over chronology and perceived contradictions in the Bible were not news to Christians and Jews. They also discussed such issues, though we

100 See Samuel-Martin Behloul, "The Testimony of Reason and Historical Reality: Ibn Ḥazm's Refutation of Christianity," in *Controversial Thinker*, eds. Adang et al, 457–83; also Behloul, *Evangelienkritik*.

101 Ibn Ḥazm, *Faṣl*, 1: 13–17. See his *al-Taqrīb*.

102 Ibn Ḥazm, *Faṣl*, 1: 251.

103 A sophisticated study of Ibn Ḥazm's theory of language is given by Rob Gleave, *Islam and Literalism* (Edinburgh: EUP 2012), 146–74. Jessica Coope, "With Heart, Tongue and Limbs: Ibn Ḥazm on the essence of faith," *ME* 6 (2000), 109, argues that Ibn Ḥazm uses his theory of language to exclude Jews and Christians from toleration.

cannot establish any clear lines of influence upon Ibn Ḥazm.[104] Overall, Ibn Ḥazm's views are distinctive not for their content but for three other reasons – being offered by a Muslim, in such detail, and with such hostility.[105]

5.3.2.1.4 Motivation

The Distinction is well-known for its strident critique of the Bible. But is this its central aim? It has been termed "a political call to action," an attempt to stir up Muslims to overthrow their wayward Muslim rulers who were allowing Jews too prominent a political role.[106] To assess this interpretation of Ibn Ḥazm takes us back to Ibn Naghrīla, the Jewish vizier of Granada, against whom Ibn Ḥazm wrote a refutation. Pulcini argues that all the invective against the Bible is not primarily about the Bible at all but is aimed at social change, namely the overthrow of lax Muslim rulers who fail to treat non-Muslims with appropriate severity. The criticism is indirect, so it is argued, because of the hazards of calling for the overthrow of rulers in direct terms, but is designed to show how misguided are any Muslim rulers who give a prominent public role to Jews and Christians. Ibn Naghrīla is only the most prominent example of people whose faith and scripture are to be utterly despised.[107]

But is a call for rebellion a fair portrayal of the aim of the Biblical criticism in *The Distinction?* One passage stands out in this context. "What would you say of a sultan who puts Jews at the head of his kingdom and Christians in the ranks of his army?"[108] Ibn Ḥazm calls for rebellion against such rulers as obligatory. However, this passage occurs in the context of a completely different section of *The Distinction*, hundreds of pages after the treatise against the Bible. It is found in a chapter on "commanding right and forbidding wrong" *(al-amr bi'l-ma'rūf)*, a well-known category of Islamic thought which explores what measures can be

---

104 Sweetman, *Islam and Christian Theology,* Part 2, vol I: 260 – 61, mentions, as an example, Ishodad of Merv (fl c. 850), near Mosul.

105 For another example from al-Andalus of unusually hostile language which stands out from other writers, see Alejandro García-Sanjuán, "Jews and Christians in Almoravid Seville as Portrayed by the Islamic Jurist Ibn 'Abdūn," *Medieval Encounters* 14 (2008), 83 and passim. Ibn 'Abdūn, two generations later than Ibn Ḥazm, writes about the social roles of Jews and Christians, rather than their scriptures.

106 Pulcini, *Exegesis,* 196.

107 Wasserstein, *Rise and Fall,* 190 – 223, mentions other prominent Jewish figures in the royal courts of al-Andalus.

108 Ibn Ḥazm, *Faṣl,* 3: 105 – 06.

taken against a sinful or erring Muslim.[109] The context shows that Ibn Ḥazm's main concern is to demonstrate the legitimacy of rebellion against an errant ruler. In this he offers what is for him an important example, the overly generous treatment of Jews and Christians. But this is one of various examples legitimising uprising.[110] It is hard to see it as incorporating in veiled form the core purpose of the Biblical critique which occurs in a different part of the work. Ibn Ḥazm's attack has many causes, of which the issue of Jewish and Christian social prominence is only one.

The idea of a call to rebellion could more justly be applied to Ibn Ḥazm's *Refutation.* Ibn Naghrīla, the vizier of Granada targeted in this work, was allegedly the author of a lost critique of the Qu'ran, ("allegedly" because there has been speculation that someone so politically shrewd would never have written a tract critical of the Qur'an while his career flourished under Muslim rulers).[111] Ibn Ḥazm's anger against the Muslim rulers of his day is more clearly apparent in *The Refutation of Ibn Naghrīla* than in *The Distinction.* In *The Refutation* he writes, "For whosoever amongst Muslim princes has listened to all this and still continues to befriend the Jews, holding intercourse with them, well deserves to be overtaken by the same humiliation... May God keep us from rebelling against Him and His decision, from honouring those whom he has humiliated".[112] Such a stance is not surprising. Ibn Ḥazm voices similar objections in other works, and other writers voiced similar opposition to the political role of the People of the Book, including the role of the Christian powers in Northern Spain.[113] So there is some justification for seeing a political aim behind Ibn

109 See Michael Cook, *Commanding Right and Forbidding Wrong in Islamic Thought* (Cambridge: CUP, 2001).

110 Cook, *Commanding Right*, 511 n.39, calls Ibn Ḥazm's passage on this issue, "the most sustained statement of the revolutionary implications of *al-amr bi'l-ma'rūf* I have seen in pre-modern Sunnī literature." Ibn Ḥazm is thus atypical in calling for armed uprising against a Muslim ruler who commits even relatively minor transgressions.

111 See Adang *Muslim Writers*, 68–69, for a summary of recent discussion of the possible identity of the author of the tract which Ibn Ḥazm attacks. For further treatment see Maribel Fierro, "Ibn Ḥazm and the Jewish *Zindīq*," in *Controversial Thinker*, eds. Adang et al, 497–509, and Sarah Stroumsa, "From Muslim Heresy to Jewish-Muslim Polemics: Ibn al-Rāwandī's *Kitāb al-Dāmigh*," *JAOS* 107 (1987): 767–772.

112 *Al-Radd*, 88, 91; trans from Moshe Perlmann, "Eleventh Century Andalusian Authors on the Jews of Granada," *Proceedings of the American Academy for Jewish Research* 18 (1948–49), 281, 283.

113 See Ljamai, *Polémique*, 37–40. For a succinct yet insightful overview of the highly complex power relations between the Muslim party kings and Christian powers in Northern Spain, see Lynn Nelson, "Christian-Muslim Relations in Eleventh-Century Spain," *Military Affairs* 43 (1979): 195–98.

Ḥazm's anti-Biblical writings, but that argument is better based on *The Refutation* than on *The Distinction.* Ibn Ḥazm's criticisms of the Bible in *The Distinction* are driven by religious as well as socio-political concerns, as can be seen from his vehement attacks on Muslims whom he sees as religiously misguided. Of course, the religious and the political are closely intertwined in 11th century al-Andalus, but need not be entirely collapsed into one another.

5.2.3.1.5 Influence

From the modern perspective it would appear that Ibn Ḥazm has exerted huge influence on creating what is an almost routine Muslim view that the Bible is beset by textual corruption. He clearly did exert influence, but the number of manuscripts of *The Distinction* is relatively few.[114] In Spain, he influenced al-Khazrajī, (d. 519/1125), Aḥmad Ibn 'Umar al-Qurṭubī (d. 656/1258) and 'Abd Allāh al-Tarjumān (d.c. 837/1430).[115] In the Islamic east, Ibn Ḥazm is indebted for the spread of his works to his disciple al-Ḥumaydī, who travelled to Baghdad sometime around or after 448/1056 (and who will reappear in the discussion of al-Juwaynī, below). The Jewish convert to Islam, Samā'ul al-Maghribī (d. 570/1175) adopts both a similarly aggressive approach and also borrows many of the same Biblical texts in his *Silencing the Jews* (*Ifḥām al-yahūd*), indicating that he may have read Ibn Ḥazm.[116] Ibn Ḥazm's subsequent influence on Ibn Taymiyya (d. 728/1328), Ibn Qayyim al-Jawziyya (d. 751/1350) and al-Bājī (d. 714/1314) can be seen, though the first two of these writers regularly disagreed with Ibn Ḥazm as well as drawing on him.[117]

Aside from his influence on Muslims, it is sometimes held that Ibn Ḥazm is an influence on modern critical biblical scholarship.[118] This view is based on the role of Ibn Ezra (d.1167), a Spanish Jew and near contemporary of Ibn Ḥazm, who raised tentative questions over the authorship of the Pentateuch. Ibn Ezra's

---

114 Ljamai, *Polémique*, 170. To what extent this is related to his sometimes unpopular views on Islam is unclear. On this unpopularity see Samir Kaddouri, "Refutations of Ibn Ḥazm by Mālikī authors of al-Andalus and North Africa," in *Controversial Thinker*, eds. Adang et al: 539–600.

115 Ljamai, *Polémique*, 145–73.

116 Arabic text and English translation in Moshe Perlmann, *Samā'ul al-Maghribī: Ifḥām al-yahūd. Silencing the Jews* (New York: American Academcy for Jewish Research, 1964).

117 The influence of Ibn Ḥazm in the ensuing centuries will be discussed further in volume 2 of the present study.

118 Lazarus-Yafeh, *Intertwined Worlds*, 73, 140. This view is regularly repeated, citing Lazarus-Yafeh; see, e.g., Walid Saleh, "The Hebrew Bible in Islam," in *The Cambridge Companion to the Hebrew Bible/ Old Testament*, eds. Stephen Chapman, Marvin Sweeney (Cambridge: CUP, 2016), 418.

name was then used by Spinoza (d. 1677), albeit in an exaggerated way, to raise further questions over Biblical authorship. Yet Ibn Ezra appears to have been no admirer of Ibn Ḥazm. He criticises the influence of an unnamed Muslim who is very likely Ibn Ḥazm, and other Jewish writers were already raising questions about the Biblical text independently of Ibn Ḥazm.[119] So Ibn Ezra did not need the presence of Ibn Ḥazm in order to provoke questions about the Biblical text, and there is no compelling reason to give Ibn Ḥazm such a significant place in the history of Biblical criticism.

Ibn Ḥazm stands as the archetypal exponent of detailed criticisms of the Bible amongst Muslims. But another author draws our attention back from Spain to Iran and also Baghdad. His short work on the Bible carries echoes of Ibn Ḥazm's efforts, even though they lived far apart at almost the same time.

5.4 Al-Juwaynī

5.4.1 Biography and context

Abū'l-Ma'ālī al-Juwaynī, (419 – 478/1028 – 1085), Persian by birth, was a famous theologian in the Ash'arite tradition. Whether or not he would welcome the epithet, he is equally or more famous as the teacher of Abū Ḥāmid al-Ghazālī (d. 505/1111), possibly the most prominent classical period Muslim theologian of all time. Alongside some major works of theology,[120] al-Juwaynī also wrote a short work critical of the Bible and with some resemblance to Ibn Ḥazm's *Distinction*, entitled *Assuaging the Thirst* (*Shifā' al-Ghalīl*).[121] Although this work cannot be precisely dated, he most likely wrote it during or after his stay in Baghdad which lasted from around 440/1048 until the mid to late 440's/1050's, following his exile from his native Nishapur.[122] This is likely since Baghdad would have provided a more religiously mixed environment than al-Juwaynī would have en-

119 See Whittingham, "Ezra," 264 – 67.

120 On his life and major works see Paul Walker, 'Introduction' in al-Juwayni, *A Guide to Conclusive Proofs for the Principles of Belief: Kitāb al-irshād ilā qawāti' al-adilla fī uṣūl al-i'tiqād*, trans. Paul Walker, GBIC (Reading: Garnet, 2000), xix–xxxvii.

121 Al-Juwaynī, *Shifā' al-ghalīl fī bayān mā waqa'a fi'l-Tawrāt wa'l-Injīl min al-tabdīl* (*Assuaging the Thirst in explanation of the alterations occurring in the Torah and* Gospel) in Michel Allard, *Textes apologetiques de Ǧuwainī* (Beirut: Dār al-Machreq, 1968), 38 – 83 (edition and French translation). As al-Juwaynī makes clear (40), the title is an allusion to Q24:39, which refers to the works of unbelievers as being "like a mirage in a desert which the thirsty man thinks (to be) water, until, when he comes to it he finds it (to be) nothing."

122 The dates are approximate. See Walker, 'Introduction', xxii-xxiv.

countered elsewhere on his travels. Given certain similarities to Ibn Ḥazm's work, it is important to explore the possibility of any relationship between the two works, after first outlining al-Juwaynī's arguments.

5.4.2 Al-Juwaynī and the Old Testament

Al-Juwaynī considers first the theoretical possibility, then actual examples, of what he considers to be textual corruption of the Old Testament. He then follows the same procedure for the New Testament. He argues that the loss of the original *Tawrāt* is plausible because of Nebuchadnezzar's sack of Jerusalem (which occurred in the 6th century BCE), and adds that Ezra, or possibly one of his followers, re-wrote the text so as to enhance his own power and prominence.[123]

As for an actual example of textual corruption, al-Juwaynī cites the difference in ages of the descendants of Adam found between Jews and Christians (reflecting differences between the Masoretic text and the Septuagint). This passage follows very closely parts of Ibn Ḥazm's account of the same issue, though with some minor differences.[124]

5.4.3 Al-Juwaynī and the New Testament

Beginning once more with the theoretical possibility of corruption, al-Juwaynī cites the familiar issue of unreliable transmission. He also adds a list of how many years passed after the death of Jesus before each gospel writer composed his work. This list has both correspondence with and difference from that of Ibn Ḥazm. However, Ibn Ḥazm also discusses both of these issues, faulty transmission and the length of time which elapsed between the end of Jesus' life and the composition of the gospels, at the outset of his account of New Testament corruption.

Turning to actual examples, al-Juwaynī offers five instances of alleged corruption, the first four of which are also given by Ibn Ḥazm. First, there are errors in counting the number of generations in the genealogies of Jesus.[125] Secondly, when and how often did the cock crow before Peter's denial of Jesus? Thirdly, did Jesus ride a donkey or a colt at the Triumphal Entry into Jerusalem? Fourthly,

---

123 Al-Juwaynī, *Shifā'*, 47.

124 Al-Juwaynī, *Shifā'*, 51–57; cf. Ibn Ḥazm, Faṣl, 1: 257–58.

125 As an example of discussion of this issue, see Stephen Carlson, "The Davidic Key for Counting the Generations in Matthew 1:17," *CBC* 76 (2014), 665–83.

were both thieves crucified with Jesus wicked, or was one repentant, as Luke narrates (Luke 23:39–43)? The final issue, not found in Ibn Ḥazm, concerns why only Matthew amongst all the gospel writers would record an event as extraordinary as the dead rising from their graves at the moment Jesus died (Matt 27: 52–53).

5.4.4 Reflection

Al-Juwaynī clearly asserts the textual corruption of both testaments.[126] As for the quality of al-Juwaynī's Biblical knowledge, he reveals at one point that he may well be using a compilation of Biblical texts rather than a whole Bible. Where Ibn Ḥazm merely notes the number of years after which each gospel writer composed his work, al-Juwaynī makes the bolder but incorrect claim that the gospels themselves state these figures.[127] Reading the actual gospels would have spared him this error.

But is there any relationship between Ibn Ḥazm's *Distinction* and al-Juwaynī's *Assuaging the Thirst?* Though this seems unlikely given the geographical distance between these near contemporaries, a connection is in fact possible, though not proven. The solution may lie with Ibn Ḥazm's disciple al-Ḥumaydī (d. 488/1095). If *Assuaging the Thirst* were written in Baghdad sometime in the period 440–450/1048–58, this would coincide with al-Ḥumaydī's possible presence in that city sometime after 448/1056. Al-Ḥumaydī tells us that he left al-Andalus in that year, after which we know that he made the pilgrimage to Mecca and travelled in the Arab East, settling in Baghdad.[128] It is possible, if by no means certain that he may have encountered al-Juwaynī either in Baghdad or

126 He makes the same claim about the *Injīl* in a brief comment in his longest work of theology, *Kitāb al-Shāmil fi uṣūl al-dīn* (*The Complete Book on the Principles of Religion*), ed. A. Nashshār (Alexandria: Musha'at al-Ma'ārif, 1969), 607. This passage, paradoxically, is mainly concerned with using, not dismissing, Biblical verses, by interpreting them in such a way as to prove that Jesus was not divine.

127 Al-Juwaynī, *Shifā'*, 59.

128 Ljamai, *Polémique*, 9, seems to oversimplify matters in noting that al-Ḥumaydī had emigrated to Baghdad in 448/1056. Satisfying as this would be for strengthening the possibility of a clear link between al-Ḥumaydī and al-Juwaynī, what al-Ḥumaydī actually states twice in his biographical dictionary *Jadhwat al-Muqtabis fi dhikr wulāt al-Andalus* (*The Firebrand for the one seeking Illumination about the rulers of al-Andalus*), ed. Muḥammad Ṭanjī (Cairo: Maktabat Nashr al-Thaqāfat al-Islāmiyya, 1953), 128, 346, is that "my departure from al-Andalus was in 448 [=1056CE]". We also know that he settled in Baghdad, but at what exact date after his departure from al-Andalus is unknown.

other locations. If al-Ḥumaydī played a role in spreading Ibn Ḥazm's critique of the Bible, then even though the opportunity for influence is narrow in Baghdad itself, it is also possible that al-Juwaynī absorbed the influence, and could have written his work either in Baghdad itself, or some time during the 25 or so years he lived after leaving that city.[129]

It is clear that al-Juwaynī's work, while much shorter than Ibn Ḥazm's *The Distinction*, exhibits some striking similarities to it. However, there are also differences, and the work seems to resemble more closely the tradition attributed to al-Ḥasan ibn Ayyūb, (active early 3rd/ mid 10th century) which is only available as quoted by two later sources. One of these is by Naṣr b. Yaḥya (d.589/1193, or 558/1163).[130] However, it has been argued that Naṣr b. Yahya is actually producing his own criticism of the Bible, rather than, as is sometimes thought, reproducing wholesale the thought of Ibn Ayyub.[131] In other words, it is Naṣr b. Yaḥya himself who is critical of the Biblical text, not the earlier Ibn Ayyūb. This seems likely since the other source preserving the work of Ibn Ayyūb, Ibn Taymiyya's *The Correct Response to whoever alters the Religion of the Messiah* (*al-Jawāb al-ṣaḥīḥ li-man baddala dīn al-masīḥ*), gives a quite different picture of Ibn Ayyūb. Ibn Taymiyya includes none of the criticisms of the Biblical text, but instead presents Ibn Ayyūb as quoting the Bible to prove that when rightly interpreted it supports the truth of Islamic views.[132] This contradiction between the "Ibn Ayyūb" preserved by Ibn Taymiyya and the "Ibn Ayyūb" preserved by Naṣr b. Yaḥya may suggest that al-Juwaynī and others are in fact the unnamed sources of Nasr b. Yahya's account, rather than al-Juwaynī drawing on an earlier 'source' allegedly preserved by Naṣr b. Yaḥya.[133]

Returning to the implications of the similarities in the works of Ibn Ḥazm and al-Juwaynī, there is no decisive answer as yet regarding whether al-Juwaynī had any access to Ibn Ḥazm's work. Given the marked similarities between the

---

129 Al-Juwaynī's work would have arrived in al-Andalus too late to influence even the final revisions of *The Distinction*. See Sabine Schmidtke, 'Ibn Ḥazm's sources on Ash'arism and Mu'tazilism', in Adang et al (eds.), *Controversial Thinker*, 387–88.

130 Naṣr ibn Yaḥya, *Al-Naṣīḥa al-imāniyya fī faḍīḥat al-milla al-Naṣrāniyya* (*Faithful Counsel concerning the ignominy of the Christian Religion*), ed. M. al-Sharqāwī (Cairo: Dār al-ṣaḥwa, 1986). This text was unavailable to me; see Lejla Demiri, "Naṣr ibn Yaḥya," in *CMR*, 3:750–54.

131 Accad, 'Corruption', 61.

132 See Ibn Taymiyya, *al-Jawāb al-ṣaḥīḥ li-man baddala dīn al-masīḥ* (Cairo: Maṭba'at al-nīl, 1323/1905), 2: 312–45, 352–63, and 3: 2–3.

133 Discussion of al-Juwaynī and these tangled connections is found in Martin Accad, "Corruption and/or misinterpretation of the Bible: the story of the Islamic usage of *taḥrīf*," in *Christian Presence and Witness among* Muslims, ed. Peter Penner (Schwarzenfeld: Neufeld Verlag, 2005), 36–87.

two works discussed, it seems plausible that al-Ḥumaydī brought Ibn Ḥazm's work to Baghdad in time for al-Juwaynī to learn about it. But if he did not, the similarities in the points they make are sufficiently strong as to suggest some form of prior tradition of criticism of the Biblical text available to al-Juwaynī. The works are too similar to indicate that al-Juwaynī produced a work unconnected either to Ibn Ḥazm or to some prior shared tradition. At this point in our knowledge of the period, the question of the relationship between the Biblical criticism of these two men must be left open. But since it seems likely that Ibn Ḥazm did influence al-Juwaynī, al-Ḥumaydī is the prime candidate to be a link between the two.[134] If al-Juwaynī is so influenced, then Ibn Ḥazm's reach extended eastward at an early stage, through his writing on the Bible, if not in other ways.

5.5 Conclusion

'Abd al-Jabbār elaborated on the account of Paul as conspirator which can be traced back to the Jewish anti-Christian work *Toledot Yeshu*. Ibn Ḥazm launched a full-scale assault on many parts of the Hebrew Bible and New Testament, explicitly condemning the idea that Biblical corruption only extended to corrupt interpretations. For him, the text itself was his main target of criticism. Al-Juwaynī most likely (though it cannot currently be proven) absorbed the influence of Ibn Ḥazm during his years in Baghdad in the 440's/1050's, given the marked similarities between his text and the concerns of Ibn Ḥazm himself. None of the three writers discussed in this chapter wrote in a void, isolated from previous influence. All were drawing on prior traditions. And yet in Rayy, Baghdad (perhaps) and in Spain, the tide turned decisively against the acceptance of the Bible. Decisively does not mean exclusively, of course, but the views expressed in this chapter flowed into the mainstream of Muslim Biblical criticism. Where before they had surfaced either in passing, or as one among a series of points in interfaith exchanges, explicit criticism of textual reliability gradually assumes a more dominant position. All three writers were famous for many other works. Criticising the Bible was carried out in the context of lives spent writing at length on other subjects. Contextual factors alone do not explain why these authors should take this new turn in focussing their criticism of Christianity and Judaism squarely on the Biblical text. Clearly there were such contextual factors, such as

134 This departs from my earlier view, expressed in "Ezra as the Corrupter of the Torah?", in which I considered the influence of Ibn Ḥazm to be unlikely.

the complex religious and political situation in al-Andalus at the time of Ibn Ḥazm. But the works can also be seen as part of the writers' impulse to refute perceived error, an impulse which also characterised their writings about intra-Muslim matters. The stone which they collectively threw into the pool of Muslim reception of the Bible, with Ibn Ḥazm giving it the greatest effort, continued to send its ripples outwards in the ensuing centuries.

6 Conclusions and Prospects: Looking Back and Looking Ahead

It is time to pause, part-way along the journey of tracing Muslim responses to the Bible. First we can look back, and then more briefly glimpse the terrain lying ahead for discussion in Volume 2. In looking back, it is important to recall how elements of the story so far impact modern discussion, but also to recognise that the picture emerging from the early centuries is not identical to a typical understanding of Muslim views today. To draw a broad but foundational conclusion, in comparison with the modern assumptions about Muslim views, there is less impulse to condemn large parts of the Bible, more impetus to use it, and the accusation of corruption of the text lingers in the background, present but not dominant, until the $5^{th}/11^{th}$ century.

Chapter 2 showed that selected early Qur'anic commentators carefully limited the applications of apparently positive verses about the previous scriptures. This phenomenon occurs in the commentaries of Muqātil b. Sulaymān and al-Ṭabarī, who sought to draw clear boundary lines and assert identity by downplaying the importance of Judaism and Christianity. The application of positive verses is narrowed, while the application of verses on corruption, conversely, is widened. Passages seemingly referring to specific groups of Jews concealing or occasionally altering their scriptures become the basis for allegations of general and widespread corruption of the text. One can only infer here that the needs of the community to assert their primacy in the contested religious space became a key concern controlling interpretation.

In Chapter 3 we saw that hadith literature, both Sunni and Shia, contains very few narratives of textual corruption. Where references to previous scripture occur, they are much more likely to involve supporting a particular idea or individual. The notion of textual corruption (*taḥrīf al-lafẓ*) is only found in a handful of references. Likewise the earliest biographical literature on Muhammad, as evidenced by Ibn Isḥāq, is more concerned to use the Biblical scriptures rather than criticise them. Ibn Isḥāq, the most famous early biographer of Muhammad, seeks to link the 'Abbāsids, the newly ruling dynasty of his latter years, to pre-Islamic prophetic history.

Chapter 4 took a broader view of a variety of Islamic literature in the period up to the death of Ibn Ḥazm in 456/1064. Here the use of previous scriptures to support the prophethood of Muhammad and the truth of Islam more generally is in evidence. A range of Biblical predictions are taken to refer to Muhammad, and to his use of force to combat idolatry and bring about obedience to God. References to Mecca are also identified in the Biblical text. A number of historical

https://doi.org/10.1515/9783110335880-009

works continue the tendency of Ibn Isḥāq to link ʻAbbāsid and Muslim history with God's global purposes since creation. These draw on Biblical background to provide information about previous prophets and other events. The Ismāʻīlī use of Biblical literature is less well-known, and appears to have had the aim of supporting specific Ismāʻīlī doctrines and building the confidence of devotees in the belief that they possessed special knowledge unavailable to other Muslims.

However, alongside this appropriation of Biblical material there existed clear challenges to the Biblical text. Theological literature seeks to rebut claims for the Bible, often by arguing that verses have been misinterpreted and should be understood in a way that aligns with Islamic beliefs. Legal literature grants previous scripture a limited space. While in early works of legal theory the scriptures of "those who came before us" are received positively as a potential theoretical source of law, this has no bearing on actual legal rulings. Furthermore, it is clear from Christian responses throughout this period that the charge of textual corruption of the Bible troubled them, since Christian writers regularly tackle it. This indicates that the general assumption by Muslims of such textual corruption was more widespread than the evidence recorded in early Muslim texts suggests.

The 4th–5th/11th century brings winds of change. For reasons which remain unclear, two major thinkers both attack the Bible more directly at around the same time. They do so from geographically opposite wings of the Muslim world of the day, present-day Spain and Iran, and there appears to be no direct influence linking Ibn Ḥazm and ʻAbd al-Jabbār. Yet their combined efforts, particularly those of Ibn Ḥazm, produce a swing towards harsher rejection of the Bible. ʻAbd al-Jabbār increases the pressure on Paul as the culprit who distorted the pure teachings of Jesus, but it is Ibn Ḥazm who directs his wrath most vehemently at the Bible.

What general reflections emerge from the writings explored so far? The role of accusations of corruption is complex. These charges seem necessary since, as the Qur'an itself records, Jews and Christians did not accept the Muslim claim of continuity with these faith traditions. It can be argued that Muslim discourses on corruption are actually not about the Biblical texts at all. They are about validating the Qur'anic text and Muslim identity, in the light of Qur'anic claims which both assert continuity with these scriptures, yet simultaneously contradict aspects of them.[1] We shall see in Volume 2 that some writers attempt to tackle

1 As noted by Anne-Sylvie Boisliveau, "Qur'ānic Discourse on the Bible: Ambivalence and *taḥrīf* in the Light of Self-Reference," *MIDEO* 33 (2018), 3–38.

one point directly, unlike anyone in these early centuries – the point that the Qur'an affirms not only some form of previous scripture but indicates that the scriptures extant in the 7th century CE were themselves conveyors of the "guidance and light" mentioned in Q 5:44 and 5:46.

The foundations of the charge of *taḥrīf* are therefore less clear and emphatic than might be presumed. The Qur'anic evidence is mixed, while the Hadith literature, the second authoritative source of Islamic law and practice, has very little to say – almost nothing if the statements are weighed alongside the thousands of other hadiths in circulation. As a result the charge of corruption does not take centre stage for some centuries. There is clearly also an emphasis in the early centuries on any corruption being primarily about interpretation. Yet it is questionable whether this charge of corrupt interpretation is meaningful, since even those writers who lean towards this lenient version of corruption affirm the traditional view that the Qur'an denies the crucifixion of Jesus. But it is difficult to read the New Testament as doing anything but affirming the death by crucifixion of Jesus, especially since the New Testament gospels devote more space to events surrounding the crucifixion than to any other single happening. It is also central to the theology of the New Testament.[2] Overall, where charges of textual corruption are made, they are more routinely levelled at the New Testament than at the Hebrew Bible, since the New Testament's teachings are more obviously in conflict with the Qur'an, notably over the life and identity of Jesus. The Hebrew Bible is more likely to be criticised for errors of chronology than of doctrine.

Another clear conclusion to emerge is that an appeal to the Bible, whether general or very specific, is useful to Muslim writers. A recent study of the role of Jews and Christians in prominent positions in the early 'Abbāsid period provides a helpful parallel in understanding the Muslim resort to the Bible. "In earlier periods Muslims were ready to learn and adopt anything valuable from the experiences of other communities".[3] The key word here is "valuable". The context for this remark is the role of *dhimmīs*, or protected peoples, who were predominantly Jews and Christians, in the 'Abbāsid administration. But a similar dynamic is at play in attitudes to the Bible. Many aspects of Islam could be given added confirmation (though not of course their ultimate basis) through the Bible. These included the prophethood of Muhammad, the legitimisation of conquest, and of Islam itself as the culmination of God's plan, along with

2 For more on the charge of corrupt interpretation, see Martin Whittingham, "The Value of *taḥrīf ma'nawī* (corrupt interpretation) as a category for analyzing Muslim views of the Bible: evidence from *Al-radd al-jamīl* and Ibn Khaldūn," *ICMR* 22 (2011), 209–22.

3 Mun'im Sirry, "The Public Role of *Dhimmīs* during 'Abbāsid Times," in *BSOAS* 74 (2011), 204.

the importance of Arabs in that plan. Genealogies were expanded, prophecies of Muhammad or Islam identified, and identity reinforced, all through Biblical texts. Much of this usage seems to relate to the emergence and rise of the 'Abbāsid dynasty from around 132/750 CE. The new ruling power, surrounded by much larger populations of Christians and Jews, brought a desire to reinforce a clearer Muslim identity and to emphasise the position of Muslims as integrally related to God's purposes in history, indeed the culmination of these purposes.

Yet for all this partial openness, it is clear that the Bible was also a suspect text. As noted, the Hadith exhibit only a minuscule record of charges of corruption. Yet Christians from an early stage record the suspicion or charge coming from Muslims that something has been not only misinterpreted, but has been subject to textual alteration. Christian writers' brief references to this charge, and the lengthy discussion of 'Ammār al-Baṣrī, all indicate sensitivity to this accusation. Yet it remains surprising how limited this charge appears to be in most Muslim writings before the 4th–5th/11th century. The charge of textual *taḥrīf* was not the central hub of discussions and debates, yet nor is the accusation of textual corruption "virtually non-existent".[4] The reality lies somewhere in between. But even the Qur'an, if carefully interpreted, levels charges only at specific groups, rather than a broad-ranging dismissal of the Biblical text, contrary to what many today assume. This is affirmed by the approach of early exegetes such as Muqātil b. Sulaymān, who are more concerned with the error of concealment of news about Muhammad in the Bible than about the error of widespread Biblical corruption. Perhaps the regular minor adjustments of Biblical quotations by authors such as al-Rassī, who are more concerned to use the Bible than to criticise it, capture the ambiguous situation best. The ambiguity is evident in trying to understand the motives for their alterations to Biblical quotations. Are these minor alterations an indirect endorsement of the Bible, since authors willingly use it once these alterations are inserted? This is a positive interpretation of such alterations, seeing a glass half-full. Or is the glass instead half-empty? That is to say, do the alterations to fit Islamic assumptions emphasise that writers do not trust extant Biblical texts, to an extent which amounts to a charge of corruption? It is hard to answer this without more information about the attitudes behind the alterations made. But to sum up, the impetus for some Muslim responses is not necessarily overall suspicion, but an absolute assumption that if something appears to deviate from the Qur'an and other Muslim

4 Accad, *Gospels*, 246. Accad here comments in relation to the gospels exclusively, rather than the whole New Testament, but the remark understates the situation, especially given the regular refutations of the charge in Christian works surveyed above.

norms, some kind of error must have occurred, and a change needs making, presumably for the benefit of all.

Having looked back over the first four centuries of Islam, it is time to look forward. In Volume 2, the starting point will be the ongoing influence of the 4th–5th/11th century attacks, and the content and tone of discussions of the Bible in the late classical period more generally. As new Muslim dynasties arise, notably the Ottomans, the Safavids in Iran (from 907/1501), and the Mughals in India, along with the Muslim societies of Africa and the Malay-Indonesian world, our enquiry will follow them to see what was written about the Bible. By the nineteenth century, British India, among other places, provides a forum for Muslim-Christian encounter where the power balance is reversed. Powerful Muslim empires have been replaced by Muslim subjugation. This pattern of relative Muslim weakness provides the backdrop for discussion in the 20th century, along with the emergence of significant Muslim minorities in Europe, the USA and elsewhere, and resurgent Islamic movements in the wake of the Iranian revolution. In the 21st century there are signs of new engagements with the Biblical text. It is important to trace in what ways the arguments of the early centuries continue to influence more recent discussions, and where these discussions forge new paths.

Appendix: Qur'anic Verses on the Previous Scriptures

Translation taken from A.J. Droge *The Qur'ān: A New Annotated Translation* (Sheffield: Equinox, 2013, reprinted with corrections 2017).

Note that the text quoted may not be the first sentence in the verse cited. Occasionally a verse occurs in both sections of this appendix if it contains elements relevant to each section.

Material in rounded brackets is given by the translator. I add material in square brackets to provide context where needed.

1 Positive Attitude

2 Some Form of Corruption Assumed

1 Positive Attitude

2:4	[Regarding the ones who guard themselves] who believe in what has been sent down to you, and what was sent down before you.
2:41	Believe in what I have sent down, confirming what is with you.
2:44	Do you command the people to piety and forget yourselves, though you recite the Book?
2:53	And (remember) when we gave Moses the Book and the Deliverance.
2:87	Certainly we gave Moses the Book.
2:89	When (there) came to them a Book from God, confirming what was with them.
2:91	When it is said to them, "Believe in what God has sent down", they say, "We believe in what has been sent down on us," but they disbelieve in anything after that, when it is the truth confirming what is with them.
2:97	Say: "Whoever is an enemy to Gabriel – surely he has brought it down on your heart by the permission of God, confirming what was before it."
2:101	When a messenger came to them from God, confirming what was with them, a group of those who were given the Book tossed the Book of God behind their backs, as if they did not know (about it).
2:121	Those to whom We have given the Book recite it as it should be recited. Those (people) believe in it.
2:136	Say: "We believe in God, and what has been sent down to us, and what has been sent down to Abraham, and Ishmael, and Isaac, and Jacob, and the tribes, and what was given to Moses and Jesus, and what was given to the prophets from their Lord. We make no distinction between any of them, and to Him we submit."
2:140	[Regarding Jews and Christians] Who is more evil than the one who conceals a testimony which he has from God?

https://doi.org/10.1515/9783110335880-010

2:144 Surely those who have been given the Book know indeed that it is the truth from their Lord.

2:146 Those to whom We have been given the Book recognize it as they recognize their (own) sons, yet surely a group of them indeed conceals the truth – and they know (it).

2:174 Surely those who conceal what God has sent down of the Book, and sell it for a small price, those – they will not eat (anything) but the Fire in their bellies.

2:211 Ask the Sons of Israel how many of the clear signs We gave them. Whoever changes the blessing of God after it has come to him – surely God is harsh in retribution.

2:213 The people were (once) one community. Then God raised up the prophets as bringers of good news and warners, and with them He sent down the Book with the truth to judge among the people concerning their differences. Only those who had been given it differed concerning it, after the clear signs had come to them, (because of) envy among themselves.

2:285 Each one believes in God, and His angels, and His Books, and His messengers. We make no distinction between any of His messengers.

3:3–4 He has sent down on you the Book with the truth, confirming what was before it, and He sent down the Torah and the Gospel [4] before (this) as guidance for the people, and He sent down the Deliverance.

3:19 Those who were given the Book did not differ until after the knowledge had come to them, (because of) envy among themselves.

3:23 Have you not seen those who were given a portion of the Book? They were called to the Book of God in order that it might judge between them. Then a group of them turned away in aversion.

3:48 And He will teach him [Jesus] the Book and the wisdom, and the Torah and the Gospel.

3:50 [Jesus says] And (I come) confirming what was before me of the Torah, and to make permitted to you some things which were forbidden to you (before).

3:53 [The disciples say] Our Lord, we believe in what You have sent down, and we follow the messenger.

3:65 People of the Book! Why do you dispute about Abraham, when the Torah and the Gospel were not sent down until after him. Will you not understand?

3:70–71 People of the Book! Why do you disbelieve in the signs of God, when you are witnesses (to them)? [71] People of the Book! Why do you mix the truth with falsehood, and conceal the truth, when you know (better)?

3:81 (Remember) when God took a covenant with the prophets: "Whatever indeed I have given you of the Book and wisdom, when a messenger comes to you confirming what is with you, you are to believe in him and you are to help him."

3:84 Say: "We believe in God, and what has been sent down on us, and what has been sent down on Abraham, and Ishmael, and Isaac, and Jacob, and the tribes, and what was given to Moses, and Jesus, and the prophets from their Lord. We make no distinction between any of them, and to Him we submit.

3:93 All food was permitted to the Sons of Israel, except for what Israel forbade himself before the Torah was sent down. Say: "Bring the Torah and read it, if you are truthful."

3:100 You who believe! If you obey a group of those who have been given the Book, they will turn you back (into) disbelievers after having believed.

3:119 There you are! You are those who love them, but they do not love you. You believe in the Book – all of it.

3:184 If they call you a liar, (know that) messengers have been called liars before you, who brought the clear signs, and the scriptures, and the illuminating Book.

3:187 (Remember) when God took a covenant with those who had been given the Book: "You shall indeed make it clear to the people, and shall not conceal it." But they tossed it behind their backs, and sold it for a small price. Evil is what they purchased!

3:199 Surely (there are) some of the People of the Book who indeed believe in God, and what has been sent down to you, and what has been sent down to them, humbling themselves before God. They do not sell the signs of God for a small price.

4:44 Do you not see those who have been given a portion of the Book? They purchase error and wish that you would go astray from the way.

4:47 You have been given the Book! Believe in what We have sent down, confirming what is with you, before We obliterate faces, and turn them on their backs, or curse them as We cursed the men of the Sabbath, and God's command is done.

4:51 Do you not see those who have been given a portion of the Book? They believe in al-Jibt and al-Ṭāghūt, and they say to those who disbelieve, "These are better guided (as to the) way than those who believe."

4:136 You who believe! Believe in God and his messenger, and the Book He has sent down on His messenger, and the Book which he sent down before (this). Whoever disbelieves in God and His angels, and His Books and His messengers, and the Last Day, has gone very far astray.

4:162–64 But the ones who are firm in knowledge among them – and the believers – believe in what has been sent down to you, and what has been sent down before you.

5:32 [Regarding the death of Abel] From that time We prescribed for the Sons of Israel that whoever kills a person, except (in retaliation) for another, or (for) fomenting corruption on the earth, (it is) as if he had killed all the people.

5:43–48 Yet how will they make you (their) judge, when they have the Torah, containing the judgment of God, (and) then turn away after that? Those (people) are not with the believers. [44] Surely We sent down the Torah, containing guidance and light. By means of it the prophets who had submitted rendered judgment for those who were Jews, and (so did) the rabbis and the teachers, with what they were entrusted of the Book of God, and they were witnesses to it. So do not fear the people, but fear Me, and do not sell My signs for a small price. Whoever does not judge by what God has sent down, those – they are the disbelievers. [45] We prescribed for them in it: "The life for the life, and the eye for the eye, and the nose for the nose, and the ear for the ear, and the tooth for the tooth, and (for) the wounds retaliation." But whoever remits it as a freewill offering, it will be an atonement for him. Whoever does not judge by what God has sent down, those – they are the evildoers. [46] And in their footsteps We followed up with Jesus, son of Mary, confirming what was with him of the Torah, and We gave him the Gospel, containing guidance and light, and confirming what was with him of the Torah, and as guidance and admonition to the ones who guard (themselves). [47] So let the People of the Gospel judge by what God has sent down in it. Whoever does not judge by what God has sent down, those – they are the wicked. [48] And We have sent down to you the Book with the truth, confirming what was with him [i.e. Jesus] of the Book, and as a preserver of it. So judge between them by what God has sent down, and do not follow their (vain) desires (away) from what has come to you of the truth.

5:59 Say: "People of the Book! Do you take vengeance on us (for any other reason) than that we believe in God and what has been sent down to us, and what was sent down before (this), and because most of you are wicked?

5:66 [Regarding the People of the Book] Had they observed the Torah and the Gospel, and what was sent down to them from their Lord, they would indeed have eaten from (what was) above them and from (what was) beneath their feet. Some of them are a moderate community, but most of them – evil is what they do.

5:68 Say: "People of the Book! You are (standing) on nothing until you observe the Torah and the Gospel, and what has been sent down to you from your Lord."

5:110 [Regarding Jesus] And when I taught you the Book and the wisdom, and the Torah and the Gospel.

6:89 [Regarding former prophets] Those are the ones to whom we gave the Book, and the judgment, and the prophetic office.

6:91–2 They [probably Jews] have not measured God (with) due measure, when they said, "God has not sent down anything on a human being." Say: "Who sent down the Book which Moses brought as a light and a guidance for the people? You make it (into) sheets of papyrus – you reveal (some of) it, but you hide much (of it). And you were taught what you did not know – neither you nor your fathers." Say: "God," and leave them in their banter (while) they jest. [92] This is a Book: We have sent it down, blessed, confirming that which was before it.

6:114–15 Shall I seek (anyone) other than God as a judge? He (it is) who has sent down to you the Book, set forth distinctly. Those to whom We have (already) given the Book know that it is sent down from your Lord with the truth. Do not be one of the doubters. [115] Perfect is the word of your Lord in truth and justice. No one can change his words. He is the hearing, the knowing.

6:154 Then We gave Moses the Book, complete for the one who does good, and a distinct setting forth of everything, and a guidance and mercy, so that they might believe in the meeting with their Lord.

7:145 And we wrote for him [Moses] on the Tablets an admonition of everything, and a distinct setting forth of everything: "So hold it fast, and command your people to take the best of it. I shall show you the home of the wicked".

7:154 When the anger of Moses abated, he took (up) the Tablets, and in their inscription (there was) a guidance and mercy for those who fear their Lord.

7:156–57 [Regarding God's mercy] I shall prescribe it for the ones who guard (themselves), and give the alms, and those who – they believe in Our signs – [157] those who follow the messenger, the prophet of the common people, whom they find written in their Torah and Gospel.

9:111 Surely God has purchased from the believers their lives and their wealth with (the price of) the Garden (in store) for them. They fight in the way of God and they kill and are killed. (That is) a promise binding on Him in the Torah, and the Gospel, and the Qur'ān.

10:37 This Qur'ān is not the kind (of Book) that it could have been forged apart from God. (It is) a confirmation of what was before it, and a distinct setting forth of the Book – (there is) no doubt about it – from the Lord of the worlds.

10:94 If you [Muhammad] are in doubt about what We have sent down to you, ask those who have been reciting the Book before you.

11:17 Is the one who (stands) on a clear sign from his Lord, and recites it as a witness from Him, and before it was the Book of Moses as a model and mercy?

12:111 It is not a forged proclamation, but a confirmation of what was before it, and a distinct setting forth of everything, and a guidance and mercy for a people who believe.

16:43–4 We have not sent (anyone) before you except men whom We inspired – just ask the People of the Reminder, if you do not know (it) – [44] with the clear signs and the scriptures.

17:2 We gave Moses the Book, and made it a guidance for the Sons of Israel: "Do not take any guardian other than Me!"

17:55 Certainly We have favored some of the prophets over others, and We gave David (the) Psalms.

17:107 Say: "Believe in it, or do not believe. Surely those who were given the knowledge before it – when it is recited to them, they fall down on their chins in prostration.

18:27 Recite what you have been inspired (with) of the Book of your Lord. No one can change His words, and you will find no refuge other than Him.

19:12 "John! Hold fast the Book!"

19:30 He [Jesus] said: "Surely I am a servant of God. He has given me the Book and made me a prophet".

20:133 They say, "If only he would bring us a sign from his Lord." Has there not come to them a clear sign (of) what was in the former pages?

21:7 We have not sent (anyone) before you except men whom We inspired – just ask the People of the Reminder if you do not know (it).

21:48 Certainly we gave Moses and Aaron the Deliverance, and a light, and a reminder to the ones who guard (themselves).

21:105 Certainly We have written in the Psalms, after the Reminder: "The earth – My righteous servants will inherit it."

25:35 Certainly We gave Moses the Book, and appointed his brother Aaron as an assistant with him.

26:196–97 Surely it is indeed in the scriptures of those of old. [197] Was it not a sign for them that it was known to the learned of the Sons of Israel?

28:43 Certainly We gave Moses the Book, after We had destroyed the former generations, as evidence for the people, and a guidance and mercy, so that they might take heed.

28:48–49 Yet when the truth did come to them from Us, they said, "If only he were given the same as what Moses was given." Did they not disbelieve in what was given to Moses before?

28:52 Those to whom we gave the Book before it – they believe in it.

29:27 [Regarding Abraham] And we granted him Isaac and Jacob, and We placed among his descendants the prophetic office and the Book.

29:46–47 Do not dispute with the People of the Book except with what is better – except for those of them who do evil. And say: "We believe in what has been sent down to us, and what has been sent down to you. Our God and your God is one, and to Him we submit." [47] In this way We have sent down the Book to you. Those to whom We have given the Book believe in it, and among these (people) (there are) some who believe in it.

32:23–24 Certainly We gave Moses the Book – so do not be in doubt of meeting Him – and We made it a guidance for the Sons of Israel. [24] And we appointed from among them leaders (who) guide (others) by Our command, when they were patient and were certain of Our signs.

35:25 If they call you a liar, (know that) those who were before them called (their messengers) liars. Their messengers brought them the clear signs, and the scriptures, and the illuminating Book.

35:31 What We have inspired you (with) of the Book – it is the truth, confirming what was before it

37:37 No! He has brought the truth and confirmed the envoys.

37:117 [Regarding Moses and Aaron] We gave them both the clarifying Book.

40:53–54 Certainly We gave Moses the guidance, and caused the Sons of Israel to inherit the Book, [54] as a guidance and reminder to those with understanding.

41:43 Nothing is said to you except what has already been said to the messengers before you.

41:45 Certainly We gave Moses the Book, and then differences arose about it.

42:3 In this way He inspires you [Muhammad], and those who were before you.

42:13 He has instituted for you from the religion what he charged Noah with, and that which We have inspired you (with), and what We charged Abraham, and Moses, and Jesus with: "Observe the religion, and do not become divided in it."

42:14 They did not become divided until after the knowledge had come to them.

45:16–17 Certainly We gave the Sons of Israel the Book, and the judgment, and the prophetic office. We provided them with good things and favored them over the worlds. [17] And We gave them clear signs of the matter. They did not differ until after the knowledge had come to them.

46:10 Say: "Do you see? If it is from God, and you disbelieve in it, and a witness from the Sons of Israel has borne witness to (a Book) like it, and believed, and you became arrogant – surely God does not guide the people who are evildoers."

46:12 Yet before it was the Book of Moses as a model and mercy; and this is a book confirming (it) in the Arabic language.

46:30 They [the jinn] said, "Our people! Surely we have heard a Book (which) has been sent down after Moses, confirming what was before it, guiding to the truth and to a straight road."

48:29 Muhammad is the messenger of God. Those who are with him are harsh against the disbelievers, (but) compassionate among themselves. You see them bowing and prostrating themselves, seeking favor from God and approval. Their marks on their faces are the trace of prostration. That is their image in the Torah, and their image in the Gospel is like a seed (that) puts forth its shoot, and strengthens it, and it becomes stout and stands straight on its stalk, pleasing the sowers – so that He may enrage the disbelievers by means of them.

53:36–37 [Regarding the one who turns away] Or has he not been informed about what is in the pages of Moses [37] and Abraham, who paid (his debt) in full?

57:16 Is it not time for those who believe that their hearts become humble before the Reminder of God, and (before) what has come down of the truth, and (that) they not be like those to whom the Book was given before, and for whom the time lasted too long, so that their hearts became hard, and many of them were wicked?

57:25 Certainly We sent Our messengers with the clear signs, and We sent down with them the Book and the scale, so that the people might uphold justice.

57:26 Certainly We sent Noah and Abraham, and We placed among his descendants the prophetic office and the Book.

57:27 Then in their footsteps We followed up with Our messengers, and We followed up with Jesus, son of Mary, and gave him the Gospel, and placed in the hearts of those who followed him kindness and mercy.

61:6 And (remember) when Jesus, son of Mary, said, "Sons of Israel! Surely I am the messenger of God to you, confirming what was before me of the Torah, and bringing good news of a messenger who will come after me, whose name will be Aḥmad."

62:5 Those who have been loaded down with the Torah, (and) then have not carried it, are like a donkey carrying books.

66:12 And Mary, daughter of ʿImrān, who guarded her private part: We breathed into it some of Our spirit, and she affirmed the words of her Lord and His Books, and became one of the obedient.

87:18–19 Surely this is indeed in the former pages, [19] the pages of Abraham and Moses.

98:4 Those who were given the Book did not become divided until after the clear sign had come to them.

2 Some Form of Corruption Assumed

2:42 Do not mix the truth with falsehood, and do not conceal the truth when you know (better).

2:59 But those who did evil exchanged a word other than that which had been spoken to them. So We sent down on those who did evil wrath from the sky, because they were acting wickedly.

2:75–79 Are you eager that they should believe you, even though a group of them has already heard the words of God, (and) then altered it after they had understood it – and they know (they have done this)? 76 When they meet those who believe, they say, "We believe," but when some of them meet with others, they say, "Do you report to them what God has disclosed to you, so that they may dispute with you by means of it in the presence of your Lord? Will you not understand?" [77] Do they not know that God knows what they keep secret and what they speak aloud? [78] Some of them are common people – they do not know the Book, only wishful thinking, and they only conjecture. [79] So woe to those who write the Book with their (own) hands, (and) then say, "This is from God," in order to sell it for a small price.

2:101 When a messenger came to them from God, confirming what was with them, a group of those who were given the Book tossed the Book of God behind their backs, as if they did not know (about it).

2:140 Or do you say, "Abraham, and Ishmael, and Isaac, and Jacob, and the tribes were Jews and Christians?" Say: "Do you know better, or God? Who is more evil than the one who conceals a testimony which he has from God? God is not oblivious of what you do."

2:146 Those to whom We have given the Book recognize it, as they recognize their (own) sons, yet surely a group of them indeed conceals the truth – and they know (it).

2:174 Surely those who conceal what God has sent down of the Book, and sell it for a small price, those – they will not eat (anything) but the Fire in their bellies.

3:71 People of the Book, why do you mix the truth with falsehood, and conceal the truth, when you know (better)?

3:78 Surely (there is) indeed a group of them who twist their tongues with the Book, so that you will think it is from the Book, when it is not from the Book. And they say, "It is from God," when it is not from God. They speak lies against God, and they know (it).

3:187 (Remember) when God took a covenant with those who had been given the Book: "You shall indeed make it clear to the people, and shall not conceal it." But they tossed it behind their backs, and sold it for a small price. Evil is what they purchased!

4:46: Some of those who are Jews alter words from their positions, and they say, "We hear and disobey," and "Hear, and do not hear," and "Observe us," twisting with their tongues and vilifying the religion. If they had said, "We hear and obey," and "Hear," and "Regard us," it would indeed have been better for them, and more just. But God has cursed them for their disbelief, and so they do not believe, except for a few.

5:13: For their breaking their covenant, We cursed them and made their hearts hard. They alter words from their positions, and have forgotten part of what they were reminded of.

5:15 People of the Book! Our messenger has come to you, making clear to you much of what you have been hiding of the Book, and overlooking much. Now a light and a clear Book from God has come to you.

5:41 Messenger! Do not let those who are quick to disbelief cause you sorrow. (They are) among those who say with their mouths, "We believe," but their hearts do not believe. Among those who are Jews (there are) those who listen to lies, (and who) listen to (other) people who have not come to you. They alter words from their positions, (and) say, "If you are given this, take it, but if you are not given it, beware." If God wishes to test anyone, you will not have any power for him against God. Those are the ones whose hearts God does not wish to purify. For them (there is) disgrace in this world, and in the Hereafter (there will be) a great punishment for them.

6:91 They [probably Jews] have not measured God (with) due measure, when they said, "God has not sent down anything on a human being." Say: "Who sent down the Book which Moses brought as a light and a guidance for the people? You make it (into) sheets of papyrus – you reveal (some of) it, but you hide much (of it). And you were taught what you did not know – neither you nor your fathers." Say: "God," and leave them in their banter (while) they jest.

7:161–62 (Remember) when it was said to them [the people of Moses], 'Inhabit this town and eat of it wherever you please, and say: "Ḥiṭṭa," and enter the gate in prostration. We shall forgive you your sins and increase the doers of good.' [162] But those of them who did evil exchanged a word other than that which had been spoken to them. So We sent down on them wrath from the sky, because of the evil they were doing.

Bibliography

Note: the prefixes "al" and "el" and the term "Abū" are disregarded for alphabetical purposes.

Primary Sources

'Abd al-Jabbār, Abū'l-Ḥasan. *Tathbīt dalā'il al-nubuwwa,* ed. 'Abd al-Karīm 'Uthmān. Beirut: Dār al-ʿArabīyah li'l-Ṭibā'ah wa'l-Nashr wa'l-Tawzī', 1966.

'Abd al-Jabbār, Abū'l-Ḥasan. *Tathbīt dalā'il al-nubuwwa*, partial translation as Reynolds, Gabriel Said, and Samir Khalil Samir, eds. and trans., *The Critique of Christian Origins.* Middle Eastern Texts Initiative. Provo,UT: Brigham Young University Press, 2010.

Aḥmad ibn Hanbal. *Masā'il al-imām Aḥmad ibn Hanbal, riwāyat Isḥāq ibn Ibrāhīm ibn Hānī al-Nīsābūrī,* ed. Isḥāq Nīsābūrī. Al-Manṣūrah: Dār al-Ta'sīl, Dār al-Mawaddah, 2008.

Aḥmad ibn Hanbal. *Musnad,* 52 vols., ed. Shu'ayb al-Arna'ūt. Beirut: al-Risalah, 1993–.

Aḥmad ibn Hanbal. *Kitāb al-Zuhd,* 2 vols., ed. Muḥammad Sharaf. Alexandria: Dār al-Fikr al-Jāmi'ī, 1980.

al-'Āmirī, Abū al-Ḥasan. *Al-I'lām bi Manāqib al-Islām,* ed. Aḥmad Ghurāb. Cairo: Dār al-Kātib al-'Arabī, 1967.

'Ammār al-Baṣrī. *Kitāb al-burhān,* in *'Ammar al-Baṣrī: Apologie et Controverses*, ed. Michel Hayek, 21–90. Beirut: Dār al-Mashriq, 1977.

'Ammār al-Baṣrī. *Kitāb al-masā'il wa'l-ajwiba,* in *'Ammar al-Baṣrī: Apologie et Controverses,* ed. Michel Hayek, 91–266. Beirut: Dār al-Mashriq, 1977.

Augustine. *City of God (De civitate Dei*). Turnhout: Brepols, 1955.

Augustine. *City of God*, in Philip Schaff, ed. *Nicene and Post-Nicene Fathers*, Series 1, vol. 2. Grand Rapids, MI: Christian Classics Ethereal Library, 1819–1893.

al-Bayhaqī, Abū Bakr. *Dalā'il al-Nubuwwa*, 7 vols., ed. 'Abd al-Mu'ṭī. Beirut: Dār al-Kutub al-'Ilmiyya, 1985.

The Book of Jubilees: James VanderKam, ed., *The Book of Jubilees: a critical text.* Corpus Scriptorum Christianorum Orientalium, Scriptores Aethiopici 88. Leuven: Peeters, 1989.

The Book of Jubilees, trans. James VanderKam. Corpus Scriptorum Christianorum Orientalium, 511. Leuven: Peeters, 1989.

al-Bīrūnī, Abū Rayḥān. *Al-Āthār al-bāqiya 'an al-qurūn al-khāliya*, ed. Eduard Sachau. Leipzig: Brockhaus, 1878.

al-Bīrūnī, Abū Rayḥān. *Chronology of Ancient Nations*, trans. Eduard Sachau. London: William Allen, 1879. Reprinted in *Theology, Ethics and Metaphysics: Royal Asiatic Society Classics of Islam. Volume III: The Chronology of Ancient Nations.* London: RoutledgeCurzon, 2003.

al-Bukhārī, Muḥammad ibn Ismā'īl. *Ṣaḥīḥ al-Bukhārī.* 9 vols. Riyadh: Darussalam, 1997.

al-Bunnāhī (also al-Nubāhī). *Al-Marqaba al-'ulyā fī man yastaḥiqq al-qaḍā' wa'l-futya.* Beirut: Dār al-Kutub al-'Ilmiyyah, 1995.

A Common Word (website). A Common Word Between Us and You initiative. Consulted online on 12 May 2020, www.acommonword.com.

al-Dabūsī, Abū Zayd.*Taqwīm al-adilla fi uṣūl al-fiqh,* ed. Khalīl Mays. Beirut: Dār al-Kutub al-'Ilmiyya, 2001.

https://doi.org/10.1515/9783110335880-011

al-Damīri, Kamāl al-Dīn. *Ḥayāt al-ḥayawān al-kubrā*, 2 vols. Cairo: al-Maṭba'at al-Khayrīyah, 1309 (1891 CE).

al-Dārimī, 'Abd Allāh. *Sunan al-Dārimī*, 2 vols., ed. Fawwāz Zamarlī and Khālid 'Alamī. Beirut: Dār al-Kitāb al-'Arabī, 1987.

Abū Dāwūd al-Sijistānī. *Sunan Abū Dāwūd*, 5 vols. Riyadh: Darussalam, 2008.

4 Ezra. See Drint, Adriana, *The Mount Sinai Arabic Version of IV Ezra*, Corpus Scriptorum Christianorum Orientalium, Scriptores Arabici 48–49. Leuven: Peeters, 1997.

The Gospel of Barnabas, trans. Lonsdale and Laura Ragg. Oxford: Clarendon, 1907; reprinted as *The Gospel of Barnabas*. New Delhi: Islamic Book Service, 1998.

al-Ḥarrāni, Ibn Shu'ba. *Tuḥaf al-'Uqūl*. Tehran: Maktabat al-Ṣadūq, 1376/ 1956–57.

al-Ḥarrāni, Ibn Shu'ba. *Tuhaf al-Uqoul* [sic]: *The Masterpieces of the Mind*, trans. Badr Shahin. Qom: Ansariyan, 2000.

Hassanabadi, Mahmoud, and Roubik Jahani and Carina Jahani, eds. with English preface by Robert Crellin, *A Unified Gospel in Persian: An Old Variant of the Gospels along with Exegetical Comments*. Studia Iranica Upsaliensia 33. Uppsala: University of Uppsala, 2018.

Hūd b. Muḥakkam. *Tafsīr Kitāb Allāh al-'Azīz*, 4 vols., ed. Balḥajj Sharīfī. Beirut: Dār al-Gharb al-Islāmī, 1990.

al-Ḥumaydī, Abū 'Abd Allāh. *Jadhwat al-Muqtabis fī dhikr wulāt al-Andalus*, ed. Muḥammad Ṭanjī. Cairo: Maktabat Nashr al-Thaqāfat al-Islāmiyya, 1953.

Ibn 'Abd al-Barr. *Bayān al-'ilm wa faḍlihi*, ed. Mas'ad Sa'danī. Beirut: Dār al-Kutub al-'Ilmiyya, 2000.

Ibn al-'Arabī. *Divine Sayings: 101 Ḥadīth Qudsī*, trans. Stephen Hirtenstein and Martin Notcutt. Oxford: Anqa Publishing, 2004.

Ibn Bābawayh al-Qummī. *Risālat al-i'tiqādāt*, published as Shaykh al-Mufīd, *Muṣannafāt al-Shaykh al-Mufīd*, vol. 5. Qom: al-Mu'tamar al-'Ālamī bi-Munāsabat Dhikrā Alfīyat al-Shaykh al-Mufīd, 1413 (1993 CE).

Ibn Bābawayh al-Qummī. *A Shi'ite Creed*, trans. Asaf Fyzee. Tehran: World Organization for Islamic Services, 1402 (1982 CE) revised edition.

Ibn Bābawayh al-Qummī. *Man lā yaḥḍuruhu al-faqīh*. 4 vols., ed. Ḥasan Kharasān. Beirut: Dār Ṣa'b, 1981.

Ibn Bābawayh al-Qummī. *'Uyūn akhbār al-Riḍā*. Qom: Chāpkhānah-I Dār al-'Ilm, 1377/1958.

Ibn Bābawayh al-Qummī. *Kitab al-Tawḥīd*, trans. Ali Adam, ed. Michael Mumisa as The *Book of Divine Unity*. Birmingham: AMI Press, 2013.

Ibn Ḥabīb, Muḥammad. *Kitāb al-Muḥabbar*, ed. Ilse Lichtenstädter. Hyderabad: Maṭba'at Jām'iyat Dā'irat al-Ma'ārif al-'Uthmāniyya, 1942.

Ibn Ḥazm, Abū Muḥammad. *Kitāb al-Faṣl fī'l-milal wa'l-ahwā' wa'l-niḥal*, 3 vols., ed. Aḥmad Shams al-Dīn. Beirut: Dār al-kutub al-'Ilmiyya, 2007.

Ibn Ḥazm, Abū Muḥammad. *Al-Uṣūl wa'l-furū'*, 2 vols in 1, ed. M. 'Irāqī. Cairo: Dār al-Nahḍa al-'Arabiyya, 1978.

Ibn Ḥazm, Abū Muḥammad. *Al-Radd 'alā ibn al-naghrīla wa rasā'il ukhrā*, ed. Iḥsān 'Abbas. Cairo: Dār al-'Urūba, 1960.

Ibn Ḥazm, Abū Muḥammad. *Al-iḥkām li uṣūl al-aḥkām*, 2 vols. Cairo: Maṭba'at al-sa'āda, 1926–28.

Ibn Isḥāq, Muḥammad, in Ibn Hishām, Abū Muḥammad. *Das Leben Muhammeds*, ed. F. Wüstenfeld. Göttingen: Dieterichsche Universitäts-Buchhandlung, 1858–60.

Ibn Isḥāq, Muḥammad. *The Life of Muhammad*, trans. Alfred Guillaume. New Delhi: OUP, 1955.
Ibn al-Jawzī. *Al-Wafā' bi aḥwāl al-muṣṭafā*, ed. Muṣṭafā 'Abd al-Wāḥid. Cairo: Dār al-Kutub al-Ḥadītha,1966.
Ibn Kathīr, Ismā'īl. *Tafsīr*, ed. Muḥammad Khinn and Muṣṭafā Khinn. Beirut: Mu'assassat al-Risāla, 2000.
Ibn al-Layth. *Risāla*. In *Jamharat rasā'il al-'Arab fī 'uṣūr al-'arabiyya al-zāhira*, ed. A.Z. Ṣafwat, vol. 3, 252–324. Cairo: Mustafā al-Bābī al-Ḥalabī, 1937.
Ibn al-Layth. *Risāla* in Hadi Eid, *Lettre du Calife Hārūn al-Rašīd à l'Empereur Constantin VI*. Paris: Cariscript, 1992.
Ibn Māja. *Sunan Ibn Mājah*, 5 vols. Riyadh: Darussalam, 2007.
Ibn al-Mubārak. *Kitāb al-Zuhd*, ed. Ḥabīb al-Raḥmān A'ẓamī. Beirut: Mu'assassat al-Risāla, 1971.
Ibn Qutayba, Abū Muḥammad. *Ta'wīl Mukhtalif al-Ḥadīth*, ed. Muḥammad Najjār. Cairo: Maktabat al-Kulliyāt al-Azhariya, 1966.
Ibn Qutayba, Abū Muḥammad. *Kitāb al-Ma'ārif*, ed. Tharwat 'Ukāshah. Cairo: Maṭba'at Dār al-Kutub, 1960.
Ibn Qutayba, Abū Muḥammad. *'Uyūn al-Akhbār*. 4 volumes in 2, ed. Yūsuf Ṭawīl. Dār al-kutub al-'Ilmiyya, 1986.
Ibn Rabbān, 'Alī al-Ṭabarī. *Kitāb al-Dīn wa'l-Dawla*, in Ebied, Rifaat, and David Thomas, eds. and trans., *The Polemical Works of 'Alī al-Ṭabarī*, 200–473. The History of Christian-Muslim Relations, 27. Leiden: Brill, 2016.
Ibn Rabbān, 'Alī al-Ṭabarī. *Al-Radd 'alā al-Naṣārā*, in Ebied, Rifaat, and David Thomas, eds. and trans., *The Polemical Works of 'Alī al-Ṭabarī*, 62–169. The History of Christian-Muslim Relations, 27. Leiden: Brill, 2016.
Ibn Sa'd, Abū 'Abd Allāh. *Al-Ṭabaqāt al-kubrā*, 9 vols., Beirut: Dār Ṣādir, 1957–58.
Ibn Sa'd, Abū 'Abd Allāh. *The Companions of Badr*, trans. Aisha Bewley. London: TaHa, 2013.
Ibn Sīnā, Abū 'Alī. *Al-Risāla al-Aḍḥawiyya fi'l-Ma'ād*. Beirut: al-Mu'assasat al-Jāmi'īyyat al-Dirāsāt wa'l-Nashr wa'l-Tawzī', 1984.
Ibn Taymiyya, Taqī al-Dīn. *Al Jawāb al-ṣaḥīḥ li-man baddala dīn al-masīḥ*, 4 vols in 2. Cairo: Maṭba'at al-Nīl, 1905.
Ikhwān al-Ṣafā'. *Rasā'il Ikhwān al-Ṣafā'*, 4 vols. Beirut: Dār Ṣādir, 1957.
Injīl Barnābā, trans. Khalīl Sa'ādah. Miṣr: Maṭba'at al-Manār, 1908.
al-Iṣfahānī, Ḥamza. *Ta'rīkh sinī mulūk al-arḍ wa'l-anbiyā'*. Beirut: Dār Maktabat al-Ḥayāt, 1961.
Al-Jāḥiẓ, Abū 'Uthmān. *Al-Radd 'alā al-naṣārā*, Arabic text in Joshua Finkel, ed., *Three Essays of Abū 'Othmān 'Amr ibn Baḥr al-Jāḥiẓ (d. 869)*. Cairo: Salafyah Press, 1926.
al-Jaṣṣās, Abū Bakr. *Al-Fuṣūl fī uṣūl*, ed. 'Ujayl Nashamī. Kuwait: Dawlat al-Kuwayt, Wizārat al-awqāf wa'l-shu'ūn al-islāmiyah, al-idārah al-'āmmah li'l-iftā' wa'l-buḥūth al-shar'īyah, 1994.
al-Jaṣṣās, Abū Bakr. *Aḥkām al-Qur'ān*, 3 vols in 2. Constantinople: Dār al-Khilāfah al-'Alīyah: Maṭba'at al-Awqāf al-Islāmīyah, 1917.
Josephus, *Antiquities*, Book I, Loeb Classical Library, trans. H. Thackeray. Loeb Classical Library 242. Cambridge, MA: Harvard University Press, 1998.

al-Juwayni, Abū'l-Ma'ālī. *Shifā' al-ghalīl fī bayān mā waqa'a fī'l-Tawrāt wa'l-Injīl min al-tabdīl*, in *Textes apologetiques de* Ğuwainī, ed. Michel Allard, 38–83. Beirut: Dār al-Machreq, 1968.

al-Juwayni, Abū'l-Ma'ālī. *Kitāb al-Shāmil fi uṣūl al-dīn*, ed. A. Nashshār. Alexandria: Manshā'at al-Ma'ārif, 1969.

al-Juwayni, Abū'l-Ma'ālī. *A Guide to Conclusive Proofs for the Principles of Belief: Kitāb al-irshād ilā qawāti' al-adilla fi uṣūl al-I'tiqād*, trans. Paul Walker. Great Books of Islamic Civilization. Reading: Garnet, 2000.

Khalīfa b. Khayyāṭ. *Ta'rīkh*, ed. Akram 'Umarī. Damascus: Dār al-Qalam, 1977.

Khalīfa b. Khayyāṭ. *Ta'rikh*, partial trans. by Carl Wurtzel, with Robert Hoyland, *Khalifa b Khayyat's History on the Umayyad Dynasty (660–750)*. Translated Texts for Historians 63. Liverpool: Liverpool University Press, 2015.

al-Kindī, 'Abd al-Masīḥ. *Risālat 'Abdallah ibn Ismā 'īl al-Hāshimī ilā 'Abd al-Masīḥ ibn Isḥāq al-Kindī yad 'ūhu bihā ilā'l-islām wa-risālat al-Kindī ilā'l-Hāshimī yaruddu bihā 'alayhi wa-yad 'ūhu ilā'l-naṣrāniyya*. London: SPCK, 1885.

al-Kindī, 'Abd al-Masīḥ. *The Apology*. In *Early Christian-Muslim Dialogue*, ed. N.A. Newman, 382–515. Hatfield, PA: Interdisciplinary Biblical Research Institute, 1993.

al-Kirmānī, Ḥamīd al-Dīn. *Al-Maṣābīḥ fī ithbāt al-imāma*, ed. and trans. in Paul Walker, *Master of the Age: an Islamic Treatise on the Necessity of the Imamate*. London: I.B. Tauris, 2007.

al-Kulaynī, Muḥammad. *Al-Kāfī*, 15 vols. Qom: Dār al-Ḥadīth, 1429/2008.

Maimonides, Moses. *Maimonides' Epistle to Yemen: the Arabic original and three Hebrew versions*, ed. and trans. by Abraham Halkin and Boaz Cohen. New York: The American Academy for Jewish Research, 1952.

Ma'mar ibn Rāshid. *The Expeditions: an Early Biography of Muḥammad*, ed. and trans. Sean Anthony. Library of Arabic Literature. New York: New York University Press, 2014.

al-Maqdisī, Abū Naṣr. *Al-Bad' wa'l-tar'īkh*, 6 vols., ed. and trans. Clément Huart. Paris: Leroux, 1899–1919.

al-Mas'ūdī, al-Ḥasan. *Murūj al-dhahab*, published as Maçoudi, *Les Prairies D'Or*, Arabic text and French translation, Barbier de Meynard and Pavet de Courteille. Paris: L'Imprimerie Impériale, 1861–77.

al-Mas'ūdī, al-Ḥasan. *The Meadows of Gold: the 'Abbāsids*, partial trans. By Paul Lunde and Caroline Stone. London: Kegan Paul International, 1989.

al-Mas'ūdī, al-Ḥasan. *Kitāb al-Tanbīh wa'l-ishrāf*, ed. M.J. de Goeje. Leiden: Brill, 1894.

al-Māwardī, Abū'l-Ḥasan. *al-Ḥāwī al-kabīr*, eds. Maḥmūd Maṭrajī and Shihīb al-dīn Abū 'Amr, 24 vols. Beirut: Dār al-Fikr, 1994.

Muqātil b. Sulaymān.*Tafsīr Muqātil bin Sulaymān*, ed. Aḥmad Farīd, 3 vols. Beirut: Dār al-Kutub al- 'Ilmiyyah, 2003.

al-Murtaḍā, Sharīf. *Al-Dharī'ah ilā uṣūl al-sharī'a*, 2 vols. Tehran: Dānishgāh-i Tihran, 1967–70.

Muslim ibn al-Ḥajjāj. *Ṣaḥīḥ Muslim*, 6 vols. Riyadh: Darussalam, 2007.

al-Nasā'ī, Abū 'Abd al-Raḥmān. *Sunan al-Nasā'ī*, 6 vols. Riyadh: Darussalam, 2007.

Nestor. Published as Lasker, Daniel, and Sarah Stroumsa, *The Polemic of Nestor the Priest: Qiṣṣat Mujādalat al-Usquf and Sefer Nestor Ha-Komer: Introduction, Annotated Translations and Commentary*, vol 1. Jerusalem: Ben-Zvi Institute for the Study of Jewish Communities in the East, 1996.

'Nistarot (Secrets of) R. Shimon b. Yohai', with translation by John Reeves. 'Trajectories in Near Eastern Apocalyptic', John Reeves. Consulted online on 12 May 2020, https://pages.uncc.edu/john-reeves/research-projects/trajectories-in-near-eastern-apocalyptic/nistarot-secrets-of-r-shimon-b-yohai-2.

Abū Nu'aym, *Ḥilyat al-Awliyā'*, 10 vols in 7. Cairo: Maktabat al-Khānjī: Maktabat al-Sa'āda, 1932–38.

Nu'aym b. Ḥammād. *Kitāb al-Fitan*. Mecca: Maktabat al-Tijārīyah, n.d.

Nu'aym b. Ḥammād, trans. David Cook, *The Book of Tribulations: The Syrian Muslim Apocalyptic Tradition*. Edinburgh Studies in Apocalypticism and Eschatology. Edinburgh: EUP, 2017.

al-Nu'mān, Qāḍī. *Da'ā'im al-islām*. Vol.1, Cairo: Dār al-Ma'ārif, 1963.

al-Nu'mān, Qāḍī. *The Pillars of Islam*, trans. Asaf Fyzee, 2 vols. New Delhi: OUP, 2002–04.

al-Qābisī. *Al-Risāla al-mufaṣṣala*, in Aḥmad al-Ahwānī, *al-Ta'līm fī ra'y al-Qābisī*. Cairo: Dār al-Kutub al-'Arabīya, 1945.

al-Qarāfī, Shihāb al-dīn. *Al-Dhakhīra*, ed. M. Būkhubzah, 14 vols. Beirut: Dār al-Gharb al-islāmī, 1994.

al-Qirqisānī, Ya'qūb. *Kitab al-Anwār wa'l-marāqib*, ed. Leon Nemoy, 5 vols. New York: The Alexander Kohut Foundation, 1939–1943.

al-Qummī, 'Alī bin Ibrāhīm. *Tafsīr al-Qummī*, 2 vols. Najaf: Maktabat al-Hudā, 1967.

The Qur'an: a New Annotated Translation, trans. A.J. Droge. Sheffield: Equinox, 2013, reprinted with corrections 2017.

al-Qūṭī, Ḥafs. *Le Psautier Mozarabe de Hafs le Goth*, ed. and trans. Marie-Thérèse Urvoy. Toulouse: Presses Universitaires du Mirail, 1994.

al-Rassī, al-Qāsim ibn Ibrāhīm. *Al-Radd 'alā al-Naṣārā*, in *Majmū' kutub wa rasā'il li'l-Imām al-Qāsim ibn Ibrāhīm al-Rassī*, ed. 'Abd al-Karīm Jadabān, vol.1, 387–442. Ṣan'ā': Dār al-Ḥikmah al-Yamāniyah, 2001.

al-Rāzī, Abū Ḥātim. *The Proofs of Prophecy*, Arabic text with English translation by Tarif Khalidi. Middle Eastern Texts Initiative. Provo, Utah: Brigham Young University Press, 2011.

Saḥnūn, *Al-Mudawwana al-Kubrā li Imām Mālik b. Anās*, 5 vols. Beirut: Dār al-kutub al-'ilmiyya, 1994.

al-Ṣan'ānī, Abd al-Razzāq. *Al-Muṣannaf*, ed. Ḥabīb al-Raḥmān A'ẓamī, 11 vols. Beirut: al-Majlis al-'Ilmī, 1972.

Sayf b. 'Umar al-Tamīmī. *Kitāb al-ridda wa'l-futūḥ* and *Kitāb al-Jamal wa masīr 'Ā'isha wa 'Alī*, ed. Qasim al-Samarrai (Leiden: Smitskamp, 1995); partial translation in Sean Anthony, "The Composition of Sayf b. 'Umar's Account of King Paul and his Corruption of Ancient Christianity." *Der Islam* 85 (2008): 164–202.

al-Shāfi'ī, Muḥammad ibn Idrīs. *The Epistle on Legal Theory*, ed. and trans. Joseph Lowry. New York: NYUP, 2013.

al-Shāfi'ī, Muḥammad ibn Idrīs. *Kitāb al-umm*, ed. Rabī' ibn Sulaymān Murādī, 7 volumes in 4. Bulaq: Al-Maṭba'at al-kubrā al-amīrīyya, 1903–08.

al-Sijistānī, Abū Ya'qūb. *Kitāb al-Yanābī'*, in *Trilogie Ismaélienne*, ed. Henry Corbin. Tehran: Département d'Iranologie de l'Institut francoiranien, 1961.

Sunnah.Com (website). Consulted online on 12 May 2020, https://sunnah.com.

al-Ṭabarī, Abū Ja'far. *Annales quos scripsit Abu Djafar ibn Djarir at-Tabari*, ed. M. de Goeje et al. Leiden: Brill, 1879–1901.

al-Ṭabarī, Abū Ja'far. *The History of al-Ṭabarī, vol. I: General Introduction and from Creation to the Flood*, trans. Franz Rosenthal. Albany, N.Y. SUNY Press, 1989.

al-Ṭabarī, Abū Ja'far. *The History of Al-Ṭabarī, vol. III: The Children of Israel*, trans. William Brinner. Albany, NY: SUNY Press, 1991.

al-Ṭabarī, Abū Ja'far. *The History of Al-Ṭabarī, vol. IV: The Ancient Kingdoms*, trans. Moshe Perlmann. Albany, N.Y.: SUNY Press, 1987.

al-Ṭabarī, Abū Ja'far. *Biographies of the Prophet's Companions and their Successors*, trans. Ella Landau-Tasseron. Albany, N.Y.: SUNY Press, 1998.

al-Ṭabarī, Abū Ja'far. *Jāmi' al-bayān 'an ta'wīl al-Qur'ān*, edited by Maḥmūd and Aḥmad Shākir, 16 vols. Cairo: Dār al-Ma'ārif, 1955.

al-Ṭabarī, Abū Ja'far. *Jāmi' al-bayān 'an ta'wīl al-Qur'ān*, 13 vols. Beirut: Dār al-Kutub al-'Ilmiyah, 1999.

al-Ṭabarī, Abū Ja'far. *The Commentary on the Qur'an by Abū Ja'far Muḥammad bin Jarīr al-Ṭabarī, Volume 1*, trans. John Cooper. Oxford: OUP, 1987.

al-Ṭabarsī, al-Nūrī. *Faṣl al-khiṭāb fī ithbāt taḥrīf kitāb rabb al-arbāb*, lithographed, n.p. 1298/1880.

al-Tanūkhī, Abū 'Alī. *Kitāb al-faraj ba'da al-shidda*, ed. 'Abbūd Shāljī. Beirut: Dār Ṣādir, 1398/1978.

al-Tha'labī, Abū Isḥāq. *Tafsīr al-Tha'labī*, ed. 'Alī 'Āshūr,10 vols. Beirut: Dār Iḥyā' al-turāth al-'arabī, 2002.

al-Tha'labī, Abū Isḥāq. *'Arā'is al-majālis fī qiṣaṣ al-anbiyā'*. Cairo: Sharikat Maktabat wa Maṭba'at Muṣṭafā al-Bābī al-Ḥalabī, 1954.

al-Tha'labī, Abū Isḥāq. *'Arā'is al-majālis fī qiṣaṣ al-anbiyā' or 'Lives of the Prophets' as recounted by Abū Isḥaq Aḥmad ibn Muḥammad ibn Ibrāhīm al-Tha'labī*, trans. William Brinner. Studies in Arabic Literature 24. Leiden: Brill, 2002.

Theodore bar Koni. *Theodorus bar Koni. Liber Scholiorum*, ed. Addai Scher. Paris: E Typographeo Reipublicae, 1910–12.

Theodore bar Koni. Théodore bar Koni, *Livre Des Scolies II: Mimrè VI–XI*, trans. Robert Hespel and René Draguet. Corpus Scriptorum Christianorum Orientalium 432. Louvain: Peeters, 1982.

Timothy, Patriarch. *Timotheus I, Ostsyrischer Patriarch: Disputation mit den Kalifen al-Mahdi*, German translation by Martin Heimgartner (Leuven: Peeters, 2011), 39–40, sections 8.23–8.39, keyed to same sections in *Timotheus I, Ostsyrischer Patriarch: Disputation mit den Kalifen al-Mahdi*, Syriac text, ed. Heimgartner (Leuven: Peeters, 2011).

Timothy, Patriarch. *The Dialogue of Patriarch Timothy I and the Caliph al-Mahdi*, trans. Alphonse Mingana. In *The Early Christian-Muslim Dialogue: a Collection of Documents from the First Three Islamic Centuries (632–900 A.D.). Translations With Commentary*, ed. N.A. Newman. Hatfield, PA: Interdisciplinary Biblical Research Institute, 1993, 174–267.

al-Tirmidhī, Abū 'Īsā. *Jāmi' al-Tirmidhī*, 6 vols. Riyadh: Darussalam, 2007.

al-Ṭūsī, Muḥammad. *Tahdhīb al-aḥkām*, 10 vols. Tehran: Dār al-Kutub al-Islāmiyah, 1390/1970–71.

al-Ṭūsī, Muḥammad. *Al-Istibsār*. Tehran: Dār al-Kutub al-Islāmī, 1405/1984.

al-Ṭūsī, Muḥammad. *'Uddat al-uṣūl*. Qom: Chapkhaneh Setarah, 1417/1997.

Toledot Yeshu: *The Life Story of Jesus: two volumes and database*, ed. and trans. Michael Meerson and Peter Schäfer. Tübingen: Mohr Siebeck, 2014.

Abū ʻUbayd al-Qāsim b. Sallām. *Kitāb al-Khuṭāb wa'l-mawāʻiẓ*. Cairo: Maktabat al-Thaqāfa wa'l-Dīnīya, 1986.
Abū ʻUbayd al-Qāsim b. Sallām. *Abū ʻUbaid al-Qāsim b. Sallām's* K. al-nāsikh wa'l-mansūkh *(MS. Istanbul, Topkapi, Ahmet III A 143)*, ed. John Burton. Cambridge: E.J.W. Gibb Memorial Trust, 1987.
Abū ʻUbayd al-Qāsim b. Sallām. *Faḍā'il al-Qur'ān*. Beirut: Dār al-Kutub al-ʻIlmiyya, 1991.
al-Wansharīsī, Aḥmad. *Al-Miʻyār al-muʻrib wa'l-jāmiʻ al-mughrib ʻan fatāwī ʻulamā' ifrīqiyya wa'l-andalus wa'l-maghrib*, ed. Muḥammad Ḥajjī, 13 vols. Beirut: Dār al-Maghrib al-Islāmī, 1981–1983.
Yaḥyā b. ʻAdī. Untitled tract, in *Vingt Traités philosophiques et apologétiques*, ed. Paul Sbath, 171. Cairo: Maktabat H. Frīdrīkh, 1929. The Arabic text and an English translation by Sam Noble are also available at http://www.tertullian.org/fathers/sbath_16_yahya_ibn_adi_02.htm, consulted on 10th October 2018.
al-Yaman, Jaʻfar ibn Manṣūr. *Sarā'ir wa'l-asrār al-nuṭaqā'*, ed. Muṣṭafā Ghālib. Beirut: Dār al-Andalus, 1984.
al-Yaʻqūbī, Ibn Wāḍiḥ. *Ta'rīkh*, published as *Ibn Wāḍiḥ qui dicitur al-Yaʻqūbī, Historiae*, ed. M. Houtsma, 2 vols. Leiden: Brill, 1883.
al-Yaʻqūbī, Ibn Wāḍiḥ. *The Works of Ibn Wāḍiḥ al-Yaʻqūbī: an English Translation*, eds. Matthew Gordon, Chase Robinson, Everett Rowson and Michael Fishbein, 3 vols. Islamic History and Civilization 152. Leiden: Brill, 2017.

Secondary Sources

Abbott, Nabia. "Wahb B. Munabbih: A Review Article," *Journal of Near Eastern Studies* 36 (1977): 112.
Abulafia, Anna Sapir. "The Bible in Jewish-Christian Dialogue." In *The New Cambridge History of the Bible, vol. 2, From 600–1450*, edited by Richard Marsden and Ann Matter, 616–37. Cambridge: Cambridge University Press, 2012.
Abd al-Rauf, Muhammad. "Hadith Literature – 1: The Development of the Science of Hadith." In: *The Cambridge History of Arabic Literature*, vol. 10, edited by A.F.L. Beeston, T.M. Johnstone, R.B. Serjeant, G.R. Smith, 271–88. Cambridge: CUP: 1983–.
Accad, Martin. *Sacred Misinterpretation: Reaching Across the Christian-Muslim Divide*. Grand Rapids, MI: Eerdmans, 2019.
Accad, Martin.*The Gospels in the Muslim and Christian Exegetical Discourse from the Eighth to the Fourteenth Century*. Oxford: unpublished D.Phil thesis, 2001.
Accad, Martin. "Corruption and/or misinterpretation of the Bible: the story of the Islamic usage of *taḥrīf*." In *Christian Presence and Witness among Muslims*, edited by Peter Penner, 36–87. Schwarzenfeld: Neufeld Verlag, 2005.
Accad, Martin. "Corruption and/or Misinterpretation of the Bible: the story of the Islamic usage of *taḥrīf*." *Theological Review of the Near Eastern School of Theology* 24 (2003): 67–87.
Accad, Martin. "The Gospels in the Muslim Discourse of the Ninth to the Fourteenth Centuries: an exegetical inventorial table (part I)." *Islam and Christian-Muslim Relations* 14 (2003): 67–91, Part II, 205–20, Part III, 337–52, Part IV, 459–79.

Accad, Martin. "The Ultimate Proof-Text: the Interpretation of John 20.17 in Muslim-Christian Dialogue (Second/Eighth-Eighth/Fourteenth Centuries)." In *Christians at the Heart of Islamic Rule: Church Life and Scholarship in 'Abbāsid Iraq*, edited by David Thomas, 199–214. Leiden: Brill, 2003.

Adang, Camilla. *Muslim Writers on Judaism and the Hebrew Bible*. Islamic Philosophy Theology and Science: Texts and Studies 22. Leiden: Brill, 1996.

Adang, Camilla. "The Chronology of the Israelites According to Ḥamza al-Iṣfahānī." *Jerusalem Studies in Arabic and Islam* 32 (2006): 286–310.

Adang, Camilla. "A Fourth/Tenth Century Tunisian Muftī on the Sanctity of the Torah of Moses." In*The Intertwined Worlds of Islam: Essays in Memory of Hava Lazarus–Yafeh*, edited by Nahem Ilan et al, vii–xxxiv. Jerusalem: Ben Zvi Institute for the Study of Jewish Communities in the East, 2002.

Adang, Camilla. "Some Hitherto Neglected Biblical Material in the work of Ibn Ḥazm." *Al-Masāq* 5 (1992): 17–28.

Adang, Camilla. "Torah." In: *Encyclopaedia of the Qur'ān*, Volume 5.

Adang, Camilla, and Sabine Schmidtke. *Muslim Perceptions and Receptions of the Bible*. Atlanta, GA: Lockwood Press, 2016.

Adang, Camilla, Fierro, Maribel, and Sabine Schmidtke, eds. *Ibn Ḥazm of Cordoba: the life and works of a controversial thinker*. Handbook of Oriental Studies: Section 1, the Near and Middle East, 103. Leiden: Brill, 2012.

Ahmed, Shahab. Review of Bar-Asher, *JAOS* 123 (2003): 183–85.

Alexander, Philip. "The *Toledot Yeshu* in the Context of Jewish–Muslim Debate." In *Toledot Yeshu... Revisited*, edited by Peter Schäfer, 137–58. Tübingen: Mohr Siebeck, 2011.

Algermissen, Ernst. *Die Pentateuchzitate Ibn Ḥazms: ein Beitrag zur Geschichte der arabischen Bibelübersetzungen*. University of Münster: dissertation, 1933.

Amanat, Abbas. "*Mujtahids* and Missionaries: Shi'ī responses to Christian polemics in the early Qajar period." In *Religion and Society in Qajar Iran* edited by Robert Gleave. London: RoutledgeCurzon, 2005.

Amir-Moezzi, Muhammad Ali. "The Silent Qur'an and the Speaking Qur'an: History and Scriptures through the Study of Some Ancient Texts." *Studia Islamica* 108 (2013): 143–74.

Ananikian, M. "*Tahrif* or the Alteration of the Bible According to the Moslems," *Muslim World* 14 (1924): 61–84.

Andersson, Tobias. *Early Sunni Historiography: a Study of the* Tārīkh *of Khalīfa b. Khayyāṭ*. Islamic History and Civilization 157. Leiden: Brill, 2018.

Anthony, Sean. *The Caliph and the Heretic: Ibn Saba' and the Origins of Shī'ism*. Islamic History and Civilization 91. Leiden: Brill, 2012.

Anthony, Sean. "Muḥammad, Menaḥem, and the Paraclete: New Light on Ibn Isḥāq's (d.150/767) Arabic version of John 15:23–16:1." *Bulletin of the School of Oriental and African Studies* 79 (2016): 255–78.

Anthony, Sean. "Was Ibn Wāḍiḥ al-Ya'qūbī a Shi'ite Historian? The State of the Question." *Al-'Uṣūr al-Wusṭa* 24 (2016): 15–41.

Anthony, Sean. "Muḥammad, the Keys to Paradise, and the Doctrina Iacobi: a Late Antique puzzle." *Der Islam* 91 (2014): 243–65.

Anthony, Sean. "Who was the Shepherd of Damascus? The Enigma of Jewish and Messianist Responses to the Islamic Conquests in Marwānid Syria and Mesopotamia." In *The*

Lineaments of Islam: Studies in Honor of Fred McGraw Donner, edited by Paul Cobb, Islamic History and Civilization 95, 21–59. Leiden: Brill, 2012.

Anthony, Sean. "The Composition of Sayf b. 'Umar's Account of King Paul and his Corruption of Ancient Christianity." *Der Islam* 85 (2008): 164–202.

Armstrong, Lyall. *The* Quṣṣāṣ *of Early Islam*. Islamic History and Civilization 139. Leiden: Brill, 2017.

Ayoub, Mahmoud. "'Uzayr in the Qur'an and Muslim Tradition." In *Studies in Islamic and Judaic Traditions*, edited by William Brinner and Stephen Ricks, 3–18. Atlanta: Scholars' Press, 1986.

al-A'ẓamī, Muhammad. *The History of the Qur'anic Text*. Leicester: UK Islamic Academy, 2003.

Bakhos, Carol. *Ishmael on the Border: Rabbinic Portrayals of the First Arab*. Judaica: Hermeneutics, Mysticism and Religion. Albany, N.Y.: SUNY Press, 2006.

Bar-Asher, Meir. *Scripture and Exegesis in Early Imāmī Shiism*. Islamic Philosophy, Theology and Science 37. Leiden: Brill, 1999.

Bar-Asher, Meir. "Shī'ism and the Qur'ān." In *Encyclopaedia of the Qur'ān*, Volume 4.

Barzegar, Abbas. "The Persistence of Heresy: Paul of Tarsus, Ibn Sabā', and Historical Narrative in Sunni Identity Formation." *Numen* 58 (2011), 207–31.

Bashear, Suliman. "Riding Beasts on Divine Missions: An Examination of the Ass and Camel Traditions." *Journal of Semitic Studies* 37 (1991): 37–75.

Bashear, Suliman. "Qibla Musharriqa and Early Muslim Prayer in Churches." *Muslim World* 81 (1991): 267–82.

Bashear, Suliman. "Abraham's Sacrifice of his Son and Related Issues." *Der Islam* 67 (1990): 243–77.

Bashear, Suliman. "The Title 'Fārūq', and its Association with 'Umar I," *Studia Islamica* 72 (1990): 47–70.

Bashear, Suliman. "Qur'ān 2:114 and Jerusalem." *Bulletin of the School of Oriental and African Studies* 52 (1989): 215–238.

Baumstark, Anton. "Markus Kap. 2 in der arabischen Übersetzung des Isaak Velasquez." *Oriens Christianus* 31 (1934): 226–39.

Beaumont, Mark. "'Ammār al-Baṣrī on the Alleged Corruption of the Gospels." In *The Bible in Arab Christianity*, edited by David Thomas, 241–55. The History of Christian-Muslim Relations, 6. Leiden: Brill, 2007.

Bedir, Murteza. *The Early Development of Ḥanafī* uṣūl al-fiqh. Unpublished Ph.D. thesis, University of Manchester, 1999.

Bedir, Murteza. "Revelation and Reason: Abū Zayd al-Dabbūsī on Rational Proofs." *Islamic Studies* 43 (2004): 227–245.

Behloul, Samuel-Martin. *Ibn Ḥazms Evangelienkritik: Eine Methodische Untersuchung*. Islamic Theology, Philosophy and Science 50. Leiden: Brill, 2002.

Behloul, Samuel-Martin. "The Testimony of Reason and Historical Reality: Ibn Ḥazm's Refutation of Christianity." In *Controversial Thinker*, edited by Adang et al, 457–83. Leiden: Brill, 2012.

Bekkum, Wout Jac. Van. "The Karaite Jacob al-Qirqisānī (Tenth Century) on Christianity and the Christians." In *Syriac Polemics*, edited by Wout Jac. Van Bekkum, Jan Willem Drijvers, Alex Klugkist, 173–92. Leuven: Peeters, 2007.

Ben-Ari, Shosh. "The Stories About Abraham in Islam: a Geographical Approach." *Arabica* 54 (2007): 526–53.

Berchman, Robert. *Porphyry Against the Christians*. Studies in Platonism, Neoplatonism, and the Platonic Tradition 1. Leiden: Brill, 2005.

Berg, Herbert. "Ṭabarī's Exegesis of the Qur'ānic Term *al-Kitāb*." *Journal of the American Academy of Religion* 63 (1995): 761–74.

Berg, Herbert. *The Development of Exegesis in Early Islam*. Richmond: Curzon, 2000.

Bertaina, David. "Early Muslim Attitudes to the Bible." In *Routledge Handbook on Christian-Muslim Relations*, edited by David Thomas, 98–106. London: Routledge, 2018.

El-Bizri, Nader, ed. *The* Ikhwān al-Ṣafā' *and their* Rasā'il: *an introduction*. Oxford: OUP 2008.

Bori, Caterina. "'All We Know is What we Have Been Told': Reflections on Emigration and Land as Divine Heritage in the Qur'ān." In *The Coming of the Comforter: When, Where and to Whom?: Studies on the Rise of Islam and Various Other Topics in Memory of John Wansbrough*, edited by Carlos Segovia and Basil Lourié, 303–40. Piscataway, NJ: Gorgias Press, 2012.

Borrut, Antoine. *Entre mémoire et pourvoir: L'espace syrien sous les derniers Omeyades et les premiers Abbassides (v.72–193/692–809)*. Leiden: Brill, 2011.

Bottini, Laura. "al-Kindī, 'Abd al-Masīḥ ibn Isḥāq (pseudonym)." In *Christian–Muslim Relations: A Bibliographical* History. *Volume 1 (600–900)*.

Bray, Julia. "Lists and Memory: Ibn Qutayba and Muḥammad b. Ḥabīb." In *Culture and Memory in Medieval Islam: essays in honour of Wilferd Madelung*, edited by Farhad Daftary and Josef Meri, 210–31. London: I.B. Tauris, 2003.

Brinner, William. "An Islamic Decalogue." In *Studies in Islamic and Judaic Traditions*, edited by William Brinner and Stephen Ricks, vol 1: 67–84. Atlanta: Scholars Press, 1986.

Brock, Sebastian. "Jewish Traditions in Syriac Sources." *Journal of Jewish Studies* 30 (1979): 212–32.

Brown, Jonathan. *The Canonization of al-Bukhārī and Muslim: the Formation and Function of the Sunni Ḥadīth Canon*. Islamic History and Civilization, 69. Leiden: Brill, 2007.

Brunner, Rainer. "The Dispute About the Falsification of the Qur'ān Between Sunnīs and Shī'īs in the 20th Century." In *Studies in Arabic and Islam*, edited by Stefan Leder et al., 437–46. Leuven: Peeters, 2002.

Brunner, Rainer. *Die Schia und die Koranfälschung*. Würzburg: Ergon Verlag, 2001.

Buckley, Ron. "On the Origins of Shī'i Ḥadīth." *Muslim World* 88 (1998): 165–184.

Burton, John. *The Sources of Islamic Law: Islamic Theories of Abrogation*. Edinburgh: EUP, 1990.

Burton, John. "The Corruption of the Scriptures." *Occasional Papers of the School of 'Abbāsid Studies* 4 (1992): 95–106.

Busse, Heribert. "Omar's Image as the Conqueror of Jerusalem." *Jerusalem Studies in Arabic and Islam* 8 (1986): 149–68.

Calder, Norman. "From Midrash to Scripture: The Sacrifice of Abraham in early Islamic Tradition." In *The Formation of the Classical Islamic* World, edited by Andrew Rippin, 81–108. Aldershot: Ashgate Variorum, 1999.

Callataÿ, Godefroid de. *Ikhwān al-Ṣafā': A Brotherhood of Idealists on the Fringe of Orthodox Islam*. Makers of the Muslim World. Oxford: Oneworld, 2005.

Campbell, Sandra. "It must be the end of time: Apocalyptic Aḥādīth as a record of the Islamic Community's Reactions to the Turbulent First Centuries." *Medieval Encounters* 4 (1998): 178–87.

Carlson, Stephen. "The Davidic Key for Counting the Generations in Matthew 1:17." *Catholic Biblical Quarterly* 76 (2014): 665–83.
Chapman, Colin. *The Bible Through Muslim Eyes and a Christian Response.* Cambridge: Grove Books, 2008.
Charfi, Abdelmajid "Christianity in the Qur'an Commentary of Ṭabarī." *Islamochristiana* 6 (1980): 105–48.
Christian-Muslim Relations: A Bibliographical History. Edited by David Thomas. *Volume 1 (600–900).* Edited by David Thomas and Barbara Roggema. Leiden: Brill, 2009.
Christian-Muslim Relations: A Bibliographical History. Edited by David Thomas. *Volume 2 (900–1050).* Edited by David Thomas and Alex Mallett. Leiden: Brill, 2010.
Christian-Muslim Relations: A Bibliographical History. Edited by David Thomas. *Volume 3 (1050–1200).* Edited by David Thomas and Alex Mallett. Leiden: Brill, 2011.
Clivaz, Claire and Sara Schulthess. "On the Source and Rewriting of 1 Corinthians 2:9 in Christian, Jewish and Islamic Traditions (*1Clem* 34.8, *GosJud* 47.10–13; a *ḥadīth qudsī*)." *New Testament Studies* 61 (2015): 183–200.
Conrad, Lawrence. "The *Mawālī* and Early Arabic Historiography." In *Patronate and Patronage in Early and Classical Islam*, edited by Monique Bernards and John Nawas, 370–424. Islamic History and Civilization 61. Leiden: Brill, 2005.
Conrad, Lawrence. "Recovering Lost Texts: Some methodological issues." *Journal of the American Oriental Society* 113 (1993): 258–63.
Constable, Olivia ed. *Medieval Iberia: readings from Christian, Muslim and Jewish Sources.* Philadelphia: University of Pennsylvania Press, 1997.
Cook, David. *Studies in Muslim Apocalyptic.* Studies in Late Antiquity and Early Islam 21. Princeton: Darwin Press, 2002.
Cook, David. "Christians and Christianity in ḥadīth works before 900." In *Christian-Muslim Relations: A Bibliographical History, Volume 1 600–900,* 73–82.
Cook, David. "New Testament Citations in the Ḥadīth Literature and the Question of Early Gospel Translations into Arabic." In *The Encounter of Eastern Christianity with Early Islam,* edited by Emmanouela Grypeou, Mark Swanson, David Thomas, 185–223. The History of Christian-Muslim Relations 5. Leiden: Brill, 2006.
Cook, Michael. *Commanding Right and Forbidding Wrong in Islamic Thought.* Cambridge: CUP, 2001.
Coope, Jessica. "With Heart, Tongue and Limbs: Ibn Ḥazm on the essence of faith." *Medieval Encounters* 6 (2000): 101–13.
Cooper, John. *The Commentary on the Qur'an by Abū Ja'far Muḥammad bin Jarīr al-Ṭabarī,* vol. 1. Oxford: OUP, 1987.
Cragg, Kenneth. *Jesus and the Muslim.* Oxford: Oneworld, 1985.
Crone, Patricia, and Michael Cook. *Hagarism.* Cambridge: CUP, 1977.
Cuffel, Alexandra. "Between Epic Entertainment and Polemical Exegesis: Jesus as antihero in *Toledot Yeshu.*" In *Medieval Exegesis and Religious Difference: Commentary, Conflict and Community in the Predmodern Mediterranean*, edited by Ryan Szpiech, 155–170. New York: Fordham University Press, 2015.
Daftary, Farhad. *The Ismā'īlīs: Their History and Doctrines.* Cambridge: CUP, 1992.
Déclais, Jean-Louis. *Un Récit musulmane sur Isaïe.* Paris: Cerf, 2001.
Déclais, Jean-Louis. *David raconté par le musulmanes.* Paris: Cerf, 1991.

Demiri, Lejla. “Naṣr ibn Yaḥya.” In *Christian-Muslim Relations: A Bibliographical History. Volume 3 (1050–1200).*

Dikken, Berend Jan. “Some Remarks About Middle Arabic and Sa‘adya Gaon’s Arabic Translation of the Pentateuch in Manuscripts of Jewish, Samaritan, Coptic Christian, and Muslim Provenance.” In *Middle Arabic and Mixed Arabic: Diachrony and Synchrony*, edited by Liesbeth Zack and Arie Schippers, 51–81. Studies in Semitic Languages and Linguistics 64. Leiden: Brill, 2012.

Donaldson, Dwight. “Al-Ya‘qūbī’s Chapter About Jesus Christ.” *The Macdonald Presentation Volume* (no editor) 89–105. Princeton: PUP, 1933.

Donner, Fred. *Muhammad and the Believers.* Cambridge, MA: Harvard University Press, 2010.

Donner, Fred. “Talking About Islam’s Origins.” *Bulletin of the School of Oriental and African Studies* 81 (2018): 1–23.

Donohue, John. *The Buwayhid Dynasty in Iraq 334H./945 to 403H./1012: Shaping Institutions for the Future.* Islamic History and Civilization 44. Leiden: Brill, 2003.

Dunlop, D.M. “A Letter of Hārūn ar-Rashīd to the Emperor Constantine VI.” In *In Memoriam Paul Kahle*, edited by Matthew Black and Georg Fohrer, 106–115. Berlin: A. Töpelmann, 1968.

Ebied, Rifaat and L.R. Wickham. “Al-Ya‘ḳūbī’s Account of the Israelite Prophets and Kings.” *Journal of Near Eastern Studies* 29 (1970): 80–98.

Einboden, Jeffery. *The Qur’ān and Kerygma: Biblical Reception of the Muslim Scripture across a Millennium.* Themes in Qur’anic Studies. Sheffield: Equinox, 2019.

Encyclopaedia Iranica. Edited by Ehsan Yarshater. London: Routledge, 1982.

Encyclopaedia of Islam, Second Edition. Edited by P. Bearman, Th. Bianquis, C.E. Bosworth, E. van Donzel, W.P. Heinrichs. Leiden, Brill: 1954–2005. Available online at https://referenceworks.brillonline.com/browse/encyclopaedia-of-islam-2.

Encyclopaedia of Islam, THREE. Edited by Kate Fleet, Gudrun Krämer, Denis Matringe, John Nawas, Everett Rowson. Leiden, Brill: 2007–. Available online at https://referenceworks.brillonline.com/browse/encyclopaedia-of-islam-3.

Encyclopaedia of the Qur’ān. Edited by Jane McAuliffe, 6 volumes. Leiden: Brill, 2001–06.

Eph’al, Israel. “‘Ishmael’ and ‘Arabs’: a transformation of ethnological terms.” *Journal of Near Eastern Studies* 35 (1976): 225–235.

Estes, Yusuf. ‘Gospel of Barnabas: Fact or Fake?’. Islam Newsroom. Published 16 November 2010, https://www.islamnewsroom.com/news-we-need/730-gospelofbarnabasfactorfake.

The European Qur’an. Islamic Scripture in European Culture and Religion 1150–1850 (website). The European Qur’an research project. Consulted online on 12 May 2020, https://euqu.eu.

Fierro, Maribel. “Ibn Ḥazm and the Jewish *Zindīq*.” In *Controversial Thinker*, edited by Adang et al, 497–509. Leiden: Brill, 2012.

Fierro, Maribel. “Ibn Waḍḍāḥ.” In *Christian-Muslim Relations: A Bibliographical History. Volume 1 (600–900).*

Finkel, Joshua. “A *Risāla* of al-Jāḥiẓ.” *Journal of the American Oriental Society* 47 (1927): 311–34.

Firestone, Reuven. “Ishmael.” In: *Encyclopaedia of the Qur’ān*, Volume 2.

Fischel, Walter. “The Bible in Persian Translation.” *Harvard Theological Review* 45 (1952): 3–45.

Fisher, Greg ed., *Arabs and Empires before Islam.* Oxford: OUP, 2015.

Fletcher, Charles. *Anti-Christian Polemic in Early Islam: A Translation and Analysis of Abū 'Uthmān 'Amr B. Baḥr al-Jāḥiẓ's Risāla: Radd 'alā al-Naṣārā (A Reply to the Christians).* Unpublished M.A. thesis, McGill University, Montreal, 2002.

Frank, Daniel. *Search Scripture Well: Karaite Exegetes and the Origins of the Jewish Bible Commentary in the Islamic East.* Études sur le judaïsme médiéval 29. Leiden: Brill, 2004.

Friedenreich, David. "The Use of Islamic Sources in Saadiah Gaon's *Tafsir* of the Torah." *Jewish Quarterly Review* 93 (2003): 353–95.

Friedenreich, David. "Holiness and Impurity in the Torah and the Quran: Differences within a Common Typology." *Comparative Islamic Studies* 6 (2010): 5–22.

Frolov, Dmitry. "The Problem of the 'Seven Long' Sūrahs." In *Studies in Arabic and Islam: Proceedings of the 19th Congress, Union Européenne des Arabisants et Islamisants, Halle 1998,* edited by Stefan Leder, Hilary Kilpatrick et al, 193–203. Leuven: Peeters, 2002.

Gager, John. "Simon Peter, Founder of Christianity or Saviour of Israel?" in Toledot Yeshu... *Revisited*, edited by Schäfer, Meerson and Deutsch, 236–41. Tübingen: Mohr Siebeck, 2011.

Gallagher, Edmon, and John Meade. *The Biblical Canon Lists from Early Christianity: Texts and Analysis.* Oxford: OUP, 2018.

García-Sanjuán, Alejandro. "Jews and Christians in Almoravid Seville as Portrayed by the Islamic Jurist Ibn 'Abdūn." *Medieval Encounters* 14 (2008): 78–98.

Gaudeul, Jean-Marie. *Encounters and Clashes,* 2 vols., Rome: PISAI, 2000 edn.

Gaudeul, Jean-Marie, and Robert Caspar. "Textes de la tradition musulmane concernant le *taḥrīf* (falsification) des écritures." *Islamochristiana* 6 (1980): 61–104.

Gibson, Nathan. "A Mid-Ninth Century Arabic Translation of Isaiah? Glimpses from al-Jāḥiẓ." In *Senses of Scripture, Treasures of Tradition: the Bible in Arabic among Jews, Christians and Muslims*, edited by Miriam Hjälm, 327–69. Biblia Arabica 5. Leiden: Brill, 2017.

Gilliot, Claude. "Le Commentaire coranique de Hūd B. Muḥakkam/Muḥkim." *Arabica* 44 (1997): 179–233.

Gilliot, Claude. "Ṭabarī et les chrétiens Taġlibites." In *Annales du Département des études arabes, Université Saint-Joseph, Beyrouth. In Memoriam Jean Maurice Fiey 1914–1995,* 1991–92 (1996): 145–59.

Gilliot, Claude. "Christians and Christianity in Islamic Exegesis." In *Christian-Muslim Relations: A Bibliographical History. Volume 1 600–900,* 31–56.

Giudetti, Mattia. *In the Shadow of the Church: the Building of Mosques in Early Medieval Syria.* Arts and Archaeology of the Islamic World 8. Leiden: Brill, 2016.

Gleave, Robert. *Islam and Literalism: Literal Meaning and Interpretation in Islamic Legal Theory.* Edinburgh: EUP 2012.

Gleave, Robert. "Between *Ḥadīth* and *Fiqh:* the 'Canonical' Imāmī Collections of *Akhbār.*" *Islamic Law and Society* 8 (2001): 350–82.

Gobillot, Geneviève. "Qur'an and Torah: the Foundations of intertextuality." In *A History of Jewish-Muslim Relations: From the origins to the present day,* edited by Abdelwahab Meddeb and Benjamin Stora, 611–21. Princeton: PUP, 2013.

Goldstein, Miriam. "Sa'adya's *Tafsīr* in Light of Muslim Polemic Against Ninth-Century Arabic Bible Translations." *Jerusalem Studies in Arabic and Islam* 36 (2009): 173–99.

Goldziher, Ignaz. "The Ḥadīth and the New Testament." In *Muslim Studies,* vol 2, trans. C.R. Barber and S.M. Stern, 346–62. London: George Allen and Unwin, 1971.

Goldziher, Ignaz. "Über Muhammadanische Polemik gegen Ahl al-Kitāb." *Zeitschrift der deutschen morgenländischen Gesellschaft* 32 (1878): 341–87.

Görke, Andreas. "Authorship in the *Sīra* Literature." In *Concepts of Authorship in Pre-Modern Arabic Texts,* edited by Lale Behzadi and Jaakko Hämeen-Antilla, 63–92. Bamberg: University of Bamberg Press, 2015.

Görke, Andreas. "The Relationship Between Maghāzī and Ḥadīth in early Islamic Scholarship." *Bulletin of the School of Oriental and African Studies* 74 (2011): 171–85.

Grafton, David. "'The Arabs' in the Ecclesiastical Historians of the 4th/5th centuries: Effects on Contemporary Christian–Muslim Relations." *Het Teologiese Studies* 64 (2008): 177–92.

Graham, William. *Beyond the Written Word: oral aspects of scripture in the history of religion.* Cambridge: CUP, 1987.

Graham, William. "The Earliest Meaning of 'Qur'ān'." In *The Qur'an: Style and Contents,* edited by Andrew Rippin, 361–77. Aldershot: Ashgate, 2001. First printed in *Die Welt des Islams* 23–24 (1984): 101–39.

Griffith, Sidney. *The Bible in Arabic.* Jews, Christians and Muslims from the Ancient to the Modern World. Princeton: PUP, 2013.

Griffith, Sidney. *The Church in the Shadow of the Mosque.* Jews, Christians and Muslims from the Ancient to the Modern World. Princeton: PUP, 2008.

Griffith, Sidney. *The Reformation of Morals: a parallel English–Arabic Text.* Middle Eastern Texts Initiative. Provo, UT: Brigham Young University Press, 2002.

Griffith, Sidney. "When did the Bible Become an Arabic Scripture?" *Intellectual History of the Islamicate World* 1 (2013): 7–23.

Griffith, Sidney. "The Gospel in Arabic: an Inquiry into its Appearance in the First 'Abbāsid Century." *Oriens Christianus* 69 (1985): 126–67.

Griffith, Sidney. "Arguing from Scripture: The Bible in the Christian/Muslim Encounter in the Middle Ages." In *Scripture and Pluralism: Reading the Bible in the religiously plural worlds of the Middle Ages and Renaissance,* edited by Thomas Heffernan and Thomas Burman, 29–58. Studies in the History of Christian Traditions 123. Leiden: Brill, 2005.

Griffith, Sidney. "The Gospel, the Qur'ān, and the presentation of Jesus in al-Ya'qūbī's *Ta'rīkh.*" in *Bible and Qur'an: Essays in Scriptural Intertextuality,* edited by John Reeves, 133–60. Atlanta GA: Society of Biblical Literature, 2003.

Griffith, Sidney. "Disputing with Islam in Syriac: the Case of the Monk of Bêt Ḥālê and a Muslim Emir." *Hugoye* 3 (2000): 29–54.

Griffith, Sidney. *Arabic Christianity in the Monasteries of Ninth Century Palestine.* Aldershot: Variorum, 1992.

Griffith, Sidney. "The Prophet Muḥammad, his Scripture and his Message according to the Christian Apologies in Arabic and Syriac From the First 'Abbāsid Century." in Griffith, *Arabic Christianity in the Monasteries of Ninth Century Palestine*, I. Aldershot: Variorum, 1992.

Griffith, Sidney. "'Ammār al-Baṣrī's *Kitāb al-Burhān:* Christian Kalām in the First 'Abbāsid Century." *Le Muséon* 96 (1983): 145–81.

Gruber, Christiane, and Frederick Colby, eds. *The Prophet's Ascension: Cross-Cultural Encounters with the Islamic Mi'raj Tales.* Bloomington, IN: Indiana University Press, 2010.

Guillaume, Alfred. *New Light on the Life of Muhammad.* Manchester: MUP, 1960.

Günther, Sebastian. "*O People of the Scripture! Come to a Word Common to You and Us* (Q.3:64): The Ten Commandments and the Qur'an." *Journal of Quranic Studies* 9 (2007): 28–58.

Gutas, Dimitri. *Avicenna and the Aristotelian Tradition*, 2nd edition. Leiden: Brill, 2014.

Güzelmansur, Timo ed. *Hat Jesus Muhammad angekündigt? Der Paraklet des Johannesevangeliums und seine koranische Bedeutung*. Regensburg: Verlag Friedrich Pustet, 2012.

Hackenburg, Clint. *Voices of the Converted: Christian Apostate Literature in Medieval Islam*. Unpublished Ph.D thesis, Ohio State University, 2015.

Hahn, Ernest, and Gustave Adelphi. *The Integrity of the Bible According to the Qur'an and Hadith*. Hyderabad: Henry Martyn Institute of Islamic Studies, 1977.

Hakim, Avraham. "Muḥammad's Authority and Leadership Reestablished: The Prophet and 'Umar b. al-Khaṭṭāb." *Revue de l'histoire de religions* 226 (2009): 189–92.

Hakim, Avraham. "The Biblical Annunciation made to 'Umar b. al-Khaṭṭab." *Jerusalem Studies in Arabic and Islam* 42 (2015): 130–31.

Hakim, Avraham. "The Death of an Ideal Leader: Predictions and Premonitions." *Journal of the American Oriental Society* 126 (2006): 1–16.

Hakim, Avraham. "Context: 'Umar b. al-Khaṭṭāb." In *The Blackwell Companion to the Qur'ān*, edited by Andrew Rippin, 205–20. Oxford: Blackwell, 2006.

Hawting, Gerald. "The Development of the Doctrine of the Infallibility (*'iṣma*) of Prophets and the Interpretation of Qur'ān 8:67–69." *Jerusalem Studies in Arabic and Islam* 39 (2012): 141–63.

Hawting, Gerald. "The Religion of Abraham and Islam." In *Abraham, the Nations and the Hagarites: Jewish, Christian and Islamic Perspectives on kinship with Abraham*, edited by Martin Goodman, George van Kooten and Jacques van Ruiten, 477–501. Leiden: Brill, 2010.

el-Hibri, Tayeb. *Parable and Politics in Early Islamic History*. New York: Columbia University Press, 2010.

el-Hibri, Tayeb. "'Umar b. al-Khaṭṭāb and the 'Abbāsids." *Journal of the American Oriental Society* 136 (2016): 763–83.

Hillenbrand, Robert. "The Edinburgh Biruni Manuscript: a Mirror of its Time?" *Journal of the Royal Asiatic Society* Series 3, 26 (2016): 171–99.

Hillenbrand, Robert. "Images of Muhammad in al-Biruni's Chronology of Ancient Nations." In *Persian Painting from the Mongols to the Qajars: Studies in Honour of Basil W. Robinson*, edited by Robert Hillenbrand, 129–46. London: I.B. Tauris in association with the Centre of Middle Eastern Studies, Cambridge, 2000.

Hirschfeld, Hartwig. "Mohammedan Criticism of the Bible." *Jewish Quarterly Review* (1900–01): 222–240.

Hollenberg, David. *Beyond the Qur'an*. Columbia, SC: University of South Carolina Press, 2016.

Hollenberg, David. "Disrobing Judges with Veiled Truths: an Early Ismā'īlī Torah Interpretation (*ta'wīl*) in service of the Fāṭimid mission." *Religion* 33 (2003): 127–45.

Horbury, William. "Tertullian on the Jews in the Light of *De Spectaculis* XXX. 5–6." *Journal of Theological Studies* (1972): 455–59.

Hoyland, Robert. *Seeing Islam as Others Saw it: a Survey and Evaluation of Christian, Jewish and Zoroastrian Writings on Early Islam.* Studies in Late Antiquity and Early Islam 13. Princeton: Darwin Press, 1997.

Hoyland, Robert. "Sebeos, the Jews and the Rise of Islam." *Studies in Muslim-Jewish Relations* 2 (1995): 89–102.

Hoyland, Robert. "Reflections on the Identity of the Arabian Conquerors of the Seventh-Century Middle East." *Al-'Uṣūr al-Wusṭā* 25 (2017): 113–40.

Hoyland, Robert. Review of Lecker, *Bulletin of the School of Oriental and African Studies* 61 (1998): 129–31.

Isteero, Albert. *'Abdullāh Muslim Ibn Qutayba's Biblical Quotations and Their Source: an Inquiry into the Earliest Existing Arabic Bible Translations.* Unpublished Ph.D. thesis, Johns Hopkins University, 1991.

Jeffery, Arthur. *The Foreign Vocabulary of the Qur'an.* Baroda: Oriental Institute, 1938.

Johns, Anthony. "David and Bathsheba: a Case Study in the Exegesis of Qur'anic Storytelling." *Mélanges de l'Institut dominicain d'études orientales* 19 (1989): 225–66.

Joosse, Peter. "An Introduction to the Arabic Diatessaron." *Oriens Christianus* 83 (1999): 72–129.

Joosten, Jan. "The *Gospel of Barnabas* and the Diatessaron." *Harvard Theological Review* 95 (2002): 73–96.

Kaddouri, Samir. "Refutations of Ibn Ḥazm by Mālikī authors of al-Andalus and North Africa." In *Controversial Thinker,* edited by Adang et al: 539–600. Leiden: Brill, 2012.

Kashouh, Hikmat. *The Arabic Versions of the Gospels: the manuscripts and their families.* Arbeiten zur neutestamentlichen Textforschung 42. Berlin: Walter deGruyter, 2011.

Keating, Sandra Tonies. *Defending the People of Truth in the Early Islamic Period. The Christian Apologies of Abū Rā'iṭa.* History of Christian-Muslim Relations 4. Leiden: Brill, 2006.

Keating, Sandra Tonies. "Refuting the Charge of *taḥrīf.* Abū Rā'iṭa (d.ca. 835 CE) and his first *Risāla* on the Holy Trinity." In *Ideas, Images, and Methods of Portrayal. Insights into Classical Arabic Literature and Islam*, edited by Sebastian Günther, 41–57. Islamic History and Civilization 58. Leiden: Brill, 2005.

Keating, Sandra Tonies. "The Paraclete and the Integrity of Scripture." In *Theological Issues*, edited by Charles Tieszen, 15–25. Eugene, OR: Wipf and Stock, 2018.

Kendall, Calvin. "Bede and Islam." In *Bede and the Future*, edited by Peter Darby and Faith Wallis (Farnham: Ashgate, 2014): 93–114.

Kennedy, Hugh ed. *Al-Ṭabarī: a Medieval Muslim Historian and his Work.* Studies in Late Antiquity and Islam 15. Princeton: Darwin Press, 2008.

Kessler, Christel. "'Abd Al-Malik's Inscription on the Dome of the Rock: a reconsideration." *Journal of the Royal Asiatic Society of Great Britain and Ireland* 1 (1970): 2–14.

Khalidi, Tarif. *The Muslim Jesus: Sayings and Stories in Islamic Literature.* Cambridge, MA: Harvard University Press, 2001.

King, Daniel. "A Christian Qur'ān? A Study in the Syriac Background to the Language of the Qur'ān as Presented in the Work of Christoph Luxenberg." *Journal for Late Antique Religion and Culture* 3 (2009): 44–71.

Kister, M.J. "*Ḥaddithū 'an banī isrā'il wa-lā ḥaraja:* a Study of an Early Tradition." *Israel Oriental Studies* 2 (1972): 215–239.

Kister, M.J. *Studies in Jāhiliyya and Early Islam.* London: Variorum, 1980.

Khoury, R.G. "Quelques réflexions sur les citations de la Bible dans les premières générations islamiques du premier et du deuxième siècles de l'hégire." *Bulletin d'études orientales* 29 (1977): 269–78.

Klar, Marianna. *Interpreting al-Thaʿlabī's Tales of the Prophets: Temptation, Responsibility and Loss.* Routledge Studies in the Qur'an. Abingdon: Routledge, 2009.

Klorman, Bat-Zion Eraqi. "Muslim Supporters of Jewish Messiahs in Yemen." *Middle East Studies* 29 (1993): 714–25.

Koertner, Mareike. *"We Have Made Clear the Signs": Dalāʾil al-Nubuwa* [sic] – *Proofs of Prophecy in Early Hadith.* Unpublished Ph.D. thesis, University of Yale, 2014.

Koertner, Mareike. "*Dalāʾil al-Nubuwwa* Literature as Part of the Medieval Scholarly Discourse on Prophecy." *Der Islam* 95 (2018): 91–109.

Kohlberg, Etan. "Authoritative Scriptures in Early Imāmī Shīʿism." In *Les Retours aux Écritures: fondamentalismes présents et passes,* edited by Évelyne Patlagean and Alain le Boulluec, 295–312. Louvain: Peeters, 1993.

Kohlberg, Etan. "Some Shīʿī views of the Antediluvian World." *Studia Islamica* 52 (1980): 41–66.

Kohlberg, Etan. "Shīʿī Ḥadīth." In *The Cambridge Companion to Arabic Literature*, vol. 12, edited by A.F.L. Beeston, T.M. Johnstone, R.B.Serjeant, G.R. Smith, 299–307. Cambridge: CUP, 1983–.

Kohlberg, Etan. "The Term '*Rāfiḍa*' in Imāmī Shīʿī Usage," *Journal of the American Oriental Society* 99 (1979): 677–79.

Kohlberg, Etan and Mohammad Ali Amir-Moezzi, eds. *Revelation and Falsification: the* Kitāb al-Qirāʾāt *of Aḥmad b. Muḥammad al-Sayyārī.* Texts and Studies on the Qur'an 4. Leiden: Brill, 2009.

König, Daniel. *Arabic-Islamic Views of the Latin West: Tracing the Emergence of Medieval Europe.* Oxford: OUP, 2015.

Koningsveld, P.S. van. "Christian-Arabic Manuscripts from the Iberian Peninsula and North Africa: a Historical Interpretation." *Al-Qanṭara* 15 (1994): 423–51.

Koningsveld, P.S. van. "The Islamic Image of Paul and the Origin of the Gospel of Barnabas" *Jerusalem Studies in Arabic and Islam* 20 (1996): 200–28.

Kraus, Paul. "Hebräische und syrische Zitate in ismāʿīlitischen Schriften." *Der Islam* 19 (1930): 243–63.

Kreuzer, Siegfried (ed.). *Introduction to the Septuagint*, trans. David Brenner and Peter Altmann. Waco, TX: Baylor University Press, 2019.

Kuhn, Michael. "Early Islamic Perspectives on the Apostle Paul." In *Arab Christians and the Qur'an from the Origins of Islam to the Medieval Period*, edited by Mark Beaumont, 150–73. History of Christian-Muslim Relations 35. Leiden: Brill, 2018.

Kulik, Alexander. "Genre Without a Name: Was there a Hebrew term for 'Apocalypse'?" *Journal for the Study of Judaism* 40 (2009): 540–50.

Lamoreaux, John. *Theodore Abu Qurrah.* Library of the Christian East 1. Provo, UT: Brigham Young University Press, 2005.

Lasker, Daniel. "Saadya Gaon on Christianity and Islam." In *The Jews of Medieval Islam: Community, Society and Identity,* edited by Daniel Frank, 165–77. Études sur le judaïsme médiéval 16. Leiden: Brill, 1995.

Lassner, Jacob. "The Covenant of the Prophets: Muslim Texts, Jewish Subtexts." *Association for Jewish Studies Review* 15 (1990): 207–38.

Lawson, Todd. *The Crucifixion and the Qur'an*. Oxford: Oneworld, 2009.
Lazarus-Yafeh, Hava. *Intertwined Worlds*. Princeton: PUP, 1992.
Lecker, Michael. *Muslims, Jews and Pagans*. Islamic History and Civilization 13. Leiden: Brill, 1995.
Lecker, Michael. "Notes About Censorship and Self-Censorship in the Biography of the Prophet Muhammad." *Al-Qanṭara* 35 (2014): 233–54.
Lecker, Michael. "Zayd b. Thābit, 'A Jew with Two Sidelocks': Judaism and literacy in pre-Islamic Medina (Yathrib)." *Journal of Near Eastern Studies* 56 (1997): 259–73.
Lecomte, Gérard. "Les citations de l'Ancien et du Nouveau Testament dans l'œuvre d'Ibn Qutayba." *Arabica* 5 (1958): 34–46.
Leder, Stefan. "The Attitude of the Population, especially the Jews, towards the Arab-Islamic Conquest of Bilād al-Shām and the Question of their Role Therein." *Die Welt des Orients* 18 (1987): 64–71.
Leirvik, Oddbjørn. "History as a Literary Weapon: The Gospel of Barnabas in Muslim-Christian Polemics." *Studia Theologica – Nordic Journal of Theology* 56 (2002): 4–26.
Levy-Rubin, Milka. "Why was the Dome of the Rock Built? A New Perspective on a Long-discussed Question." *Bulletin of the School of Oriental and African Studies* 80 (2017): 441–64.
Lichtenstädter, Ilse. "Muḥammad Ibn Ḥabīb and his *Kitāb al-Muḥabbar*." *Journal of the Royal Asiatic Society of Great Britain and Ireland* 1 (1939): 1–27.
Ljamai, Abdelilah. *Ibn Ḥazm et la polémique islamo-chrétienne dans l'histoire de l'Islam*. The Medieval and Early Modern Iberian World 17. Leiden: Brill, 2003.
Lowin, Shari. *The Making of a Forefather: Abraham in Islamic and Jewish Exegetical Narratives*. Islamic History and Civilization 65. Leiden: Brill, 2006.
Lowin, Shari. "Revision and Alteration." In: *Encyclopaedia of the Qur'ān*, Volume 4.
Lowry, Joseph. *Early Islamic Legal Theory: the Risāla of Muḥammad ibn Idrīs al-Shāfiʿī*. Studies in Islamic Law and Society 30. Leiden: Brill, 2007.
Lowry, Joseph. "Ibn Qutaybah (828–889)." In *Arabic Literary Culture, 500–925*, edited by Shawkat Toorawa and Michael Cooperson, 172–83. Dictionary of Literary Biography 311. Detroit: Thomson Gale, 2005.
Luxenberg, Christoph. *The Syro-Aramaic Reading of the Qur'an*. Berlin: Hans Schiler, 2007.
Macdonald, Michael. "Ancient Arabia and the Written Word." *Proceedings of the Seminar for Arabian Studies* 40, Supplement: The Development of Arabic as a Written Language (2010): 5–27.
McAuliffe, Jane. *Qur'anic Christians: An Analysis of Classical and Modern Exegesis*. Cambridge: CUP, 1991.
McAuliffe, Jane. "The Qur'anic Context of Muslim Biblical Scholarship." *Islam and Christian-Muslim Relations* 7 (1996): 141–55.
McDonald, Lee, and James Sanders, eds. *The Canon Debate*. Peabody, MA: Hendrickson, 2002.
Maalouf, Tony. *Arabs in the Shadow of Israel: the unfolding of God's prophetic plan for Ishmael's line*. Grand Rapids, MI: Kregel, 2003.
Madelung, Wilferd. *Der Imam al-Qāsim ibn Ibrāhīm and die Glaubenslehre der Zaiditen*. Studien zur Geschichte und Kultur des Islamischen Orients 1. Berlin: Walter de Gruyter, 1965.

Madelung, Wilferd. "Sayf b. 'Umar: *Akhbārī* and Ideological Fiction Writer." In *Le Shī'isme Imāmite Quarante ans après: homage à Etan Kohlberg,* edited by Mohammad Ali Amir-Moezzi, Meir Bar-Asher, Simon Hopkins, 325–37. Turnhout: Brepols, 2009.

Madelung, Wilferd. "Al-Qāsim Ibn Ibrāhīm al-Rassī and Christian Theology." *Aram* 3 (1991): 35–44.

Madigan, Daniel. *The Qur'an's Self-Image: Writing and authority in Islam's scripture.* Princeton: PUP, 2001.

Maghen, Ze'ev. *After Hardship Cometh Ease: The Jews as Backdrop for Muslim Moderation.* Studien zur Geschichte und Kultur des Islamischen Orients 17. Berlin: Walter de Gruyter, 2006.

Maghen, Ze'ev. "Davidic Motifs in the Biography of Muḥammad." *Jerusalem Studies in Arabic and Islam* 35 (2008): 91–139.

Maghen, Ze'ev. "Intertwined Triangles: Remarks on the relationship between two prophetic scandals." *Jerusalem Studies in Arabic and Islam* 33 (2007): 17–92.

Marcuzzo, Giacinto. *Le Dialogue d'Abraham de Tibériade avec 'Abd al-Raḥmān al-Hāshimī à Jérusalem vers 820.* Rome: Pontificia Universitas Lateranensis, 1986.

Marquet, Yves. "Les Iḫwan al-Ṣafā' et le Christianisme." *Islamochristiana* 8 (1982): 129–58.

Mårtensson, Ulrika. "Bund und Land in muslimischer Rezeption: Biblische Kategorien in Ṭabarī's Geschichtswerk." *Judaica* 62 (2006): 289–308.

Mårtensson, Ulrika. "Discourse and Historical Analysis: The Case of al-Ṭabarī's History of the Messengers and the Kings." *Journal of Islamic Studies* 16 (2005): 287–331.

Matteo, Ignazio di. "Il 'Taḥrīf' od alterazione della Bibbia secondo i Musulmani." *Bessarione* 26 (1922): 64–111, 223–60.

Matteo, Ignazio di. "Confutazione contro i Cristiani dello Zaydita al-Qāsim b. Ibrāhīm." *Rivista degli Studi Orientali* 9 (1921–23), 301–64.

Marx, Alexander. "The Correspondence Between the Rabbis of Southern France and Maimonides about Astrology." *Hebrew Union College Annual* 3 (1926): 311–58.

Melchert, Christopher. *Ahmad ibn Hanbal.* Makers of the Muslim World. Oxford: Oneworld, 2006.

Melchert, Christopher. "Origins and Early Sufism." In *The Cambridge Companion to Sufism*, edited by Lloyd Ridgeon, 3–23. Cambridge: CUP, 2014.

Melchert, Christopher. "Quotations of Extra-Qur'ānic Scripture in Early Renunciant Literature." In *Islam and Globalisation: Historical and Contemporary Perspectives. Proceedings of the 25th Congress of L'Union Européenne des Arabisants et Islamisants,* edited by Agostino Cilardo, 7–107. Leuven: Peeters, 2013.

Melchert, Christopher. "Whether to Keep Unbelievers Out of Sacred Zones: a Survey of Medieval Islamic Law." *Jerusalem Studies in Arabic and Islam* 40 (2013): 177–94.

Melchert, Christopher. "'God Created Adam in His Image'." *Journal of Quranic Studies* 13 (2011): 113–24.

Melchert, Christopher. "Aḥmad ibn Ḥanbal's Book of Renunciation." *Der Islam* 85 (2011): 345–59.

Melchert, Christopher. "Early Renunciants as Ḥadīth Transmitters." *Muslim World* 92 (2002): 407–18.

Mikhail, Maged. *From Byzantine to Islamic Egypt: Religion, Identity and Politics after the Arab Conquest.* London: I.B. Tauris, 2014.

Mohammed, Khaleel. *David in the Muslim Tradition: The Bathsheba Affair.* Lanham, MD: Lexington Books, 2014.
Motzki, Harald. “Dating Muslim Traditions: a Survey.” *Arabica* 52 (2005): 204–53.
Motzki, Harald. “The Muṣannaf of ʻAbd al-Razzāq al-Ṣanʻānī as a Source of Authentic Aḥādīth of the First Century A.H.,” *Journal of Near Eastern Studies* 50 (1991): 1–21.
Mourad, Suleiman. *Early Islam Between Myth and History.* Islamic Philosophy, Theology and Science 62. Leiden: Brill, 2006.
Mourad, Suleiman. “Christianity in Arabia: an Overview (4th-9th Centuries CE).” In *The Syriac Writers of Qatar in the Seventh Century*, edited by Mario Kozah, Abdulrahim Abu-Husayn, Saif Shaheen al-Murikhi, Haya al-Thani, 37–60. Piscataway, NJ: Gorgias Press, 2014.
Mourad, Suleiman. “Jesus According to Ibn ʻAsākir.” In *Ibn ʻAsākir and Early Islamic History*, edited by James Lindsay, 24–43. Studies in Late Antiquity and Early Islam 20. Princeton: Darwin Press, 2001.
Musa, Aisha. *Hadith as Scripture.* New York, N.Y.: Palgrave Macmillan, 2008.
Newby, Gordon. *The Making of the Last Prophet.* Columbia: University of South Carolina Press, 1989.
Nelson, Lynn. “Christian-Muslim Relations in Eleventh–Century Spain.” *Military Affairs* 43 (1979): 195–98.
Nickel, Gordon. *Narratives of Tampering in the Earliest Commentaries on the Qur'ān.* The History of Christian-Muslim Relations 13. Leiden: Brill, 2011.
Nickel, Gordon. “Muqātil on Zayd and Zaynab.” In *Islamic Studies Today: Essays in Honor of Andrew Rippin*, edited by Majid Daneshgar and Walid Saleh, 43–61. Leiden: Brill, 2017.
Nickel, Gordon. “Qur'anic and Islamic Interpretation of the Bible.” *The Oxford Encyclopaedia of Biblical Interpretation*, edited by Steven McKenzie, vol. 2, 167–76. Oxford: OUP, 2013.
Owens, Robert. “The Early Syriac Text of Ben Sira in the Demonstrations of Aphrahat.” *Journal of Semitic Studies* 34 (1989): 39–75.
Palombo, Cecilia. “The ‘correspondence’ of Leo III and ‘Umar II: traces of an Early Christian Arabic Apologetic Work.” *Millennium* 12 (2015): 231–64.
Perlmann, Moshe. *Samā'ul al-Maghribī: Ifhām al-yahūd. Silencing the Jews.* New York: American Academcy for Jewish Research, 1964.
Perlmann, Moshe. “Eleventh Century Andalusian Authors on the Jews of Granada.” *Proceedings of the American Academy for Jewish Research* 18 (1948–49): 269–90.
Perlmann, Moshe. “A Legendary Story of Kaʻb al-Aḥbār's Conversion to Islam.” In *The Joshua Starr Memorial Volume* (New York: Conference on Jewish Relations, 1953): 85–99.
Perlmann, Moshe. “Another Kaʻb al-Aḥbār Story.” *Jewish Quarterly Review* 45 (1954): 48–51.
Petersen, William. *Tatian's Diatessaron: its Creation, Dissemination, Signicance and History in Scholarship.* Vigiliae Christianae, Supplements 25. Leiden: Brill, 1994.
Polliack, Meira. *The Karaite Tradition of Arabic Bible Translation.* Études sur le judaïsme médiéval 17. Leiden: Brill, 1997.
Polliack, Meira. “Deconstructing the Dual Torah. A Jewish Response to the Muslim Model of Scripture.” In *Interpreting Scriptures in Judaism, Christianity and Islam: Overlapping Enquiries*, edited by Mordechai Cohen and Adele Berlin, 113–29. Cambridge: CUP, 2016.
Polliack, Meira. “The Karaite Inversion of ‘Written’ and ‘Oral’ Torah in Relation to Islamic Arch-models of Qur'an and Hadith.” *Jewish Studies Quarterly* 22 (2015): 243–302.
Potthast, Daniel. *Christen und Muslime im Andalus.* Wiesbaden: Harrassowitz, 2013.

Powers, David. *Zayd: the Little Known Story of Muḥammad's Adopted Son.* Philadelphia: University of Pennsylvania Press, 2014.
Powers, David. *Muhammad is not the Father of any of your Men.* Philadelphia: University of Pennsylvania Press, 2009.
Powers, David. "Reading/Misreading One Another's Scriptures: Ibn Ḥazm's Refutation of Ibn Nagrella al-Yahūdī." In *Studies in Islamic and Jewish Traditions,* edited by W. Brinner and S. Ricks, vol. 1, 109–21. Atlanta: Scholars' Press, 1986.
Pregill, Michael. "Isrā'iliyyāt, Myth, and Pseudepigraphy: Wahb b. Munabbih and the Early Islamic Versions of the Fall of Adam and Eve." *Jerusalem Studies in Arabic and Islam* 34 (2008): 215–284.
'Proofs of Muhammad's Prophethood in the New and Old Testament.' Updated 5 August 2000, http://www.waytotruth.org/prophetmuhammad/proofs.html.
Pruitt, Jennifer. "Method in Madness: Recontextualizing the Destruction of Churches in the Fatimid Era." *Muqarnas* 30 (2013): 119–39.
Puerta Vilchez, J.M. "Inventory of Ibn Ḥazm's works." In *Controversial Thinker,* edited by Adang et al, 683–760. Leiden: Brill, 2012.
Pulcini, Theodore. *Exegesis as Polemical Discourse.* Atlanta: Scholars Press, 1998.
Rahman, Fazlur. *Prophecy in Islam.* London: George Allen and Unwin, 1958.
Reeth, Jan van. "L'Évangile du Prophète," In *Acta Orientalia Belgica (Subsidia III): Al-Kitāb: La Sacralité du texte dans le monde de l'islam,* 155–74. Leuven: Belgian Society for Oriental Studies, 2004.
Reeves, John. "The Muslim Appropriation of a Biblical Text: the Messianic Dimensions of Isa 21:6–7." In *Shaping the Middle East. Jews, Christians and Muslims in an Age of Transition 400–800 C.E.*, edited by Kenneth Holum and Hayim Lapin, 211–22. Bethesda, MD: University Press of Maryland, 2011.
Resnick, Irven. "The Falsification of Scripture and Medieval Christian and Jewish Polemics." *Medieval Encounters* 2 (1996): 344–80.
Reynolds, Gabriel Said. *The Qur'an and its Biblical Subtext.* Routledge Studies in the Qur'an. London: Routledge, 2010.
Reynolds, Gabriel Said. *A Muslim Theologian in the Sectarian Milieu: 'Abd al-Jabbār and the* Critique of Christian Origins. Islamic History and Civilization 56. Leiden: Brill, 2004.
Reynolds, Gabriel Said. "On the Qur'anic Accusation of Scriptural Falsification (*taḥrīf*) and Christian anti-Jewish Polemic." *Journal of the American Oriental Society* 130 (2010): 189–202.
Reynolds, Gabriel Said. "The Rise and Fall of Qāḍī 'Abd al-Jabbār." *International Journal of Middle East Studies* 37 (2005): 3–18.
Ridgeon, Lloyd. "Mysticism in Medieval Sufism." In *The Cambridge Companion to Sufism,* edited by Lloyd Ridgeon, 125–49. Cambridge: CUP, 2014.
Rifat, N.A. *Ibn Ḥazm on Jews and Judaism.* University of Exeter: Unpublished Ph.D. thesis, 1988.
Rippin, Andrew. "Foreign Vocabulary." In *Encyclopaedia of the Qur'ān*, Volume 2.
Rippin, Andrew. "The Exegetical Literature of Abrogation: form and content." In *Studies in Islamic and Middle Eastern Texts and Traditions in Memory of Norman Calder*, edited by Gerald Hawting, Jawid Mojaddedi and Alexander Samely, 213–31. Oxford: OUP, 2000.
Robb, Julie. *The Prophet Like Moses: its Jewish Context and Use in the Early Christian Tradition.* Unpublished Ph.D. thesis, King's College, London, 2003.

Robinson, Chase. "Islamic Historical Writing, Eighth Through the Tenth Centuries." In *The Oxford History of Historical Writing: Volume 2: 400–1400*, edited by Sarah Foot and Chase Robinson, 238–66. Oxford: OUP, 2012.

Robinson, Chase. "Al-Ṭabarī (839–923)." In *Arabic Literary Culture, 500–925*, edited by Michael Cooperson and Shawkat Toorawa, 332–43. Dictionary of Literary Biography 311. Detroit: Thomson Gale, 2005.

Robinson, Chase. Review of Lecker, *Journal of the Royal Asiatic Society* 7 (1997): 129–31.

Robinson, James. "Reading Other People Reading Other People's Scripture: the Influence of Religious Polemic on Jewish Biblical Exegesis." *English Language Notes* 50 (2012): 77–78.

Robson, James. "The Material of Tradition II." *Muslim World* 41 (1951): 261–67.

Roggema, Barbara. *The Legend of Sergius Baḥīrā: Eastern Christian apologetics and apocalyptic in response to Islam.* The History of Christian-Muslim Relations 9. Leiden: Brill, 2009.

Roggema, Barbara. "The Debate Between Patriarch John and an Emir of the Mhaggrāyē: a Reconsideration of the Earliest Christian-Muslim Debate." In *Christians and Muslims in Dialogue in the Islamic Orient of the Middle Ages*, edited by Martin Tamcke, 21–39. Beirut: Orient Institut, 2007.

Roggema, Barbara. "Ibn al-Layth." In *Christian-Muslim Relations: A Bibliographical History. Volume 1 (600–900).*

Rosenblatt, Samuel. "Rabbinic Legends in Hadith." *Muslim World* 35 (1945): 237–52.

Rosenthal, Franz. "The Influence of the Biblical Tradition on Muslim Historiography." In *Historians of the Middle East*, ed. Peter Holt and Bernard Lewis, 35–48. London: OUP, 1962.

Ross, Samuel. *The Biblical Turn in Modern Qur'an Commentary.* Unpublished Ph.d thesis, Yale University, 2018.

Rubin, Uri. *Between Bible and Qur'ān: the Children of Israel and the Islamic Self-Image.* Princeton: The Darwin Press, 1999.

Rubin, Uri. *The Eye of the Beholder: the Life of Muhammad as Viewed by the Early Muslims: a Textual Analysis.* Princeton: Darwin Press, 1995.

Rubin, Uri. "Muḥammad the Exorcist: Aspects of Islamic-Jewish Polemics." *Jerusalem Studies in Arabic and Islam* 30 (2005): 94–111.

Rubin, Uri. "Apocalypse and Authority in Islamic Tradition: The Emergence of the Twelve Leaders." *Al-Qanṭara* 18 (1997): 11–42.

Rubin, Uri. "Prophets and Progenitors in the Early Shī'a Tradition." *Jerusalem Studies in Arabic and Islam* (1979), 41–65.

Rudolph, Ulrich. *Al-Māturīdī and the Development of Sunnī Theology in Samarqand.* Islamic History and Civilization 100. Leiden: Brill, 2012.

Sadan, J. "Some Literary Problems Concerning Judaism and Jewry in Medieval Arabic Sources." In *Studies in Islamic History and Civilization in Honour of David Ayalon*, edited by Moshe Sharon, 353–98. Jerusalem: Cana, 1986.

Saeed, Abdullah. *The Qur'an: An Introduction.* Abingdon: Routledge, 2008.

Saeed, Abdullah. "The Charge of Distortion of Jewish and Christian Scriptures." *Muslim World 92* (2002): 419–36.

Safran, Janina. *Defining Boundaries in al-Andalus: Muslims, Christians and Jews in Islamic Iberia.* Ithaca, N.Y.: Cornell Univ Press, 2013.

Sahas, Daniel. *John of Damascus on Islam*. Leiden: Brill, 1972.
Saleh, Walid. "Re-reading al-Ṭabarī through al-Māturīdī: New light on the third century hijrī." *Journal of Quranic Studies* 18 (2016): 180–209.
Saleh, Walid. "The Hebrew Bible in Islam." In *The Cambridge Companion to the Hebrew Bible/ Old Testament*, edited by Stephen Chapman and Marvin Sweeney, 407–25. Cambridge: CUP, 2016.
Saleh, Walid. "A Piecemeal Qur'ān: *Furqān* and its Meaning in Classical Islam and in Modern Qur'ānic Studies." *Jerusalem Studies in Arabic and Islam* 42 (2015): 31–71.
Saleh, Walid. "The Psalms in the Qur'an and in the Islamic Religious Imagination." In *The Oxford Handbook of the Psalms*, edited by William Brown, 281–292. Oxford: OUP, 2014.
Salem, Feryal. *The Emergence of Early Sufi Piety and Sunni Scholasticism: Abdulllāh b. al-Mubārak and the Formation of Sunni Identity in the Second Islamic* Century. Islamic History and Civilization 125. Leiden: Brill, 2017.
Samir, Samir Khalil. "Une adaptation arabe musulmane en prose rimée des Évangiles (IXe s.)." In *Graeco-Latina et Orientalia. Studia in honorem Angeli Urbani heptagenarii*, edited by Samir Khalil Samir and Juan Pedro Monferrer-Sala, 295–325. Cordoba: CNERU-CEDRAC, 2013.
Schadler, Peter. *John of Damascus and Islam: Christian Heresiology and the Intellectual Background to Earliest Christian-Muslim Relations*. The History of Christian-Muslim Relations 34. Leiden: Brill, 2017.
Schäfer, Peter, ed. Toledot Yeshu ("*The Life Story of Jesus*") *Revisited*. Texts and Studies in Ancient Judaism 143. Tübingen: Mohr Siebeck, 2011.
Schaffner, Ryan. *The Bible Through a Qur'ānic Filter: Scripture Falsification* (Taḥrīf) *in 8th- and 9th- century Muslim Disputational Literature*. Unpublished Ph.D. thesis, Ohio State University, 2016.
Schiffman, Lawrence. "Messianism and Apocalyticism in Rabbinic Texts." In *The Cambridge History of Judaism*, vol. 4, edited by Steven Katz, 1053–1072. Cambridge: CUP, 1990.
Schippers, Arie. "Ḥafṣ al-Qūṭī's Psalms in Arabic Raĝaz Metre." In *Law, Christianity and Modernism in Islamic Society*, edited by Urbain Vermeulen and Jan van Reeth, 133–46. Leuven: Peeters, 1998.
Schmidtke, Sabine. "The Muslim Reception of the Bible: Al-Māwardī and his *Kitāb A'lām al-nubuwwa*.'" In *Le Sacre Scritture e le Loro Interpretazioni*, edited by Carmela Baffioni, Anna Passoni Dell'Acqua et al, 1–27. Milan/Rome: Veneranda Biblioteca Ambrosiana, 2016.
Schmidtke, Sabine. "Biblical Predictions of the Prophet Muhammad among the Zaydis of Iran." *Arabica* 59 (2012): 218–66.
Schmidtke, Sabine. "Ibn Ḥazm's sources on Ash'arism and Mu'tazilism." In *Controversial Thinker*, edited by Adang et al, 387–88. Leiden: Brill, 2012.
Schmidtke, Sabine. "The Muslim Reception of Biblical Materials: Ibn Qutayba and his *A'lām al-nubuwwa*." *Islam and Christian-Muslim Relations* 22 (2011): 249–74.
Schmidtke, Sabine. "Abū al-Ḥusayn al-Baṣrī and his Transmission of Biblical Materials from *Kitāb al-Dīn wa-al-Dawla* by Ibn Rabban al-Ṭabarī: The Evidence from Fakhr al-Dīn al-Rāzī's *Mafātīḥ al-ghayb*." *Islam and Christian-Muslim Relations* 20 (2009): 105–118.
Schmidtke, Sabine. "Abū al-Ḥusayn al-Baṣrī on the Torah and its Abrogation." *Mélanges de l'université Saint Joseph* 61 (2008): 559–80.

Schreiner, Stefan. *Die Jüdische Bibel in Islamischer Auslegung*, edited by Friedmann Eissler, 19–31. Texts and Studies in Medieval and Early Modern Judaism 27. Tübingen: Mohr Siebeck, 2012.

Schulthess, Sara. "Liste des manuscrits arabes des lettres de Paul: Résultats Préliminaires." *Journal of Eastern Christian Studies* 66 (2014): 153–67.

El Shamsy, Ahmed. *The Canonization of Islamic Law: a Social and Intellectual History.* New York: CUP, 2013.

El Shamsy, Ahmed. "Bridging the Gap: Two Early Texts of Islamic Legal Theory." *Journal of the American Oriental Society* 137 (2013): 505–36.

Shboul, Ahmad. *Al-Mas'ūdī and his World.* London: Ithaca Press, 1979.

Shoemaker, Stephen. *The Death of a Prophet: the End of Muhammad's Life and the Beginnings of Islam.* Divinations: Rereading Late Ancient Religion. Philadelphia: University of Pennsylvania Press, 2012.

Silverstein, Adam. *Veiling Esther, Unveiling her Story: the Reception of a Biblical Book in Islamic Lands.* Oxford Studies in the Abrahamic Religions. Oxford: OUP, 2018.

Sinai, Nicolai. *The Qur'an: a Historical-Critical Introduction.* New Edinburgh Islamic Surveys. Edinburgh: EUP, 2017.

Sinai, Nicolai. "The Qur'anic Commentary of Muqātil b. Sulaymān and the Evolution of Early *Tafsīr* Literature." In Tafsīr *and Islamic Intellectual History: Exploring the Boundaries of a Genre,* edited by Andreas Görke and Johanna Pink, 113–43. Oxford: OUP, in association with the Institute of Ismaili Studies, 2014.

Sinai, Nicolai. "When did the Consonantal Skeleton of the Qur'an Reach Closure?" *Bulletin of the School of Oriental and African Studies* 77 (2014): 273–92 and 509–21.

Sindawi, Khalid. "'Fāṭima's Book': a Shī'ite Qur'ān?" *Rivista degli Studi Orientali* 78 (2004): 57–70.

Sirry, Mun'im. "The Public Role of *Dhimmīs* during 'Abbāsid Times." *Bulletin of the School of Oriental and African Studies* 74 (2011): 187–204.

Sirry, Mun'im. "'Compete With One Another in Good Works': Exegesis of Qur'an Verse 5:48 and Contemporary Muslim Discourses on Religious Pluralism." *Islam and Christian-Muslim Relations* 20 (2009): 423–38.

Sizgorich, Thomas. "Narrative and Community in Islamic Late Antiquity." *Past and Present.* No. 185 November 2004: 9–42.

Sklare, David "Responses to Islamic Polemics by Jewish Mutakallimūn in the Tenth Century." In *The Majlis. Interreligious Encounters in Medieval Islam*, edited by Hava Lazarus-Yafeh, Mark Cohen, Sasson Somekh, Sidney Griffith, 137–61. Wiesbaden: Harrassowitz, 1999.

Slomp, Jan. "The Gospel in Dispute." *Islamochristiana* 4 (1978): 67–111.

Slomp, Jan. "The 'Gospel of Barnabas in Recent Research." *Islamochristiana* 23 (1997): 81–109.

Smet, Daniel de, and Meryem Sebti. "Avicenna's Philosophical Approach to the Qur'an in the Light of his '*Tafsīr Sūrat al-Ikhlāṣ*'." *Journal of Qur'anic Studies* 11 (2009): 134–48.

Smet, Daniel de, and Jan Van Reeth. "Les Citations Bibliques dans l'oeuvre du *Dā'ī* Ismaélien Ḥamīd ad-dīn al-Kirmānī." In *Law, Christianity and Modernism in Islamic Society: Proceedings of the Eighteenth Congress of* Union Européenne des Arabisants et Islamisants *held at the Katholieke Universiteit Leuven (September 3–September 9, 1996)*, eds. Urbain Vermeulen and Jan van Reeth, 147–60. Leuven: Peeters, 1998.

Soravia, Bruno. "A Portrait of the *'Ālim* as a Young Man: the formative years of Ibn Ḥazm, 404/1013–420/1029." In *Controversial Thinker*, edited by Adang et al, 25–49. Leiden: Brill, 2012.

Speight, Marston. "A Versatile *mathal:* 'the man who hired laborers." *Islam and Christian-Muslim Relations* 14 (2004): 91–98.

Speight, Marston. "Muslim Attitudes toward Christians in the Maghrib during the Fāṭimid Period, 297/909–358/969." In *Christian-Muslim Encounters,* edited by Yvonne Yazbeck Haddad and Wadi Haddad, 180–93. Gainesville: University of Florida Press, 1995.

Steigerwald, Diana. "Ismāʿīlī *Ta'wīl.*" In *The Blackwell Companion to the Qur'ān*, edited by Andrew Rippin, 386–400. Oxford: Blackwell, 2006.

Steiner, Richard. *A Biblical Translation in the Making: the Evolution and Impact of Saadia Gaon's* Tafsīr. Cambridge, MA: Harvard University Press, 2011.

Steinschneider, Moritz. *Polemische und Apologetische Literatur in Arabische Sprache.* Leipzig 1877, reprinted Hildesheim: Georg Olms, 1966.

Stern, Samuel. "'Abd al-Jabbār's Account of how Christ's Religion was falsified by the Adoption of Roman Customs." *Journal of Theological Studies* 19 (1968): 128–85.

Stökl Ben Ezra, Daniel. "An Ancient List of Christian Festivals in 'Toledot Yeshu': Polemics as Indication for Interaction." *Harvard Theological Review* 102 (2009): 481–96.

Stroumsa, Guy. *The Making of the Abrahamic Religions in Late Antiquity.* Oxford Studies in the Abrahamic Religions. Oxford: OUP, 2015.

Stroumsa, Sarah. "Jewish Polemics Against Islam and Christianity in the Light of Judaeo-Arabic Texts." In *Judaeo-Arabic Studies; Proceedings of the Founding Conference of the Society for Judaeo-Arabic Studies*, edited by Norman Golb, 241–50. Amsterdam: Studies in Muslim-Jewish Relations, 3, 1997. Reprinted in Robert Hoyland, ed. *Muslims and Others in Early Islamic Society*, 201–210. London: Ashgate, 2004.

Stroumsa, Sarah. "Ibn al-Rāwandī's *sū' adab al-mujādala:* the Role of Bad Manners in Medieval Disputations." In *The Majlis: Interreligious Encounters in Medieval Islam,* edited by Hava Lazarus-Yafeh, Mark Cohen, Sasson Somekh, Sidney Griffith, 66–83. Wiesbaden: Harrassowitz, 1999.

Stroumsa, Sarah. "From Muslim Heresy to Jewish-Muslim Polemics: Ibn al-Rāwandī's *Kitāb al-Dāmigh.*" *Journal of the American Oriental Society* 107 (1987): 767–72.

Stroumsa, Sarah. "The Signs of Prophecy: The Emergence and Early Development of a Theme in Arabic Theological Literature." *Harvard Theological Review* 78 (1985): 101–14.

Swanson, Mark. "The Disputation of the monk Ibrāhīm al-Ṭabarānī." In: *Christian-Muslim Relations: A Bibliographical History. Volume 1 (600–900).*

Sweetman, James. *Islam and Christian Theology,* Part 2 vol. 1. London: Lutterworth Press, 1955.

Szpiech, Ryan. "Preaching Paul to the Moriscos: The *Confusión o Confutación de la Secta Mahomética y del Alcoran* (1515) of 'Juan Andres'." *La Corónica* 41 (2012): 317–43.

Tacchini, Davide. "Paul the Forgerer: Classical and modern radical views of the Apostle of Tarsus." *Islamochristiana* 34 (2008): 129–47.

Takim, Liyakat. "The Ten Commandments and the Tablets in Shīʿī and Sunnī Tafsīr Literature: a Comparative Perspective." *Muslim World* 101 (2011): 94–109.

Talmon-Heller, Daniella. "Reciting the Qur'an and Reading the Torah: Muslim and Jewish Attitudes and Practices in a Comparative Historical Perspective." *Religion Compass* 6/8 (2012): 369–380.

Talmon-Heller, Daniella. "Scriptures as Holy Objects: Preliminary Comparative Remarks on the Qur'ān and the Torah in the Medieval Middle East." *Intellectual History of the Islamicate World* 4 (2016): 210–244.

Tannous, Jack. *The Making of the Medieval Middle East: Religion, Society and Simple Believers*. Princeton: PUP, 2018.

Tayyara, Abed El-Rahman. "Ibn Ḥabīb's *Kitāb al-Muḥabbar* and its Place in Early Islamic Historical Writing." *Journal of Islamic Studies* 29 (2018): 392–416.

Thomas, David. *Christian Doctrines in Islamic Theology*. The History of Christian-Muslim Relations 10. Leiden: Brill, 2008.

Thomas, David. "The Bible in Early Muslim Anti-Christian Polemic." *Islam and Christian-Muslim Relations* 7 (1996): 29–38.

Thomas, David. "'Alī Ibn Rabbān al-Ṭabarī: A Convert's Assessment of his Former Faith." In *Christians and Muslims in Dialogue in the Islamic Orient of the Middle Ages*, edited by Martin Tamcke, 137–55. Beirut: Orient Institut, 2007.

Thomas, David. "The Miracles of Jesus in Early Islamic Polemic." *Journal of Semitic Studies* 39 (1994): 221–43.

Thomas, David. "Two Muslim-Christian Debates from the Early Shī'ite Tradition." *Journal of Semitic Studies* 33 (1988): 53–80.

Thomas, David. "'Alī al-Ṭabarī." In: *Christian-Muslim Relations: A Bibliographical History, Volume 1 (600–900)*.

Thomas, David. "Al-Ḥasan ibn Ayyūb." In: *Christian-Muslim Relations: A Bibliographical History. Volume 2 (900–1050)*.

Thomas, Kenneth. *A Restless Search: A History of Persian Translations of the Bible*. Atlanta: SBL Press/ Nida Institute for Biblical Scholarship, 2015.

Tottoli, Roberto. "Origin and Use of the Term *Isrā'īliyyāt* in Muslim Literature." *Arabica* 46 (1999): 193–210.

Tottoli, Roberto. *Biblical Prophets in the Qur'an and Muslim Literature*. Richmond: Curzon, 2002.

Tottoli, Roberto. "At Cock-crow: Some Muslim Traditions about the Rooster." *Der Islam* 76 (1999): 139–47.

Treiger, Alexander. "Origins of Kalām." In *The Oxford Handbook of Islamic Theology*, edited by Sabine Schmidtke, 27–43. Oxford: OUP, 2016.

Vajda, Georges. "Juifs et musulmanes selon le Hadit." *Journal asiatique* 229 (1937): 57–125.

Vishanoff, David. *The Formation of Islamic Hermeneutics: How Sunni Legal Theorists Imagined a Revealed Law*. American Oriental Series 93. New Haven, CT: American Oriental Society, 2011.

Vishanoff, David. "Other People's Scriptures: Mythical Texts of Imagined Communities." *Numen* 61 (2014): 329–33.

Vishanoff, David. "An Imagined Book Gets a New Text: Psalms of the Muslim David." *Islam and Christian-Muslim Relations* 22 (2011), 85–99.

Vishanoff, David. "Why do the Nations Rage? Boundaries of Canon and Community in a Muslim's Rewriting of Psalm 2." *Comparative Islamic Studies* 6 (2010), 151–79.

Vishanoff, David. "Images of David in Several Muslim Rewritings of the Psalms," forthcoming.

Vollandt, Ronny. *Arabic Versions of the Pentateuch*. Leiden: Brill, 2015.

Vollandt, Ronny. "The *Status Quaestionis* of Research on the Arabic Bible." In *Studies in Semitic Linguistics and Manuscripts: a Liber Discipulorum in Honour of Professor*

Geoffrey Khan, edited by Nadia Vidro, Ronny Vollandt, Esther-Miriam Wagner, Judith Olszowy-Schlanger, 442–67. Uppsala: University of Uppsala, 2018.

Vollers, Kurt. “Das Religionsgespräch von Jerusalem (um 800 D).” in *Zeitschrift für Kirchengeschichte* 29 (1908): 29–71, 197–221.

Waines, David. “The Bible in Muslim-Christian Encounters.” In *The New Cambridge History of the Bible, vol 2, From 600–1450*, edited by Richard Marsden and Ann Matter, 638–55. Cambridge: CUP, 2012.

Ward, Seth. “A Fragment from an Unknown Work by al-Ṭabarī on the Tradition ‘Expel the Jews and Christians from the Arabian Peninsula (and the Lands of Islam)’.” *Bulletin of the School of Oriental and African Studies* 53 (1990): 407–420.

Wasserstein, David. *The Rise and Fall of the Party-kings: politics and society in Islamic Spain, 1002–1086*. Princeton: PUP, 1985.

Wasserstein, David. “The Majlis of al-Riḍā’: A Religious debate in the court of the Caliph al-Ma’mūn as represented in a Shī‘ī hagiographical work about the Eighth Imām ‘Alī ibn Mūsā al-Riḍā.” In *The Majlis: Interreligious Encounters in Medieval Islam*, edited by Hava Lazarus-Yafeh, 108–19. Wiesbaden: Harrassowitz, 1999.

Wasserstein, David. “Samuel ibn Naghrīla Ha-Nagid and Islamic Historiography in al-Andalus.” *Al-Qanṭara* 14 (1993): 109–25.

Watt, W. Montgomery. “The Early Development of the Muslim Attitude to the Bible.” *Transactions of the Glasgow University Oriental Society* 16 (1957): 50–62, reprinted in his *Early Islam* (Edinburgh: EUP, 1990): 77–85.

Watt, W. Montgomery. *Islam and the Integration of Society*. London: Routledge and Kegan Paul, 1961.

Watt, W. Montgomery. “Created in his Image.” *Transactions of the Glasgow University Oriental Society* 18 (1961): 38–49.

Webb, Peter. “Pre-Islamic al-Shām in Classical Arabic Literature: Spatial Narratives and History-Telling.” *Studia Islamica* 110 (2015): 135–64.

Webb, Peter. *Imagining the Arabs*. Edinburgh: EUP, 2016.

Wheeler, Brannon. “Arab prophets of the Qur’an and Bible.” *Journal of Qur’anic Studies* 8 (2006): 24–57.

Whelan, Estelle. “Forgotten Witness: Evidence for the Early Codification of the Qur’ān.” *Journal of the American Oriental Society* 118 (1998): 1–14.

Whittingham, Martin. *Al-Ghazālī and the Qur’an: One Book, Many Meanings*. London: Routledge, 2007.

Whittingham, Martin. “Ezra as Corrupter of the Torah? Re-assessing Ibn Ḥazm’s role in the Long History of an Idea.” *Intellectual History of the Islamicate World* 1 (2013): 253–71.

Whittingham, Martin. “The Value of *taḥrīf ma‘nawī* (corrupt interpretation) as a Category for Analyzing Muslim Views of the Bible: Evidence from *Al-radd al-jamīl* and Ibn Khaldūn.” *Islam and Christian-Muslim Relations* 22 (2011): 209–22.

Whittingham, Martin. “How Could So Many Christians be Wrong? The Role of *Tawātur* (Recurrent Transmission of Reports) in Understanding Muslim Views of the Crucifixion.” *Islam and Christian-Muslim Relations* 19 (2008): 167–78.

Whittingham, Martin. “Muslims and the Bible.” In *Routledge Handbook on Christian-Muslim Relations*, edited by David Thomas, 269–278. London: Routledge, 2018.

Whittingham, Martin. 'What is the 'Gospel' mentioned in the Qur'an?'. *CMCS Research Briefings* 6 (2016), 3–6; consulted online 12 May 2020, https://www.cmcsoxford.org.uk/s/Research-Briefing-Spring-2016.pdf

Witztum, Joseph. "Ibn Isḥāq and the Pentateuch in Arabic." *Jerusalem Studies in Arabic and Islam* 40 (2013): 1–71.

Wright, Peter. "Critical Approaches to the 'Farewell Khutba' in Ibn Ishaq's Life of the Prophet." *Comparative Islamic Studies* 6 (2010): 217–49.

Yücesoy, Hayrettin. "Ancient Imperial Heritage and Islamic Universal History: al-Dīnawarī's Secular Perspective." *Journal of Global History* 2 (2007): 135–55.

Zaki, Vevian. "The Textual History of the Arabic Pauline Epistles: One Version, Three Recensions, Six Manuscripts." In *Senses of Scripture, Treasures of Tradition: The Bible in Arabic among Jews, Christians and Muslims*, edited by Miriam Hjälm, 392–424. Leiden: Brill, 2017.

Zewi, Tamar. *The Samaritan Version of Saadya Gaon's Translation of the Pentateuch*. Biblia Arabica 3. Leiden: Brill, 2015.

Index of Subjects and Names

'Abbāsids 5, 9, 35, 51, 59, 68, 71, 77, 168f.
'Abd al-Jabbār 138–42, 144, 146, 148, 165, 168
'Abd Allāh b. Salām 29, 50
Abraham 25, 56, 66–71, 76, 90, 98, 113, 125, 154
Abrogation 6, 19, 39–44, 84
Adam 67, 69, 79, 98, 107, 113, 162
Africa 1
Aḥmad b. Ḥanbal 58, 82, 114–15
'Alī, Caliph 15f., 34, 38, 55–57
'Ammār al-Baṣrī 132–33, 170
Apologetics 3, 49
Augustine 14

Baghdad 1, 10–11, 30, 47, 87, 89, 91, 97–98, 101, 103, 119, 129, 160–65
Barnabas, Gospel of 7–8
al-Bayhaqī 4, 64–65
Bible
– canon 4
– in Arabic 9–12
– in Persian 12f.
al-Bukhārī 9, 44, 46, 57, 59, 82
Byzantine 73f. 119, 130, 147, 155

Church 4, 93, 120–21, 130, 137
Corruption (of the Bible) [see also *taḥrīf*] 6, 18, 21, 34–37, 39, 55, 85–86, 89–90, 99, 102–03, 119, 122–25, 127–34

al-Dārimī 61
David 4, 7, 22, 52, 56, 65, 80
Diatessaron 7, 12–13

4 Ezra 14, 37, 101–03, 154

ḥadīth qudsī 81f.
Ḥafṣ al-Qūṭī 11
Hezekiah 72

Ibn 'Abbās 57, 60
Ibn 'Abd al-Barr 54
Ibn Bābawayh 16, 47, 57
Ibn Ḥazm 1, 15, 34, 72, 167f.
Ibn Hishām 48, 50f., 55, 60, 62–64, 69, 80
Ibn Isḥāq 48, 50, 55, 59f., 62–64, 69–71, 76, 79f., 167f.
Ibn Qutayba 1, 43, 51, 79, 88–89, 91–95, 98
Ibn Rabbān 89–94, 118–119, 126
Ibn Sa'd 72f.
Ikhwān al-Ṣafā' 108–09
India 1, 5, 7, 171
Injīl 2, 7, 17, 23f., 26, 29, 31, 33, 52, 55, 58–60, 65
Iran 1, 6, 12, 30, 47, 168, 171
Iraq 5, 28, 47, 71
Ishmael 55, 66–71, 75, 77, 90
Ismā'īlīs 47, 104–08, 168
Isrā'īliyyāt 8, 50

al-Jafr 56
al-Jāḥiẓ 11, 86–87
al-Jaṣṣāṣ 44, 124–25
Jerusalem 7, 34, 41f., 72–76
Jesus 2, 17, 21, 23–25, 27, 31, 52, 56, 59f., 63, 76, 80f., 168f.
John of Damascus 130–31, 134
John the Baptist 26, 95
Jubilees, Book of 68

Ka'b b. al-Aḥbār 50, 59, 72, 74, 77
Karaites 92, 129

al-Mas'ūdī 50, 101–02
al-Māturīdī 21
Mecca 34, 36, 41, 69, 76, 90, 92, 163, 167
Medina 6, 36, 39, 41, 61f., 76, 116
Midrash 5, 22, 66
Moses 2, 4, 22, 25, 35, 37, 43, 54–56, 64f., 70f., 75f.

https://doi.org/10.1515/9783110335880-012

Muhammad 3, 7, 9, 15–17, 27–34, 36–39, 41, 46–48, 51–55, 58–60, 66–70, 78–81, 83–85, 170
– Biblical proofs 4, 62–65, 167
muhaymin 26, 31
Muqātil b. Sulaymān 21, 28–32, 35 f., 167, 170
mutawātir transmission 48 f.

al-Nasā'ī 52, 58
Nu'aym b. Ḥammād 59, 73, 77 f.

Paraclete 59 f., 63, 80, 88–90, 95, 99, 127
Paul (Apostle) 7, 10, 137–150, 165, 168
Peshitta 12
Peter (Apostle) 142, 148–49
Polemics 3, 6
Promised Land 76

al-Qummī 21, 28, 32–34, 38

Ramadan 55
al-Rassī 116–19, 170
Rayy 6, 100, 105, 136, 139, 165

Sa'adya Gaon 10–11, 102, 153
al-Ṣan'ānī, 'Abd al-Razzāq 30, 47, 51–54
Sermon on the Mount 82 f.
al-Shāfi'ī 41, 47, 121–24
Spain 5, 11, 150, 159, 160–61, 165, 168
Syriac 12–14, 22, 50, 61–63, 90–94, 100–01, 107–08, 118, 126, 130, 139

al-Ṭabarī 21, 28–32, 35, 37, 42, 50, 55, 62, 64, 70, 73, 79, 167
tabdīl 29
taḥrīf 6, 18, 27, 44, 55, 56–61, 85, 94–95, 130–34, 140, 169–70
taḥrīf 6, 27, 44, 55, 85, 169 f.
– *taḥrīf al-lafẓ* 2, 167
– *taḥrīf al-ma'nā* 2, 60
Talmud 5, 22
Tawrāt 2, 9, 17, 22–25, 29, 31, 33, 35–37, 44, 49 f., 52, 54–56, 58 f., 63, 65, 71 f., 74 f., 77, 84
Ten Commandments 56
al-Tha'labī 50, 114, 144
al-Tirmidhī 46, 52 f.
al-Ṭūsī, Muḥammad 47

'Umar, Caliph 50, 53 f., 61, 71–74, 77 f.
Umayyads 71, 76, 96, 130, 147, 150

Vatican Arabic 13 (MS) 10

Wahb b. Munabbih 50, 100

al-Ya'qūbī 98–99

Zabūr 17, 22–24, 33, 55, 65

Index of Biblical References

Genesis
- 1:27 79
- 4: 9–16 100
- 5:4–32 97
- 10:22 70
- 10:24 70
- 10:25 69
- 11:10–26 97
- 12–25 66
- 16:12 90
- 17:20 77
- 21 70
- 25:13 69

Exodus
- 3:1 70
- 4:18 70
- 18:1–12 70
- 21:24 33
- 31:7 78

Leviticus
- 24:20 33

Deuteronomy
- 9:3 154
- 18:15 92
- 18:18 89–90, 92, 104, 126
- 19:21 33
- 33: 2 88, 90, 104, 126

1 Kings
- 17:9–16 79

2 Kings
- 20:1–7 72
- 25 97

Ezra 14 f., 37

Esther 103

Psalms 7, 11–13, 17, 23, 53, 56, 79
- 2 7
- 37:9 22
- 37:11 22
- 37:29 22
- 51 79
- 72 90
- 103 79
- 149: 6–8 94

Isaiah 72, 90, 100–101
- 5:1–2 114
- 21:6–7 92–93
- 21:1–10 93
- 38:1–6 72
- 40:6 79
- 42 65, 74, 88, 113
- 42:2–7 63

Jeremiah
- 52 97

Ezekiel 119
- 26–27 74
- 40–47 90

Daniel 65
- 7 90

Jonah 76

Micah
- 4:13 73, 78

Habakkuk 90, 92

Zephaniah 90

Zechariah 90

Malachi
- 4:5 95
- 1:8 105

https://doi.org/10.1515/9783110335880-013

Matthew 10, 13, 80, 83
- 1:1–17 156
- 1:17 162
- 1:18–21 98
- 3:17 119
- 4:4 99
- 4:5–7 115
- 5–7 82
- 5:7–9 89
- 5:29 82
- 5:39 144
- 5:39–41 89
- 5:43–48 86
- 6:3 83
- 6:9 89
- 6:9–13 82
- 7:3 86
- 7:24–2 7 55
- 10:34 156
- 11:11–15 95
- 12:15–21 63
- 20:1–16 83
- 25:31 107
- 25:31–46 106
- 25:36 82
- 25:40 106
- 27:52–53 163

Luke 10, 104, 155–56
- 3:23–38 156
- 11:27 82
- 12:49 156
- 13:32 156
- 22:35–36 90
- 23:39–43 163

John 60
- 3:17 156
- 5:22 156
- 5:31 119
- 6:38–39 119
- 8 115
- 12:36 105–06
- 14:16 63, 99
- 14:26 63, 127
- 14:28 89
- 15:26 63
- 16:7 63
- 19:26–27 140
- 20:17 89, 106
- 20:29 147

Acts 127
- 9:27–15:41 7

1 Corinthians
- 2:9 81
- 12:25 82

1 Peter 4

2 Peter 4

Jude 4

Revelation 4

Index of Qur'anic References

2\
– 1 30
– 4 25, 30, 33, 51
– 6 33
– 53 25
– 62 42
– 75 27, 34–37
– 79 36f., 57f., 60
– 105 41
– 106 40–44
– 127 69
– 131 66
– 136 53
– 143–44 41
– 146 36f.
– 178 33
– 285 26, 29, 31, 33, 51

3\
– 3 23
– 19 42, 44
– 48 23
– 50 25
– 65 23, 66
– 78 36f.
– 81 35
– 85 42, 44
– 184 23, 25

4\
– 37 36f.
– 46 27, 36f., 60
– 136 26, 51
– 163 67

5\
– 13 27, 34f., 37f.
– 41 27, 34f., 37
– 43–44 26
– 43–48 28, 33
– 44 2, 22, 31, 169
– 45 33
– 46 2, 23f., 27, 31, 34f., 169
– 46–47 33
– 47 23f., 28, 58
– 48 26, 31
– 66 23, 26, 29, 31, 33, 52
– 68 23, 26, 29, 31
– 110 23

6\
– 91–92 33
– 115 26, 29

7\
– 65–72 70
– 73–9 70
– 85–93 70
– 145 25
– 150 25
– 154 25
– 157 23f., 41
– 169 24

9\
– 111 23f.

10\
– 64 2
– 94 26, 29, 32f.

11\
– 17 29
– 50–60 70
– 61–8 70
– 84–95 70

14\
– 35–41 67

15\
– 9 2

16\
– 44 23
– 101 40, 42, 44

https://doi.org/10.1515/9783110335880-014

17\
- 111 59

18\
- 27 26, 29

19\
- 12 26

20\
- 133 24

21\
- 48 25
- 105 22

24\
- 2 44

25\
- 35 22

26\
- 123–40 70
- 141–59 70
- 176–91 70
- 196 23, 26

27\
- 45–53 70

29\
- 36–7 70

35\
- 25 23, 25
- 32 24

40\
- 53 24

42\
- 14 24

46\
- 21–6 70

48\
- 29 23 f., 33

52\
- 1–3 25

54\
- 23–31 70
- 43 23
- 52 23

57\
- 27 23, 58

61\
- 6 24

87\
- 19 25

91\
- 11–15 70

www.ingramcontent.com/pod-product-compliance
Lightning Source LLC
Chambersburg PA
CBHW032059230426
43662CB00035B/614
9783110991444